The Dreamings

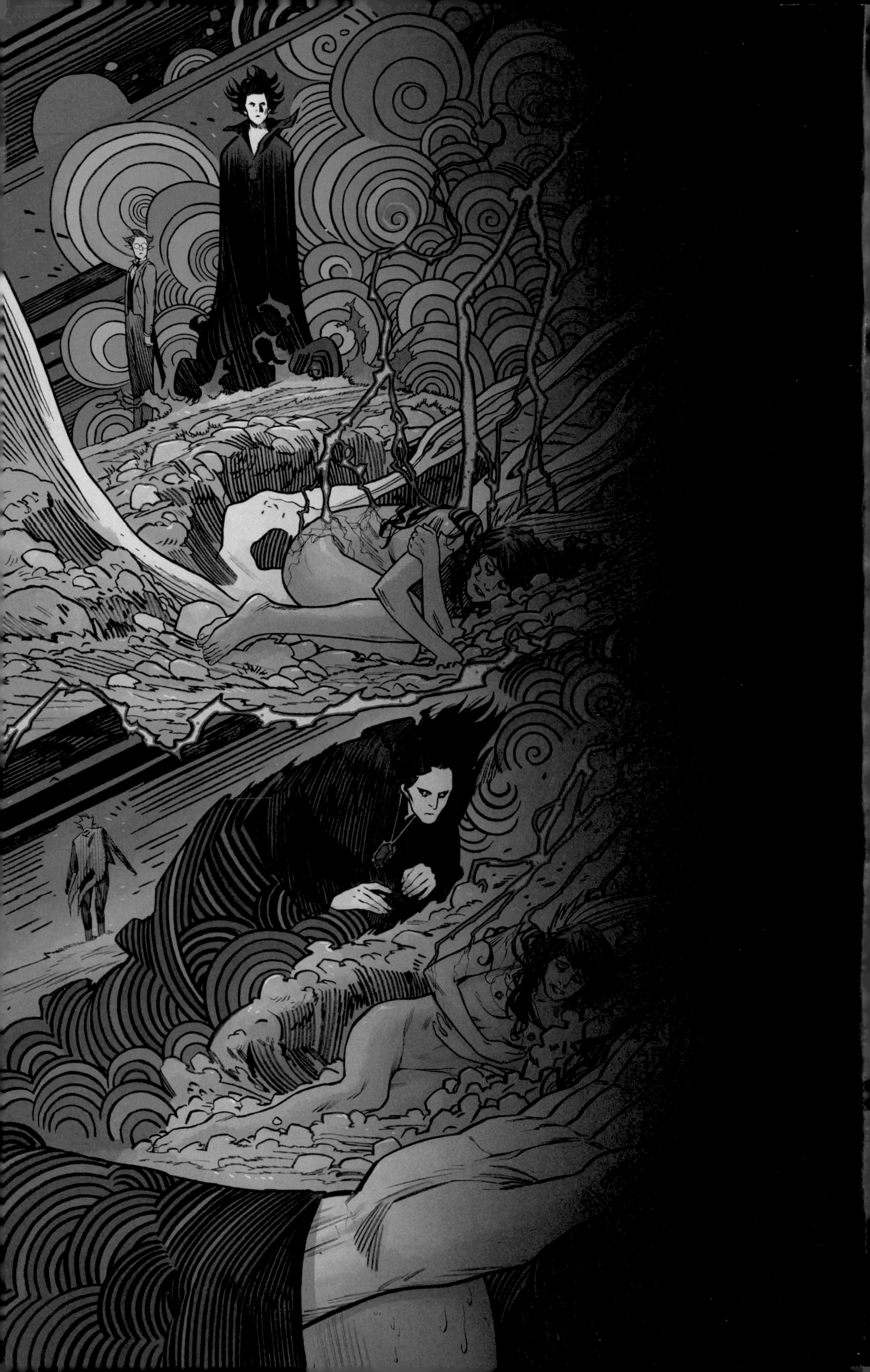

The Dreaming

VOLUME ONE

Pathways and Emanations

WRITTEN BY
Simon Spurrier
Neil Gaiman
Kat Howard
Nalo Hopkinson
Dan Watters

ART BY
Bilquis Evely
Abigail Larson
Tom Fowler
Dominike "DOMO" Stanton
Max Fiumara
Sebastian Fiumara

COLORS BY
Mat Lopes
Quinton Winter

LETTERS BY
Simon Bowland

Collection and original series
COVER ART BY
Jae Lee and *June Chung*

The Dreaming created by Neil Gaiman
The Sandman created by Neil Gaiman,
Sam Kieth, and Mike Dringenberg
The Sandman Universe curated by Neil Gaiman

MOLLY MAHAN	*Editor – Original Series*
AMEDEO TURTURRO	*Associate Editor – Original Series*
MAGGIE HOWELL	*Assistant Editor – Original Series*
JEB WOODARD	*Group Editor – Collected Editions*
SCOTT NYBAKKEN	*Editor – Collected Edition*
STEVE COOK	*Design Director – Books and Publication Design*
BOB HARRAS	*Senior VP – Editor-in-Chief, DC Comics*
MARK DOYLE	*Executive Editor, Vertigo & Black Label*
DAN DiDIO	*Publisher*
JIM LEE	*Publisher & Chief Creative Officer*
AMIT DESAI	*Executive VP – Business & Marketing Strategy, Direct to Consumer & Global Franchise Management*
BOBBIE CHASE	*VP & Executive Editor, Young Reader & Talent Development*
MARK CHIARELLO	*Senior VP – Art, Design & Collected Editions*
JOHN CUNNINGHAM	*Senior VP – Sales & Trade Marketing*
BRIAR DARDEN	*VP – Business Affairs*
ANNE DePIES	*Senior VP – Business Strategy, Finance & Administration*
DON FALLETTI	*VP – Manufacturing Operations*
LAWRENCE GANEM	*VP – Editorial Administration & Talent Relations*
ALISON GILL	*Senior VP – Manufacturing & Operations*
JASON GREENBERG	*VP – Business Strategy & Finance*
HANK KANALZ	*Senior VP – Editorial Strategy & Administration*
JAY KOGAN	*Senior VP – Legal Affairs*
NICK J. NAPOLITANO	*VP – Manufacturing Administration*
LISETTE OSTERLOH	*VP – Digital Marketing & Events*
EDDIE SCANNELL	*VP – Consumer Marketing*
COURTNEY SIMMONS	*Senior VP – Publicity & Communications*
JIM (SKI) SOKOLOWSKI	*VP – Comic Book Specialty Sales & Trade Marketing*
NANCY SPEARS	*VP – Mass, Book, Digital Sales & Trade Marketing*
MICHELE R. WELLS	*VP – Content Strategy*

THE DREAMING VOL. 1: PATHWAYS AND EMANATIONS

DC Comics, 2900 West Alameda Ave., Burbank, CA 91505
Printed by LSC Communications, Kendallville, IN, USA. 5/3/19. First Printing.
ISBN: 978-1-4012-9117-4

Library of Congress Cataloging-in-Publication Data is available.

PEFC Certified

This product is from sustainably managed forests and controlled sources

PEFC/29-31-337   www.pefc.org

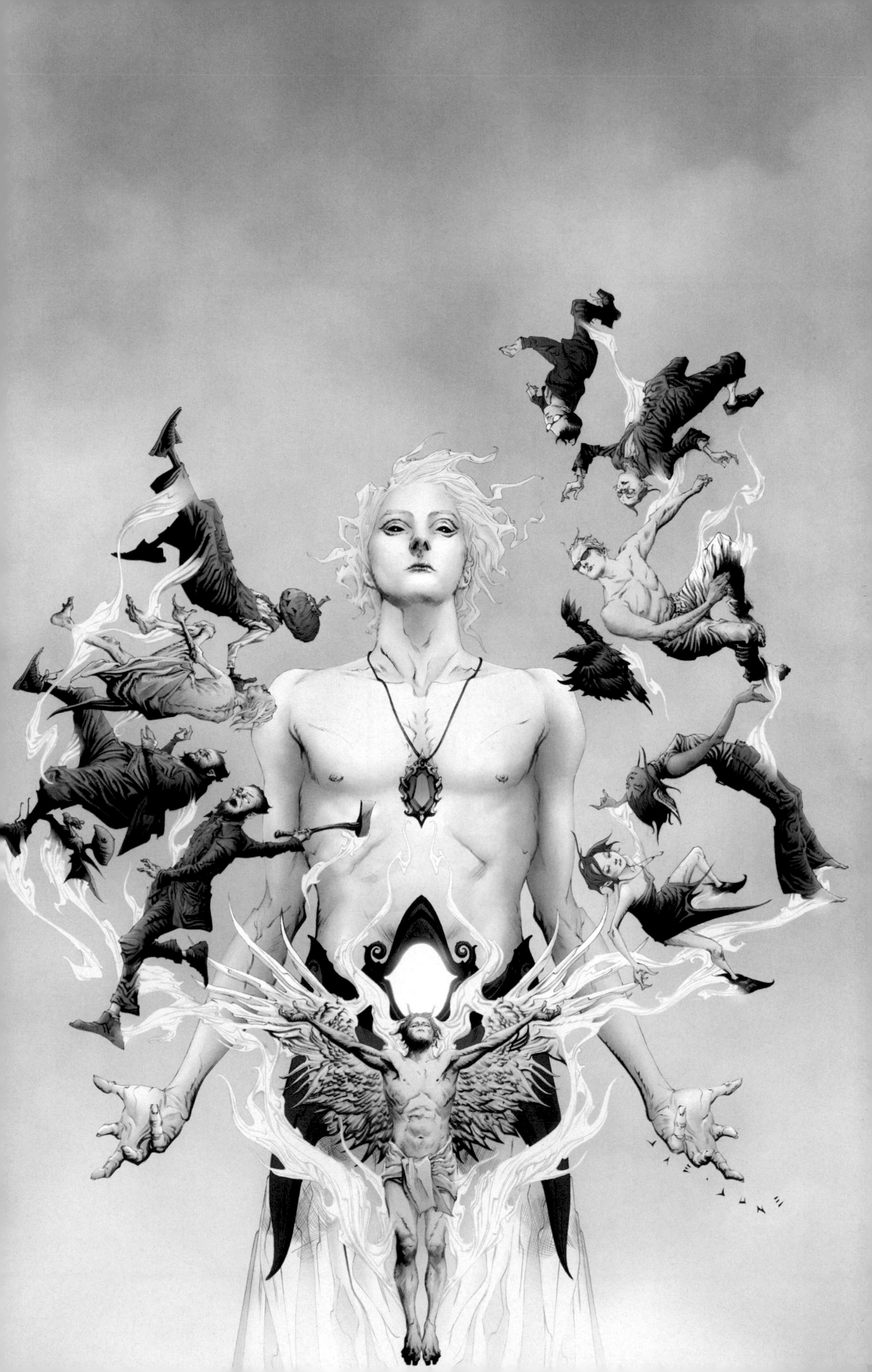

The Sandman Universe

STORY BY
Neil Gaiman

WRITTEN BY
Simon Spurrier
Kat Howard
Nalo Hopkinson
Dan Watters

ILLUSTRATED BY
Bilquis Evely
Tom Fowler
Dominike "DOMO" Stanton
Max Fiumara
Sebastian Fiumara

COLORS BY
Mat Lopes

LETTERS BY
Simon Bowland

COVER ART BY
Jae Lee and *June Chung*

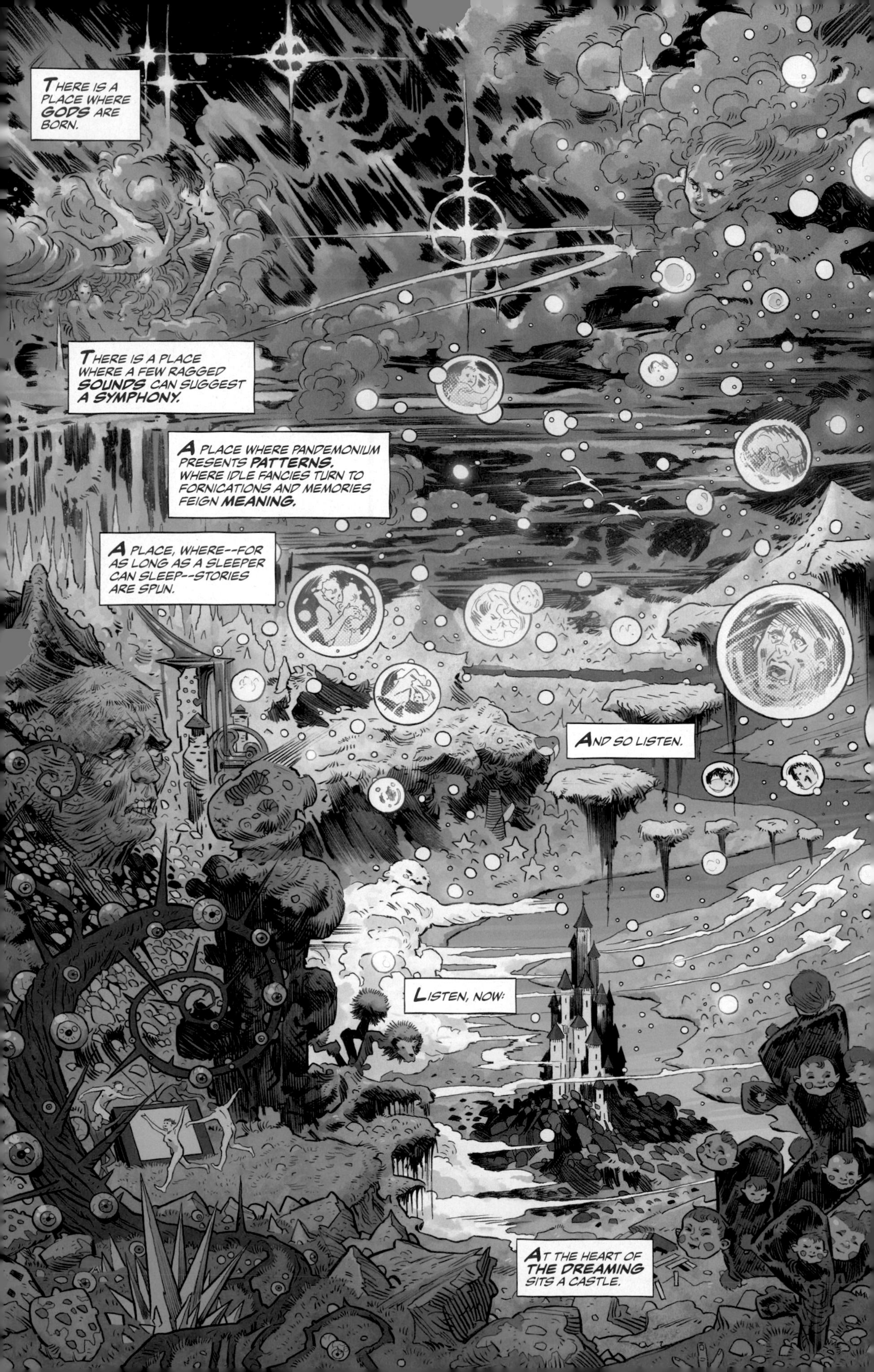
THERE IS A PLACE WHERE GODS ARE BORN.
THERE IS A PLACE WHERE A FEW RAGGED SOUNDS CAN SUGGEST A SYMPHONY.
A PLACE WHERE PANDEMONIUM PRESENTS PATTERNS. WHERE IDLE FANCIES TURN TO FORNICATIONS AND MEMORIES FEIGN MEANING.
A PLACE, WHERE--FOR AS LONG AS A SLEEPER CAN SLEEP--STORIES ARE SPUN.
AND SO LISTEN.
LISTEN, NOW:
AT THE HEART OF THE DREAMING SITS A CASTLE.

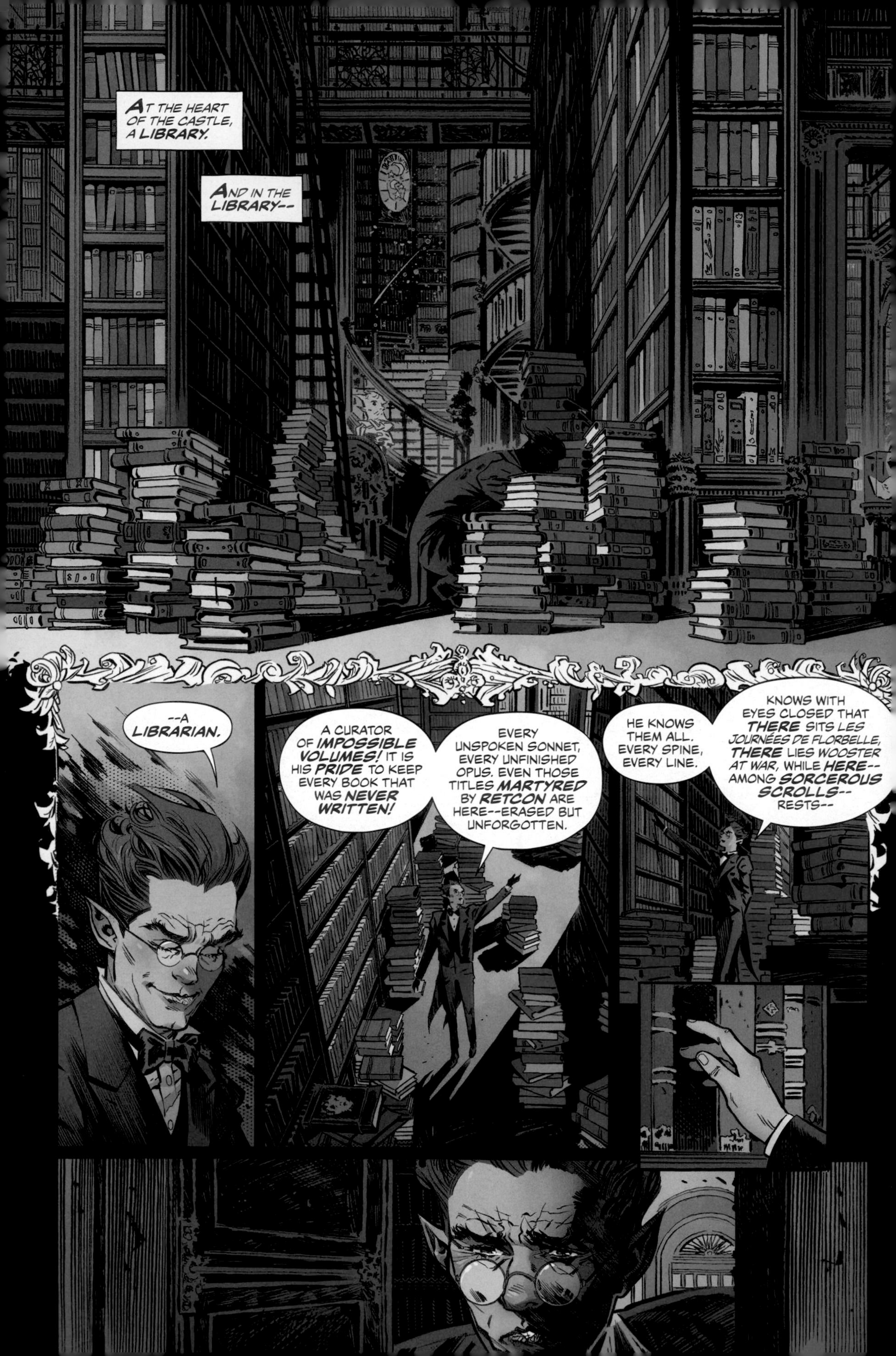

AT THE HEART OF THE CASTLE, A LIBRARY.
AND IN THE LIBRARY--
--A LIBRARIAN.
A CURATOR OF IMPOSSIBLE VOLUMES! IT IS HIS PRIDE TO KEEP EVERY BOOK THAT WAS NEVER WRITTEN!
EVERY UNSPOKEN SONNET, EVERY UNFINISHED OPUS. EVEN THOSE TITLES MARTYRED BY RETCON ARE HERE--ERASED BUT UNFORGOTTEN.
HE KNOWS THEM ALL. EVERY SPINE, EVERY LINE.
KNOWS WITH EYES CLOSED THAT THERE SITS LES JOURNÉES DE FLORBELLE, THERE LIES WOOSTER AT WAR, WHILE HERE-- AMONG SORCEROUS SCROLLS-- RESTS--

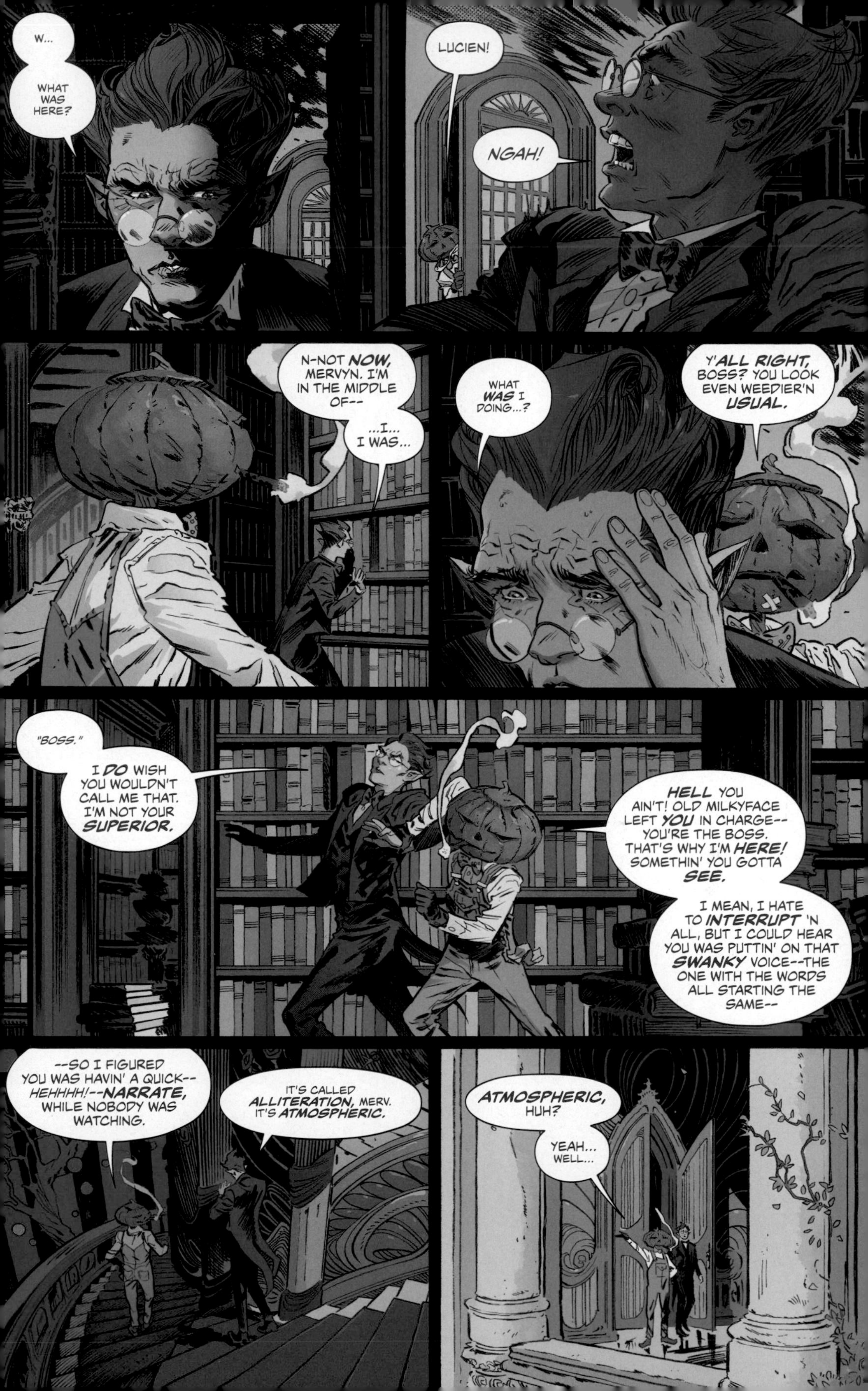
W...
WHAT WAS HERE?
LUCIEN!
NGAH!
N-NOT NOW, MERVYN. I'M IN THE MIDDLE OF--
...I... I WAS...
WHAT WAS I DOING...?
Y'ALL RIGHT, BOSS? YOU LOOK EVEN WEEDIER'N USUAL.
"BOSS."
I DO WISH YOU WOULDN'T CALL ME THAT. I'M NOT YOUR SUPERIOR.
HELL YOU AIN'T! OLD MILKYFACE LEFT YOU IN CHARGE-- YOU'RE THE BOSS. THAT'S WHY I'M HERE! SOMETHIN' YOU GOTTA SEE.
I MEAN, I HATE TO INTERRUPT 'N ALL, BUT I COULD HEAR YOU WAS PUTTIN' ON THAT SWANKY VOICE--THE ONE WITH THE WORDS ALL STARTING THE SAME--
--SO I FIGURED YOU WAS HAVIN' A QUICK-- HEHHHH!--NARRATE, WHILE NOBODY WAS WATCHING.
IT'S CALLED ALLITERATION, MERV. IT'S ATMOSPHERIC.
ATMOSPHERIC, HUH?
YEAH... WELL...

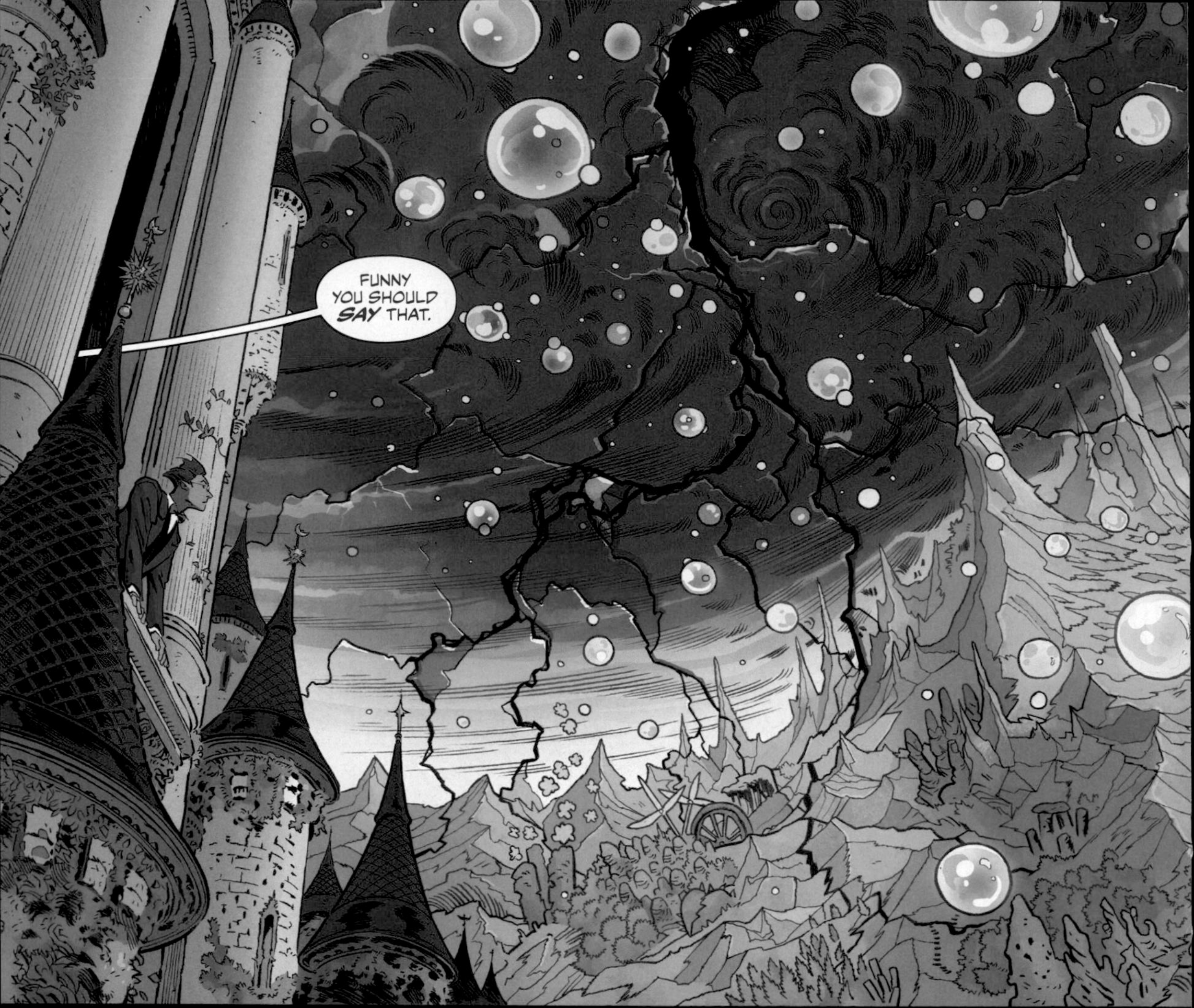
FUNNY YOU SHOULD SAY THAT.

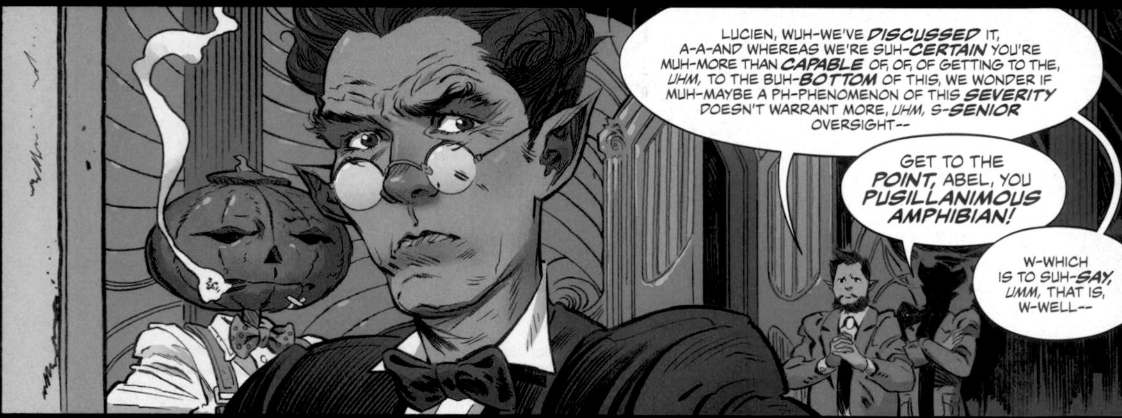
LUCIEN, WUH-WE'VE DISCUSSED IT, A-A-AND WHEREAS WE'RE SUH-CERTAIN YOU'RE MUH-MORE THAN CAPABLE OF, OF, OF GETTING TO THE, UHM, TO THE BUH-BOTTOM OF THIS, WE WONDER IF MUH-MAYBE A PH-PHENOMENON OF THIS SEVERITY DOESN'T WARRANT MORE, UHM, S-SENIOR OVERSIGHT--
GET TO THE POINT, ABEL, YOU PUSILLANIMOUS AMPHIBIAN!
W-WHICH IS TO SUH-SAY, UMM, THAT IS, W-WELL--

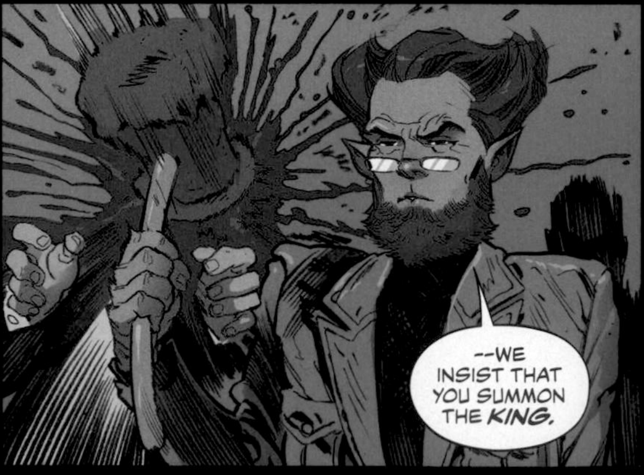
--WE INSIST THAT YOU SUMMON THE KING.

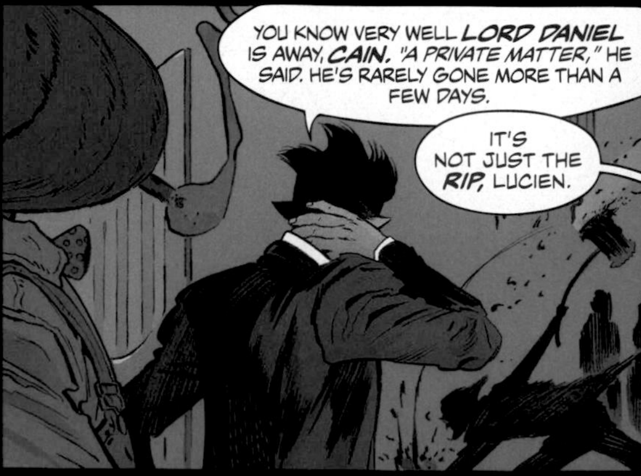
YOU KNOW VERY WELL LORD DANIEL IS AWAY, CAIN. "A PRIVATE MATTER," HE SAID. HE'S RARELY GONE MORE THAN A FEW DAYS.
IT'S NOT JUST THE RIP, LUCIEN.

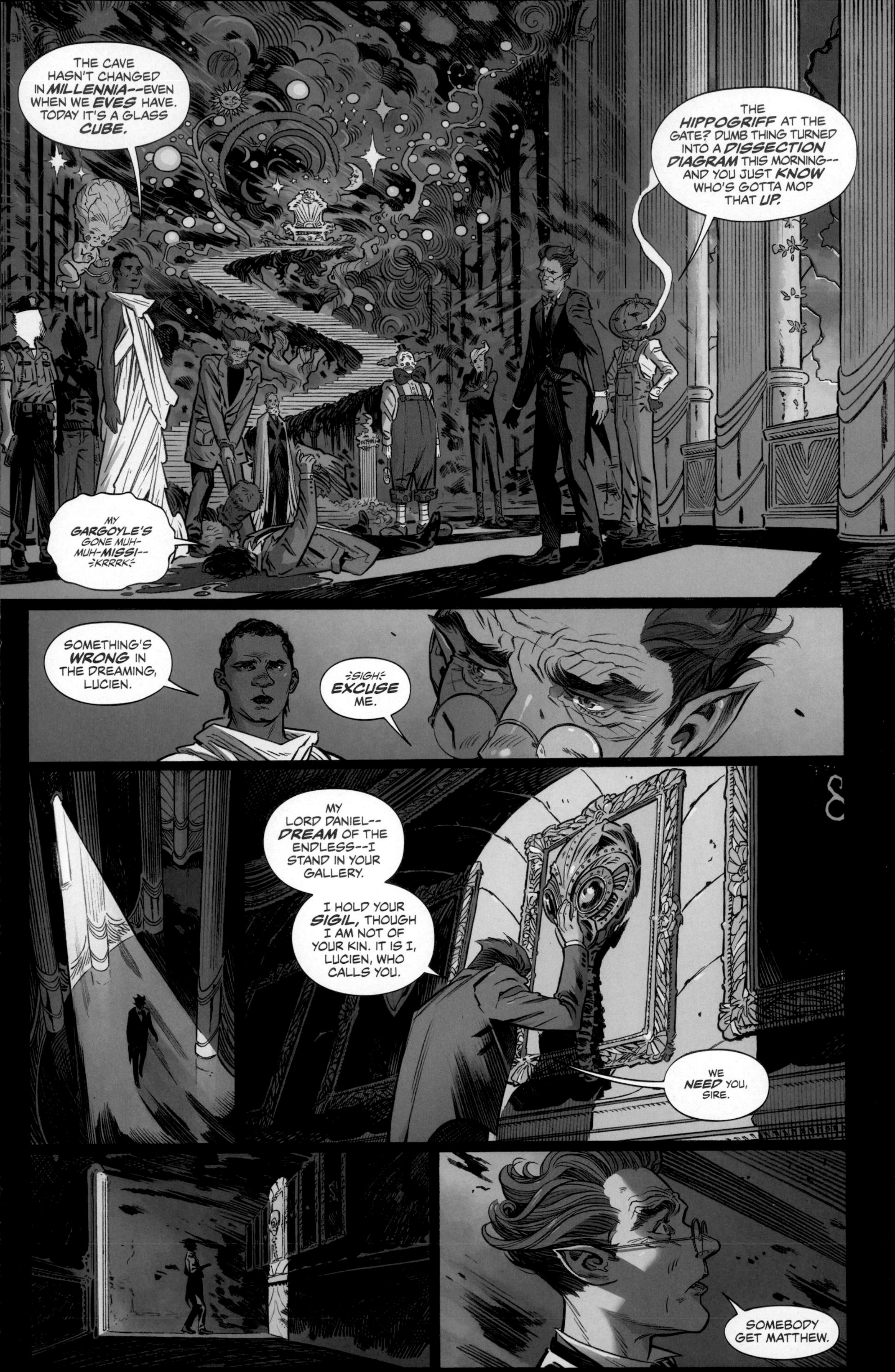
THE CAVE HASN'T CHANGED IN MILLENNIA--EVEN WHEN WE EVES HAVE. TODAY IT'S A GLASS CUBE.
THE HIPPOGRIFF AT THE GATE? DUMB THING TURNED INTO A DISSECTION DIAGRAM THIS MORNING-- AND YOU JUST KNOW WHO'S GOTTA MOP THAT UP.
MY GARGOYLE'S GONE MUH-MUH-MISSI-- KRRRK
SOMETHING'S WRONG IN THE DREAMING, LUCIEN.
SIGH EXCUSE ME.
MY LORD DANIEL-- DREAM OF THE ENDLESS--I STAND IN YOUR GALLERY.
I HOLD YOUR SIGIL, THOUGH I AM NOT OF YOUR KIN. IT IS I, LUCIEN, WHO CALLS YOU.
WE NEED YOU, SIRE.
SOMEBODY GET MATTHEW.

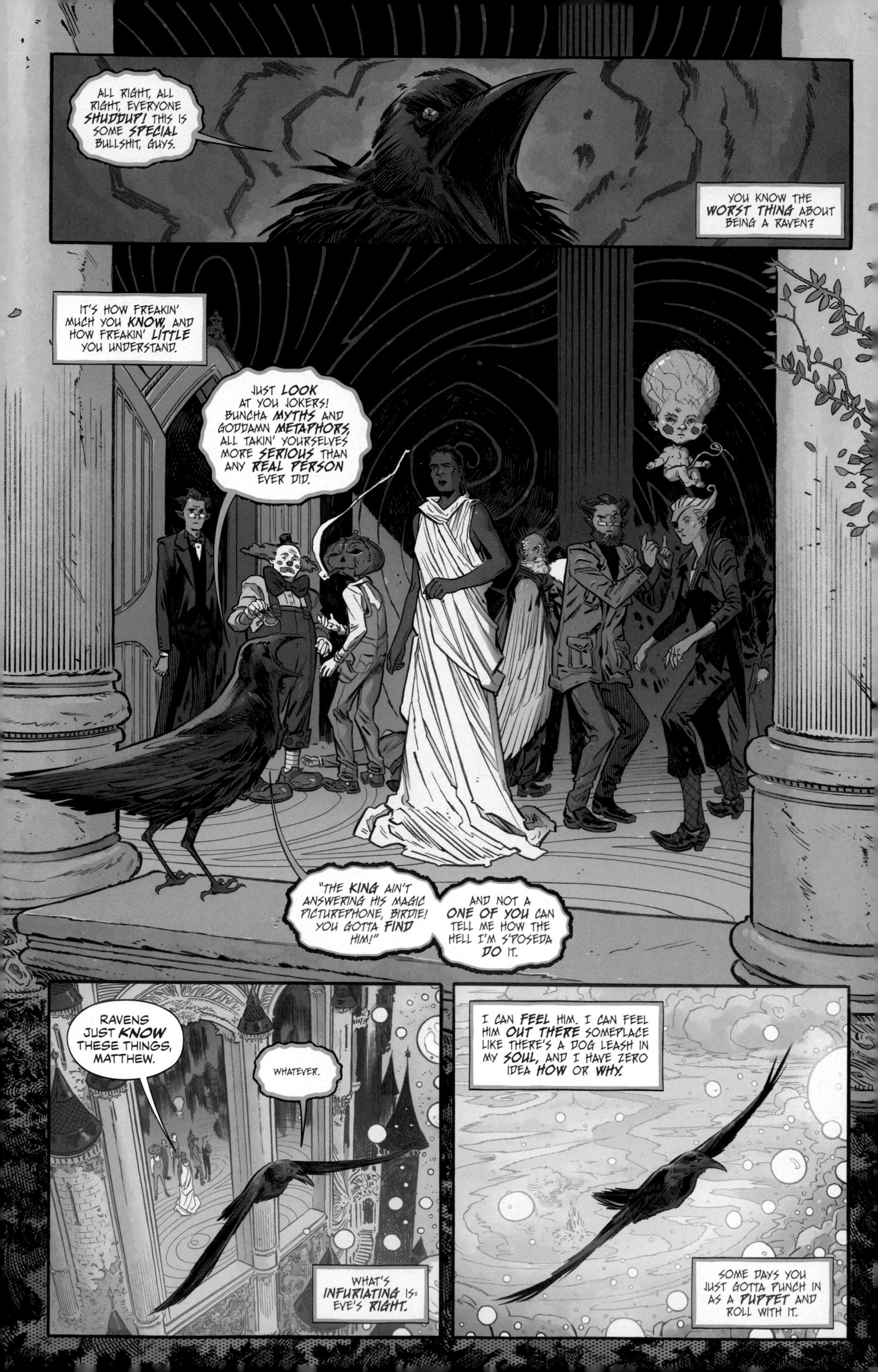
ALL RIGHT, ALL RIGHT, EVERYONE SHUDDUP! THIS IS SOME SPECIAL BULLSHIT, GUYS.
YOU KNOW THE WORST THING ABOUT BEING A RAVEN?
IT'S HOW FREAKIN' MUCH YOU KNOW, AND HOW FREAKIN' LITTLE YOU UNDERSTAND.
JUST LOOK AT YOU JOKERS! BUNCHA MYTHS AND GODDAMN METAPHORS, ALL TAKIN' YOURSELVES MORE SERIOUS THAN ANY REAL PERSON EVER DID.
"THE KING AIN'T ANSWERING HIS MAGIC PICTUREPHONE, BIRDIE! YOU GOTTA FIND HIM!"
AND NOT A ONE OF YOU CAN TELL ME HOW THE HELL I'M S'POSEDA DO IT.
RAVENS JUST KNOW THESE THINGS, MATTHEW.
WHATEVER.
WHAT'S INFURIATING IS: EVE'S RIGHT.
I CAN FEEL HIM. I CAN FEEL HIM OUT THERE SOMEPLACE LIKE THERE'S A DOG LEASH IN MY SOUL, AND I HAVE ZERO IDEA HOW OR WHY.
SOME DAYS YOU JUST GOTTA PUNCH IN AS A PUPPET AND ROLL WITH IT.

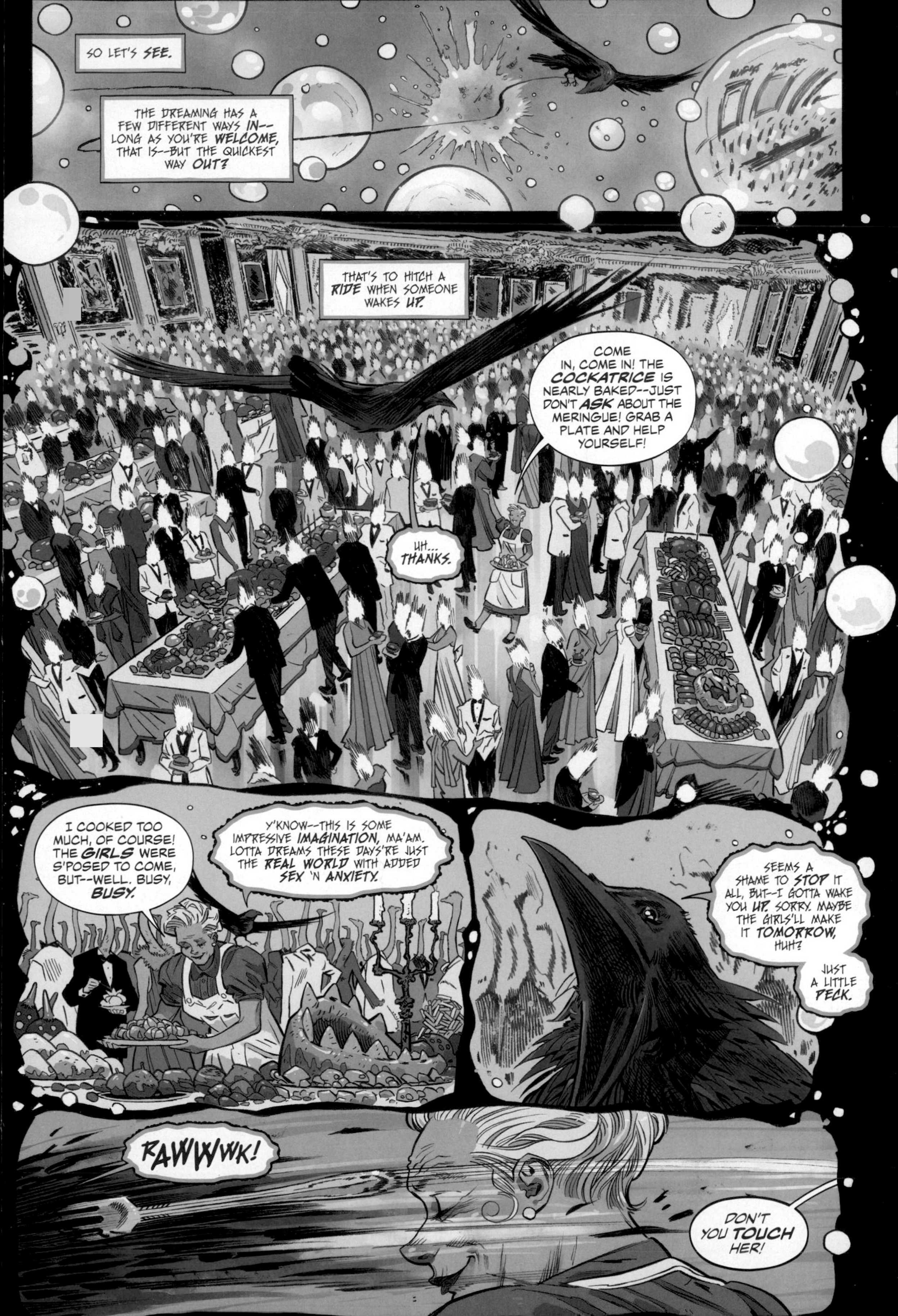
SO LET'S SEE.
THE DREAMING HAS A FEW DIFFERENT WAYS IN--LONG AS YOU'RE WELCOME, THAT IS--BUT THE QUICKEST WAY OUT?
THAT'S TO HITCH A RIDE WHEN SOMEONE WAKES UP.
COME IN, COME IN! THE COCKATRICE IS NEARLY BAKED--JUST DON'T ASK ABOUT THE MERINGUE! GRAB A PLATE AND HELP YOURSELF!
UH... THANKS.
I COOKED TOO MUCH, OF COURSE! THE GIRLS WERE S'POSED TO COME, BUT--WELL. BUSY, BUSY.
Y'KNOW--THIS IS SOME IMPRESSIVE IMAGINATION, MA'AM. LOTTA DREAMS THESE DAYS'RE JUST THE REAL WORLD WITH ADDED SEX 'N ANXIETY.
SEEMS A SHAME TO STOP IT ALL, BUT--I GOTTA WAKE YOU UP. SORRY. MAYBE THE GIRLS'LL MAKE IT TOMORROW, HUH?
JUST A LITTLE PECK.
RAWWWK!
DON'T YOU TOUCH HER!

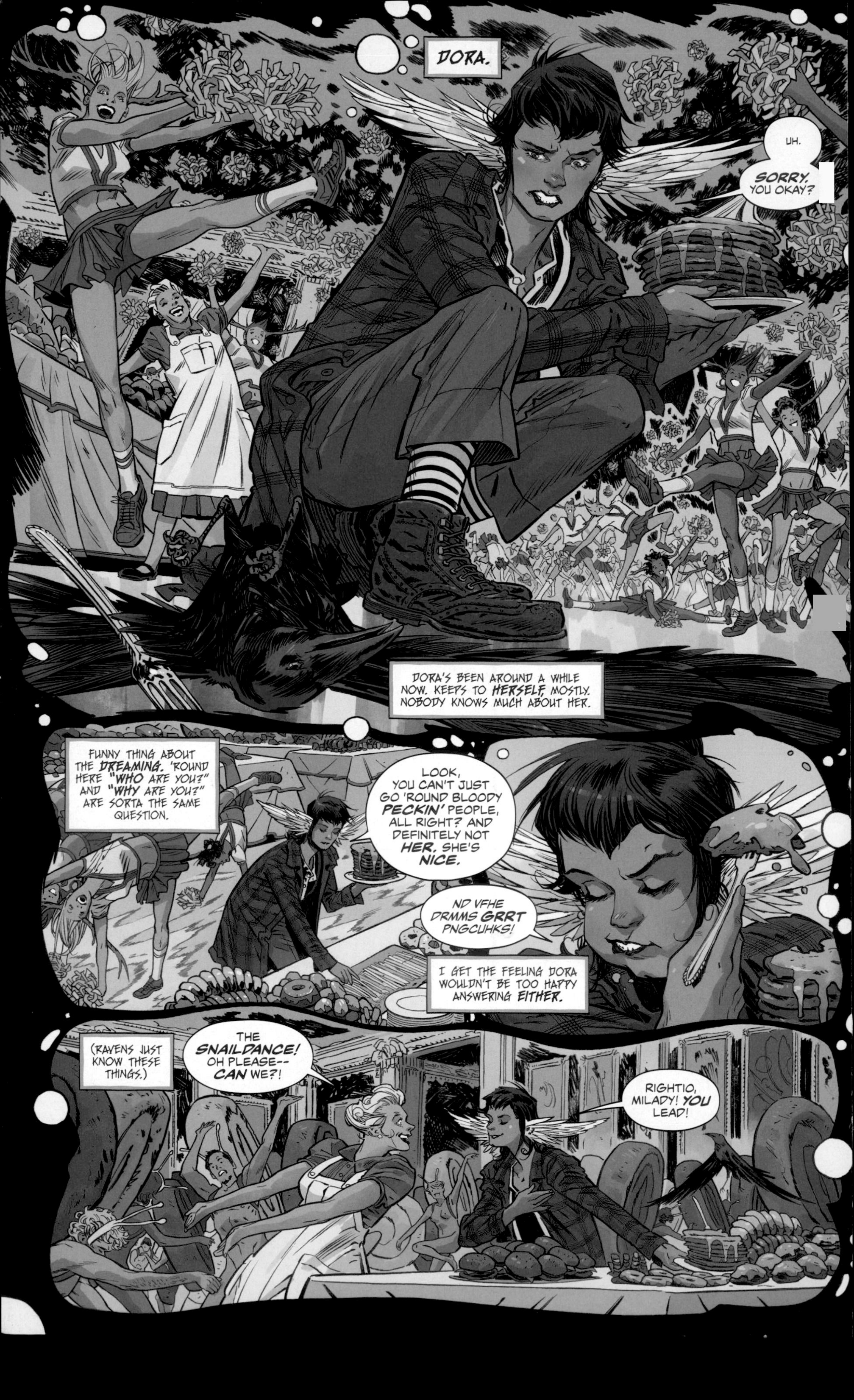
DORA.
UH.
SORRY. YOU OKAY?
DORA'S BEEN AROUND A WHILE NOW. KEEPS TO HERSELF, MOSTLY. NOBODY KNOWS MUCH ABOUT HER.
FUNNY THING ABOUT THE DREAMING. 'ROUND HERE "WHO ARE YOU?" AND "WHY ARE YOU?" ARE SORTA THE SAME QUESTION.
LOOK, YOU CAN'T JUST GO 'ROUND BLOODY PECKIN' PEOPLE, ALL RIGHT? AND DEFINITELY NOT HER. SHE'S NICE.
ND VFHE DRMMS GRRT PNGCUHKS!
I GET THE FEELING DORA WOULDN'T BE TOO HAPPY ANSWERING EITHER.
(RAVENS JUST KNOW THESE THINGS.)
THE SNAILDANCE! OH PLEASE-- CAN WE?!
RIGHTIO, MILADY! YOU LEAD!

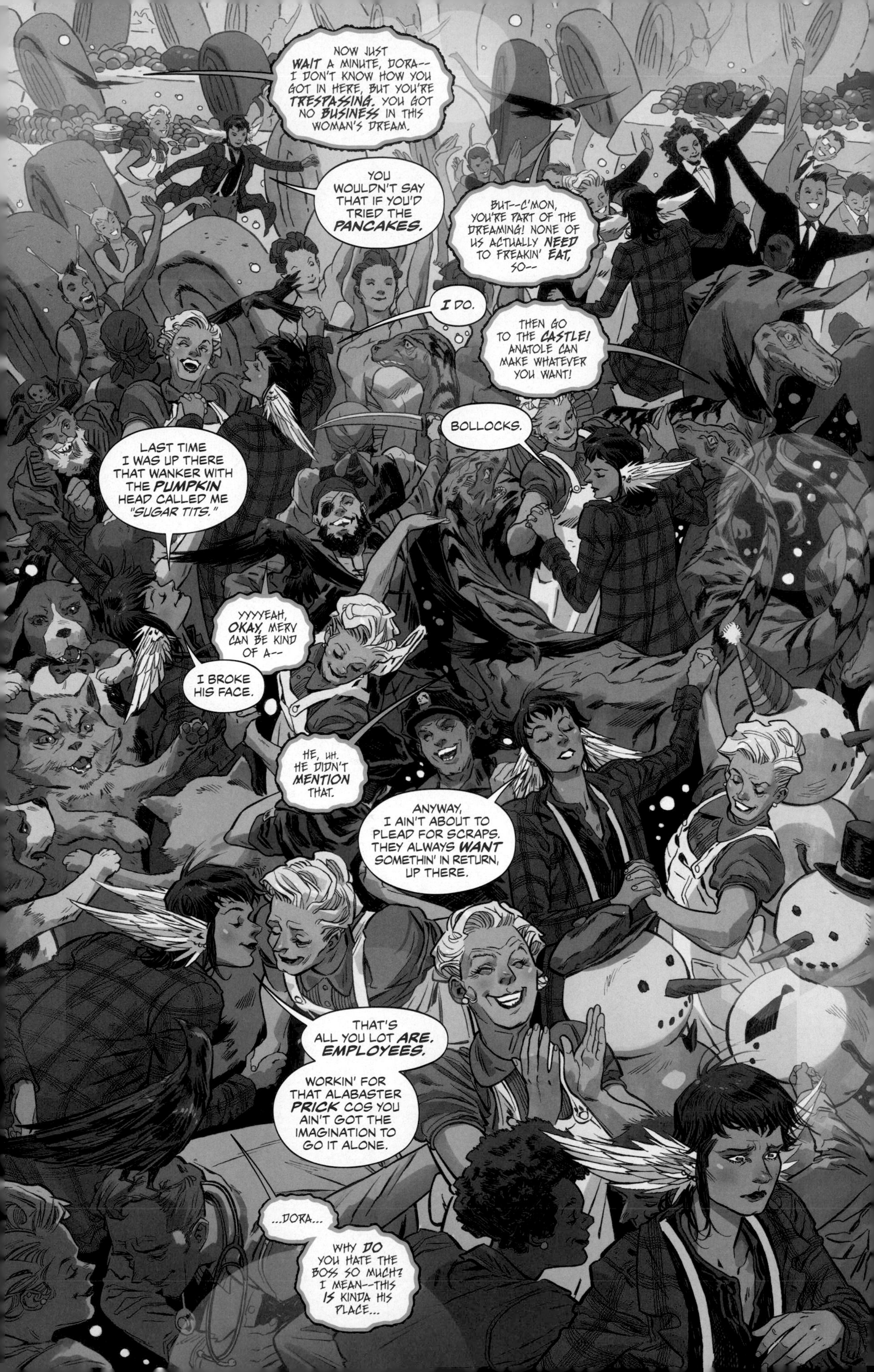
NOW JUST WAIT A MINUTE, DORA-- I DON'T KNOW HOW YOU GOT IN HERE, BUT YOU'RE TRESPASSING. YOU GOT NO BUSINESS IN THIS WOMAN'S DREAM.
YOU WOULDN'T SAY THAT IF YOU'D TRIED THE PANCAKES.
BUT--C'MON, YOU'RE PART OF THE DREAMING! NONE OF US ACTUALLY NEED TO FREAKIN' EAT, SO--
I DO.
THEN GO TO THE CASTLE! ANATOLE CAN MAKE WHATEVER YOU WANT!
BOLLOCKS.
LAST TIME I WAS UP THERE THAT WANKER WITH THE PUMPKIN HEAD CALLED ME "SUGAR TITS."
YYYYEAH, OKAY, MERV CAN BE KIND OF A--
I BROKE HIS FACE.
HE, UH. HE DIDN'T MENTION THAT.
ANYWAY, I AIN'T ABOUT TO PLEAD FOR SCRAPS. THEY ALWAYS WANT SOMETHIN' IN RETURN, UP THERE.
THAT'S ALL YOU LOT ARE. EMPLOYEES.
WORKIN' FOR THAT ALABASTER PRICK COS YOU AIN'T GOT THE IMAGINATION TO GO IT ALONE.
...DORA...
WHY DO YOU HATE THE BOSS SO MUCH? I MEAN--THIS IS KINDA HIS PLACE...

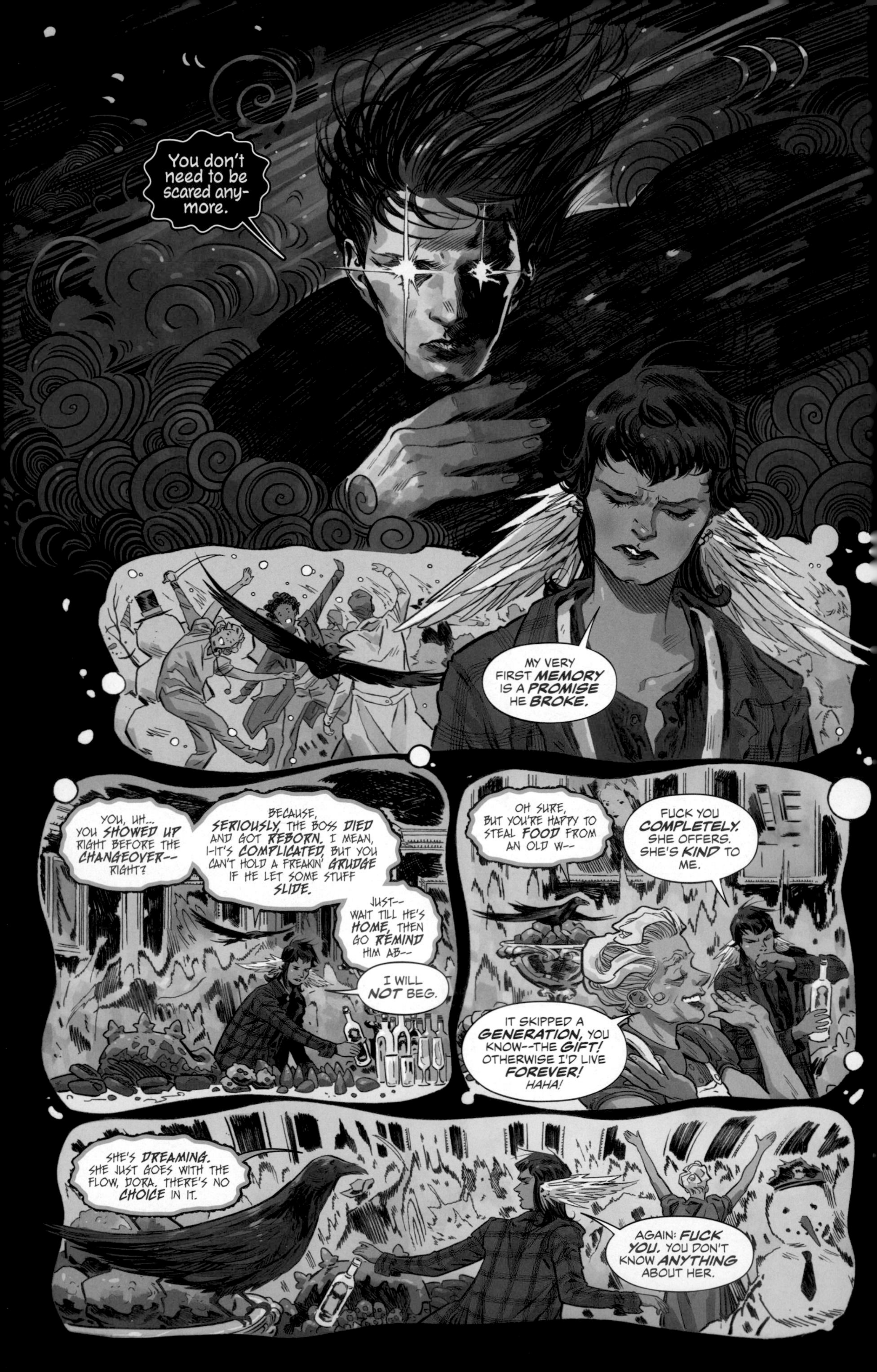
You don't need to be scared any-more.
MY VERY FIRST MEMORY IS A PROMISE HE BROKE.
YOU, UH... YOU SHOWED UP RIGHT BEFORE THE CHANGEOVER-- RIGHT?
BECAUSE, SERIOUSLY, THE BOSS DIED AND GOT REBORN. I MEAN, I-IT'S COMPLICATED, BUT YOU CAN'T HOLD A FREAKIN' GRUDGE IF HE LET SOME STUFF SLIDE.
JUST-- WAIT TILL HE'S HOME, THEN GO REMIND HIM AB--
I WILL NOT BEG.
OH SURE, BUT YOU'RE HAPPY TO STEAL FOOD FROM AN OLD W--
FUCK YOU COMPLETELY. SHE OFFERS. SHE'S KIND TO ME.
IT SKIPPED A GENERATION, YOU KNOW--THE GIFT! OTHERWISE I'D LIVE FOREVER! HAHA!
SHE'S DREAMING. SHE JUST GOES WITH THE FLOW, DORA. THERE'S NO CHOICE IN IT.
AGAIN: FUCK YOU. YOU DON'T KNOW ANYTHING ABOUT HER.

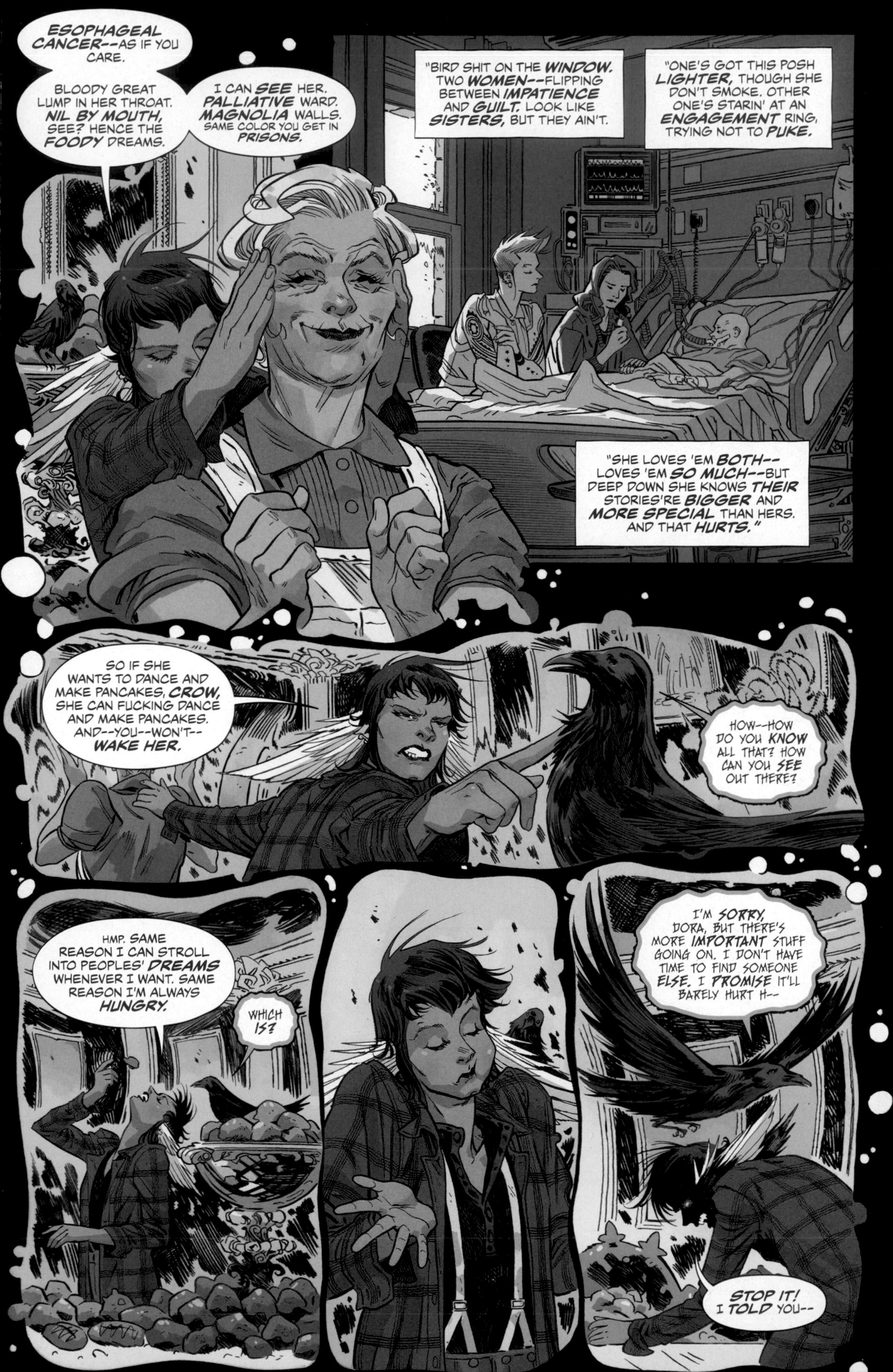
ESOPHAGEAL CANCER--AS IF YOU CARE.
BLOODY GREAT LUMP IN HER THROAT. NIL BY MOUTH, SEE? HENCE THE FOODY DREAMS.
I CAN SEE HER. PALLIATIVE WARD. MAGNOLIA WALLS. SAME COLOR YOU GET IN PRISONS.
"BIRD SHIT ON THE WINDOW. TWO WOMEN--FLIPPING BETWEEN IMPATIENCE AND GUILT. LOOK LIKE SISTERS, BUT THEY AIN'T.
"ONE'S GOT THIS POSH LIGHTER, THOUGH SHE DON'T SMOKE. OTHER ONE'S STARIN' AT AN ENGAGEMENT RING, TRYING NOT TO PUKE.
"SHE LOVES 'EM BOTH--LOVES 'EM SO MUCH--BUT DEEP DOWN SHE KNOWS THEIR STORIES'RE BIGGER AND MORE SPECIAL THAN HERS. AND THAT HURTS."
SO IF SHE WANTS TO DANCE AND MAKE PANCAKES, CROW, SHE CAN FUCKING DANCE AND MAKE PANCAKES. AND--YOU--WON'T--WAKE HER.
HOW--HOW DO YOU KNOW ALL THAT? HOW CAN YOU SEE OUT THERE?
HMP. SAME REASON I CAN STROLL INTO PEOPLES' DREAMS WHENEVER I WANT. SAME REASON I'M ALWAYS HUNGRY.
WHICH IS?
I'M SORRY, DORA, BUT THERE'S MORE IMPORTANT STUFF GOING ON. I DON'T HAVE TIME TO FIND SOMEONE ELSE. I PROMISE IT'LL BARELY HURT H--
STOP IT! I TOLD YOU--

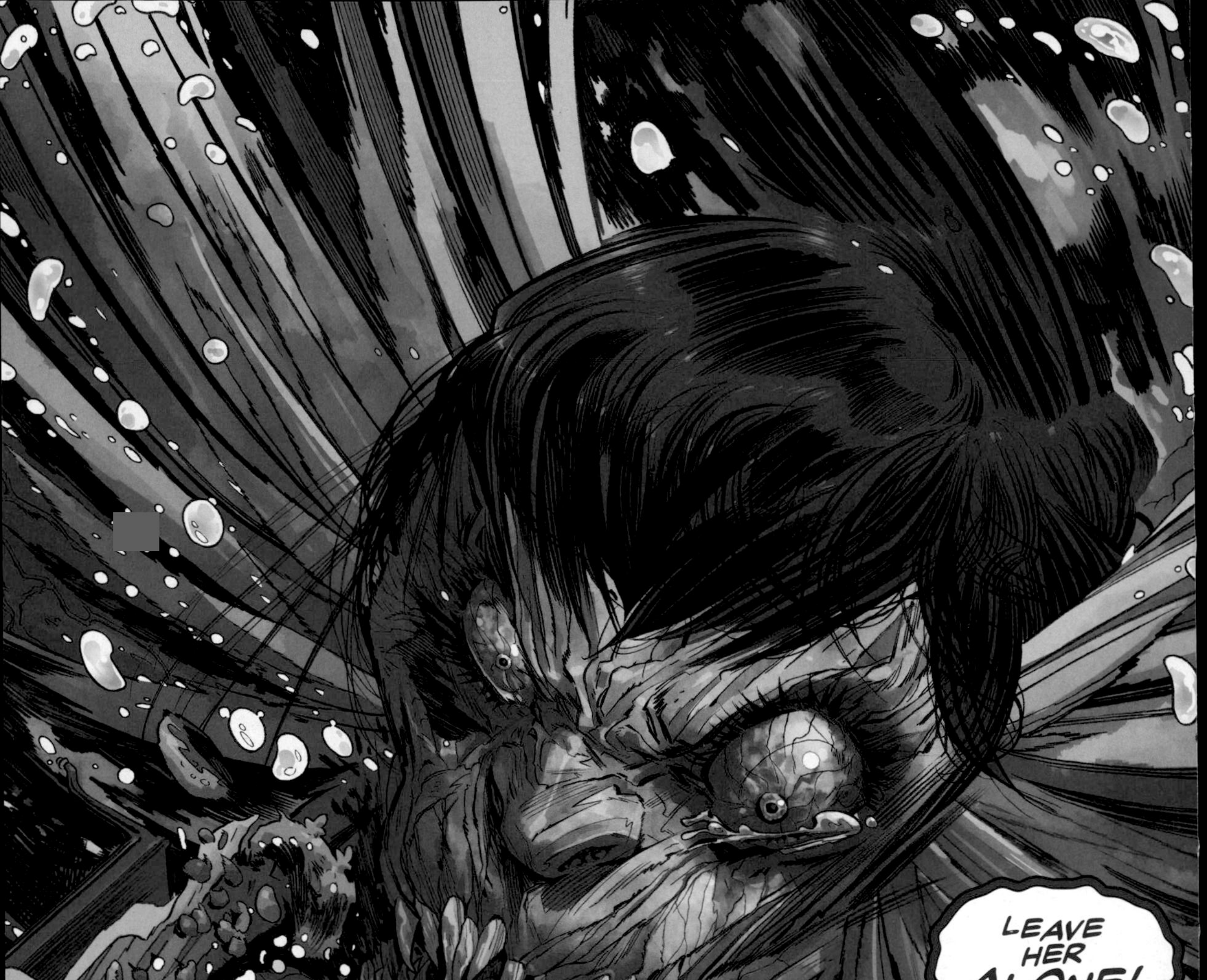
LEAVE HER ALONE!

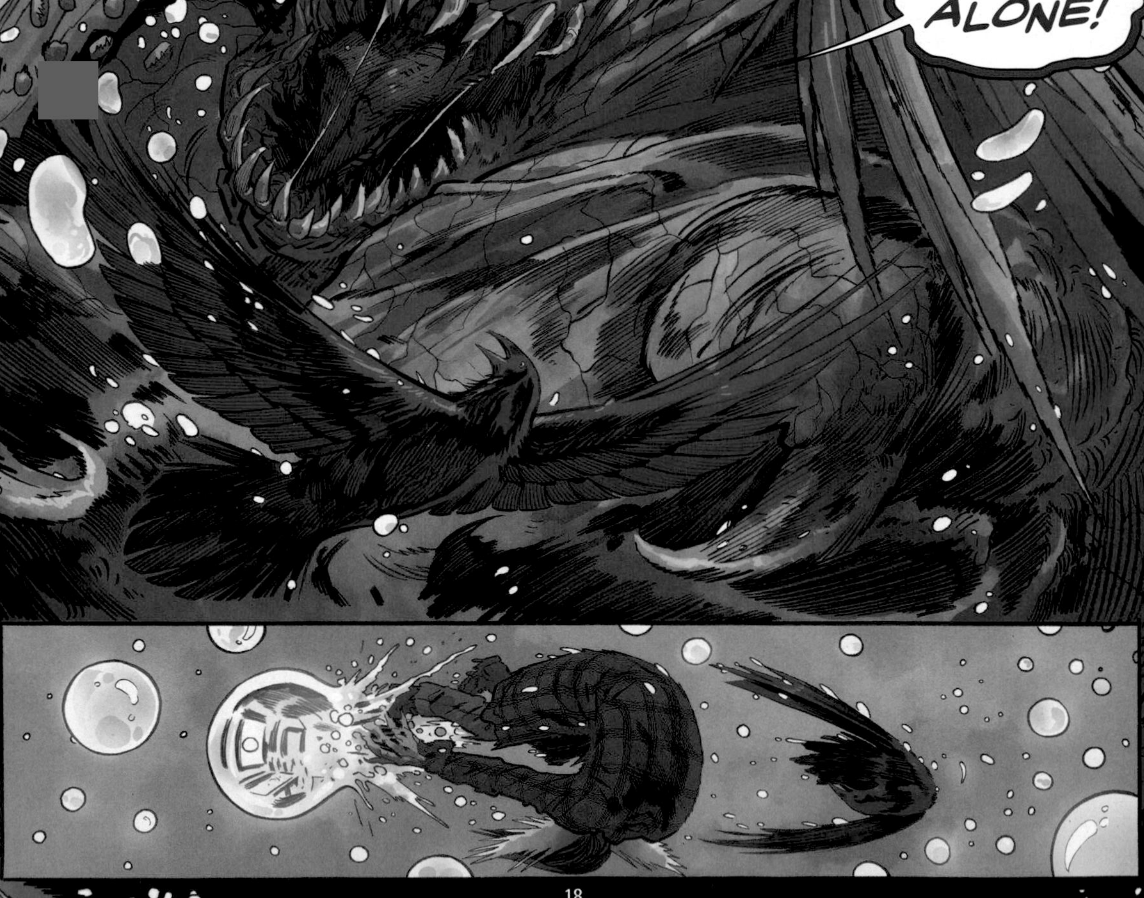

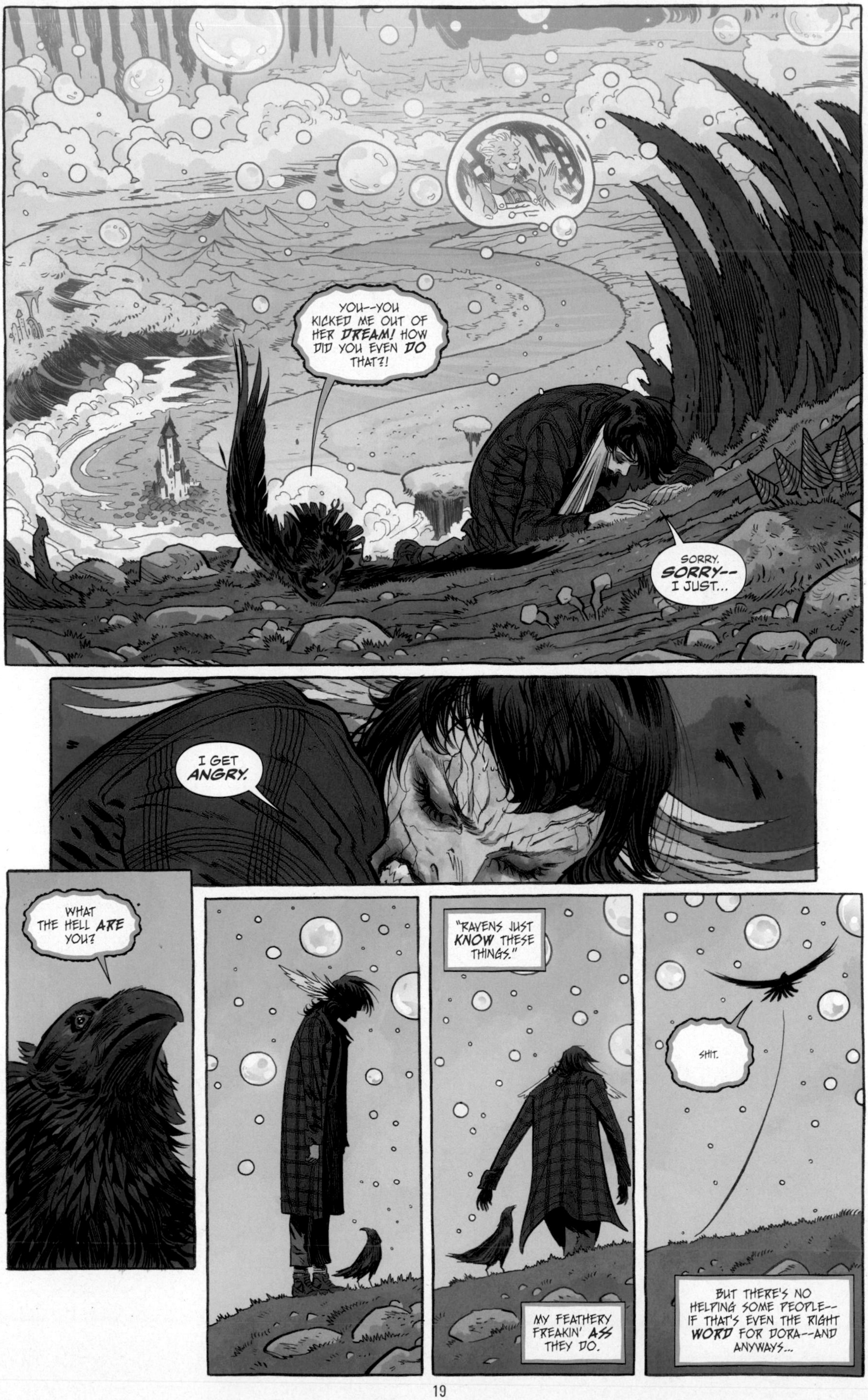
YOU--YOU KICKED ME OUT OF HER DREAM! HOW DID YOU EVEN DO THAT?!
SORRY. SORRY-- I JUST...
I GET ANGRY.
WHAT THE HELL ARE YOU?
"RAVENS JUST KNOW THESE THINGS."
MY FEATHERY FREAKIN' ASS THEY DO.
SHIT.
BUT THERE'S NO HELPING SOME PEOPLE-- IF THAT'S EVEN THE RIGHT WORD FOR DORA--AND ANYWAYS...

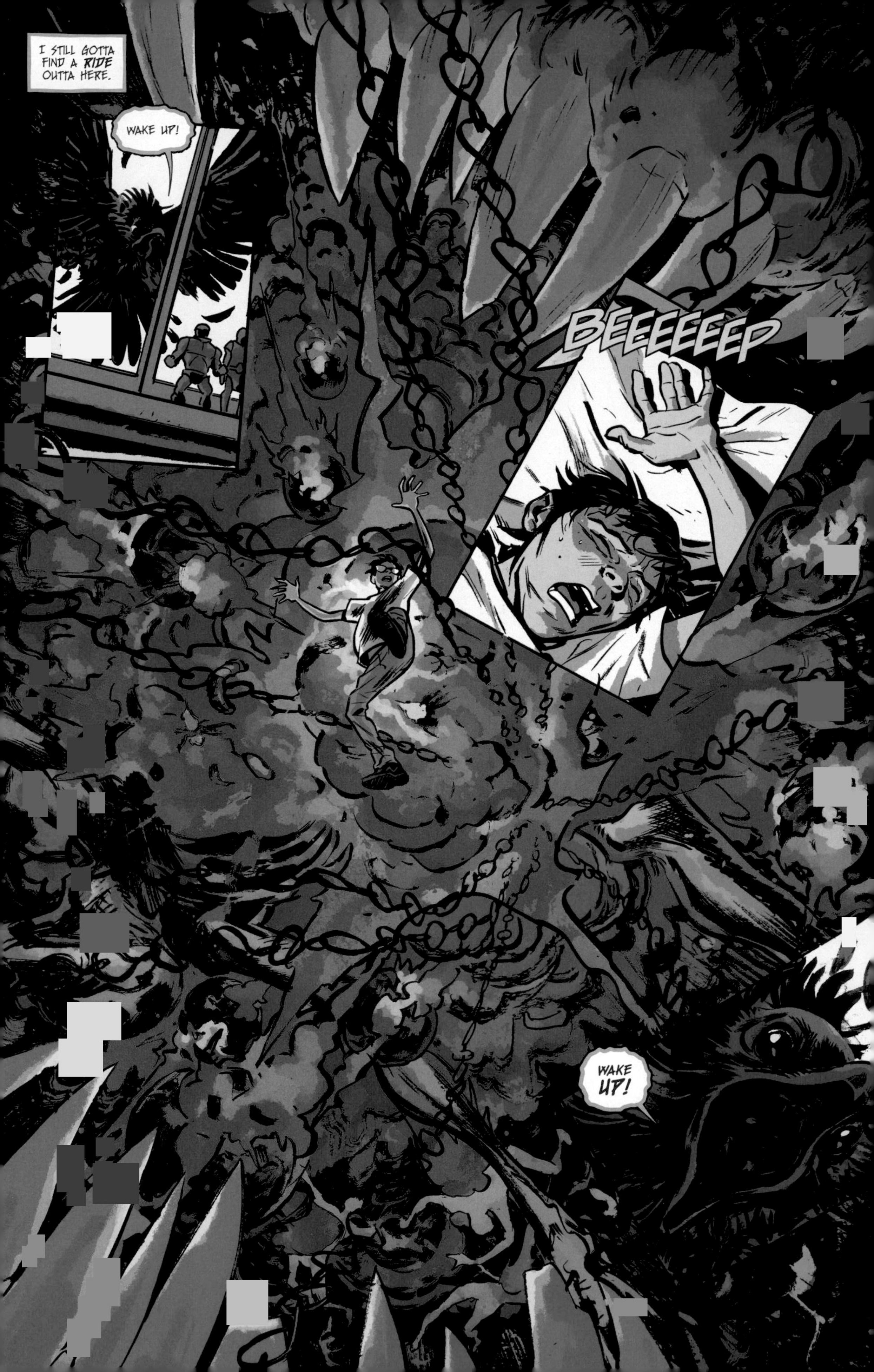
I STILL GOTTA FIND A RIDE OUTTA HERE.
WAKE UP!
BEEEEEEP
WAKE UP!

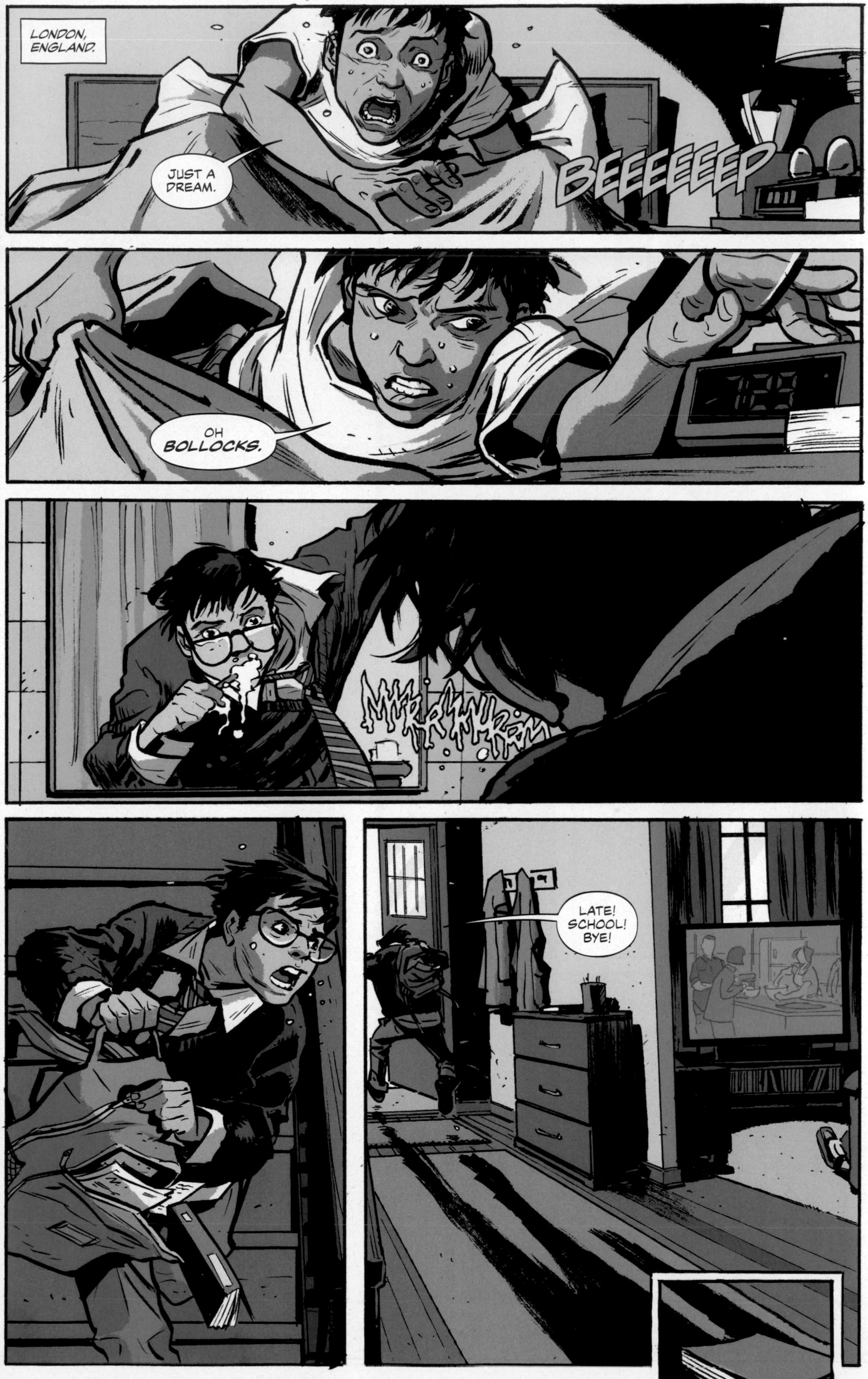
LONDON, ENGLAND.
JUST A DREAM.
BEEEEEEP
OH BOLLOCKS.
LATE! SCHOOL! BYE!

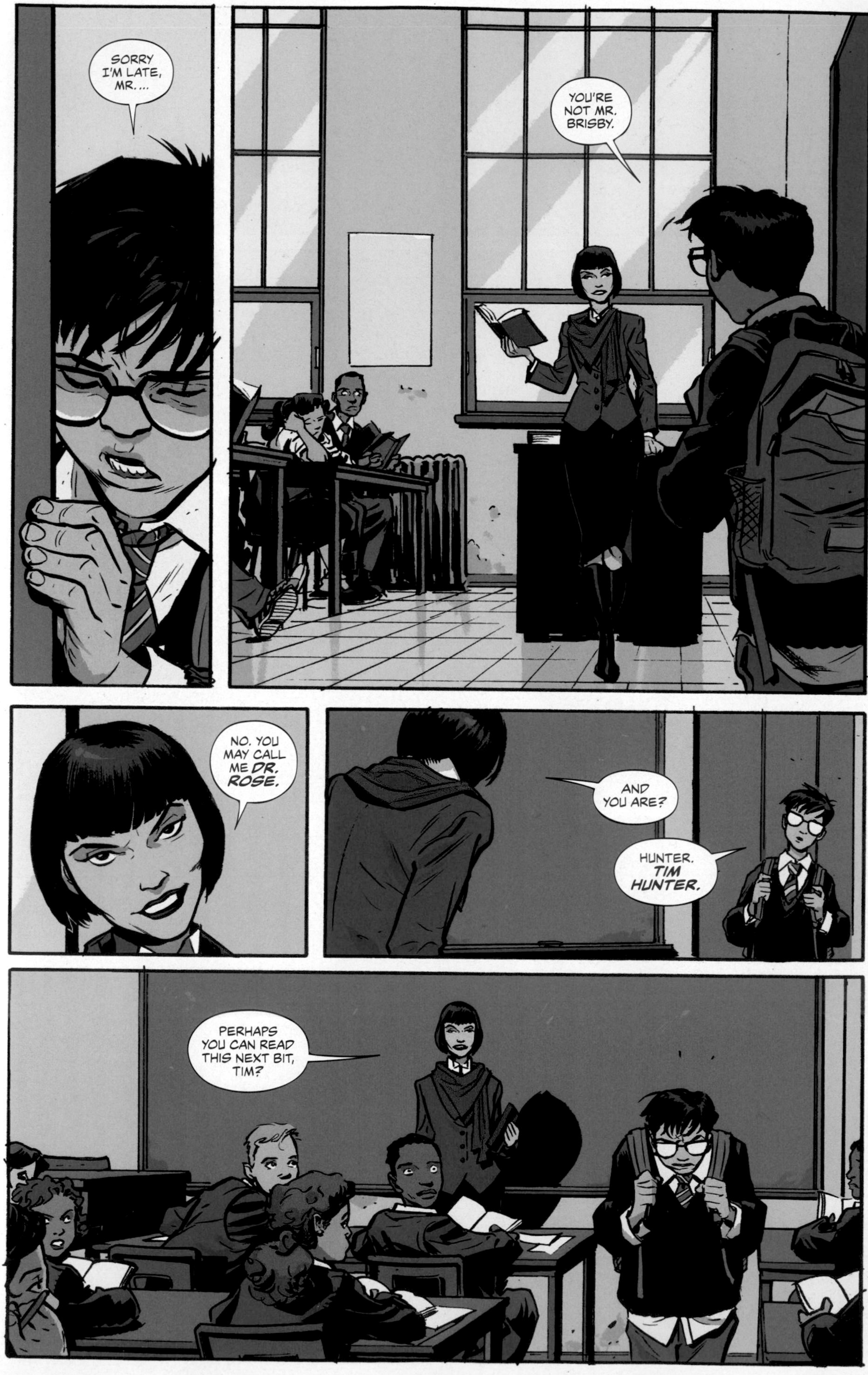
SORRY I'M LATE, MR....
YOU'RE NOT MR. BRISBY.
NO. YOU MAY CALL ME *DR. ROSE.*
AND YOU ARE?
HUNTER. *TIM HUNTER.*
PERHAPS YOU CAN READ THIS NEXT BIT, TIM?

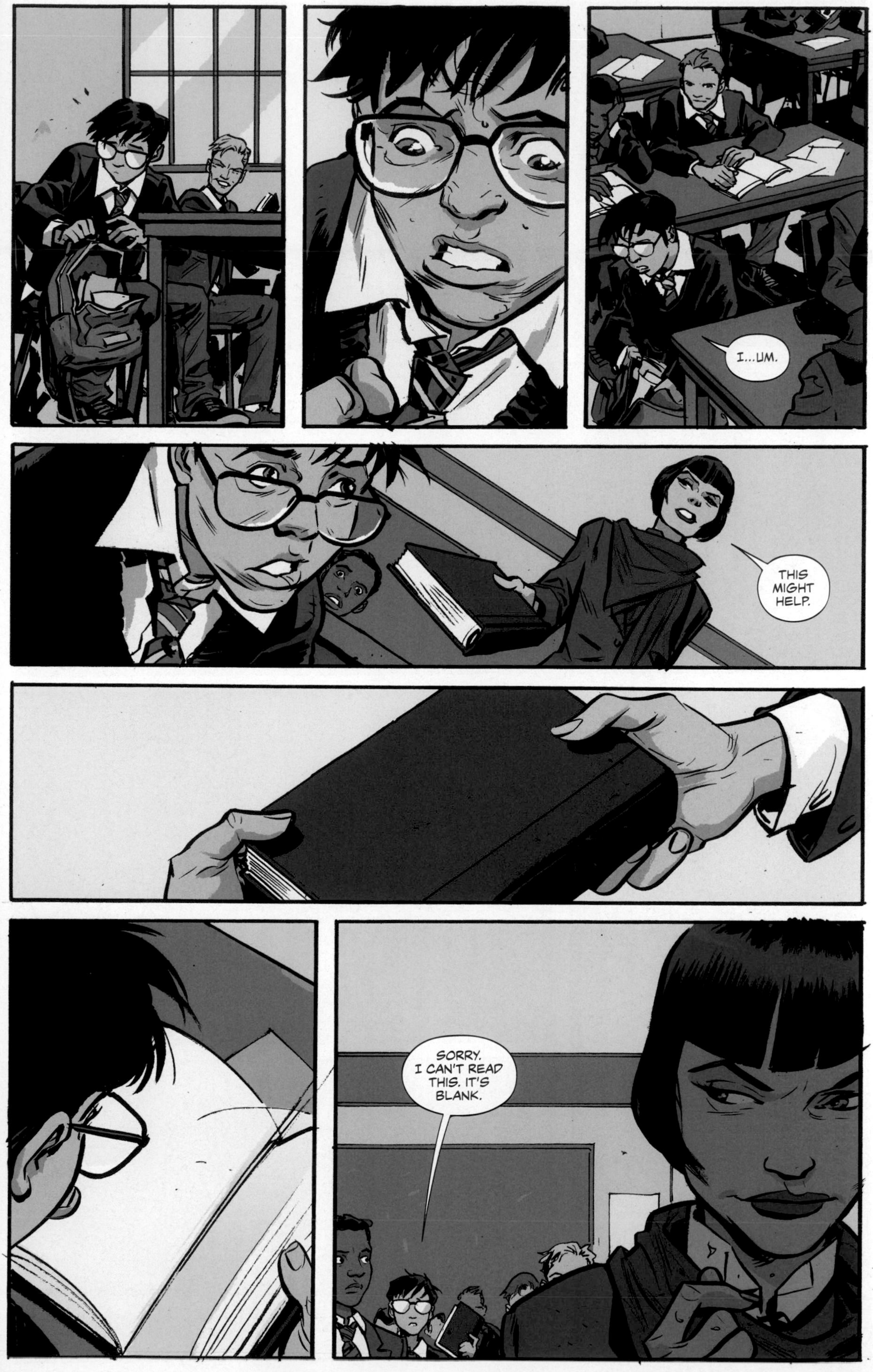
I...UM.
THIS MIGHT HELP.
SORRY. I CAN'T READ THIS. IT'S BLANK.

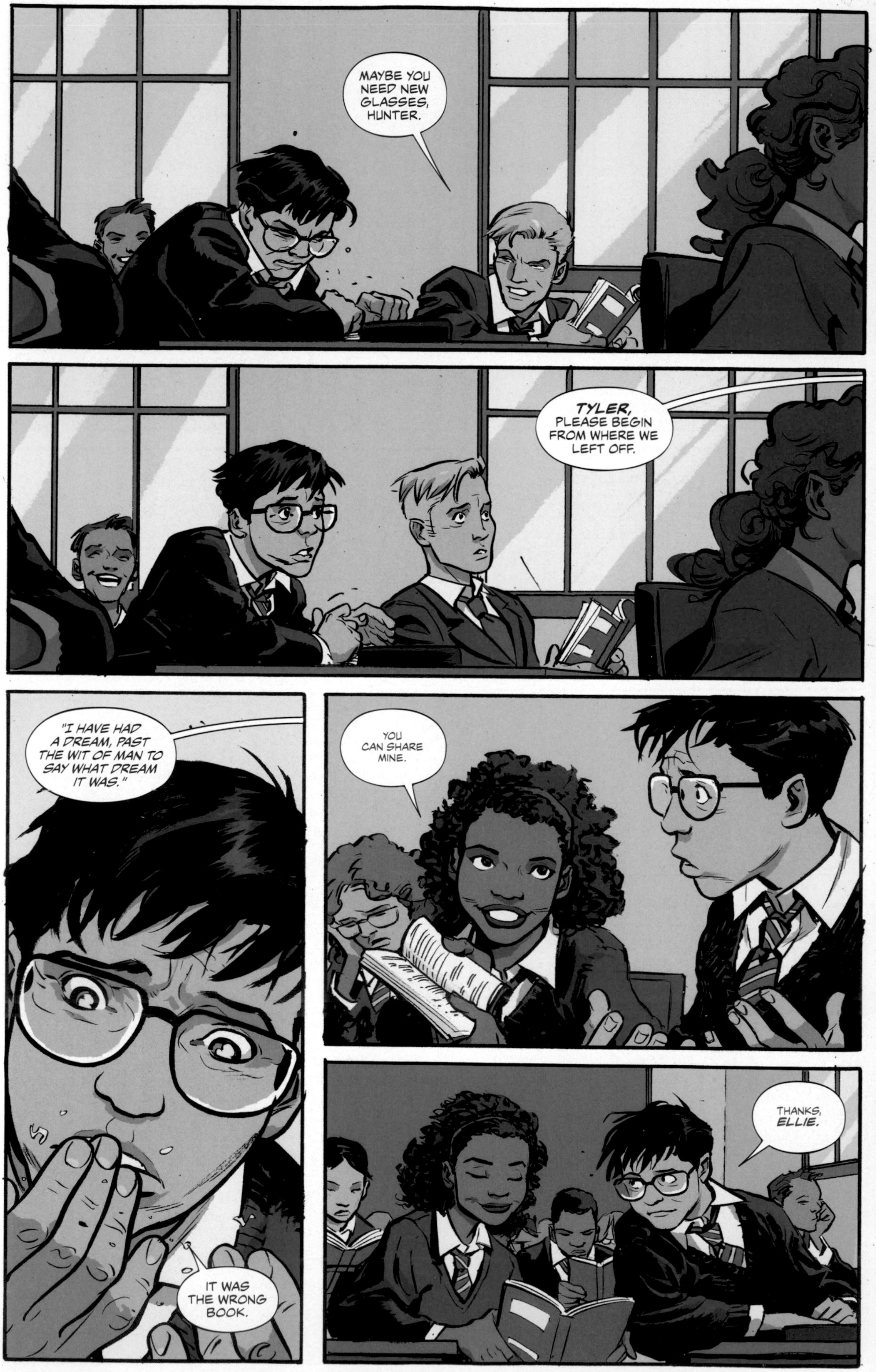
MAYBE YOU NEED NEW GLASSES, HUNTER.
TYLER, PLEASE BEGIN FROM WHERE WE LEFT OFF.
"I HAVE HAD A DREAM, PAST THE WIT OF MAN TO SAY WHAT DREAM IT WAS."
IT WAS THE WRONG BOOK.
YOU CAN SHARE MINE.
THANKS, ELLIE.

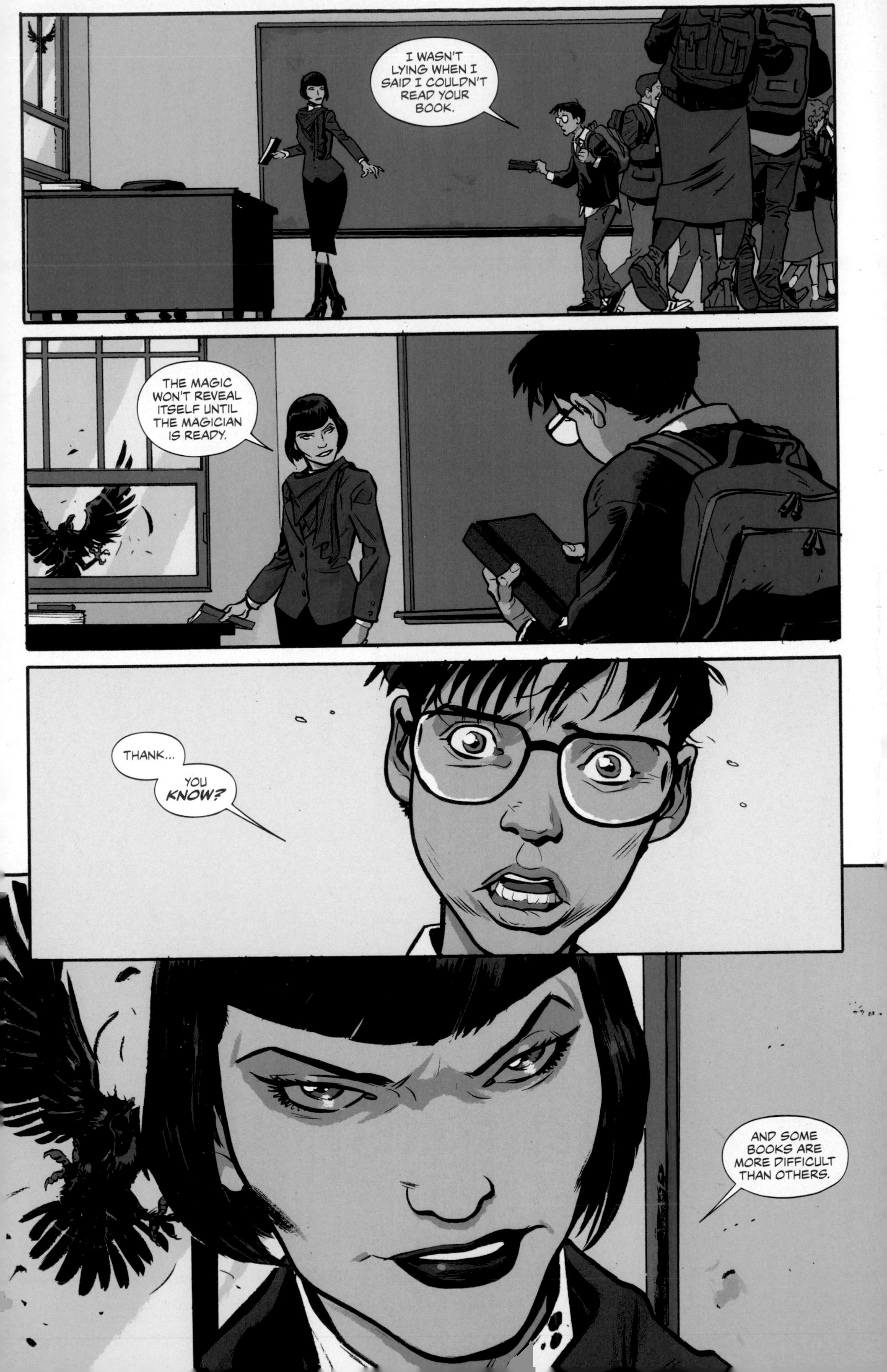
I WASN'T LYING WHEN I SAID I COULDN'T READ YOUR BOOK.
THE MAGIC WON'T REVEAL ITSELF UNTIL THE MAGICIAN IS READY.
THANK...
YOU *KNOW?*
AND SOME BOOKS ARE MORE DIFFICULT THAN OTHERS.

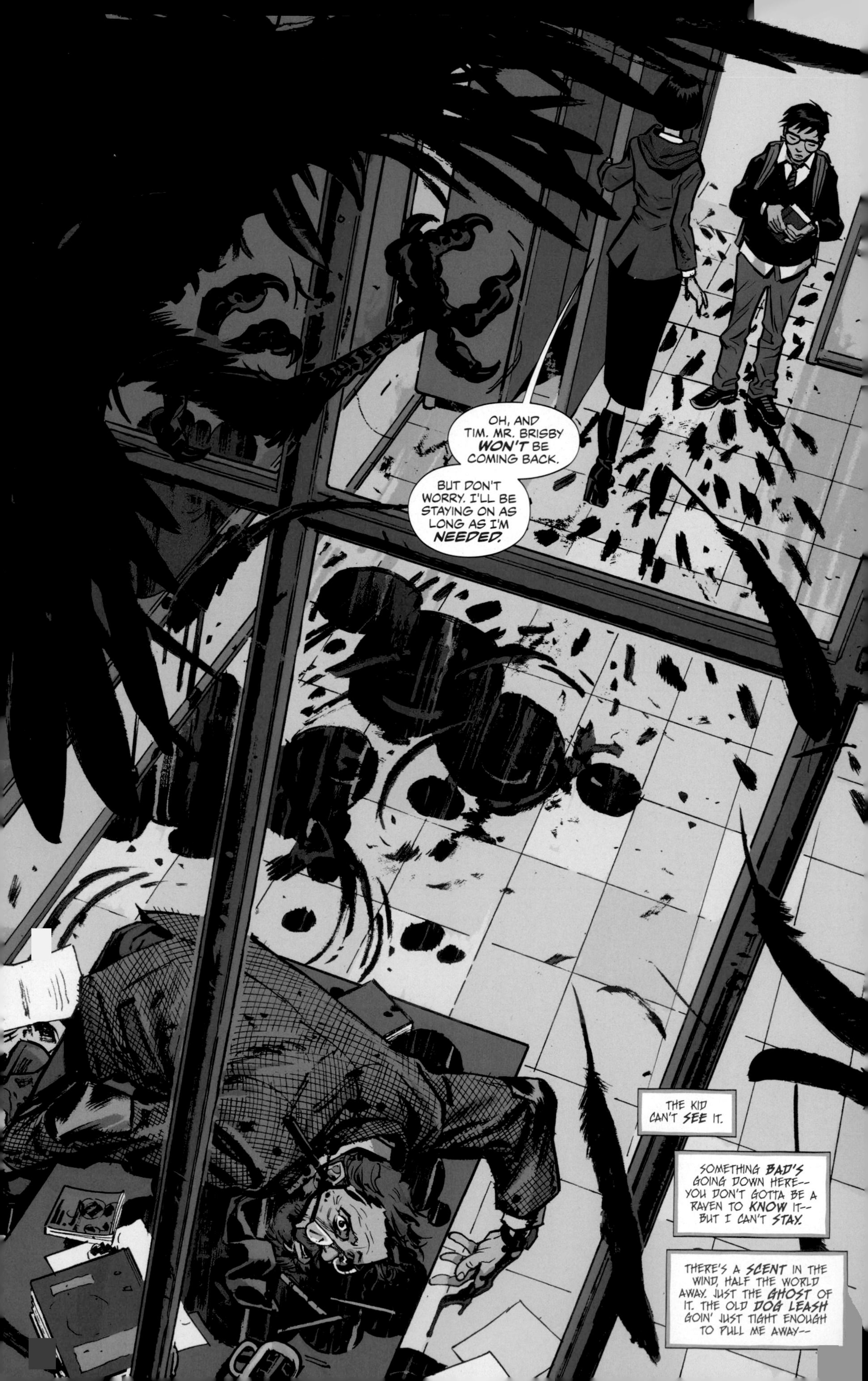
OH, AND TIM. MR. BRISBY WON'T BE COMING BACK.
BUT DON'T WORRY. I'LL BE STAYING ON AS LONG AS I'M NEEDED.
THE KID CAN'T SEE IT.
SOMETHING BAD'S GOING DOWN HERE-- YOU DON'T GOTTA BE A RAVEN TO KNOW IT-- BUT I CAN'T STAY.
THERE'S A SCENT IN THE WIND, HALF THE WORLD AWAY. JUST THE GHOST OF IT. THE OLD DOG LEASH GOIN' JUST TIGHT ENOUGH TO PULL ME AWAY--

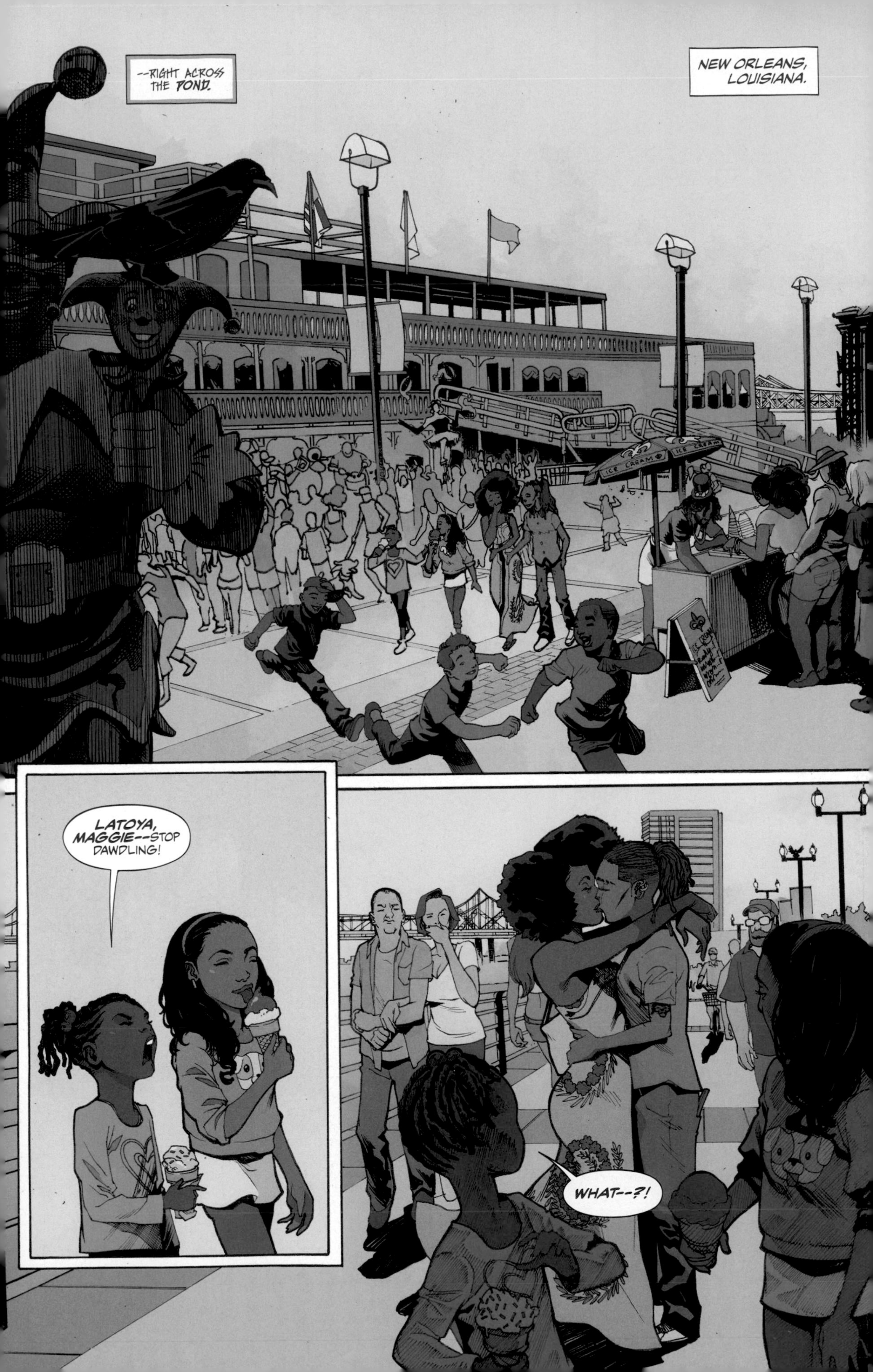
--RIGHT ACROSS THE POND.
NEW ORLEANS, LOUISIANA.
LATOYA, MAGGIE--STOP DAWDLING!
WHAT--?!

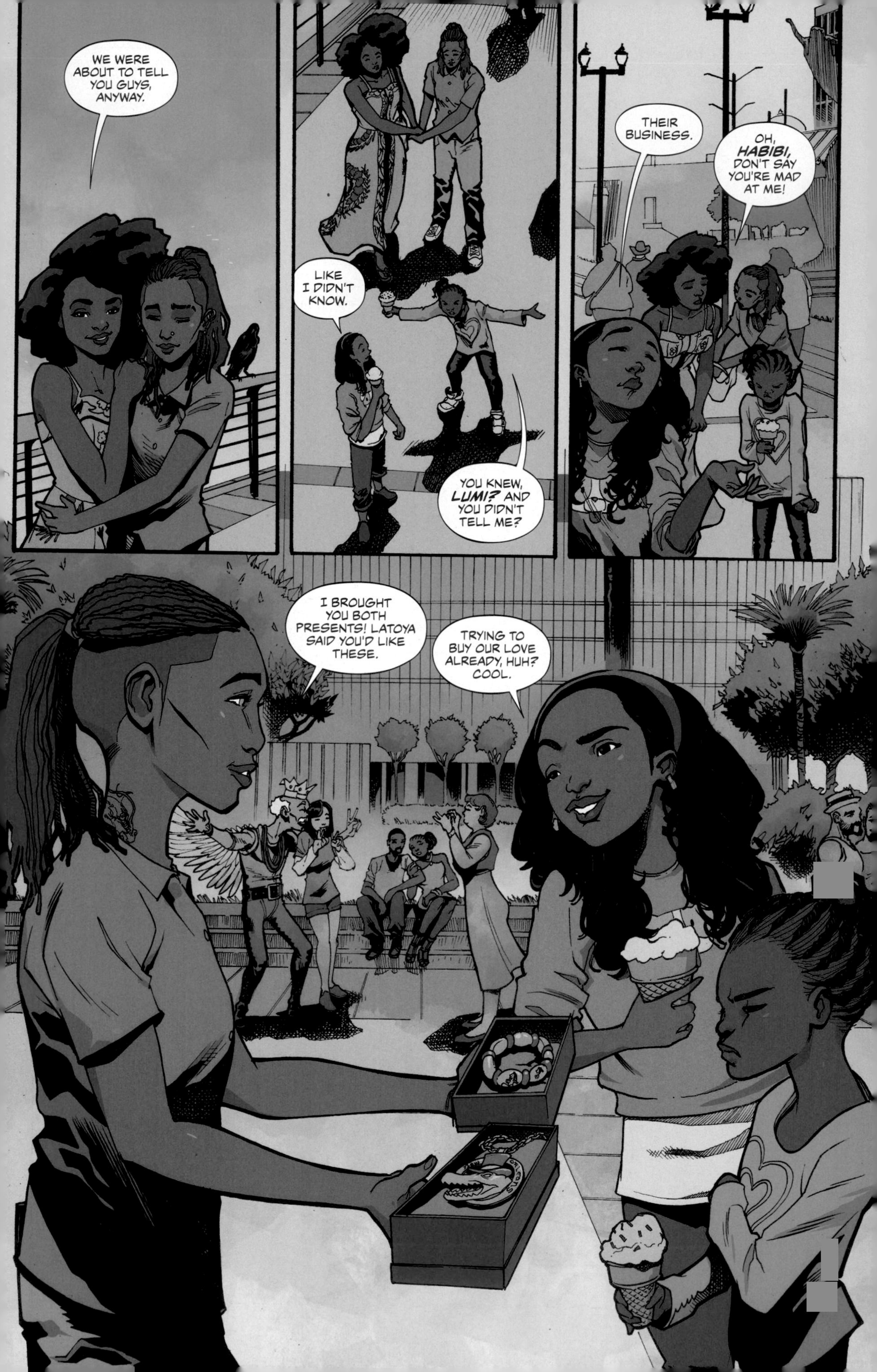
WE WERE ABOUT TO TELL YOU GUYS, ANYWAY.
LIKE I DIDN'T KNOW.
YOU KNEW, LUMI? AND YOU DIDN'T TELL ME?
THEIR BUSINESS.
OH, HABIBI, DON'T SAY YOU'RE MAD AT ME!
I BROUGHT YOU BOTH PRESENTS! LATOYA SAID YOU'D LIKE THESE.
TRYING TO BUY OUR LOVE ALREADY, HUH? COOL.

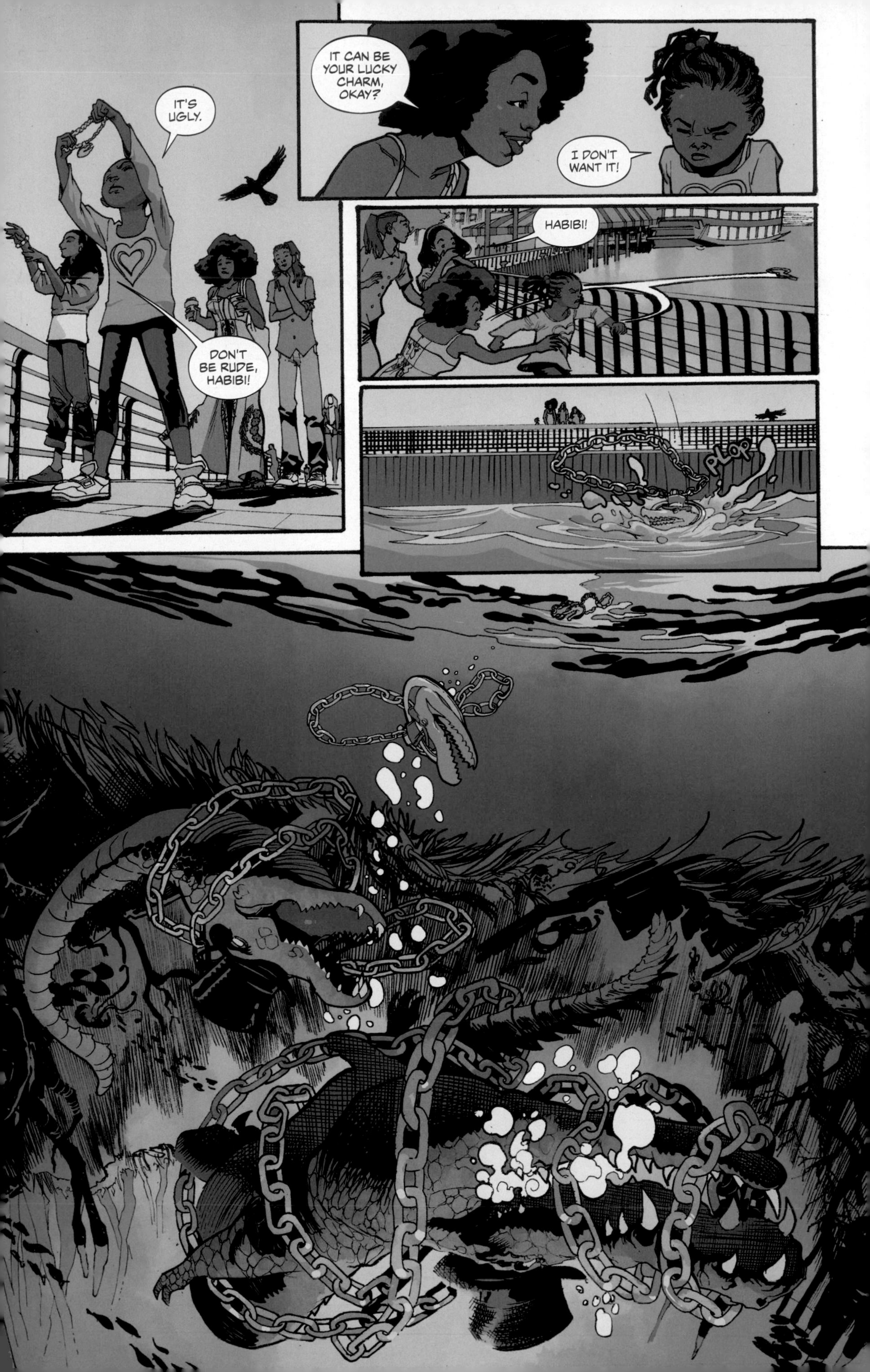
IT'S UGLY.
DON'T BE RUDE, HABIBI!
IT CAN BE YOUR LUCKY CHARM, OKAY?
I DON'T WANT IT!
HABIBI!
PLOP

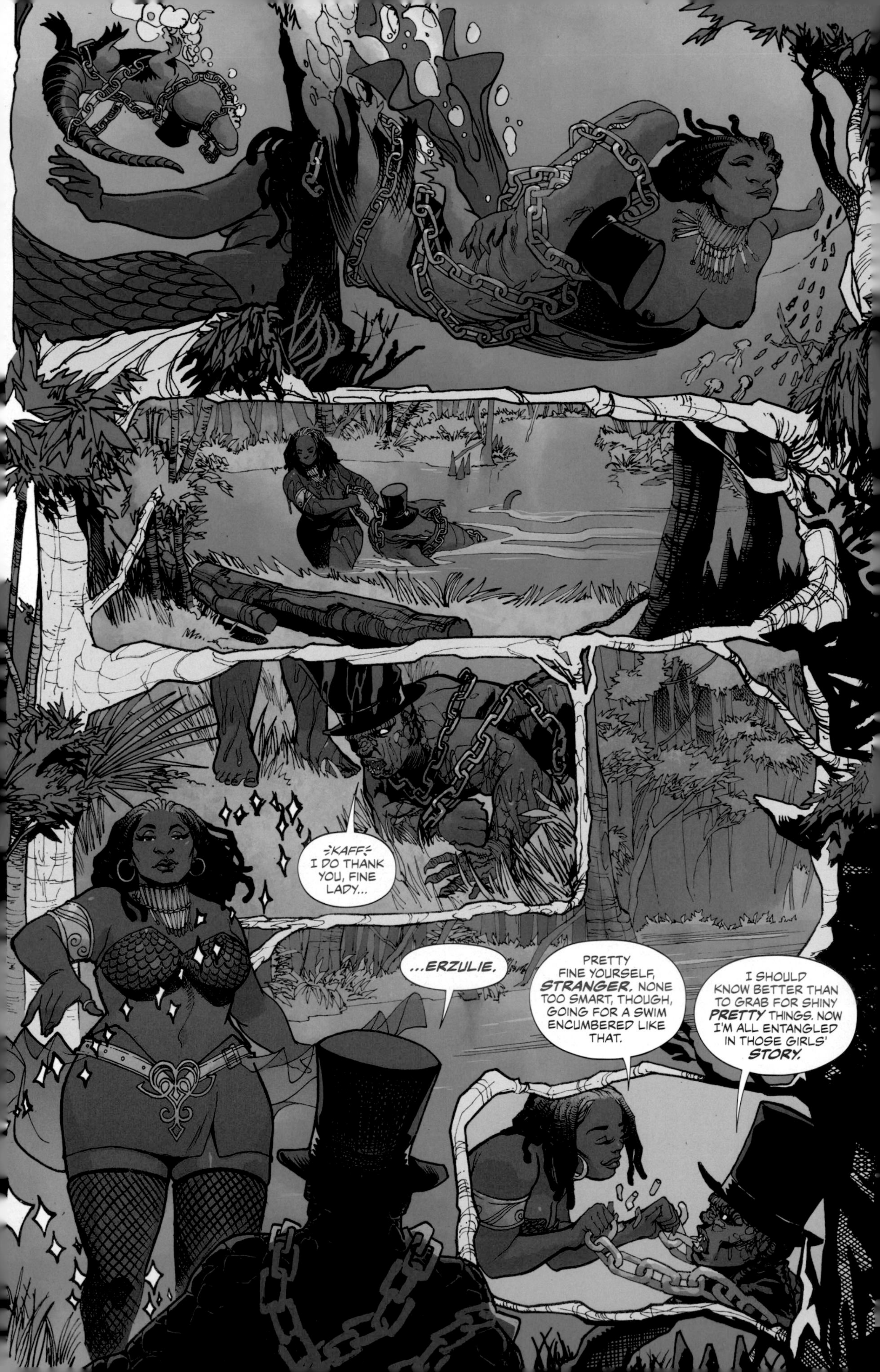

-KAFF- I DO THANK YOU, FINE LADY...
...ERZULIE.
PRETTY FINE YOURSELF, STRANGER. NONE TOO SMART, THOUGH, GOING FOR A SWIM ENCUMBERED LIKE THAT.
I SHOULD KNOW BETTER THAN TO GRAB FOR SHINY PRETTY THINGS. NOW I'M ALL ENTANGLED IN THOSE GIRLS' STORY.

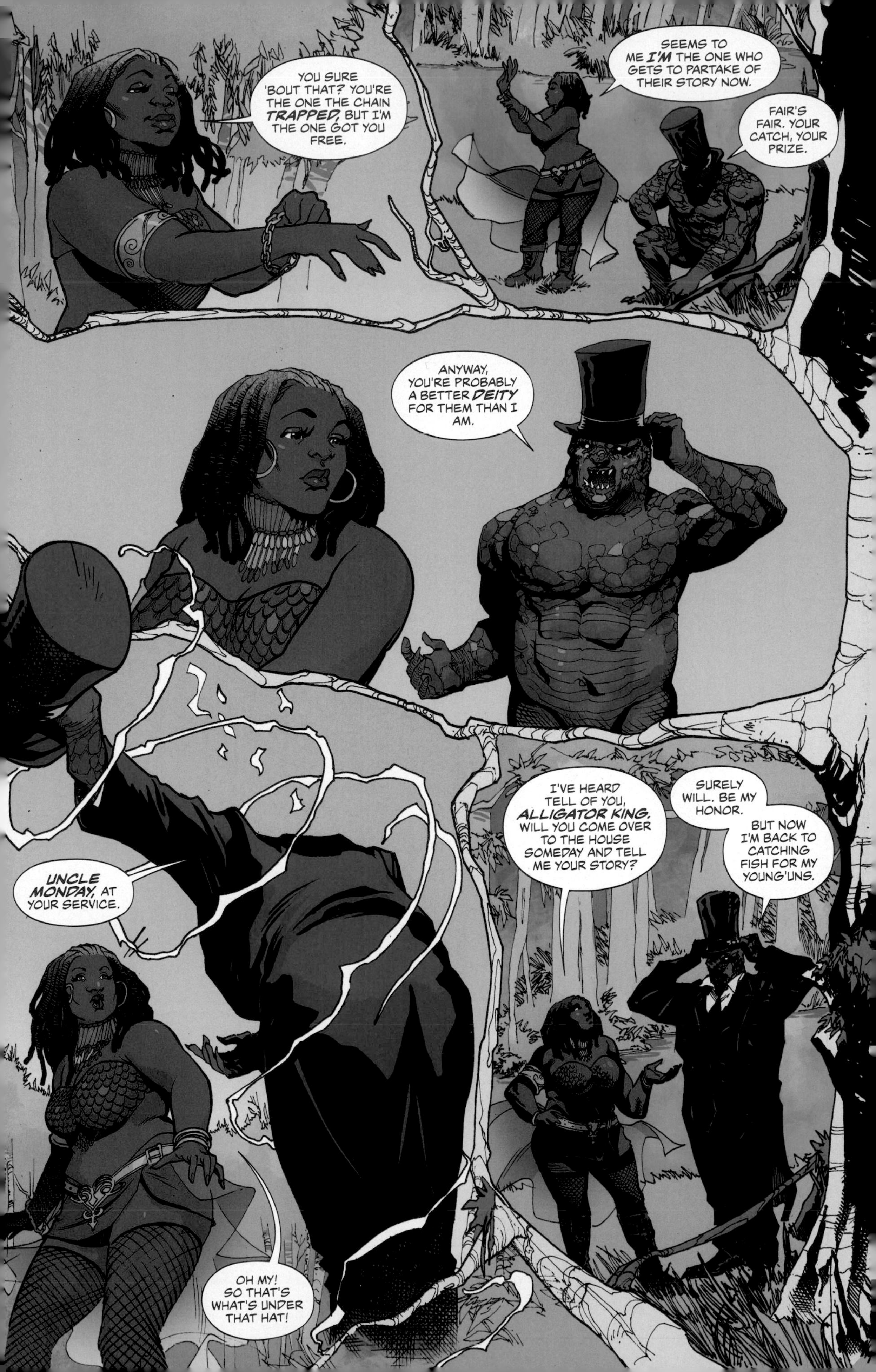
YOU SURE 'BOUT THAT? YOU'RE THE ONE THE CHAIN TRAPPED, BUT I'M THE ONE GOT YOU FREE.
SEEMS TO ME I'M THE ONE WHO GETS TO PARTAKE OF THEIR STORY NOW.
FAIR'S FAIR. YOUR CATCH, YOUR PRIZE.
ANYWAY, YOU'RE PROBABLY A BETTER DEITY FOR THEM THAN I AM.
UNCLE MONDAY, AT YOUR SERVICE.
OH MY! SO THAT'S WHAT'S UNDER THAT HAT!
I'VE HEARD TELL OF YOU, ALLIGATOR KING. WILL YOU COME OVER TO THE HOUSE SOMEDAY AND TELL ME YOUR STORY?
SURELY WILL. BE MY HONOR.
BUT NOW I'M BACK TO CATCHING FISH FOR MY YOUNG'UNS.

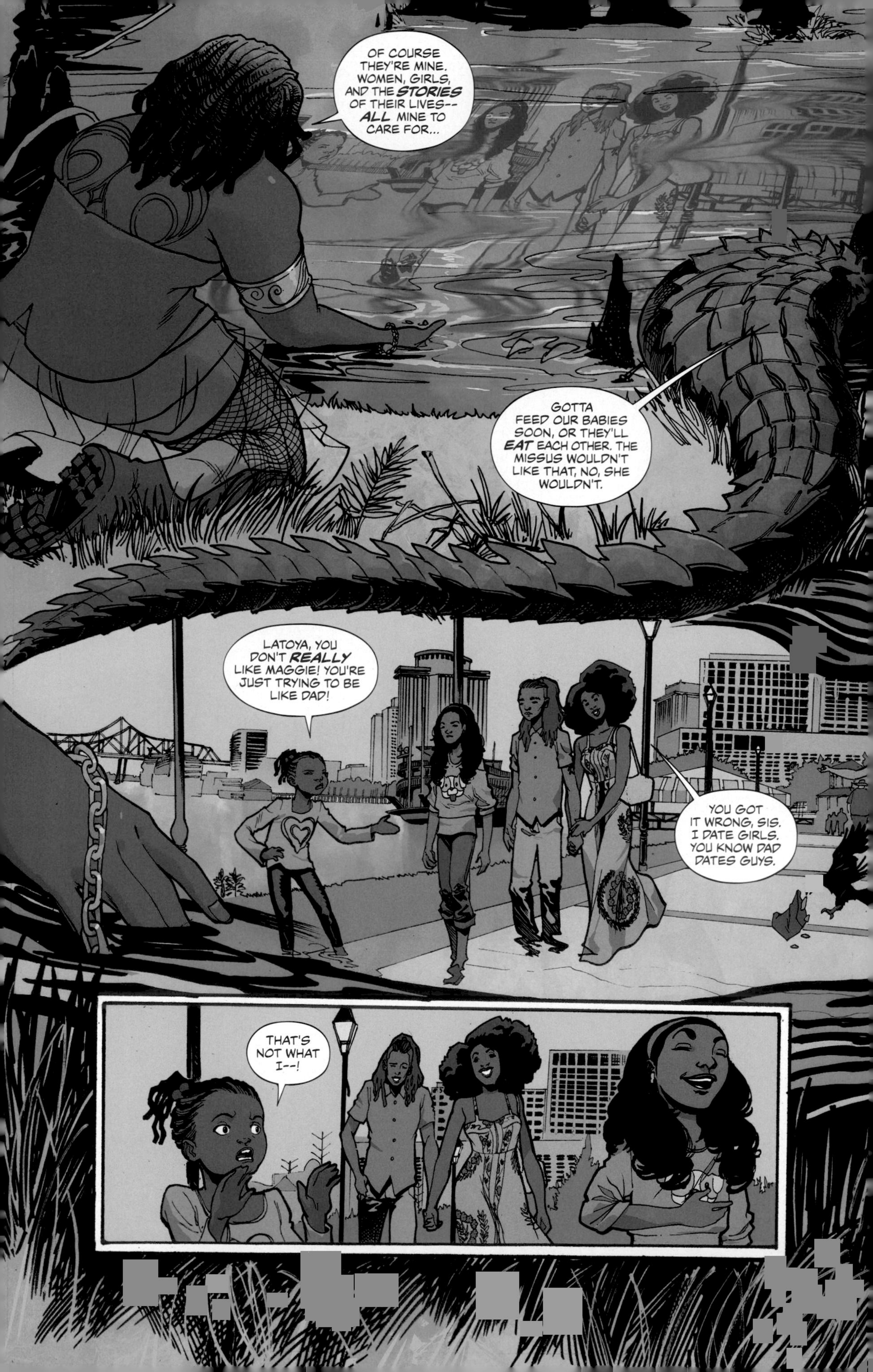
OF COURSE THEY'RE MINE. WOMEN, GIRLS, AND THE *STORIES* OF THEIR LIVES-- *ALL* MINE TO CARE FOR...
GOTTA FEED OUR BABIES SOON, OR THEY'LL *EAT* EACH OTHER. THE MISSUS WOULDN'T LIKE THAT, NO, SHE WOULDN'T.
LATOYA, YOU DON'T *REALLY* LIKE MAGGIE! YOU'RE JUST TRYING TO BE LIKE DAD!
YOU GOT IT WRONG, SIS. I DATE GIRLS. YOU KNOW DAD DATES GUYS.
THAT'S NOT WHAT I--!

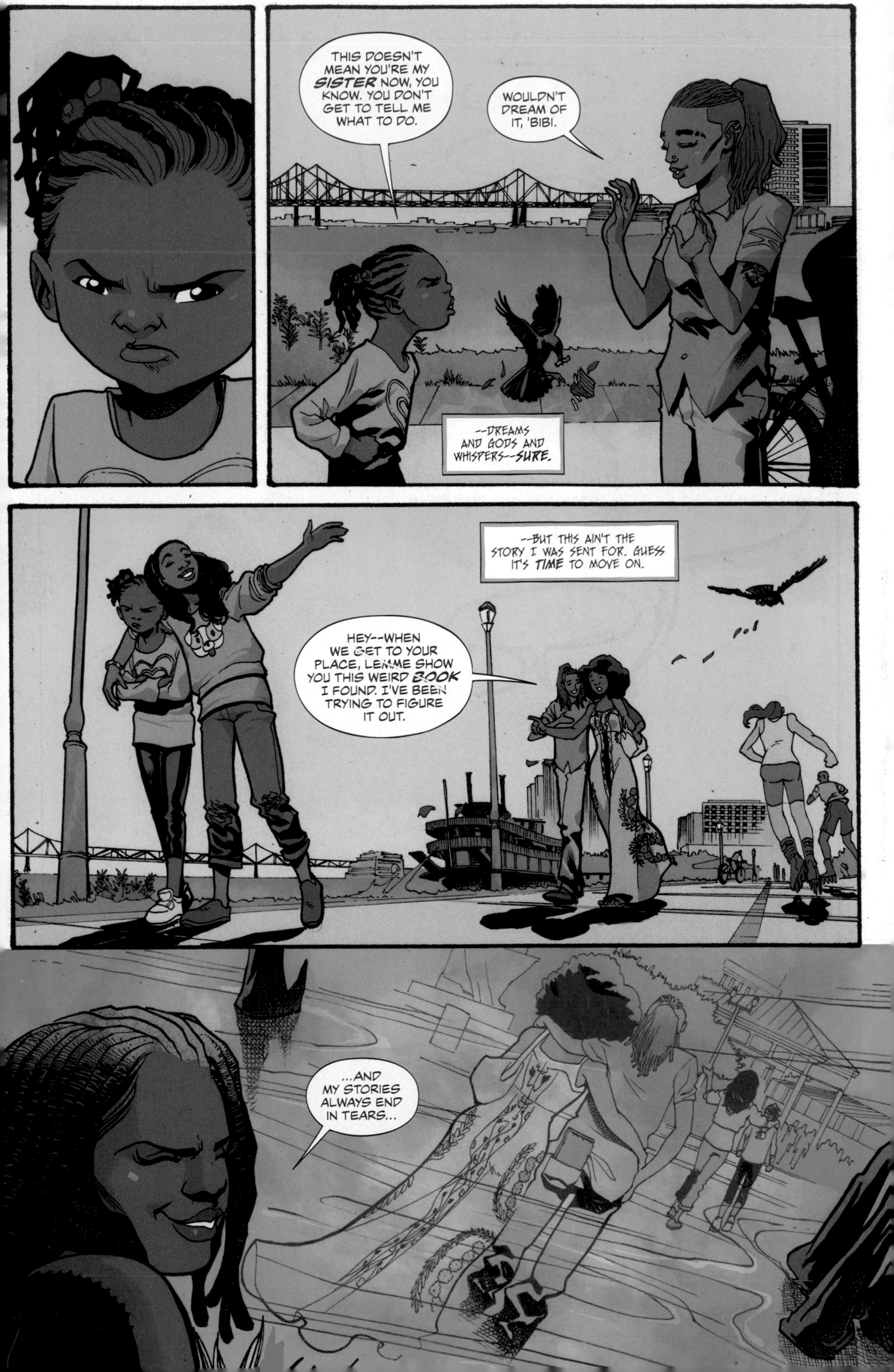
THIS DOESN'T MEAN YOU'RE MY SISTER NOW, YOU KNOW. YOU DON'T GET TO TELL ME WHAT TO DO.
WOULDN'T DREAM OF IT, 'BIBI.
--DREAMS AND GODS AND WHISPERS--SURE.
--BUT THIS AIN'T THE STORY I WAS SENT FOR. GUESS IT'S TIME TO MOVE ON.
HEY--WHEN WE GET TO YOUR PLACE, LEMME SHOW YOU THIS WEIRD BOOK I FOUND. I'VE BEEN TRYING TO FIGURE IT OUT.
...AND MY STORIES ALWAYS END IN TEARS...

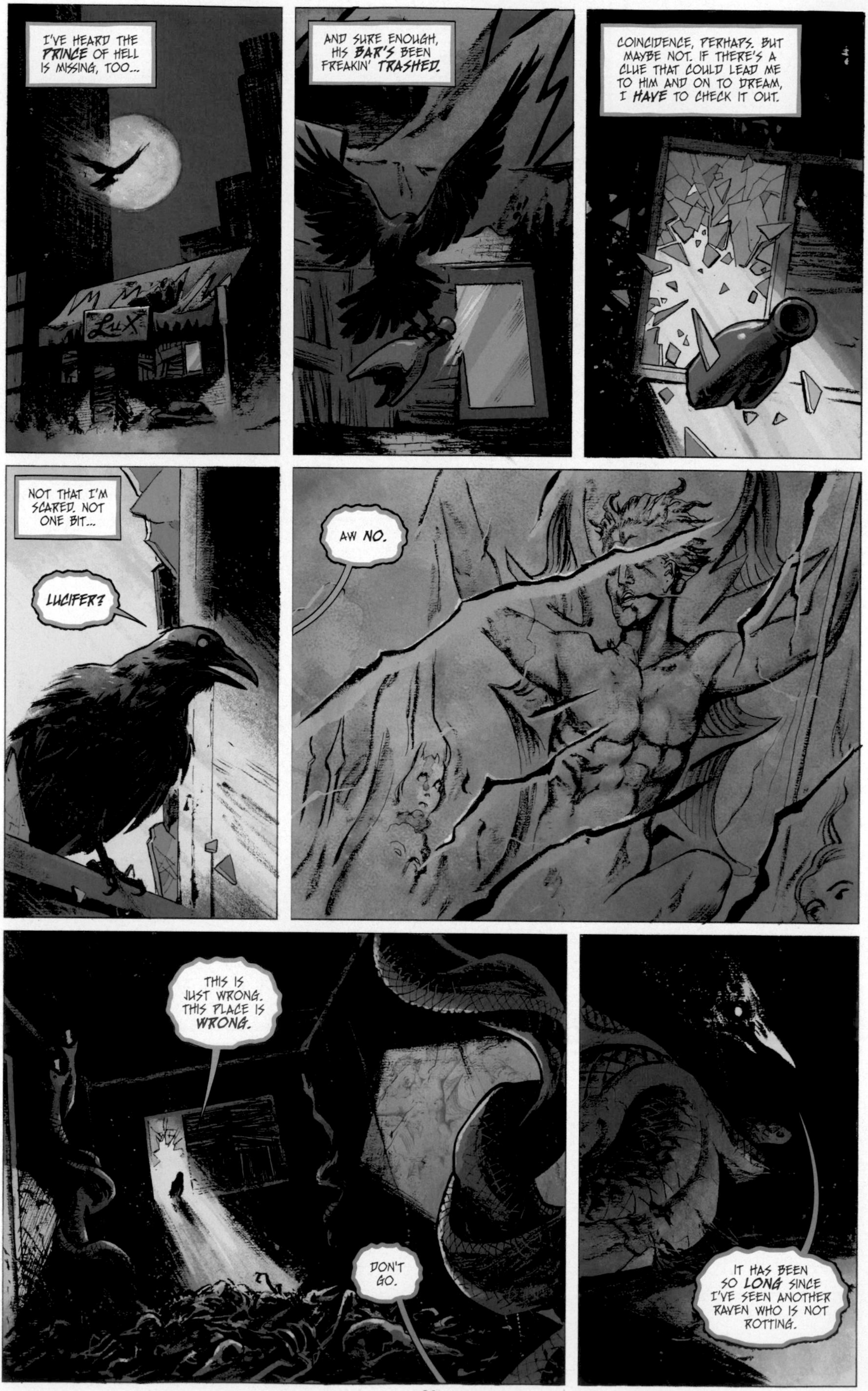
I'VE HEARD THE PRINCE OF HELL IS MISSING, TOO...
LUX
AND SURE ENOUGH, HIS BAR'S BEEN FREAKIN' TRASHED.
COINCIDENCE, PERHAPS. BUT MAYBE NOT. IF THERE'S A CLUE THAT COULD LEAD ME TO HIM AND ON TO DREAM, I HAVE TO CHECK IT OUT.
NOT THAT I'M SCARED. NOT ONE BIT...
LUCIFER?
AW NO.
THIS IS JUST WRONG. THIS PLACE IS WRONG.
DON'T GO.
IT HAS BEEN SO LONG SINCE I'VE SEEN ANOTHER RAVEN WHO IS NOT ROTTING.

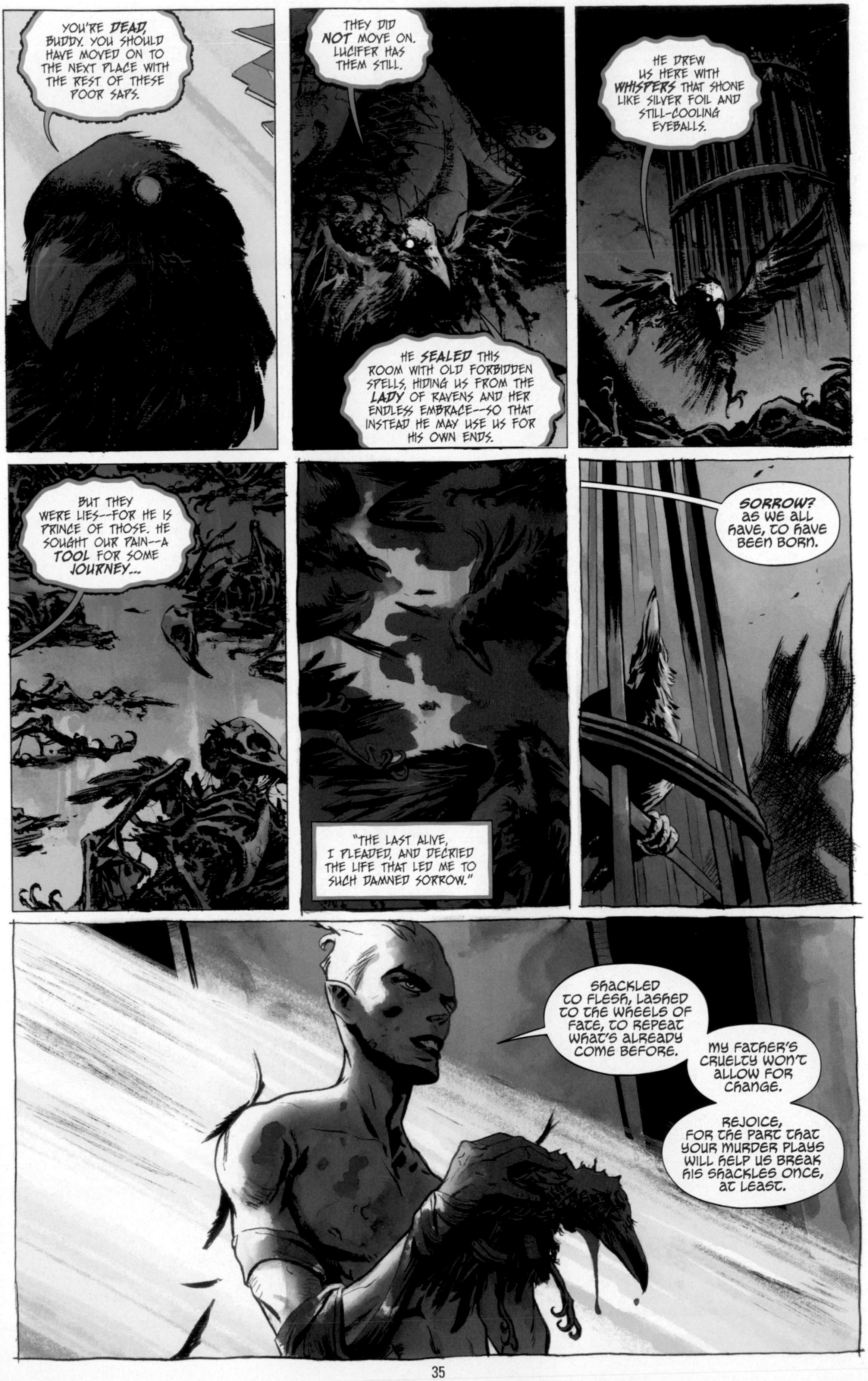
YOU'RE DEAD, BUDDY. YOU SHOULD HAVE MOVED ON TO THE NEXT PLACE WITH THE REST OF THESE POOR SAPS.
THEY DID NOT MOVE ON. LUCIFER HAS THEM STILL.
HE SEALED THIS ROOM WITH OLD FORBIDDEN SPELLS, HIDING US FROM THE LADY OF RAVENS AND HER ENDLESS EMBRACE--SO THAT INSTEAD HE MAY USE US FOR HIS OWN ENDS.
HE DREW US HERE WITH WHISPERS THAT SHONE LIKE SILVER FOIL AND STILL-COOLING EYEBALLS.
BUT THEY WERE LIES--FOR HE IS PRINCE OF THOSE. HE SOUGHT OUR PAIN--A TOOL FOR SOME JOURNEY...
"THE LAST ALIVE, I PLEADED, AND DECRIED THE LIFE THAT LED ME TO SUCH DAMNED SORROW."
SORROW? AS WE ALL HAVE, TO HAVE BEEN BORN.
SHACKLED TO FLESH, LASHED TO THE WHEELS OF FATE, TO REPEAT WHAT'S ALREADY COME BEFORE.
MY FATHER'S CRUELTY WON'T ALLOW FOR CHANGE.
REJOICE, FOR THE PART THAT YOUR MURDER PLAYS WILL HELP US BREAK HIS SHACKLES ONCE, AT LEAST.

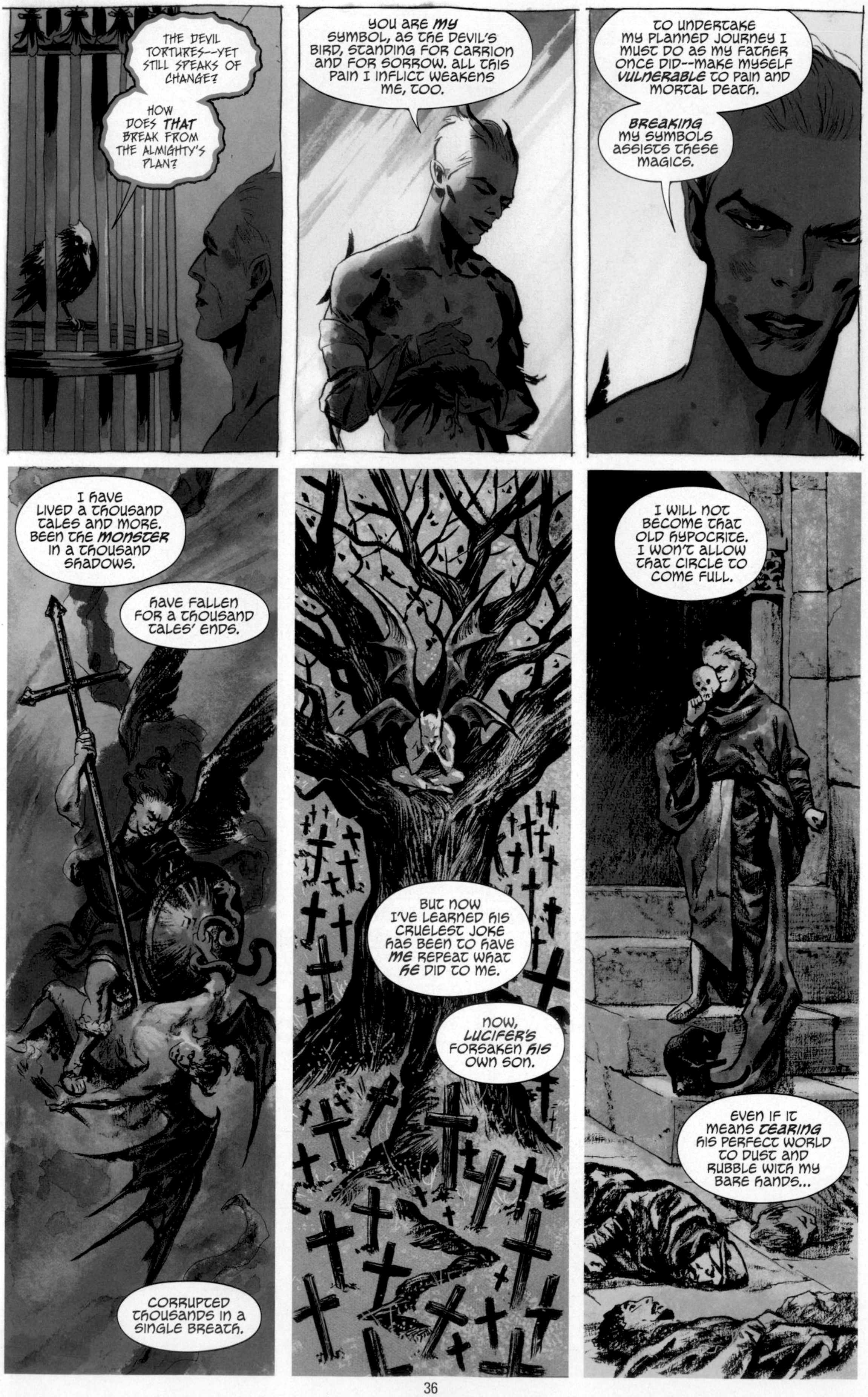
THE DEVIL TORTURES--YET STILL SPEAKS OF CHANGE?
HOW DOES THAT BREAK FROM THE ALMIGHTY'S PLAN?
YOU ARE MY SYMBOL, AS THE DEVIL'S BIRD, STANDING FOR CARRION AND FOR SORROW. ALL THIS PAIN I INFLICT WEAKENS ME, TOO.
TO UNDERTAKE MY PLANNED JOURNEY I MUST DO AS MY FATHER ONCE DID--MAKE MYSELF VULNERABLE TO PAIN AND MORTAL DEATH.
BREAKING MY SYMBOLS ASSISTS THESE MAGICS.
I HAVE LIVED A THOUSAND TALES AND MORE. BEEN THE MONSTER IN A THOUSAND SHADOWS.
HAVE FALLEN FOR A THOUSAND TALES' ENDS.
CORRUPTED THOUSANDS IN A SINGLE BREATH.
BUT NOW I'VE LEARNED HIS CRUELEST JOKE HAS BEEN TO HAVE ME REPEAT WHAT HE DID TO ME.
NOW, LUCIFER'S FORSAKEN HIS OWN SON.
I WILL NOT BECOME THAT OLD HYPOCRITE. I WON'T ALLOW THAT CIRCLE TO COME FULL.
EVEN IF IT MEANS TEARING HIS PERFECT WORLD TO DUST AND RUBBLE WITH MY BARE HANDS...

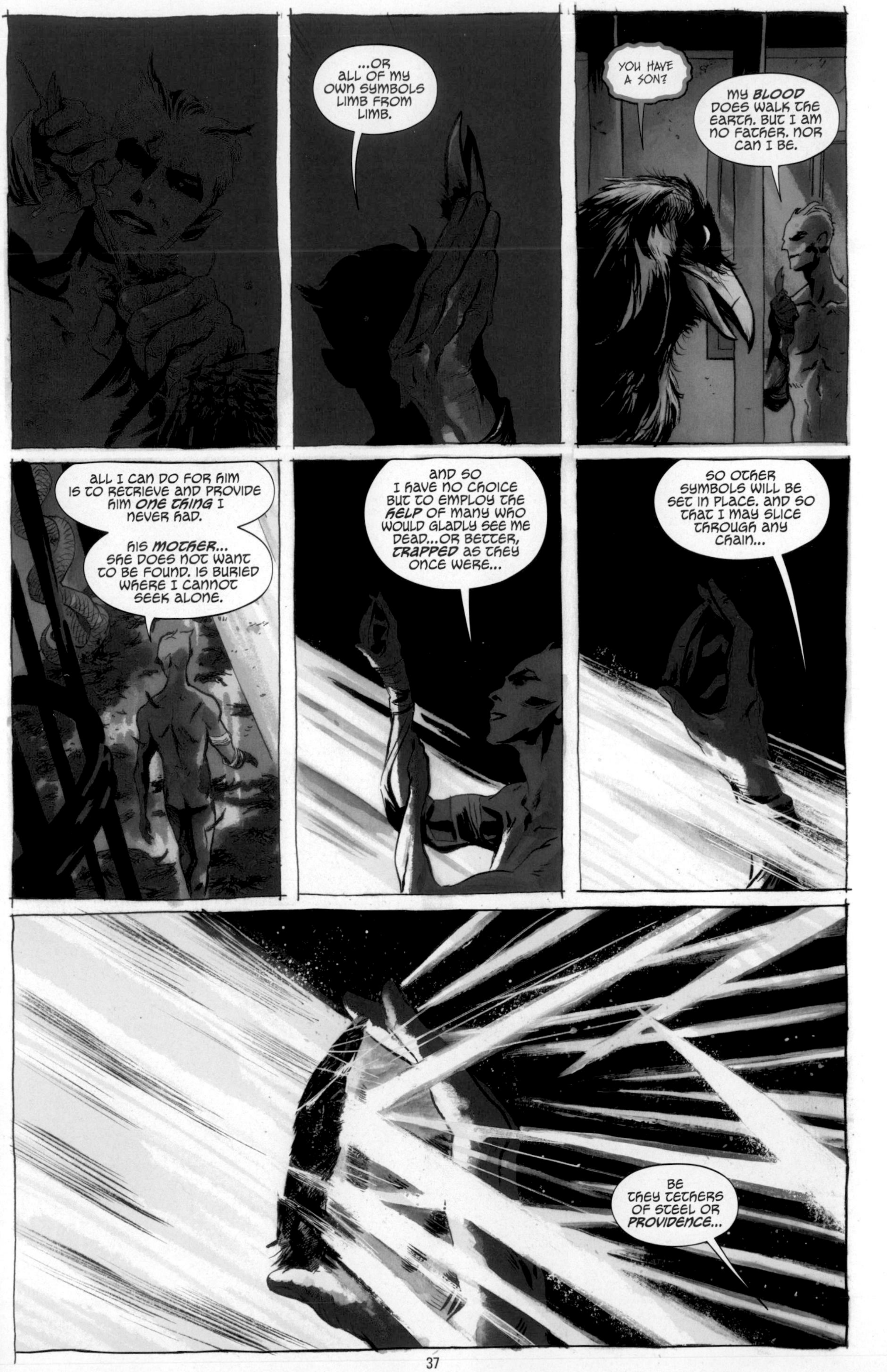
...OR ALL OF MY OWN SYMBOLS LIMB FROM LIMB.
YOU HAVE A SON?
MY BLOOD DOES WALK THE EARTH. BUT I AM NO FATHER. NOR CAN I BE.
ALL I CAN DO FOR HIM IS TO RETRIEVE AND PROVIDE HIM ONE THING I NEVER HAD.
HIS MOTHER... SHE DOES NOT WANT TO BE FOUND. IS BURIED WHERE I CANNOT SEEK ALONE.
AND SO I HAVE NO CHOICE BUT TO EMPLOY THE HELP OF MANY WHO WOULD GLADLY SEE ME DEAD...OR BETTER, TRAPPED AS THEY ONCE WERE...
SO OTHER SYMBOLS WILL BE SET IN PLACE. AND SO THAT I MAY SLICE THROUGH ANY CHAIN...
BE THEY TETHERS OF STEEL OR PROVIDENCE...

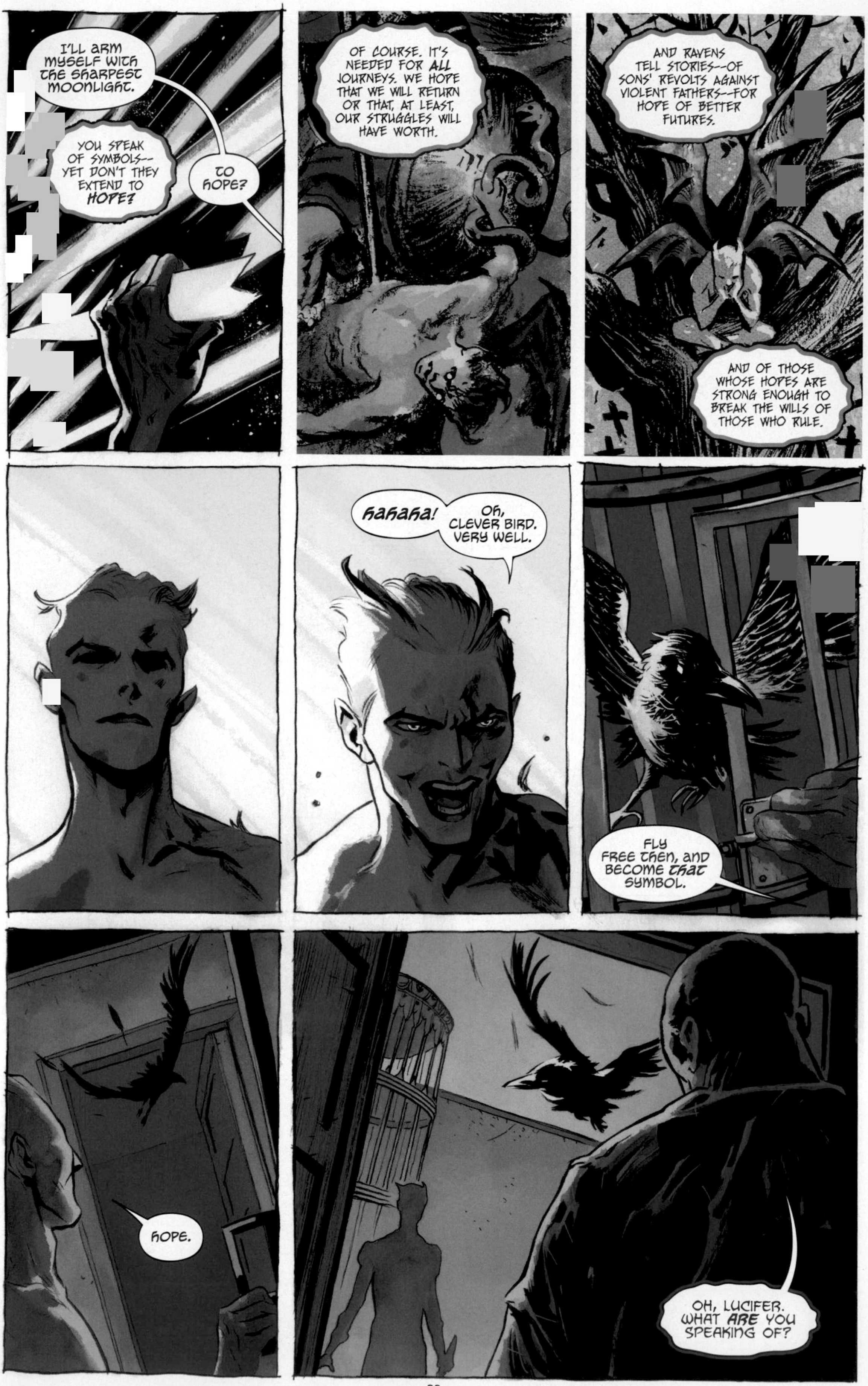
I'LL ARM MYSELF WITH THE SHARPEST MOONLIGHT.
YOU SPEAK OF SYMBOLS--YET DON'T THEY EXTEND TO HOPE?
TO HOPE?
OF COURSE. IT'S NEEDED FOR ALL JOURNEYS. WE HOPE THAT WE WILL RETURN OR THAT, AT LEAST, OUR STRUGGLES WILL HAVE WORTH.
AND RAVENS TELL STORIES--OF SONS' REVOLTS AGAINST VIOLENT FATHERS--FOR HOPE OF BETTER FUTURES.
AND OF THOSE WHOSE HOPES ARE STRONG ENOUGH TO BREAK THE WILLS OF THOSE WHO RULE.
HAHAHA!
OH, CLEVER BIRD. VERY WELL.
FLY FREE THEN, AND BECOME THAT SYMBOL.
HOPE.
OH, LUCIFER. WHAT ARE YOU SPEAKING OF?

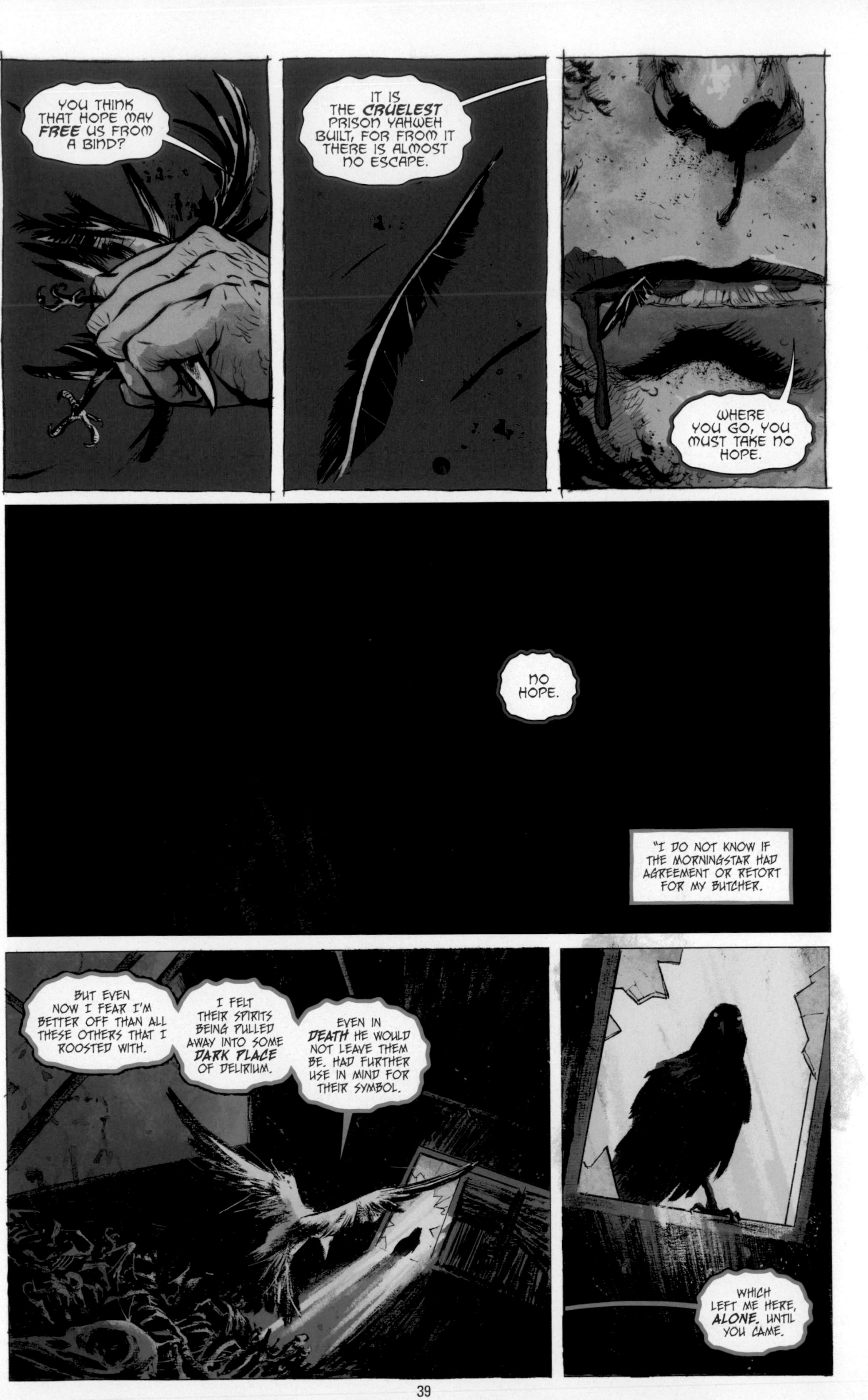
YOU THINK THAT HOPE MAY FREE US FROM A BIND?
IT IS THE CRUELEST PRISON YAHWEH BUILT, FOR FROM IT THERE IS ALMOST NO ESCAPE.
WHERE YOU GO, YOU MUST TAKE NO HOPE.
NO HOPE.
"I DO NOT KNOW IF THE MORNINGSTAR HAD AGREEMENT OR RETORT FOR MY BUTCHER.
BUT EVEN NOW I FEAR I'M BETTER OFF THAN ALL THESE OTHERS THAT I ROOSTED WITH.
I FELT THEIR SPIRITS BEING PULLED AWAY INTO SOME DARK PLACE OF DELIRIUM.
EVEN IN DEATH HE WOULD NOT LEAVE THEM BE. HAD FURTHER USE IN MIND FOR THEIR SYMBOL.
WHICH LEFT ME HERE, ALONE. UNTIL YOU CAME.

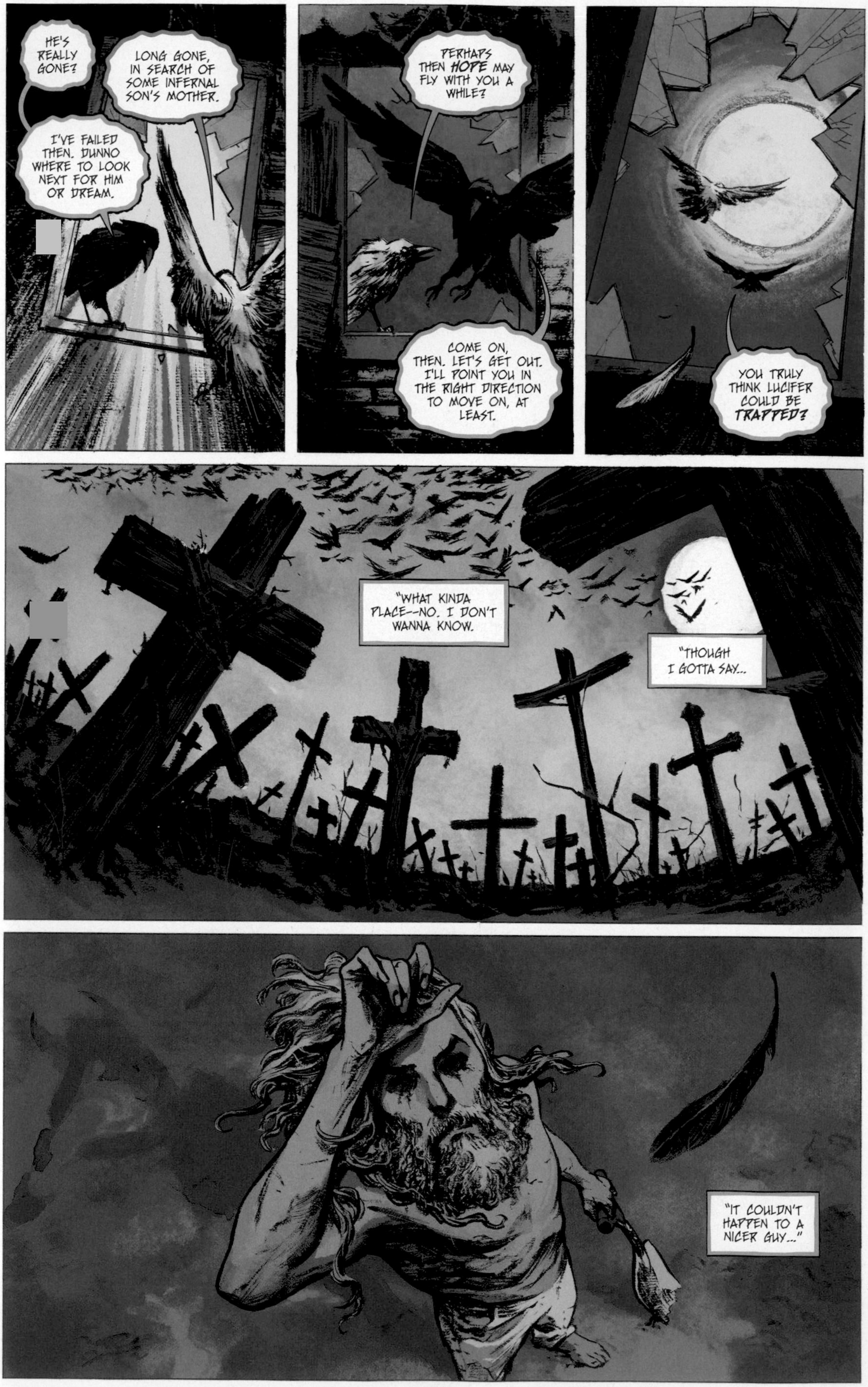
HE'S REALLY GONE?
LONG GONE, IN SEARCH OF SOME INFERNAL SON'S MOTHER.
I'VE FAILED THEN. DUNNO WHERE TO LOOK NEXT FOR HIM OR DREAM.
PERHAPS THEN HOPE MAY FLY WITH YOU A WHILE?
COME ON, THEN. LET'S GET OUT. I'LL POINT YOU IN THE RIGHT DIRECTION TO MOVE ON, AT LEAST.
YOU TRULY THINK LUCIFER COULD BE TRAPPED?
"WHAT KINDA PLACE--NO. I DON'T WANNA KNOW.
"THOUGH I GOTTA SAY...
"IT COULDN'T HAPPEN TO A NICER GUY..."

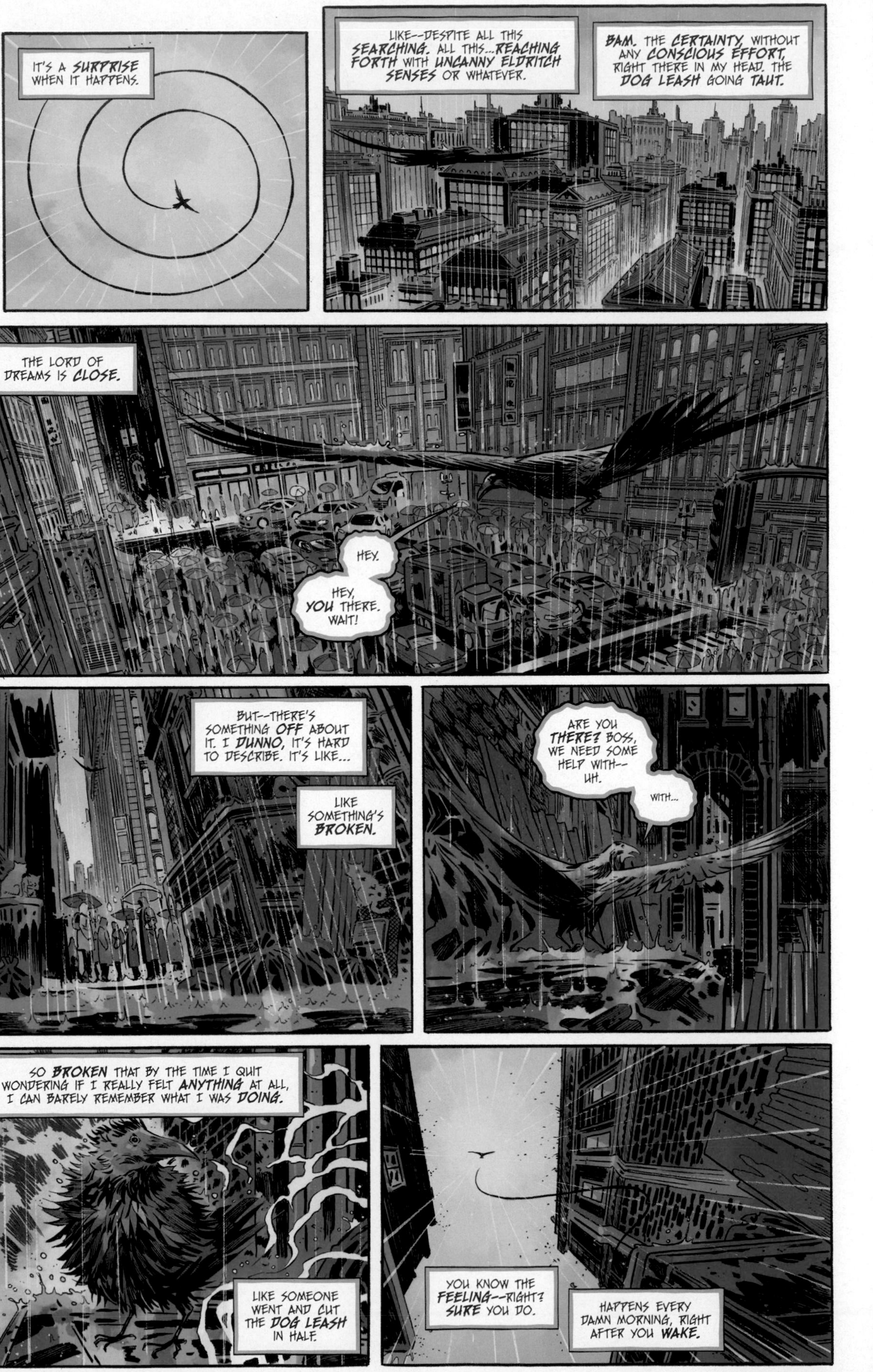
IT'S A SURPRISE WHEN IT HAPPENS.
LIKE--DESPITE ALL THIS SEARCHING. ALL THIS...REACHING FORTH WITH UNCANNY ELDRITCH SENSES OR WHATEVER.
BAM. THE CERTAINTY, WITHOUT ANY CONSCIOUS EFFORT, RIGHT THERE IN MY HEAD. THE DOG LEASH GOING TAUT.
THE LORD OF DREAMS IS CLOSE.
HEY.
HEY, YOU THERE. WAIT!
BUT--THERE'S SOMETHING OFF ABOUT IT. I DUNNO, IT'S HARD TO DESCRIBE. IT'S LIKE...
LIKE SOMETHING'S BROKEN.
ARE YOU THERE? BOSS, WE NEED SOME HELP WITH-- UH.
WITH...
SO BROKEN THAT BY THE TIME I QUIT WONDERING IF I REALLY FELT ANYTHING AT ALL, I CAN BARELY REMEMBER WHAT I WAS DOING.
LIKE SOMEONE WENT AND CUT THE DOG LEASH IN HALF.
YOU KNOW THE FEELING--RIGHT? SURE YOU DO.
HAPPENS EVERY DAMN MORNING, RIGHT AFTER YOU WAKE.

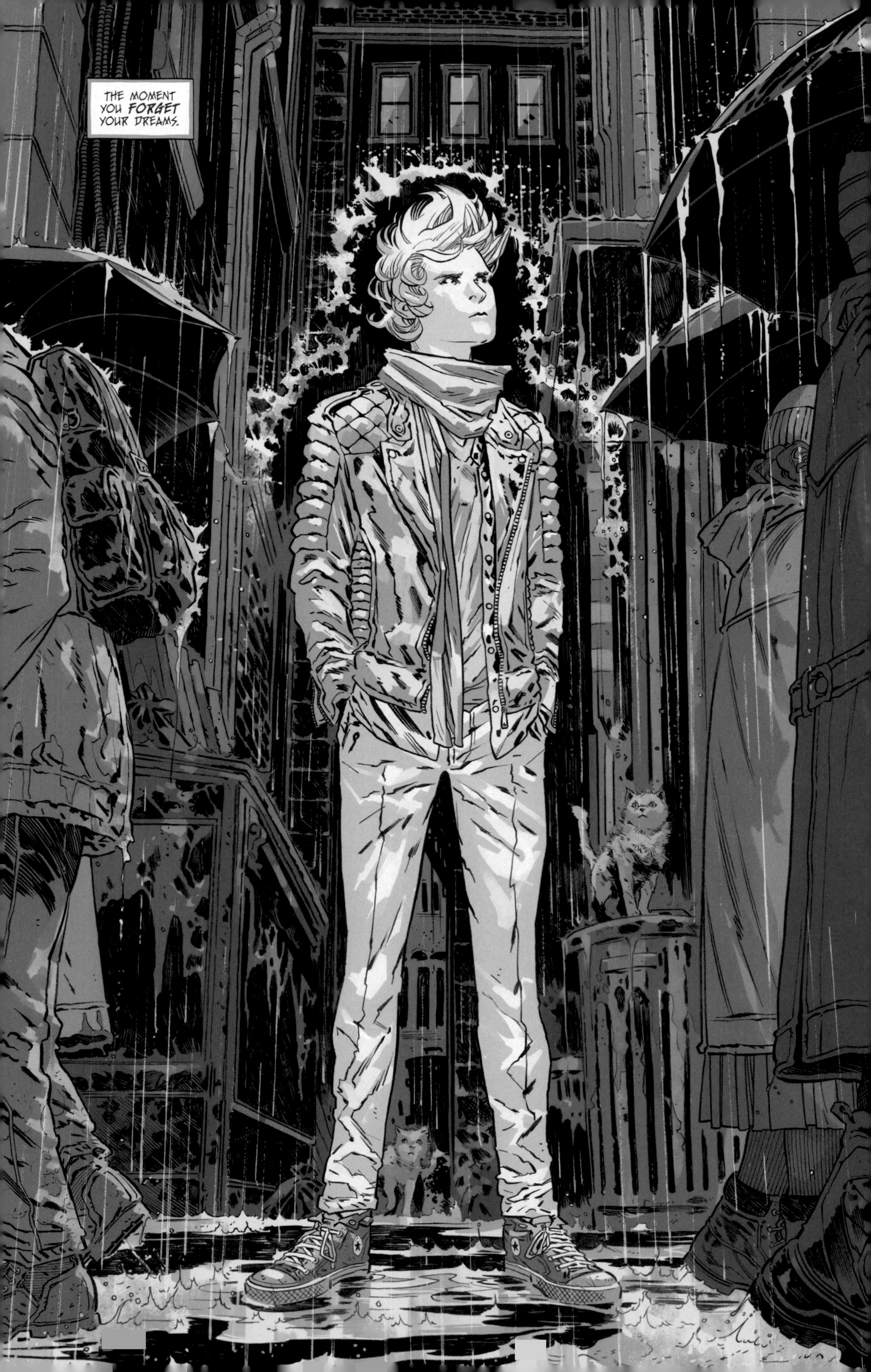
THE MOMENT YOU FORGET YOUR DREAMS.

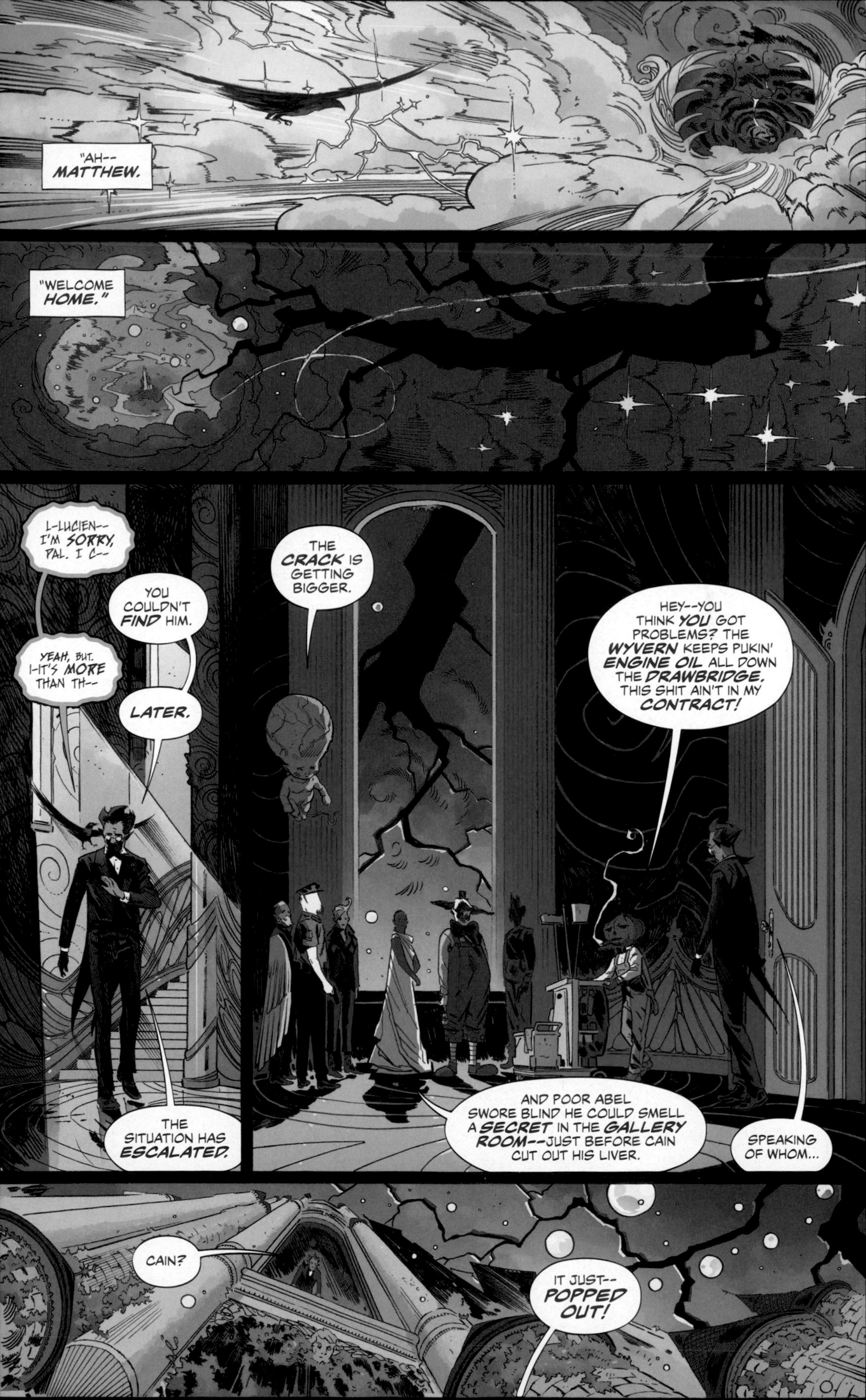
"AH-- MATTHEW.
"WELCOME HOME."
L-LUCIEN-- I'M SORRY, PAL. I C--
YOU COULDN'T FIND HIM.
YEAH, BUT. I-IT'S MORE THAN TH--
LATER.
THE SITUATION HAS ESCALATED.
THE CRACK IS GETTING BIGGER.
AND POOR ABEL SWORE BLIND HE COULD SMELL A SECRET IN THE GALLERY ROOM--JUST BEFORE CAIN CUT OUT HIS LIVER.
HEY--YOU THINK YOU GOT PROBLEMS? THE WYVERN KEEPS PUKIN' ENGINE OIL ALL DOWN THE DRAWBRIDGE. THIS SHIT AIN'T IN MY CONTRACT!
SPEAKING OF WHOM...
CAIN?
IT JUST-- POPPED OUT!

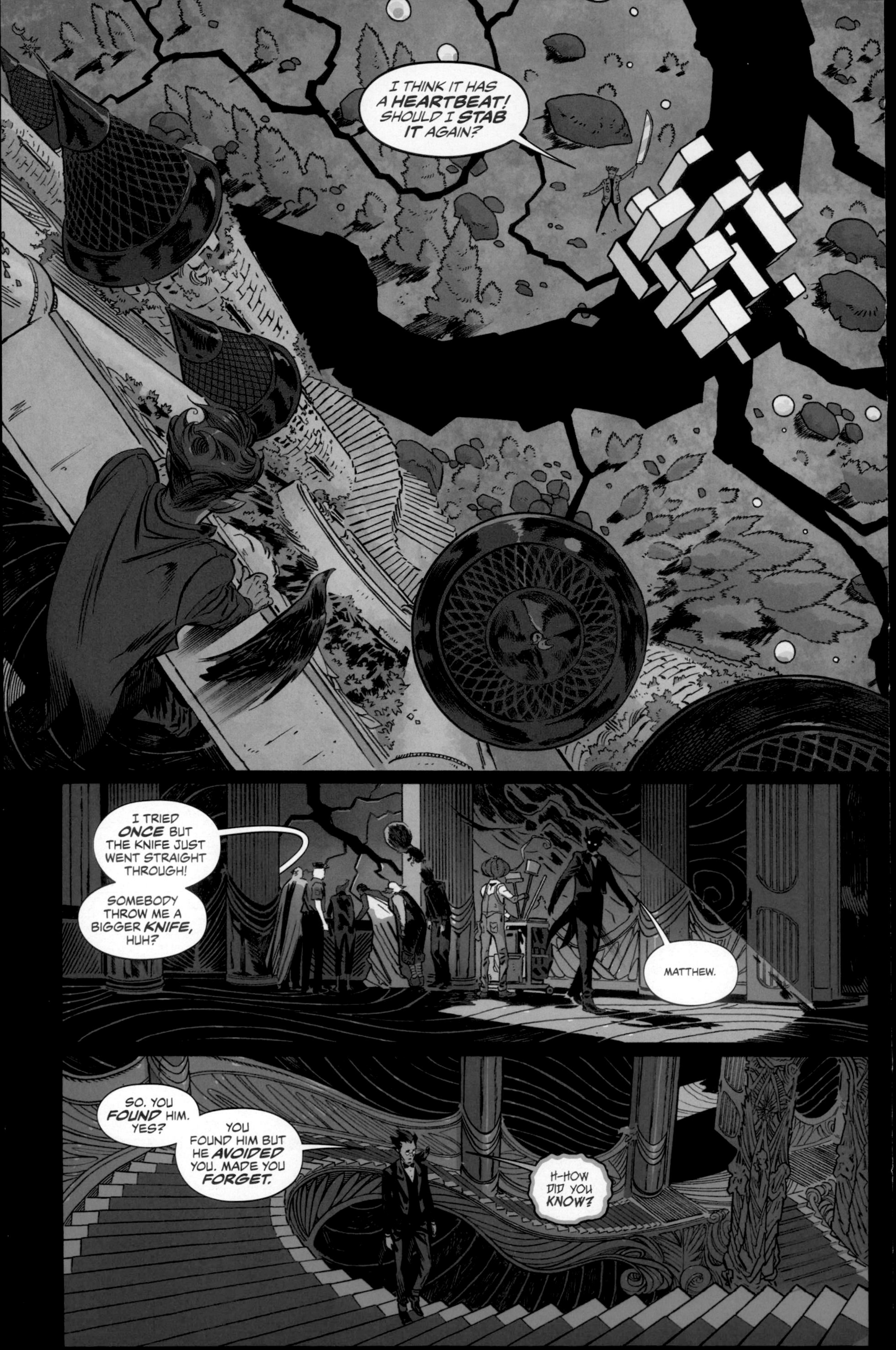

I THINK IT HAS A HEARTBEAT! SHOULD I STAB IT AGAIN?
I TRIED ONCE BUT THE KNIFE JUST WENT STRAIGHT THROUGH!
SOMEBODY THROW ME A BIGGER KNIFE, HUH?
MATTHEW.
SO. YOU FOUND HIM. YES?
YOU FOUND HIM BUT HE AVOIDED YOU. MADE YOU FORGET.
H-HOW DID YOU KNOW?

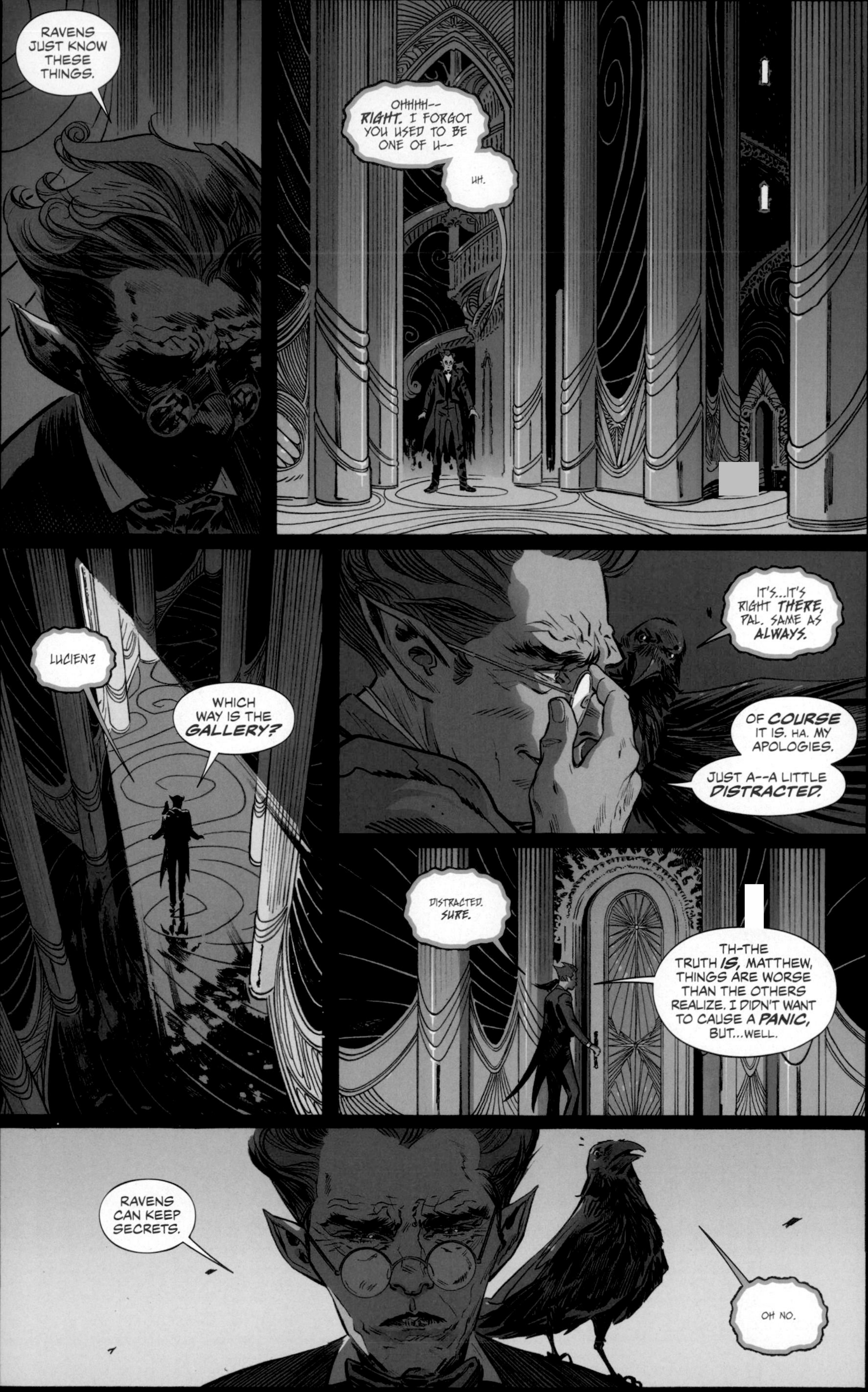

RAVENS JUST KNOW THESE THINGS.
OHHHH-- RIGHT. I FORGOT YOU USED TO BE ONE OF U--
UH.
LUCIEN?
WHICH WAY IS THE GALLERY?
IT'S...IT'S RIGHT THERE, PAL. SAME AS ALWAYS.
OF COURSE IT IS. HA. MY APOLOGIES.
JUST A--A LITTLE DISTRACTED.
DISTRACTED. SURE.
TH-THE TRUTH IS, MATTHEW, THINGS ARE WORSE THAN THE OTHERS REALIZE. I DIDN'T WANT TO CAUSE A PANIC, BUT...WELL.
RAVENS CAN KEEP SECRETS.
OH NO.

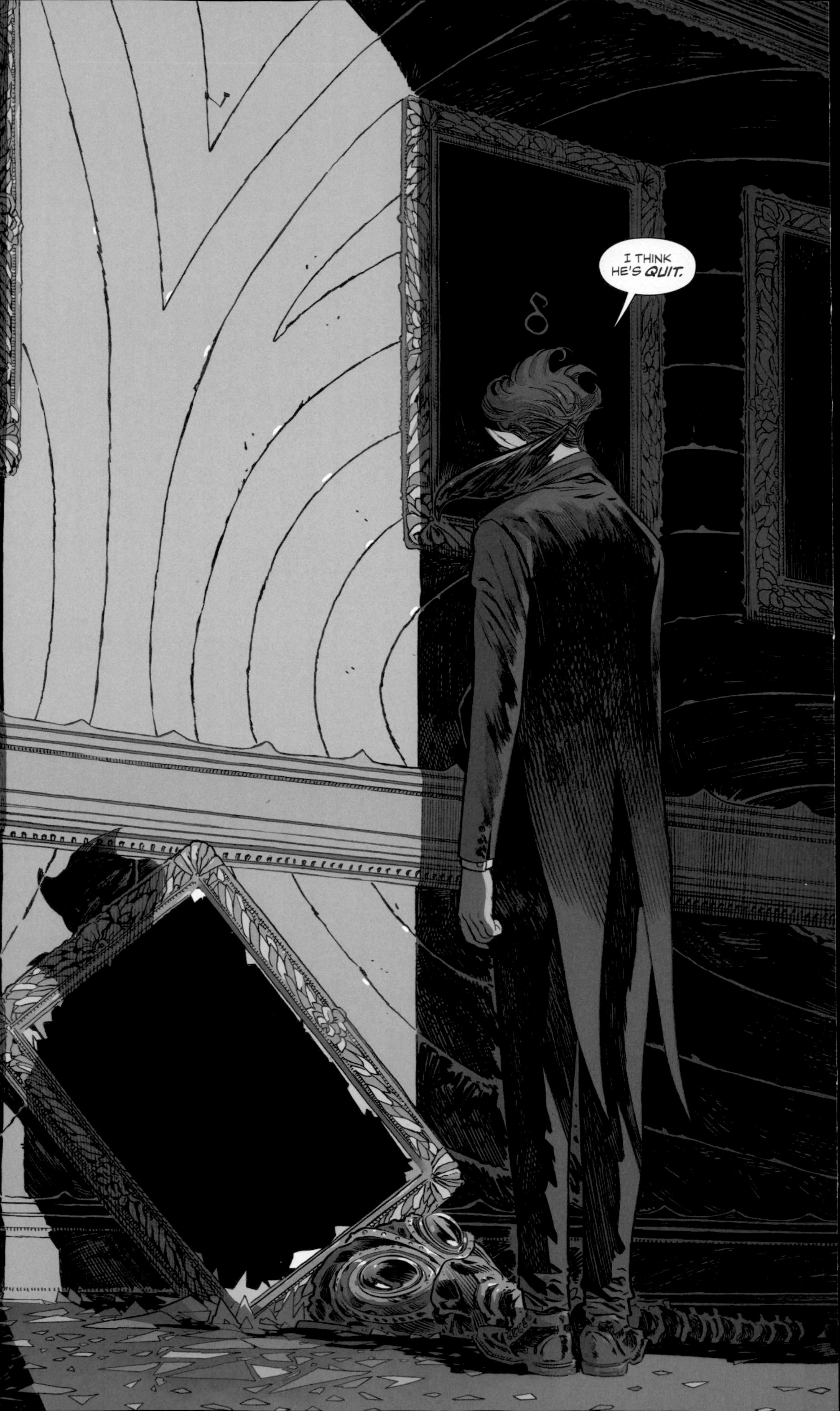
I THINK HE'S *QUIT.*

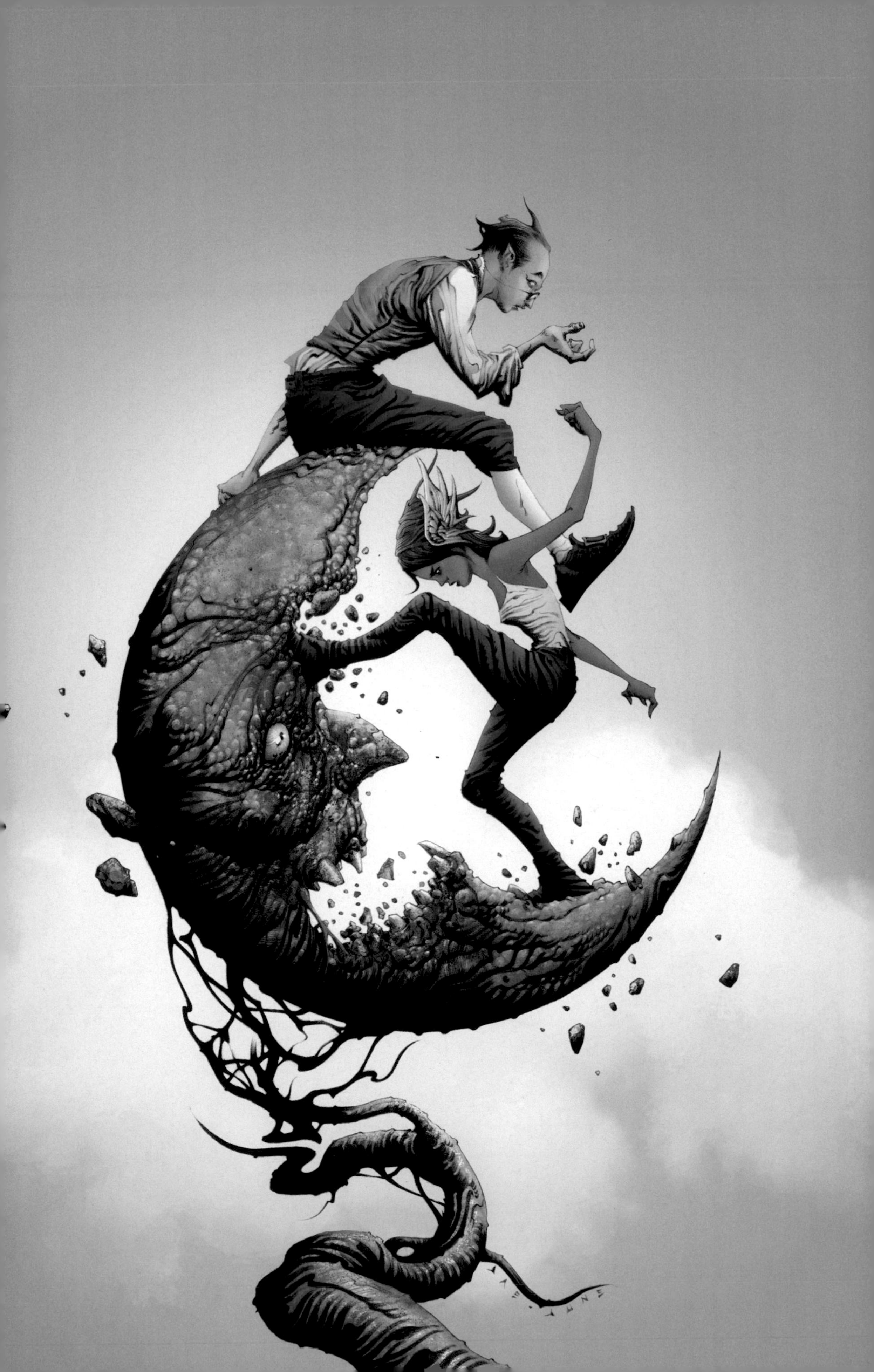

THE DREAMING

The Kingdom

WRITTEN BY
Simon Spurrier

ILLUSTRATED BY
Bilquis Evely

COLORS BY
Mat Lopes

LETTERS BY
Simon Bowland

COVER ART BY
Jae Lee and *June Chung*

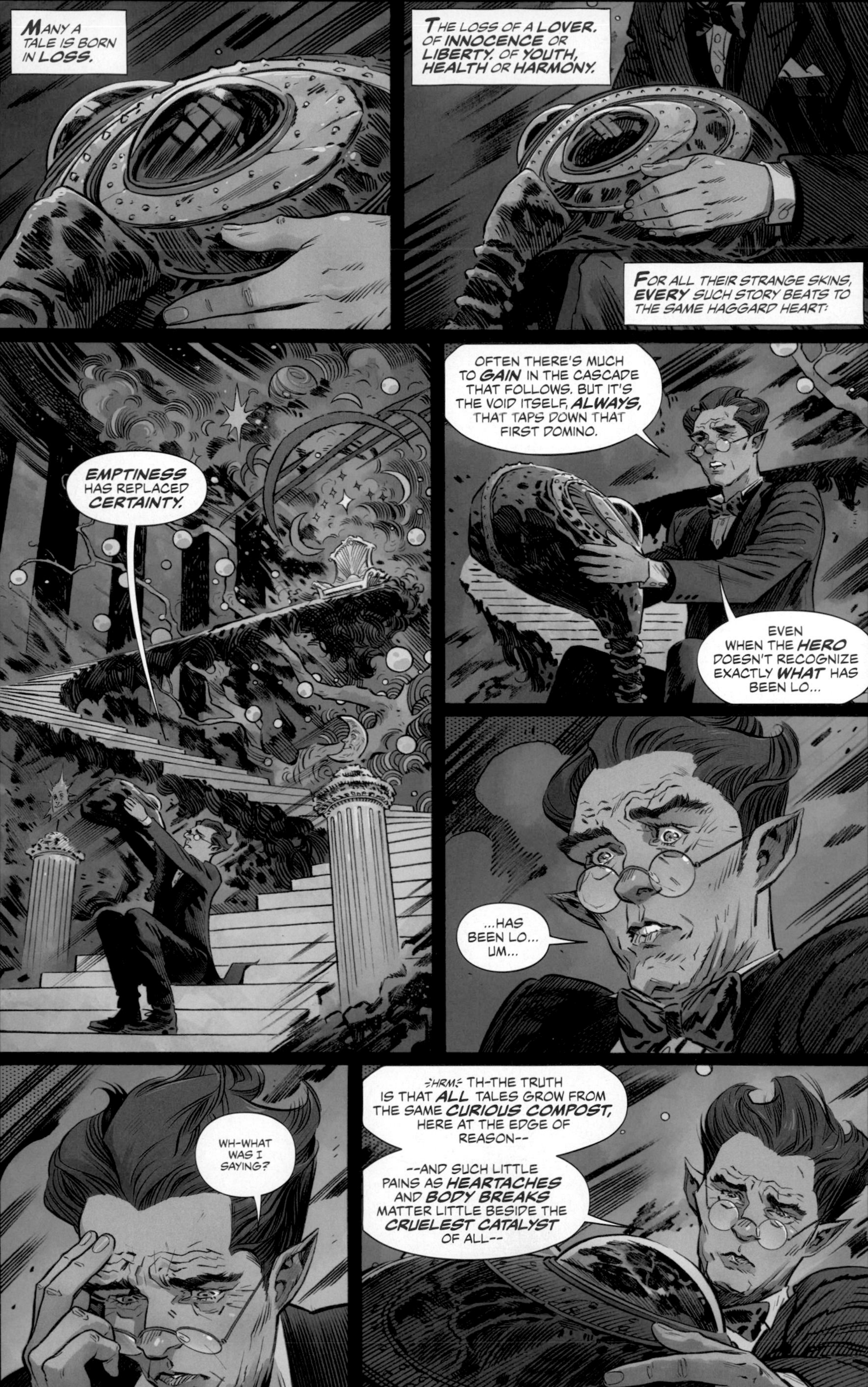
MANY A TALE IS BORN IN LOSS.
THE LOSS OF A LOVER, OF INNOCENCE OR LIBERTY, OF YOUTH, HEALTH OR HARMONY.
FOR ALL THEIR STRANGE SKINS, EVERY SUCH STORY BEATS TO THE SAME HAGGARD HEART:
EMPTINESS HAS REPLACED CERTAINTY.
OFTEN THERE'S MUCH TO GAIN IN THE CASCADE THAT FOLLOWS. BUT IT'S THE VOID ITSELF, ALWAYS, THAT TAPS DOWN THAT FIRST DOMINO.
EVEN WHEN THE HERO DOESN'T RECOGNIZE EXACTLY WHAT HAS BEEN LO...
...HAS BEEN LO... UM...
WH-WHAT WAS I SAYING?
=HRM= TH-THE TRUTH IS THAT ALL TALES GROW FROM THE SAME CURIOUS COMPOST, HERE AT THE EDGE OF REASON--
--AND SUCH LITTLE PAINS AS HEARTACHES AND BODY BREAKS MATTER LITTLE BESIDE THE CRUELEST CATALYST OF ALL--

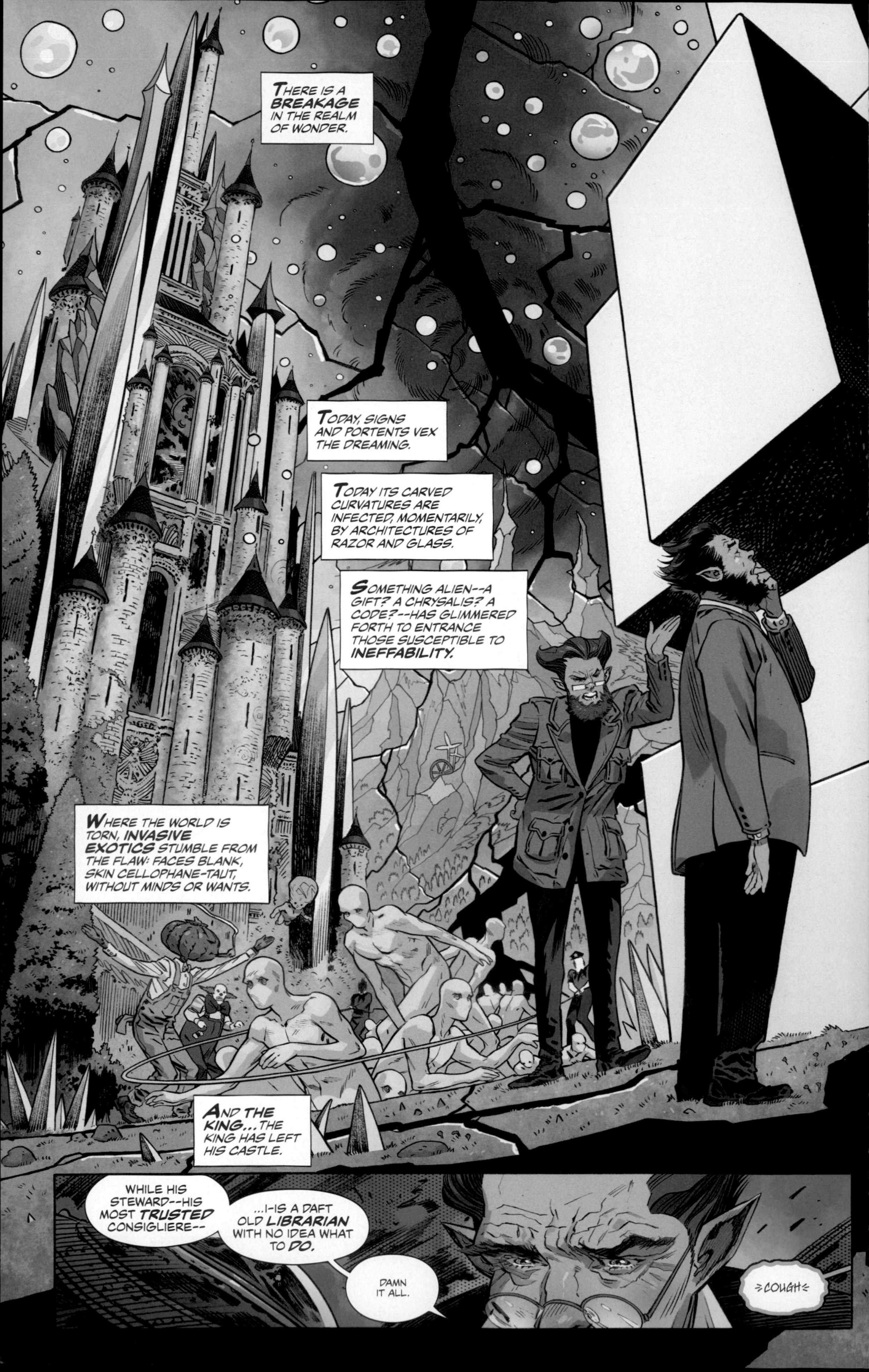

THERE IS A BREAKAGE IN THE REALM OF WONDER.
TODAY, SIGNS AND PORTENTS VEX THE DREAMING.
TODAY ITS CARVED CURVATURES ARE INFECTED, MOMENTARILY, BY ARCHITECTURES OF RAZOR AND GLASS.
SOMETHING ALIEN--A GIFT? A CHRYSALIS? A CODE?--HAS GLIMMERED FORTH TO ENTRANCE THOSE SUSCEPTIBLE TO INEFFABILITY.
WHERE THE WORLD IS TORN, INVASIVE EXOTICS STUMBLE FROM THE FLAW: FACES BLANK, SKIN CELLOPHANE-TAUT, WITHOUT MINDS OR WANTS.
AND THE KING... THE KING HAS LEFT HIS CASTLE.
WHILE HIS STEWARD--HIS MOST TRUSTED CONSIGLIERE--
...I-IS A DAFT OLD LIBRARIAN WITH NO IDEA WHAT TO DO.
DAMN IT ALL.
COUGH

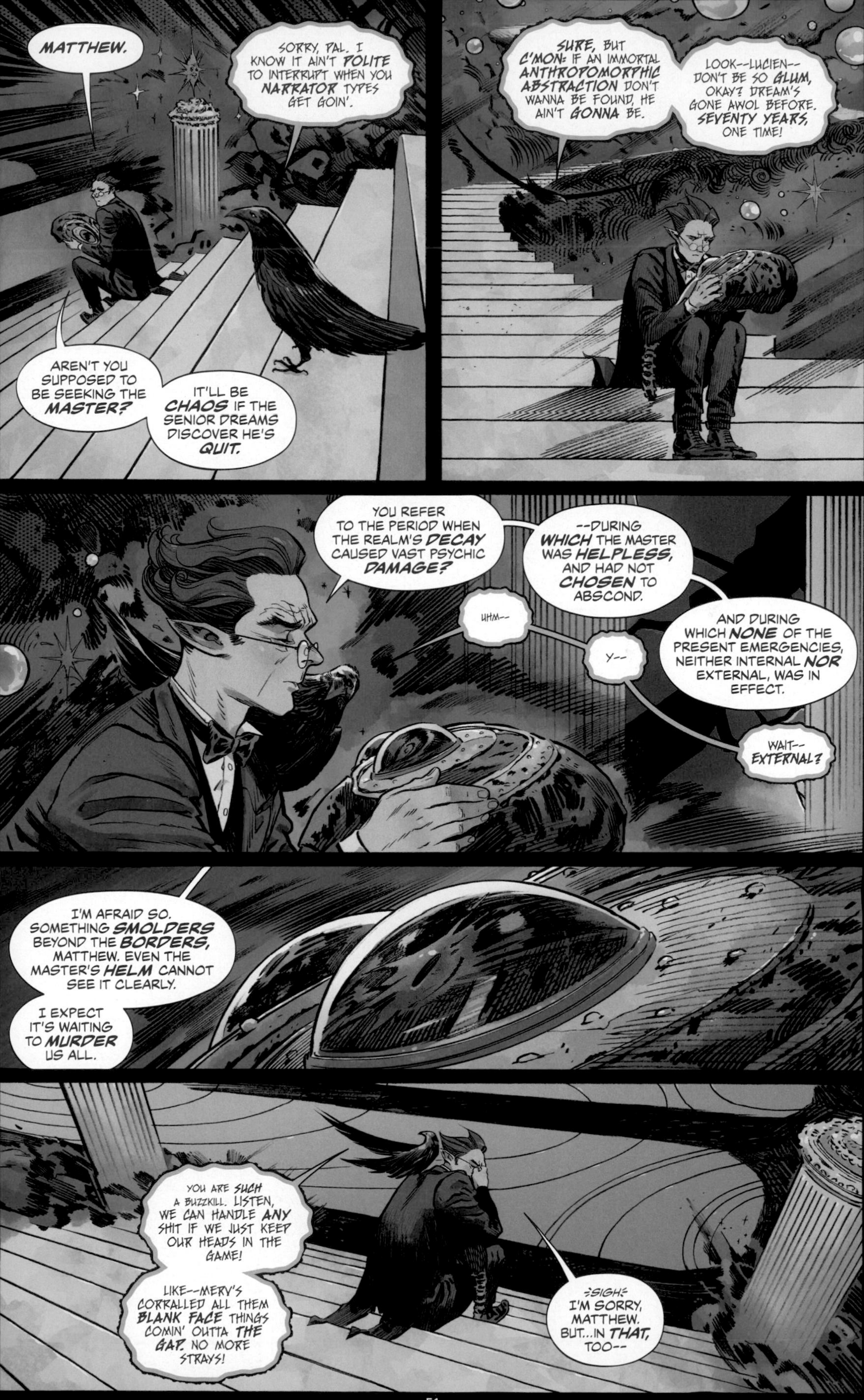
MATTHEW.
SORRY, PAL. I KNOW IT AIN'T POLITE TO INTERRUPT WHEN YOU NARRATOR TYPES GET GOIN'.
AREN'T YOU SUPPOSED TO BE SEEKING THE MASTER?
IT'LL BE CHAOS IF THE SENIOR DREAMS DISCOVER HE'S QUIT.
SURE, BUT C'MON: IF AN IMMORTAL ANTHROPOMORPHIC ABSTRACTION DON'T WANNA BE FOUND, HE AIN'T GONNA BE.
LOOK--LUCIEN-- DON'T BE SO GLUM, OKAY? DREAM'S GONE AWOL BEFORE. SEVENTY YEARS, ONE TIME!
YOU REFER TO THE PERIOD WHEN THE REALM'S DECAY CAUSED VAST PSYCHIC DAMAGE?
UHM--
--DURING WHICH THE MASTER WAS HELPLESS, AND HAD NOT CHOSEN TO ABSCOND.
Y--
AND DURING WHICH NONE OF THE PRESENT EMERGENCIES, NEITHER INTERNAL NOR EXTERNAL, WAS IN EFFECT.
WAIT-- EXTERNAL?
I'M AFRAID SO. SOMETHING SMOLDERS BEYOND THE BORDERS, MATTHEW. EVEN THE MASTER'S HELM CANNOT SEE IT CLEARLY.
I EXPECT IT'S WAITING TO MURDER US ALL.
YOU ARE SUCH A BUZZKILL. LISTEN, WE CAN HANDLE ANY SHIT IF WE JUST KEEP OUR HEADS IN THE GAME!
LIKE--MERV'S CORRALLED ALL THEM BLANK FACE THINGS COMIN' OUTTA THE GAP. NO MORE STRAYS!
SIGH I'M SORRY, MATTHEW. BUT...IN THAT, TOO--

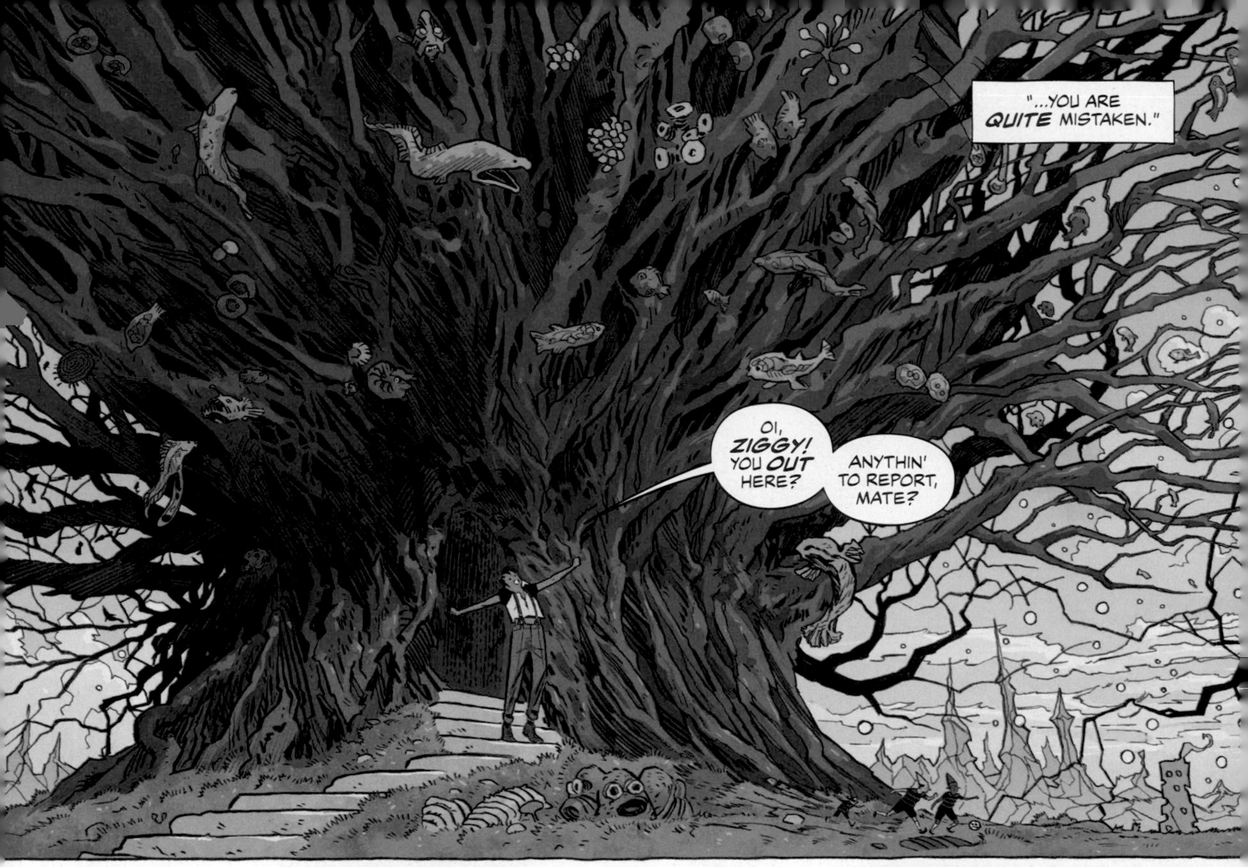
"...YOU ARE QUITE MISTAKEN."
OI, ZIGGY! YOU OUT HERE?
ANYTHIN' TO REPORT, MATE?
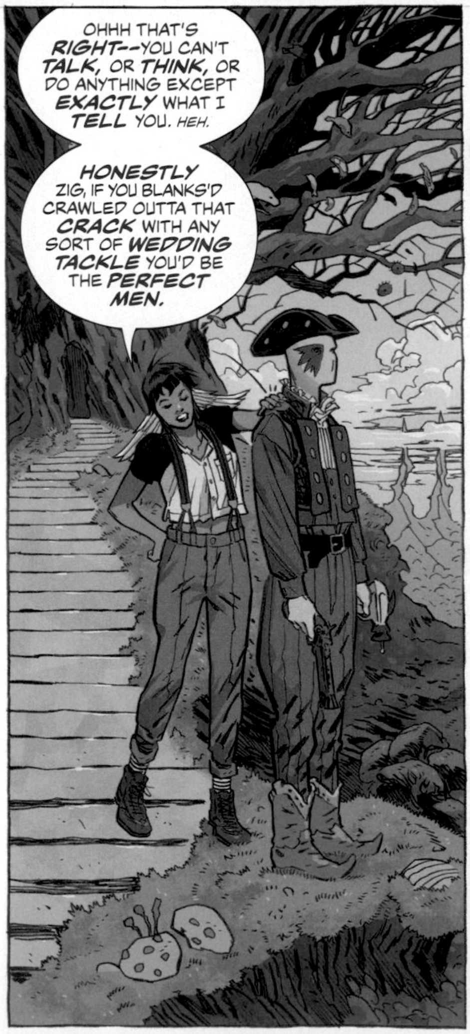
OHHH THAT'S RIGHT--YOU CAN'T TALK, OR THINK, OR DO ANYTHING EXCEPT EXACTLY WHAT I TELL YOU. HEH.
HONESTLY ZIG, IF YOU BLANKS'D CRAWLED OUTTA THAT CRACK WITH ANY SORT OF WEDDING TACKLE YOU'D BE THE PERFECT MEN.
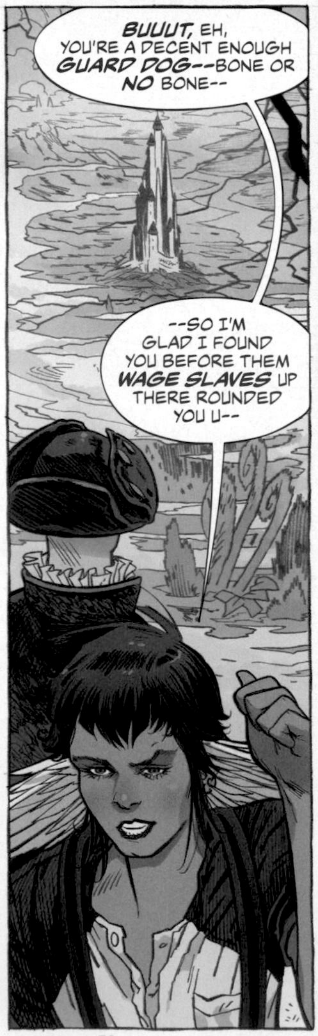
BUUUT, EH, YOU'RE A DECENT ENOUGH GUARD DOG--BONE OR NO BONE--
--SO I'M GLAD I FOUND YOU BEFORE THEM WAGE SLAVES UP THERE ROUNDED YOU U--
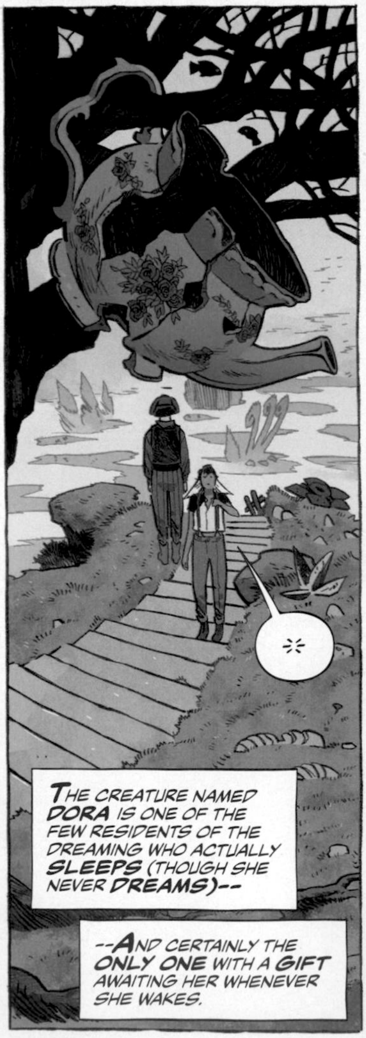
THE CREATURE NAMED DORA IS ONE OF THE FEW RESIDENTS OF THE DREAMING WHO ACTUALLY SLEEPS (THOUGH SHE NEVER DREAMS)--
--AND CERTAINLY THE ONLY ONE WITH A GIFT AWAITING HER WHENEVER SHE WAKES.

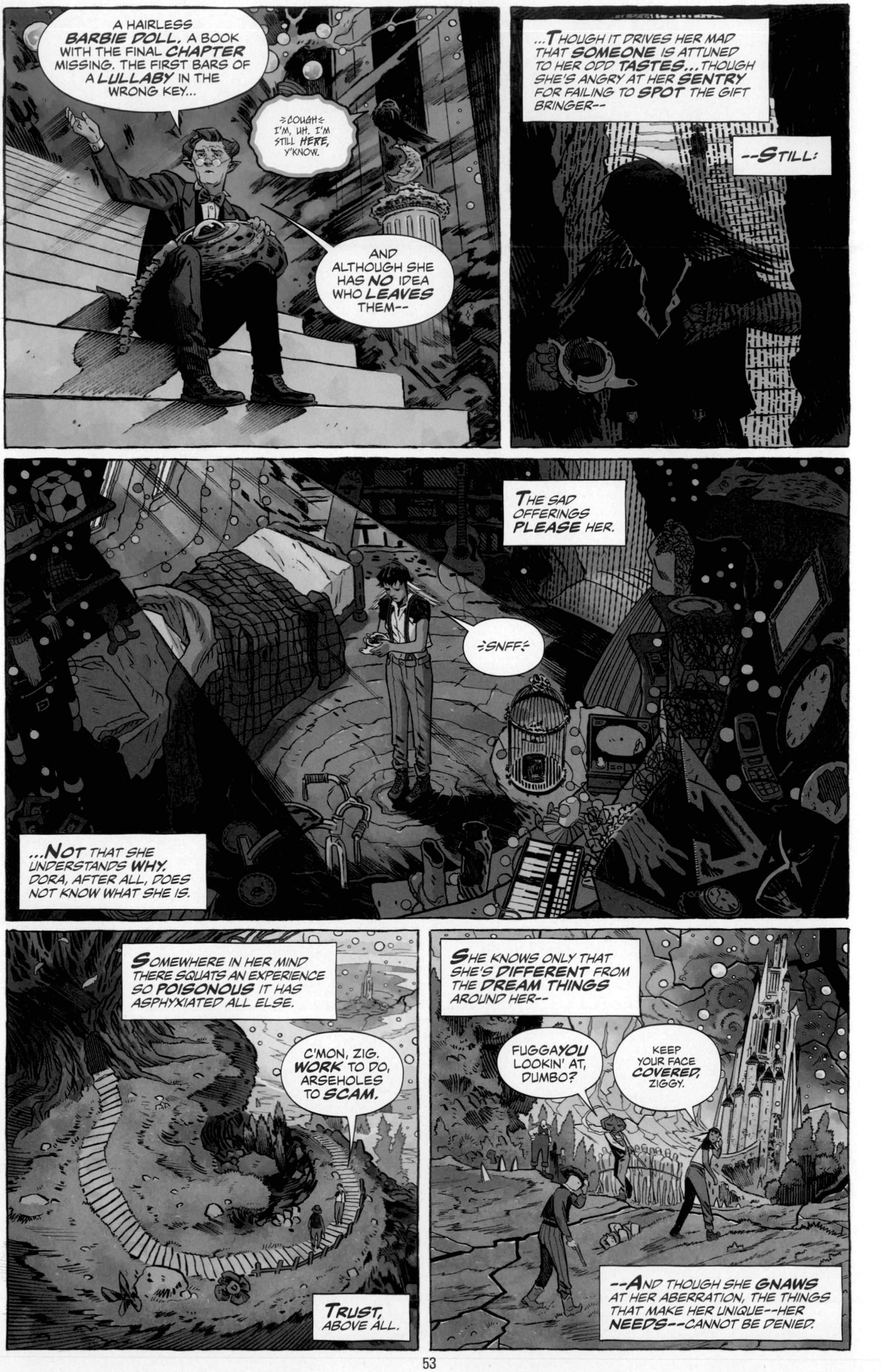
A HAIRLESS BARBIE DOLL. A BOOK WITH THE FINAL CHAPTER MISSING. THE FIRST BARS OF A LULLABY IN THE WRONG KEY...
≈COUGH≈ I'M, UH. I'M STILL HERE, Y'KNOW.
AND ALTHOUGH SHE HAS NO IDEA WHO LEAVES THEM--
...THOUGH IT DRIVES HER MAD THAT SOMEONE IS ATTUNED TO HER ODD TASTES...THOUGH SHE'S ANGRY AT HER SENTRY FOR FAILING TO SPOT THE GIFT BRINGER--
--STILL:
THE SAD OFFERINGS PLEASE HER.
≈SNFF≈
...NOT THAT SHE UNDERSTANDS WHY. DORA, AFTER ALL, DOES NOT KNOW WHAT SHE IS.
SOMEWHERE IN HER MIND THERE SQUATS AN EXPERIENCE SO POISONOUS IT HAS ASPHYXIATED ALL ELSE.
C'MON, ZIG. WORK TO DO, ARSEHOLES TO SCAM.
TRUST, ABOVE ALL.
SHE KNOWS ONLY THAT SHE'S DIFFERENT FROM THE DREAM THINGS AROUND HER--
FUGGAYOU LOOKIN' AT, DUMBO?
KEEP YOUR FACE COVERED, ZIGGY.
--AND THOUGH SHE GNAWS AT HER ABERRATION, THE THINGS THAT MAKE HER UNIQUE--HER NEEDS--CANNOT BE DENIED.

MMF. I'M *STARVING.*

HUH?

NO, YOU BLOODY *APPENDAGE,* WE ARE *NOT* GOING TO THE CASTLE KITCHENS.

LISTEN, YOU TAKE FOOD FROM *THIS* LOT, THEY'LL WANT SOMETHING *BACK*--EVEN IF IT'S JUST A *GRATEFUL SIMPER.*

BEFORE YOU *KNOW* IT YOU'RE A *DREAMSCAPE DECORATOR* OR A *ZEITGEIST RESEARCHER* OR A RACIST BLOODY *TOILET CLEANER* WITH A *VEGETABLE* FOR A HEAD.

AND *ALL* OF IT IN THE NAME OF THEIR GREAT *LORD AND MASTER.*

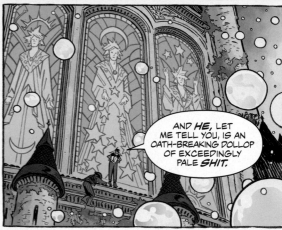

AND *HE,* LET ME TELL YOU, IS AN OATH-BREAKING DOLLOP OF EXCEEDINGLY PALE *SHIT.*

LOOK-- JUST STOP *STARING,* OKAY?

DISTRACT THE *DREAMERS* WHEN I TELL YOU TO, AND IN THE FUTURE KEEP YOUR POINTED FINGERS TO *YOURSELF.*

YOU DON'T QUESTION A *MASTER* AT WORK, ZIGGY.

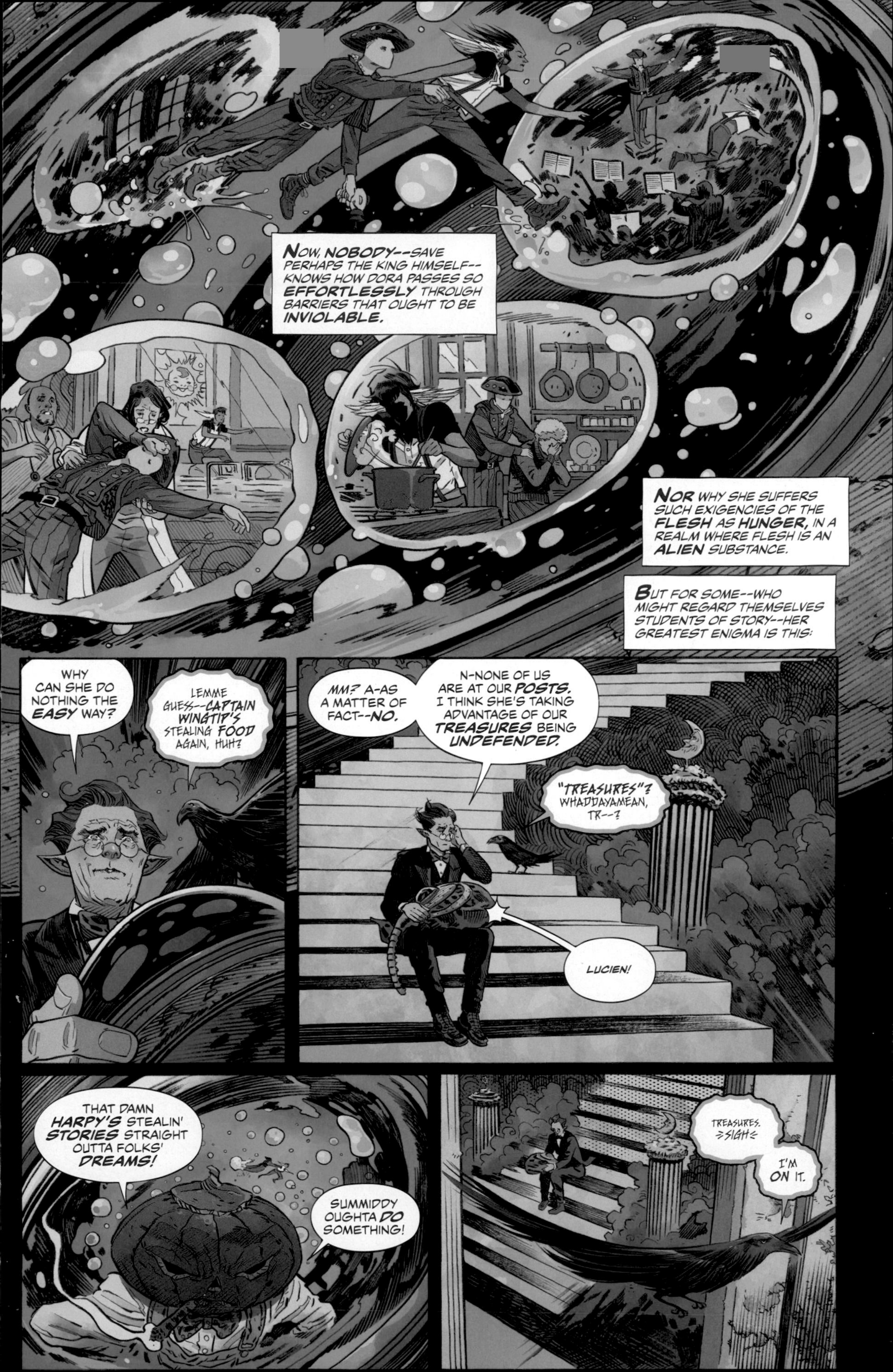
NOW, NOBODY--SAVE PERHAPS THE KING HIMSELF--KNOWS HOW DORA PASSES SO EFFORTLESSLY THROUGH BARRIERS THAT OUGHT TO BE INVIOLABLE.
NOR WHY SHE SUFFERS SUCH EXIGENCIES OF THE FLESH AS HUNGER, IN A REALM WHERE FLESH IS AN ALIEN SUBSTANCE.
BUT FOR SOME--WHO MIGHT REGARD THEMSELVES STUDENTS OF STORY--HER GREATEST ENIGMA IS THIS:
WHY CAN SHE DO NOTHING THE EASY WAY?
LEMME GUESS--CAPTAIN WINGTIP'S STEALING FOOD AGAIN, HUH?
MM? A-AS A MATTER OF FACT--NO.
N-NONE OF US ARE AT OUR POSTS. I THINK SHE'S TAKING ADVANTAGE OF OUR TREASURES BEING UNDEFENDED.
"TREASURES"? WHADDAYAMEAN, TR--?
LUCIEN!
THAT DAMN HARPY'S STEALIN' STORIES STRAIGHT OUTTA FOLKS' DREAMS!
SUMMIDDY OUGHTA DO SOMETHING!
TREASURES. >SIGH<
I'M ON IT.

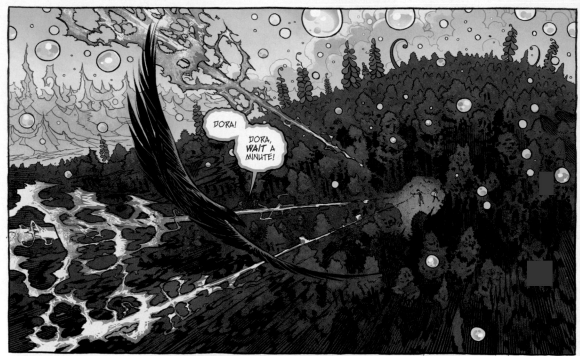

DORA!

DORA, *WAIT A* MINUTE!

C'MON, LADY, THIS IS *DUMB!* ALL I WANNA DO IS *TALK!*

I NEED TO *CONCENTRATE* FOR A SEC HERE, ZIGGY. BE A *MATE* AND SHOW THE TWEETY BIRD HOW MUCH I LIKE TO *CHAT,* WOULD YA?

ALLEZ...

OOP!

SQUAAAWK!

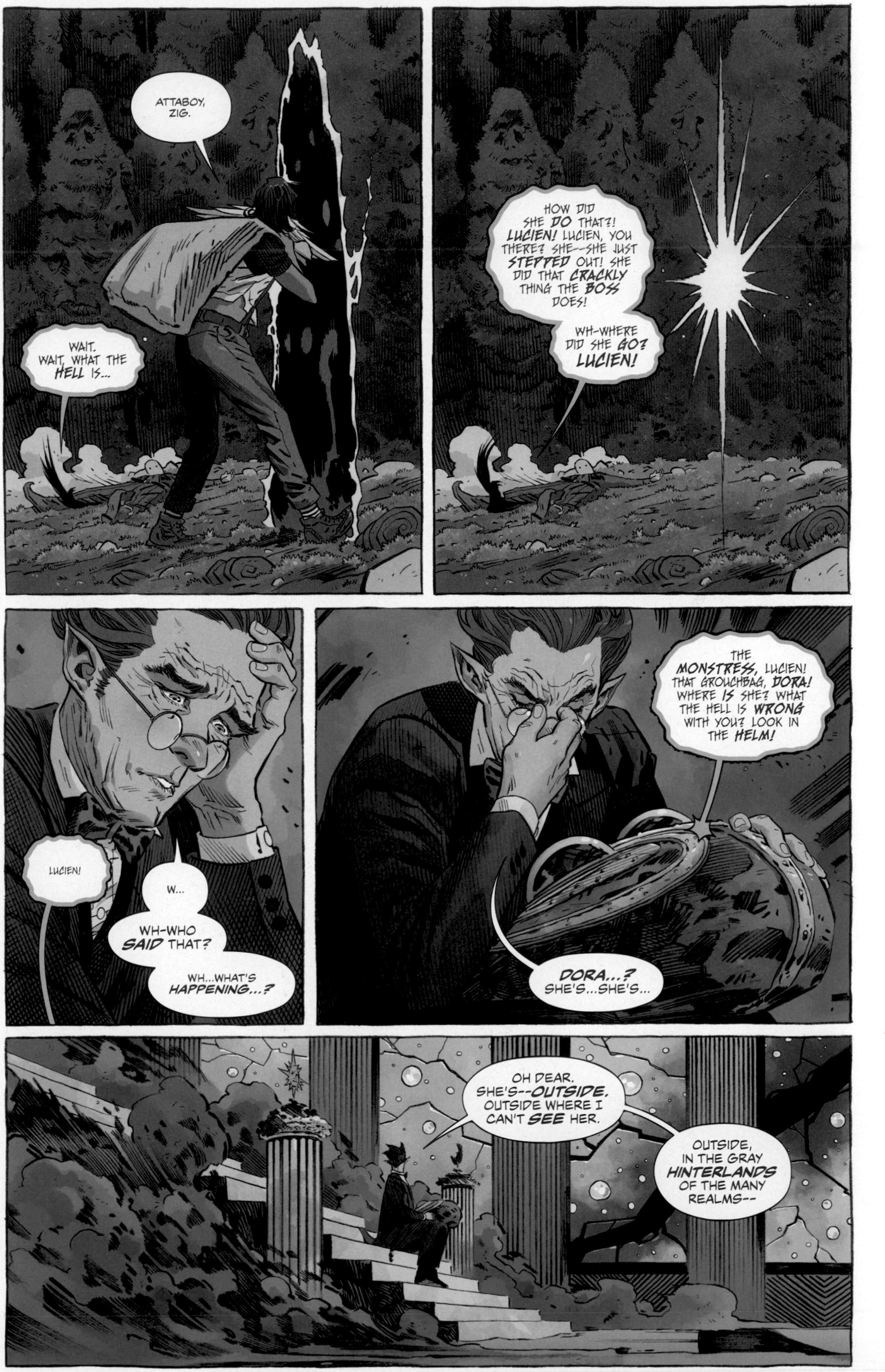
ATTABOY, ZIG.
WAIT. WAIT, WHAT THE HELL IS...
HOW DID SHE DO THAT?! LUCIEN! LUCIEN, YOU THERE? SHE--SHE JUST STEPPED OUT! SHE DID THAT CRACKLY THING THE BOSS DOES!
WH-WHERE DID SHE GO? LUCIEN!
LUCIEN!
W...
WH-WHO SAID THAT?
WH...WHAT'S HAPPENING...?
THE MONSTRESS, LUCIEN! THAT GROUCHBAG, DORA! WHERE IS SHE? WHAT THE HELL IS WRONG WITH YOU? LOOK IN THE HELM!
DORA...? SHE'S...SHE'S...
OH DEAR. SHE'S--OUTSIDE. OUTSIDE WHERE I CAN'T SEE HER.
OUTSIDE, IN THE GRAY HINTERLANDS OF THE MANY REALMS--

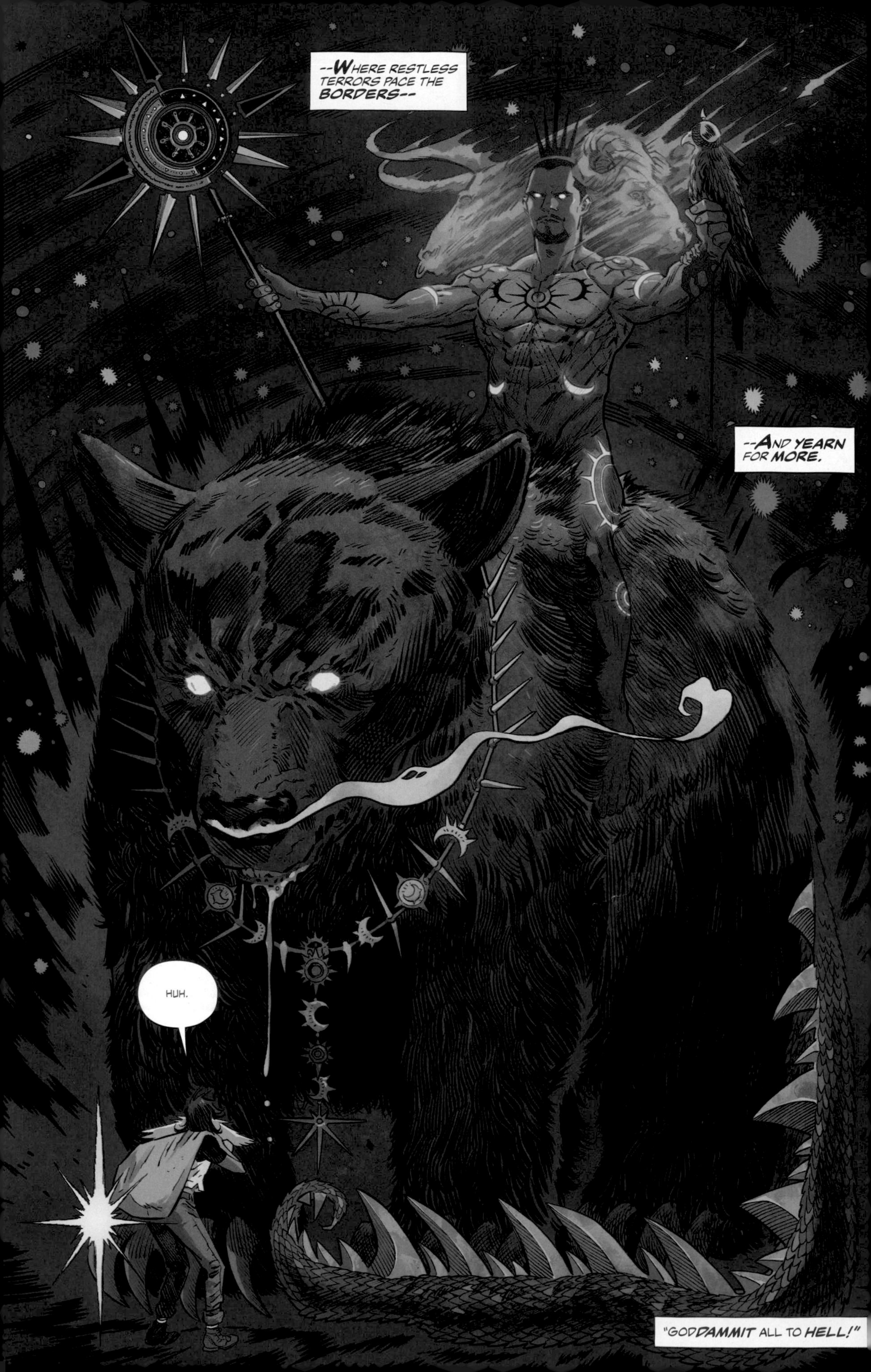
--WHERE RESTLESS TERRORS PACE THE BORDERS--
--AND YEARN FOR MORE.
HUH.
"GODDAMMIT ALL TO HELL!"

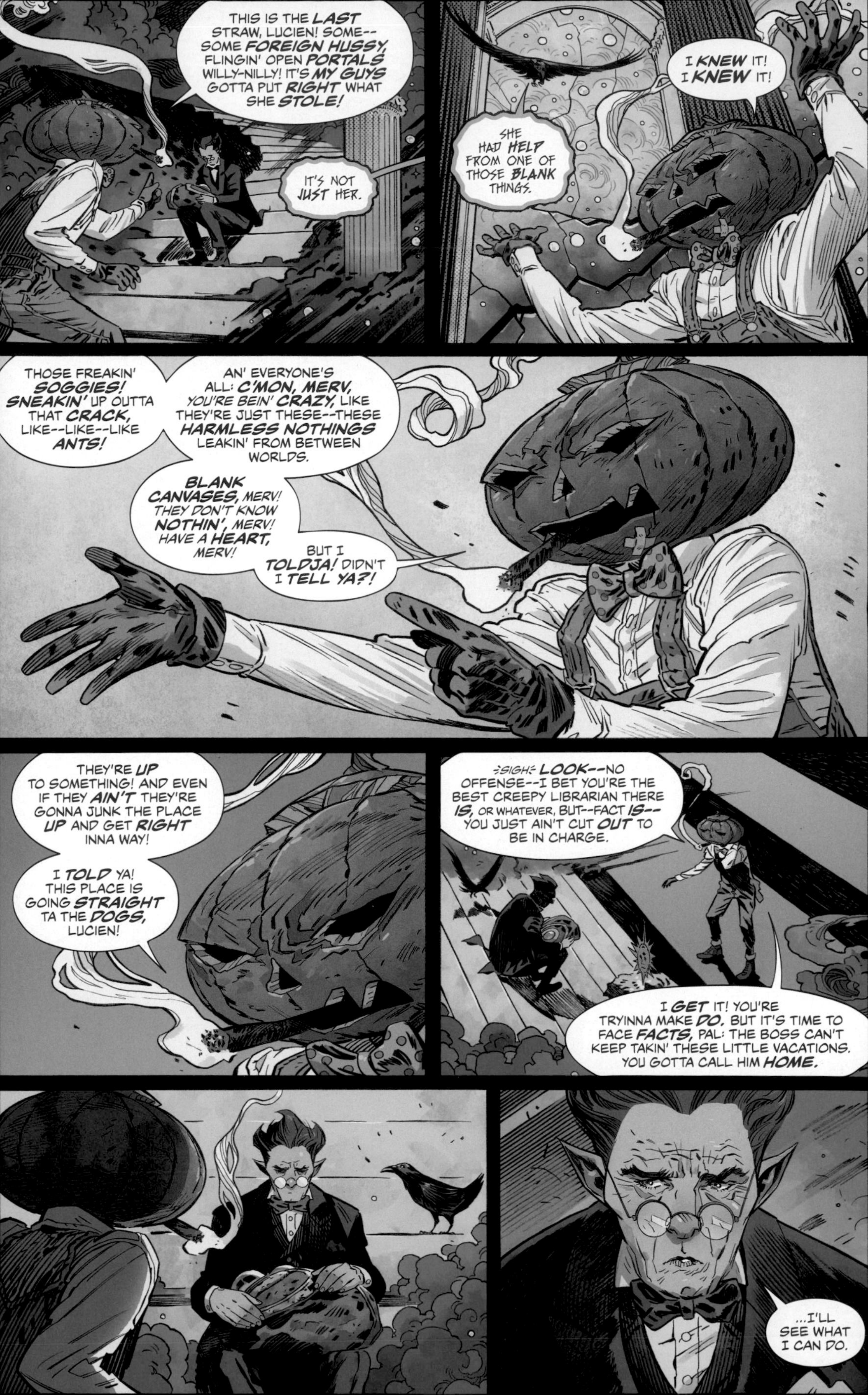
THIS IS THE LAST STRAW, LUCIEN! SOME--SOME FOREIGN HUSSY, FLINGIN' OPEN PORTALS WILLY-NILLY! IT'S MY GUYS GOTTA PUT RIGHT WHAT SHE STOLE!
IT'S NOT JUST HER.
SHE HAD HELP FROM ONE OF THOSE BLANK THINGS.
I KNEW IT! I KNEW IT!
THOSE FREAKIN' SOGGIES! SNEAKIN' UP OUTTA THAT CRACK, LIKE--LIKE--LIKE ANTS!
AN' EVERYONE'S ALL: C'MON, MERV, YOU'RE BEIN' CRAZY, LIKE THEY'RE JUST THESE--THESE HARMLESS NOTHINGS LEAKIN' FROM BETWEEN WORLDS.
BLANK CANVASES, MERV! THEY DON'T KNOW NOTHIN', MERV! HAVE A HEART, MERV!
BUT I TOLDJA! DIDN'T I TELL YA?!
THEY'RE UP TO SOMETHING! AND EVEN IF THEY AIN'T THEY'RE GONNA JUNK THE PLACE UP AND GET RIGHT INNA WAY!
I TOLD YA! THIS PLACE IS GOING STRAIGHT TA THE DOGS, LUCIEN!
SIGH LOOK--NO OFFENSE--I BET YOU'RE THE BEST CREEPY LIBRARIAN THERE IS, OR WHATEVER, BUT--FACT IS--YOU JUST AIN'T CUT OUT TO BE IN CHARGE.
I GET IT! YOU'RE TRYINNA MAKE DO, BUT IT'S TIME TO FACE FACTS, PAL: THE BOSS CAN'T KEEP TAKIN' THESE LITTLE VACATIONS. YOU GOTTA CALL HIM HOME.
...I'LL SEE WHAT I CAN DO.

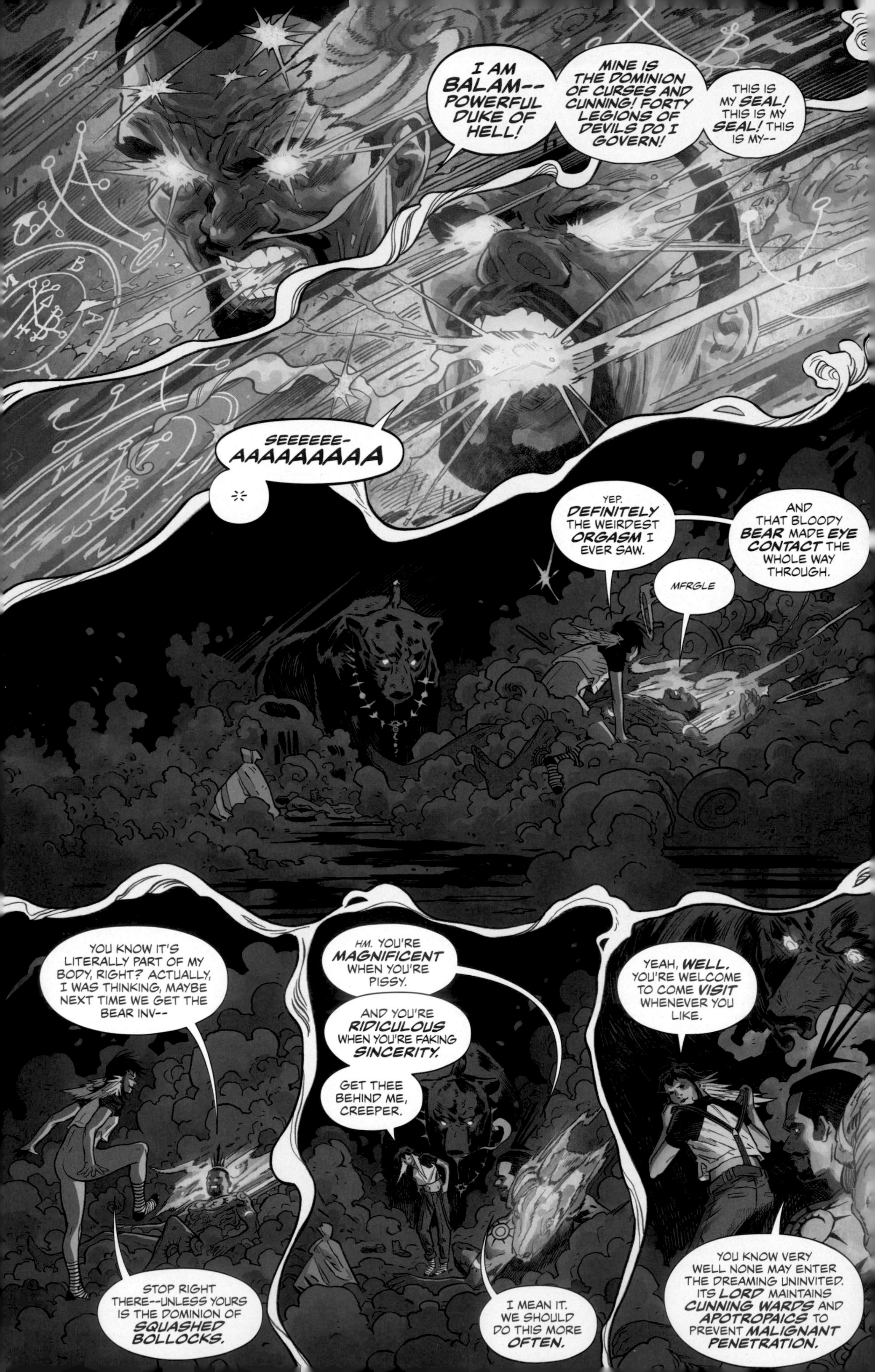
I AM BALAM-- POWERFUL DUKE OF HELL!
MINE IS THE DOMINION OF CURSES AND CUNNING! FORTY LEGIONS OF DEVILS DO I GOVERN!
THIS IS MY SEAL! THIS IS MY SEAL! THIS IS MY--
SEEEEEE-AAAAAAAAA
YEP. DEFINITELY THE WEIRDEST ORGASM I EVER SAW.
AND THAT BLOODY BEAR MADE EYE CONTACT THE WHOLE WAY THROUGH.
MFRGLE
YOU KNOW IT'S LITERALLY PART OF MY BODY, RIGHT? ACTUALLY, I WAS THINKING, MAYBE NEXT TIME WE GET THE BEAR INV--
STOP RIGHT THERE--UNLESS YOURS IS THE DOMINION OF SQUASHED BOLLOCKS.
HM. YOU'RE MAGNIFICENT WHEN YOU'RE PISSY.
AND YOU'RE RIDICULOUS WHEN YOU'RE FAKING SINCERITY.
GET THEE BEHIND ME, CREEPER.
I MEAN IT. WE SHOULD DO THIS MORE OFTEN.
YEAH, WELL. YOU'RE WELCOME TO COME VISIT WHENEVER YOU LIKE.
YOU KNOW VERY WELL NONE MAY ENTER THE DREAMING UNINVITED. ITS LORD MAINTAINS CUNNING WARDS AND APOTROPAICS TO PREVENT MALIGNANT PENETRATION.

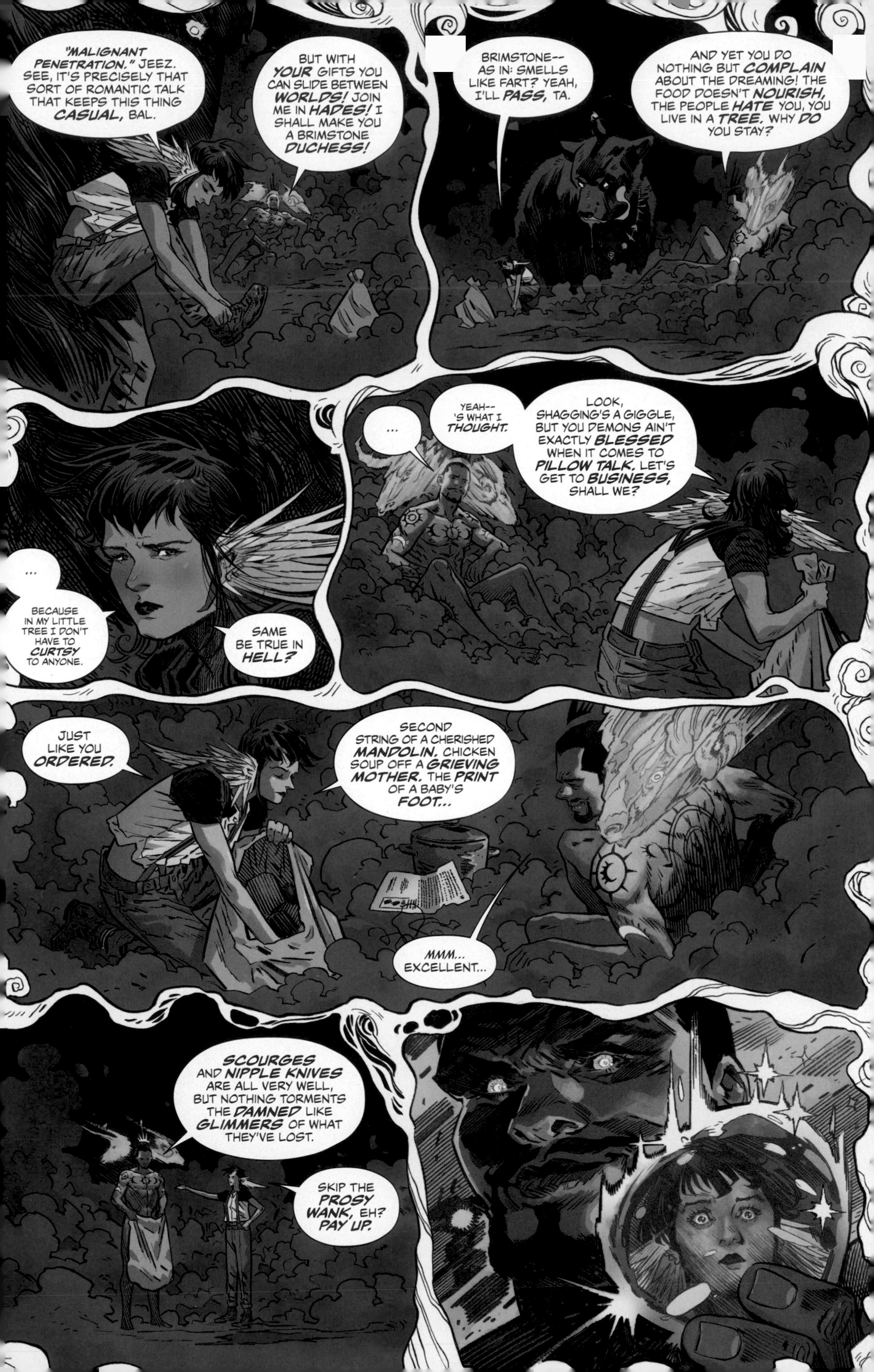
"MALIGNANT PENETRATION." JEEZ. SEE, IT'S PRECISELY THAT SORT OF ROMANTIC TALK THAT KEEPS THIS THING CASUAL, BAL.
BUT WITH YOUR GIFTS YOU CAN SLIDE BETWEEN WORLDS! JOIN ME IN HADES! I SHALL MAKE YOU A BRIMSTONE DUCHESS!
BRIMSTONE-- AS IN: SMELLS LIKE FART? YEAH, I'LL PASS, TA.
AND YET YOU DO NOTHING BUT COMPLAIN ABOUT THE DREAMING! THE FOOD DOESN'T NOURISH, THE PEOPLE HATE YOU, YOU LIVE IN A TREE. WHY DO YOU STAY?
...
BECAUSE IN MY LITTLE TREE I DON'T HAVE TO CURTSY TO ANYONE.
SAME BE TRUE IN HELL?
...
YEAH-- 'S WHAT I THOUGHT.
LOOK, SHAGGING'S A GIGGLE, BUT YOU DEMONS AIN'T EXACTLY BLESSED WHEN IT COMES TO PILLOW TALK. LET'S GET TO BUSINESS, SHALL WE?
JUST LIKE YOU ORDERED.
SECOND STRING OF A CHERISHED MANDOLIN. CHICKEN SOUP OFF A GRIEVING MOTHER. THE PRINT OF A BABY'S FOOT...
MMM... EXCELLENT...
SCOURGES AND NIPPLE KNIVES ARE ALL VERY WELL, BUT NOTHING TORMENTS THE DAMNED LIKE GLIMMERS OF WHAT THEY'VE LOST.
SKIP THE PROSY WANK, EH? PAY UP.

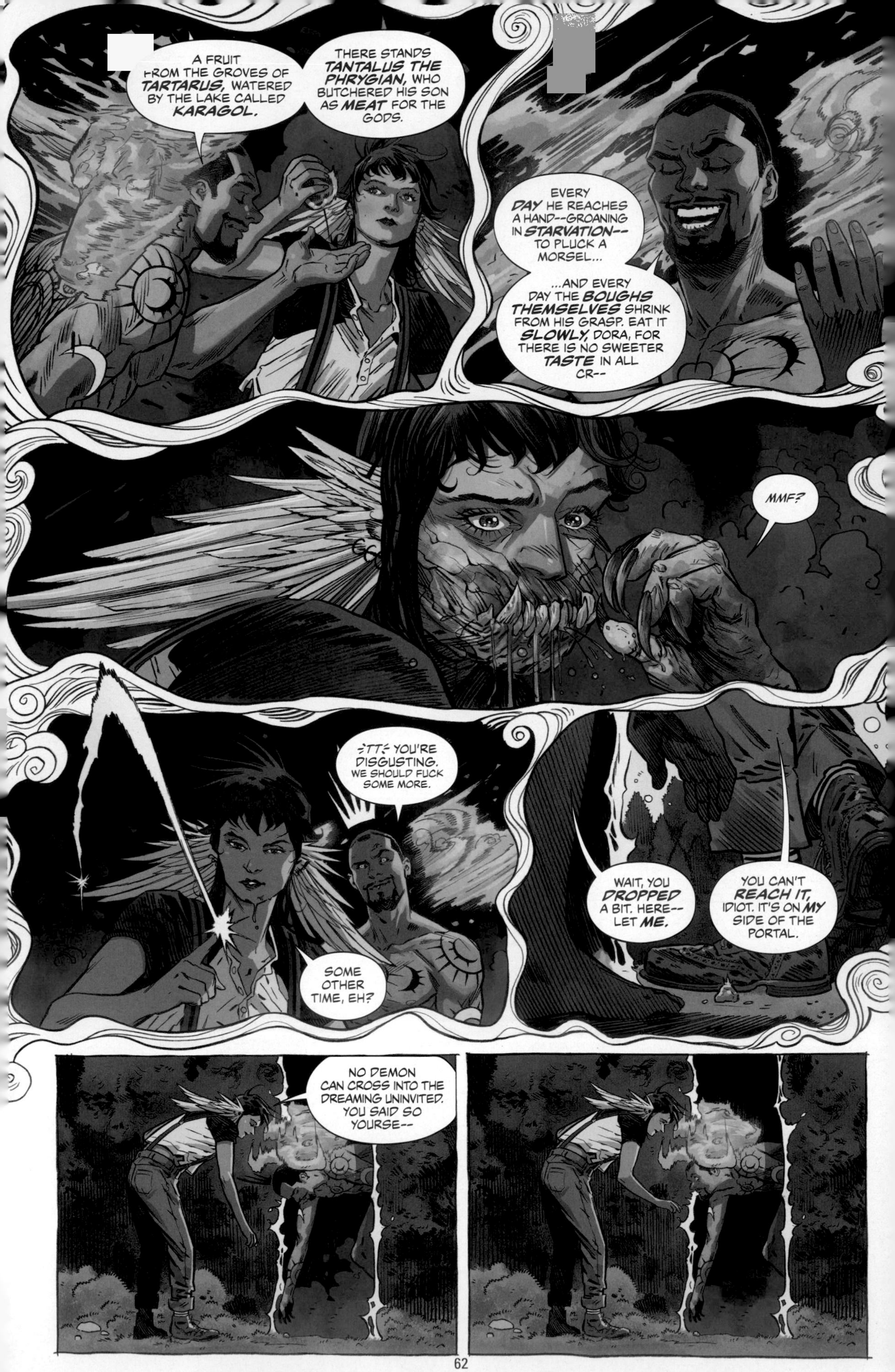
A FRUIT FROM THE GROVES OF TARTARUS, WATERED BY THE LAKE CALLED KARAGOL.
THERE STANDS TANTALUS THE PHRYGIAN, WHO BUTCHERED HIS SON AS MEAT FOR THE GODS.
EVERY DAY HE REACHES A HAND--GROANING IN STARVATION--TO PLUCK A MORSEL...
...AND EVERY DAY THE BOUGHS THEMSELVES SHRINK FROM HIS GRASP. EAT IT SLOWLY, DORA, FOR THERE IS NO SWEETER TASTE IN ALL CR--
MMF?
TT YOU'RE DISGUSTING. WE SHOULD FUCK SOME MORE.
SOME OTHER TIME, EH?
WAIT, YOU DROPPED A BIT. HERE--LET ME.
YOU CAN'T REACH IT, IDIOT. IT'S ON MY SIDE OF THE PORTAL.
NO DEMON CAN CROSS INTO THE DREAMING UNINVITED. YOU SAID SO YOURSE--

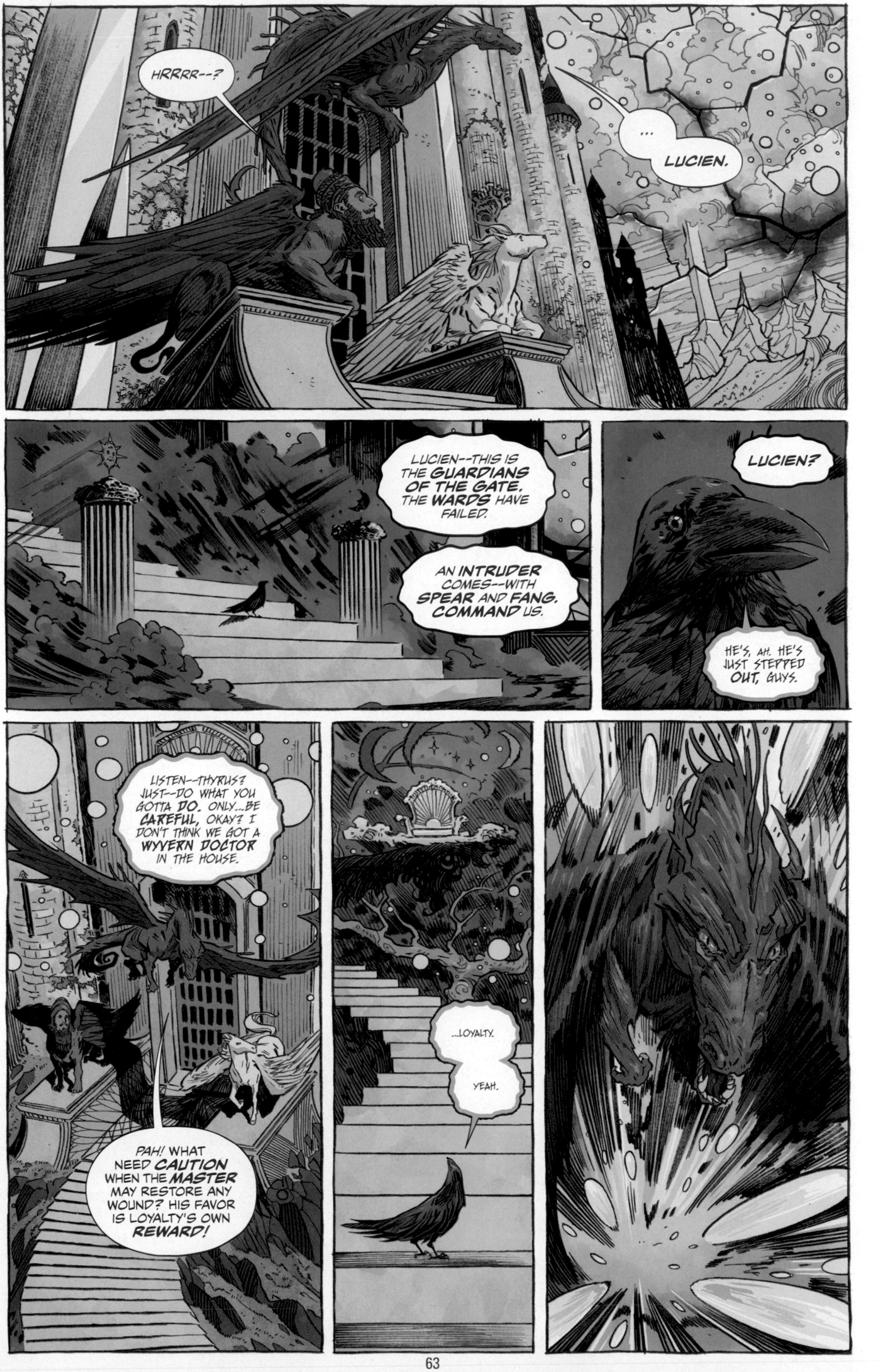
HRRRR--?
... LUCIEN.
LUCIEN--THIS IS THE GUARDIANS OF THE GATE. THE WARDS HAVE FAILED.
AN INTRUDER COMES--WITH SPEAR AND FANG. COMMAND US.
LUCIEN?
HE'S, AH. HE'S JUST STEPPED OUT, GUYS.
LISTEN--THYRUS? JUST--DO WHAT YOU GOTTA DO. ONLY...BE CAREFUL, OKAY? I DON'T THINK WE GOT A WYVERN DOCTOR IN THE HOUSE.
PAH! WHAT NEED CAUTION WHEN THE MASTER MAY RESTORE ANY WOUND? HIS FAVOR IS LOYALTY'S OWN REWARD!
...LOYALTY.
YEAH.

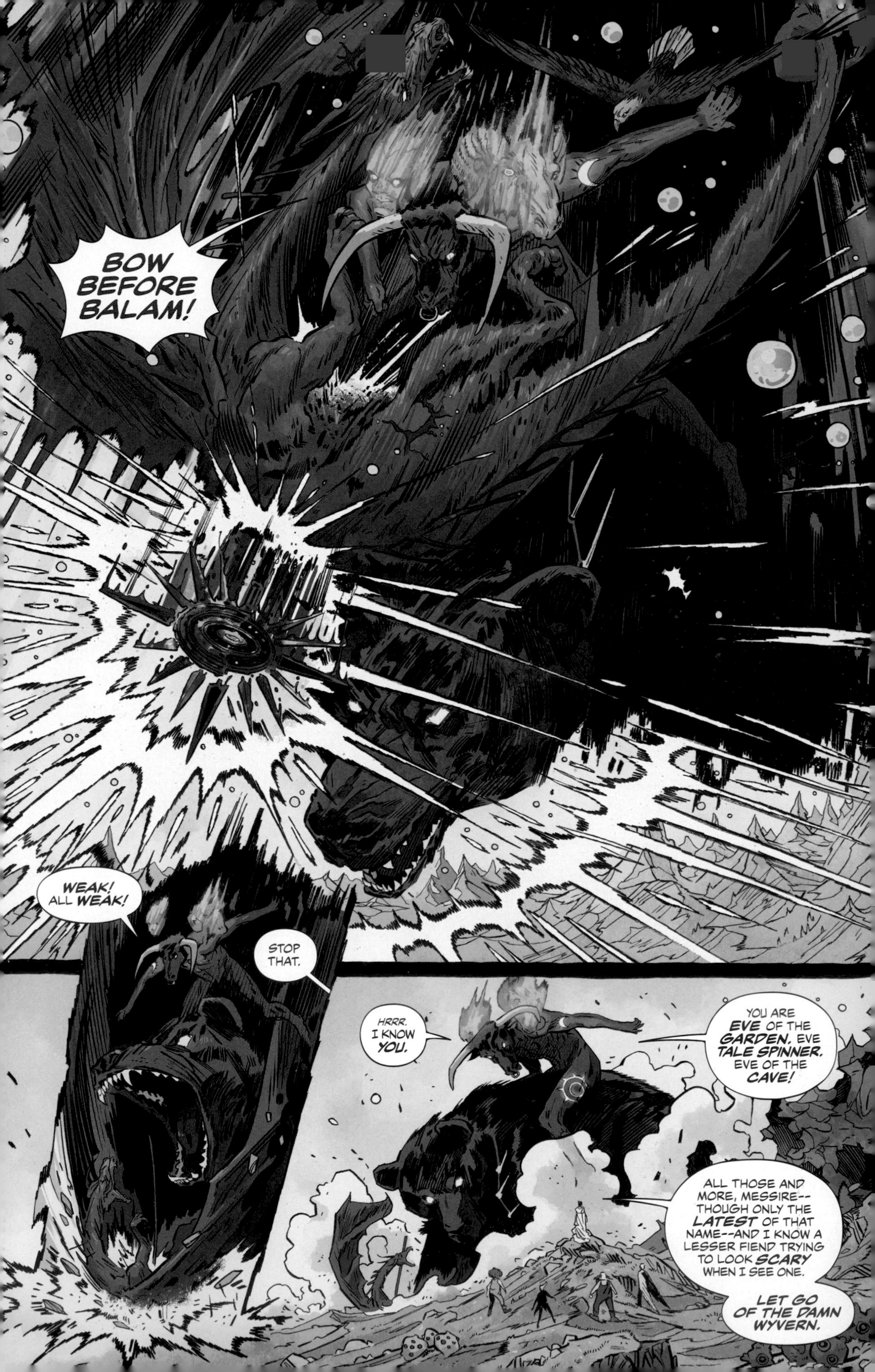
BOW BEFORE BALAM!
WEAK! ALL WEAK!
STOP THAT.
HRRR. I KNOW YOU.
YOU ARE EVE OF THE GARDEN. EVE TALE SPINNER. EVE OF THE CAVE!
ALL THOSE AND MORE, MESSIRE--THOUGH ONLY THE LATEST OF THAT NAME--AND I KNOW A LESSER FIEND TRYING TO LOOK SCARY WHEN I SEE ONE.
LET GO OF THE DAMN WYVERN.

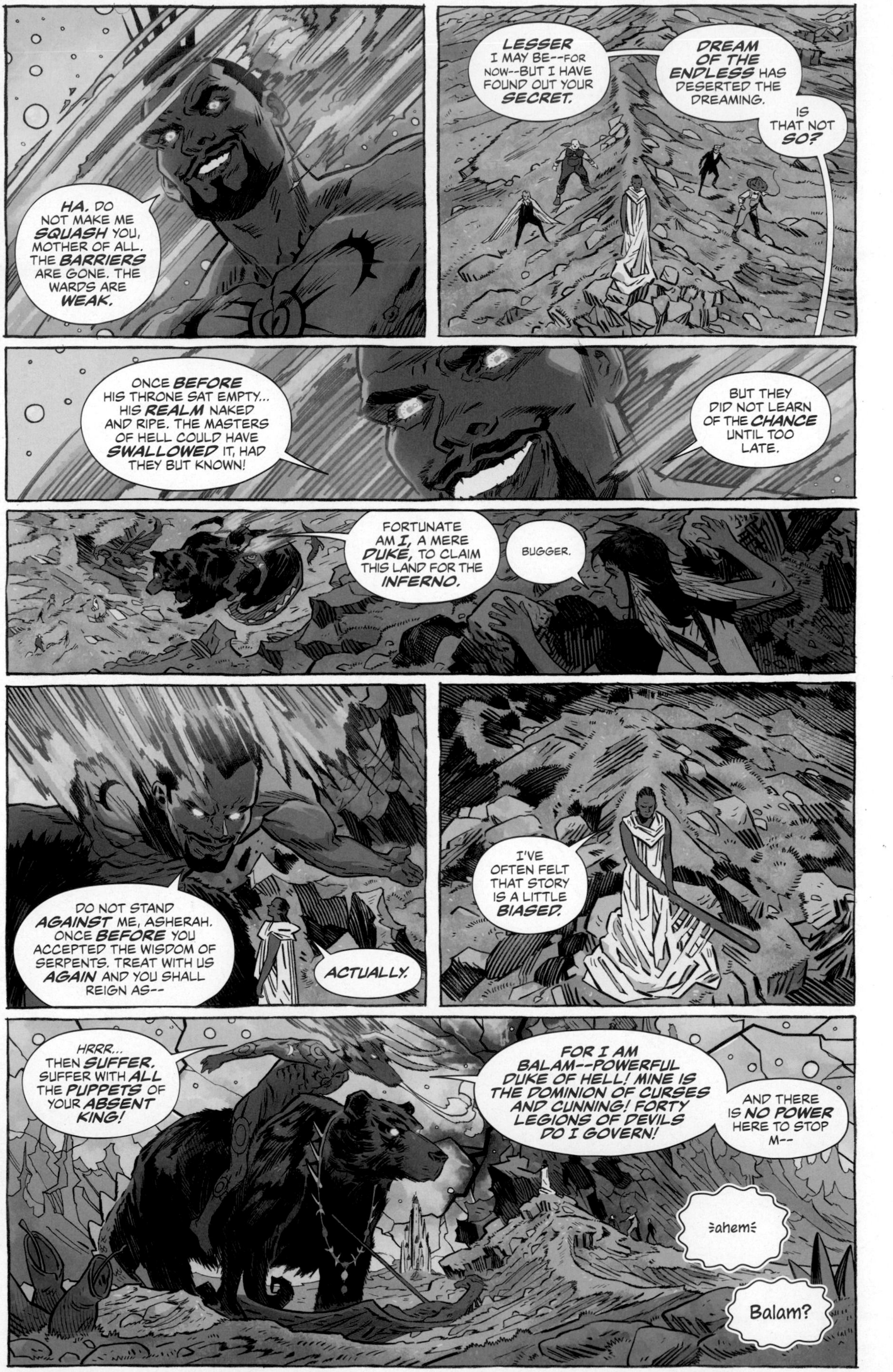
HA. DO NOT MAKE ME SQUASH YOU, MOTHER OF ALL. THE BARRIERS ARE GONE. THE WARDS ARE WEAK.
LESSER I MAY BE--FOR NOW--BUT I HAVE FOUND OUT YOUR SECRET.
DREAM OF THE ENDLESS HAS DESERTED THE DREAMING.
IS THAT NOT SO?
ONCE BEFORE HIS THRONE SAT EMPTY... HIS REALM NAKED AND RIPE. THE MASTERS OF HELL COULD HAVE SWALLOWED IT, HAD THEY BUT KNOWN!
BUT THEY DID NOT LEARN OF THE CHANCE UNTIL TOO LATE.
FORTUNATE AM I, A MERE DUKE, TO CLAIM THIS LAND FOR THE INFERNO.
BUGGER.
DO NOT STAND AGAINST ME, ASHERAH. ONCE BEFORE YOU ACCEPTED THE WISDOM OF SERPENTS. TREAT WITH US AGAIN AND YOU SHALL REIGN AS--
ACTUALLY.
I'VE OFTEN FELT THAT STORY IS A LITTLE BIASED.
HRRR... THEN SUFFER. SUFFER WITH ALL THE PUPPETS OF YOUR ABSENT KING!
FOR I AM BALAM--POWERFUL DUKE OF HELL! MINE IS THE DOMINION OF CURSES AND CUNNING! FORTY LEGIONS OF DEVILS DO I GOVERN!
AND THERE IS NO POWER HERE TO STOP M--
ahem
Balam?

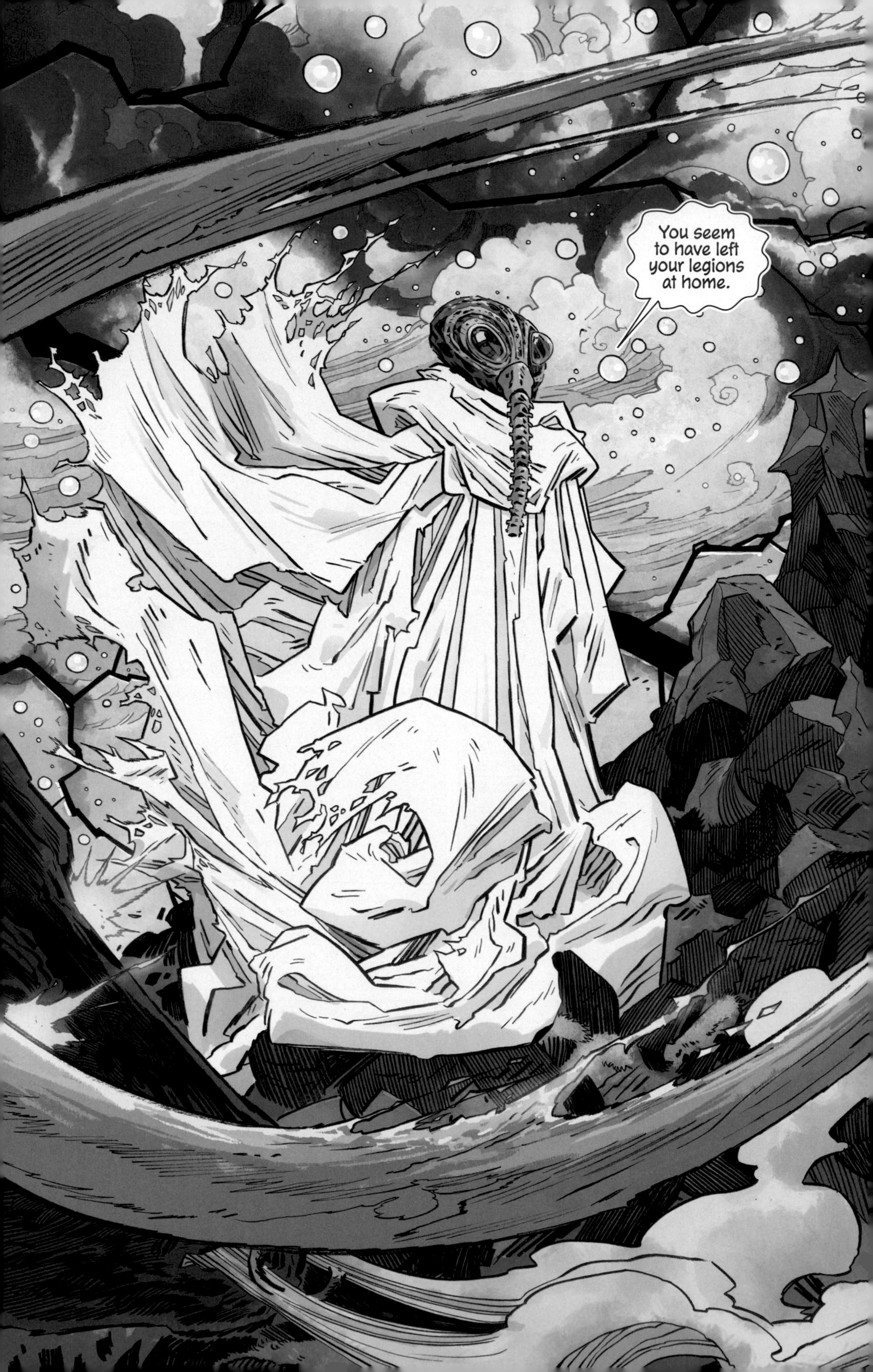
You seem to have left your legions at home.

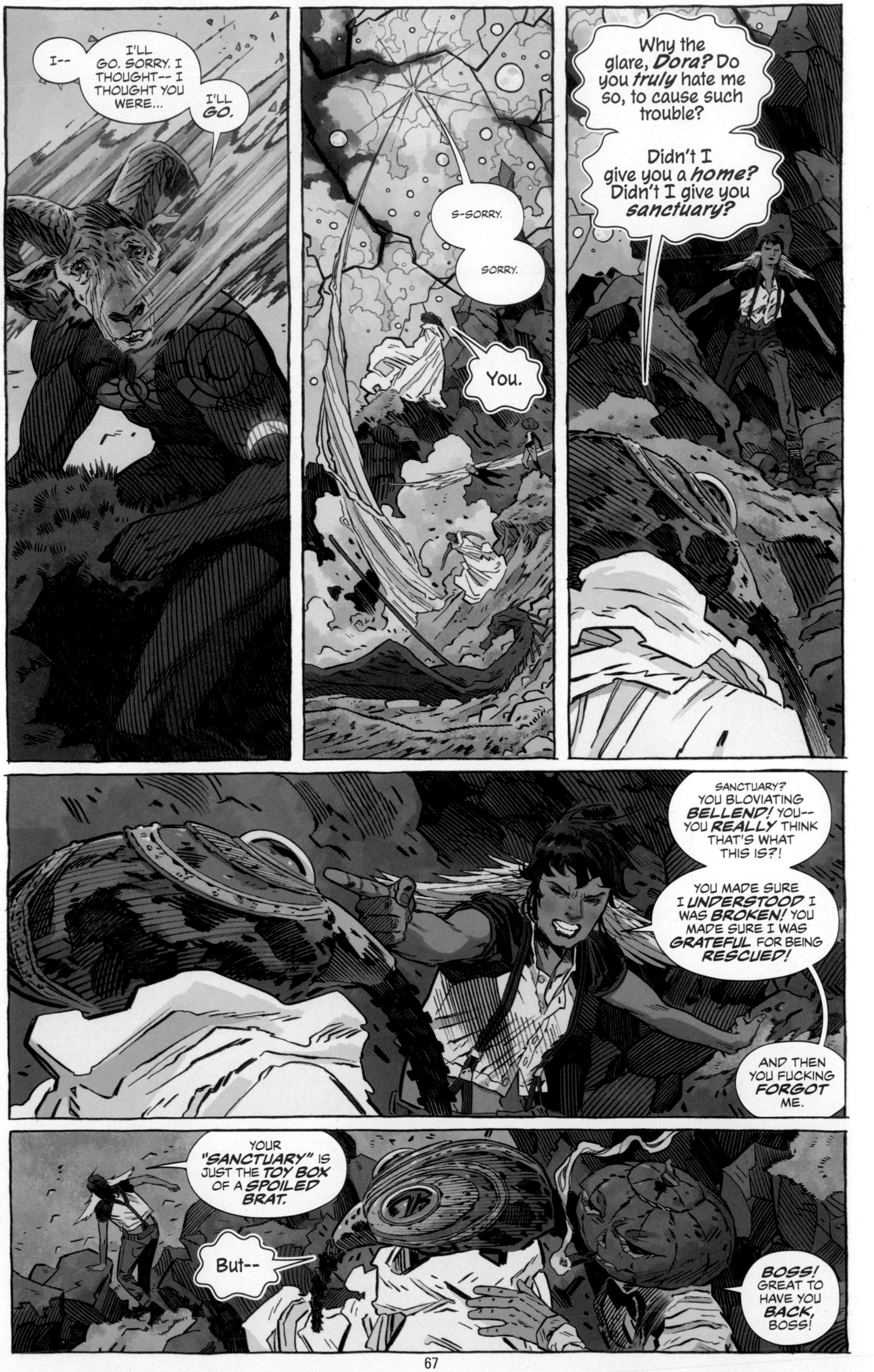
I--
I'LL GO. SORRY. I THOUGHT-- I THOUGHT YOU WERE...
I'LL GO.
S-SORRY.
SORRY.
You.
Why the glare, Dora? Do you truly hate me so, to cause such trouble?
Didn't I give you a home? Didn't I give you sanctuary?
SANCTUARY? YOU BLOVIATING BELLEND! YOU-- YOU REALLY THINK THAT'S WHAT THIS IS?!
YOU MADE SURE I UNDERSTOOD I WAS BROKEN! YOU MADE SURE I WAS GRATEFUL FOR BEING RESCUED!
AND THEN YOU FUCKING FORGOT ME.
YOUR "SANCTUARY" IS JUST THE TOY BOX OF A SPOILED BRAT.
But--
BOSS! GREAT TO HAVE YOU BACK, BOSS!

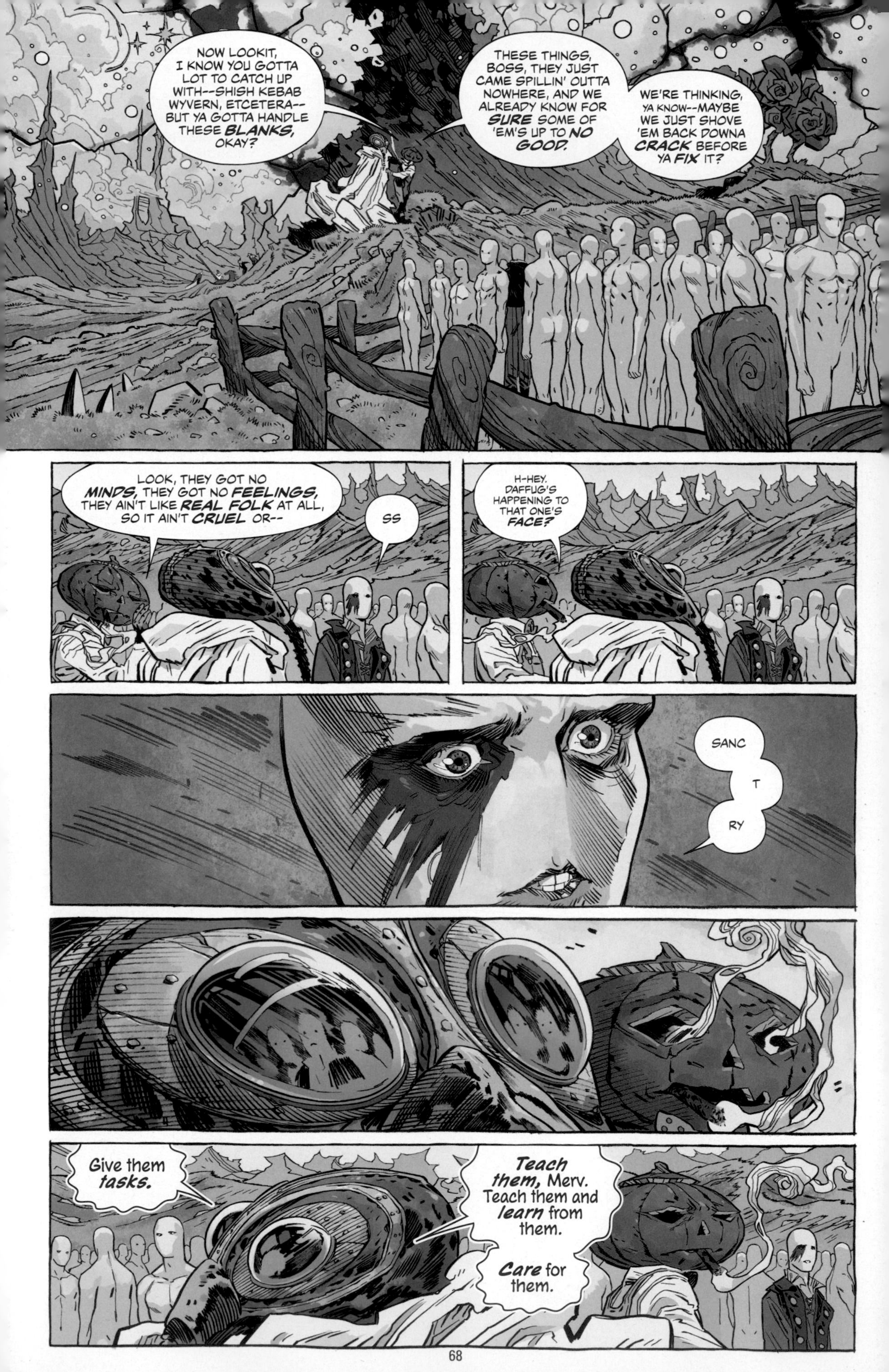
NOW LOOKIT, I KNOW YOU GOTTA LOT TO CATCH UP WITH--SHISH KEBAB WYVERN, ETCETERA--BUT YA GOTTA HANDLE THESE BLANKS, OKAY?
THESE THINGS, BOSS, THEY JUST CAME SPILLIN' OUTTA NOWHERE, AND WE ALREADY KNOW FOR SURE SOME OF 'EM'S UP TO NO GOOD.
WE'RE THINKING, YA KNOW--MAYBE WE JUST SHOVE 'EM BACK DOWNA CRACK BEFORE YA FIX IT?
LOOK, THEY GOT NO MINDS, THEY GOT NO FEELINGS, THEY AIN'T LIKE REAL FOLK AT ALL, SO IT AIN'T CRUEL OR--
SS
H-HEY. DAFFUG'S HAPPENING TO THAT ONE'S FACE?
SANC
T
RY
Give them tasks.
Teach them, Merv. Teach them and learn from them.
Care for them.

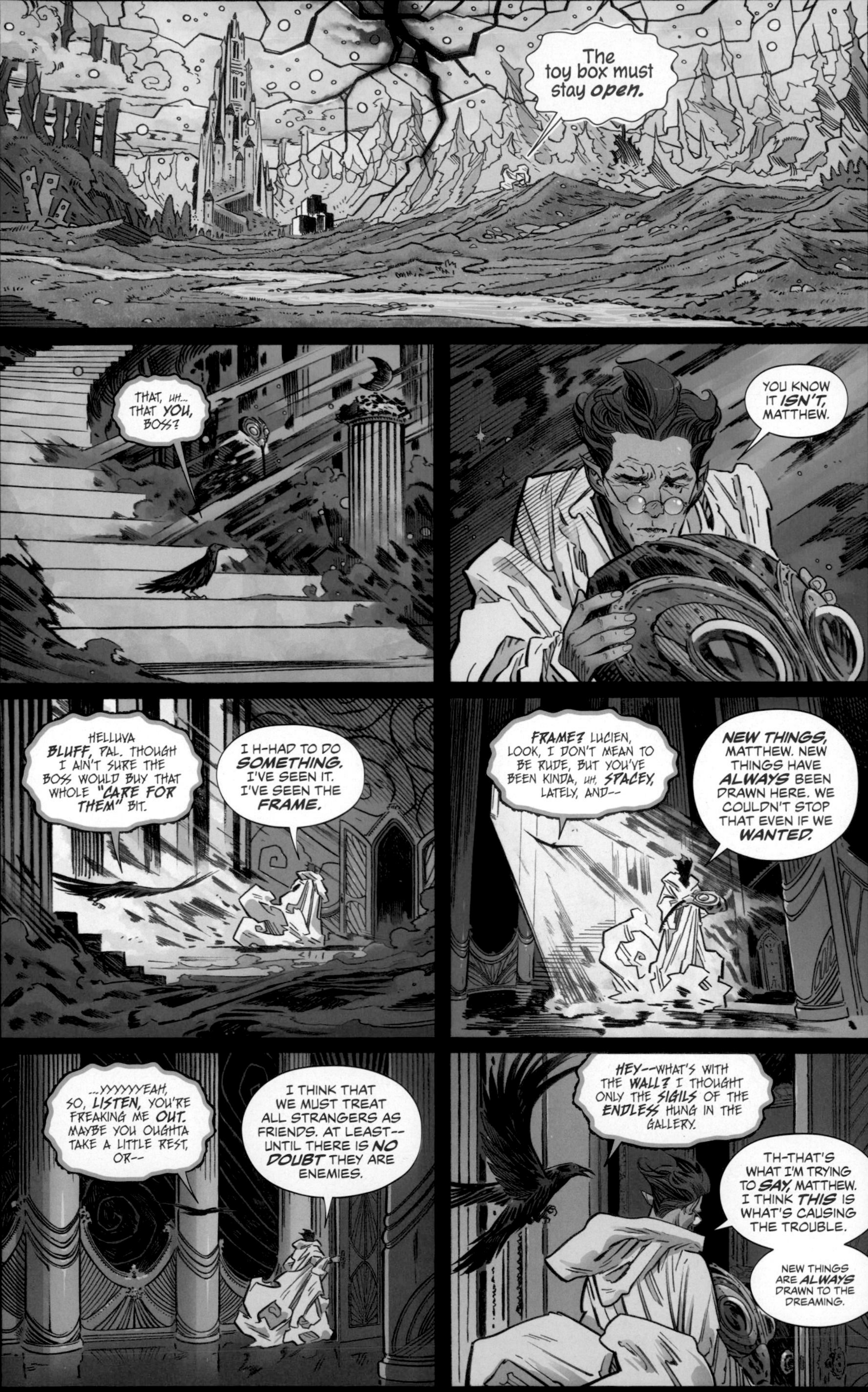
The toy box must stay *open.*
THAT, UH... THAT **YOU,** BOSS?
YOU KNOW IT ***ISN'T,*** MATTHEW.
HELLUVA **BLUFF,** PAL. THOUGH I AIN'T SURE THE BOSS WOULD BUY THAT WHOLE **"CARE FOR THEM"** BIT.
I H-HAD TO DO ***SOMETHING.*** I'VE SEEN IT. I'VE SEEN THE ***FRAME.***
FRAME? LUCIEN, LOOK, I DON'T MEAN TO BE RUDE, BUT YOU'VE BEEN KINDA, *UH,* ***SPACEY,*** LATELY, AND--
NEW THINGS, MATTHEW. NEW THINGS HAVE ***ALWAYS*** BEEN DRAWN HERE. WE COULDN'T STOP THAT EVEN IF WE ***WANTED.***
--YYYYYYEAH, SO, **LISTEN,** YOU'RE FREAKING ME **OUT.** MAYBE YOU OUGHTA TAKE A LITTLE REST, OR--
I THINK THAT WE MUST TREAT ALL STRANGERS AS FRIENDS. AT LEAST-- UNTIL THERE IS ***NO DOUBT*** THEY ARE ENEMIES.
HEY--WHAT'S WITH THE ***WALL?*** I THOUGHT ONLY THE ***SIGILS*** OF THE ***ENDLESS*** HUNG IN THE GALLERY.
TH-THAT'S WHAT I'M TRYING TO ***SAY,*** MATTHEW. I THINK ***THIS*** IS WHAT'S CAUSING THE TROUBLE.
NEW THINGS ARE ***ALWAYS*** DRAWN TO THE DREAMING.

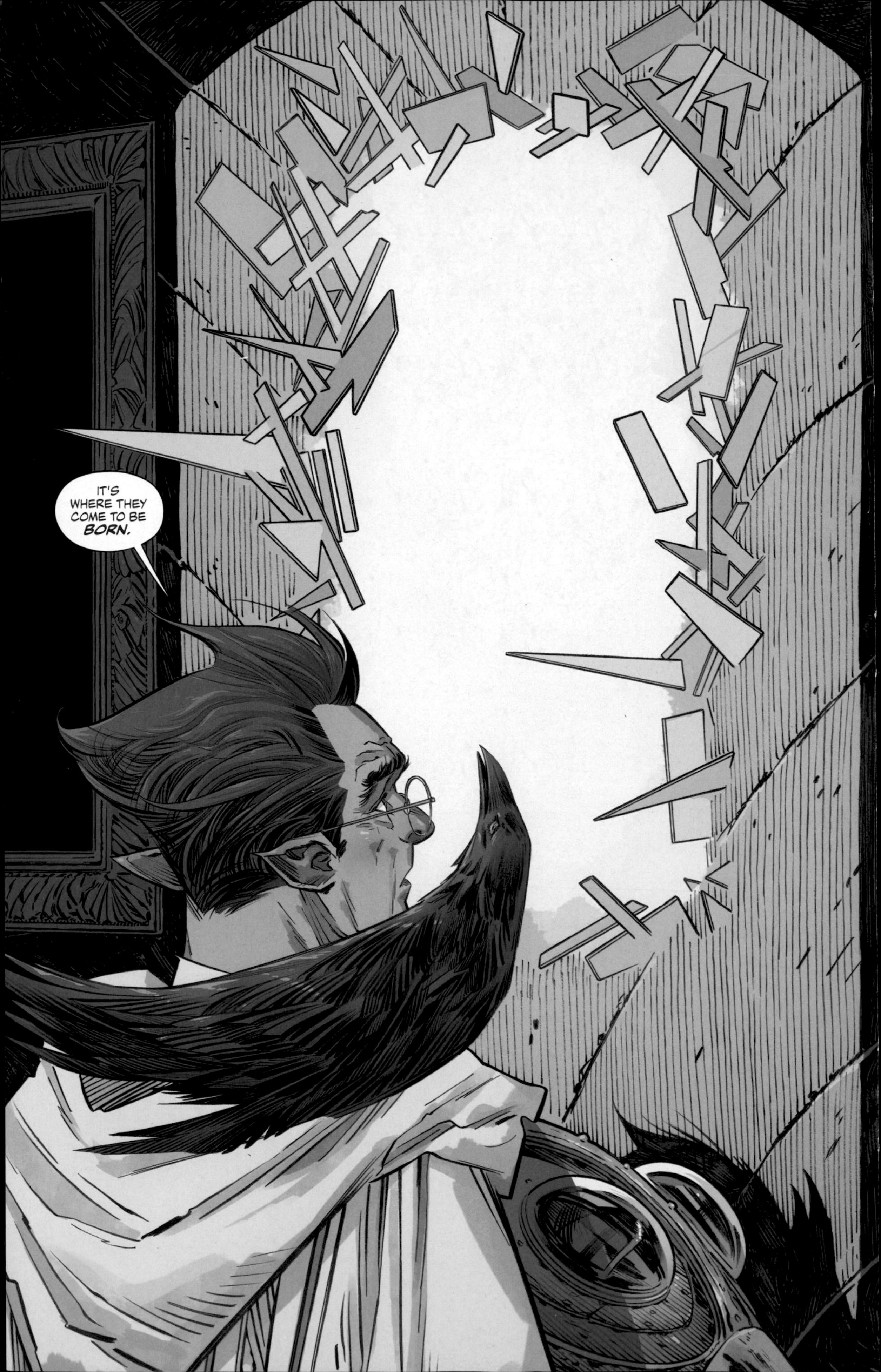
IT'S WHERE THEY COME TO BE *BORN.*

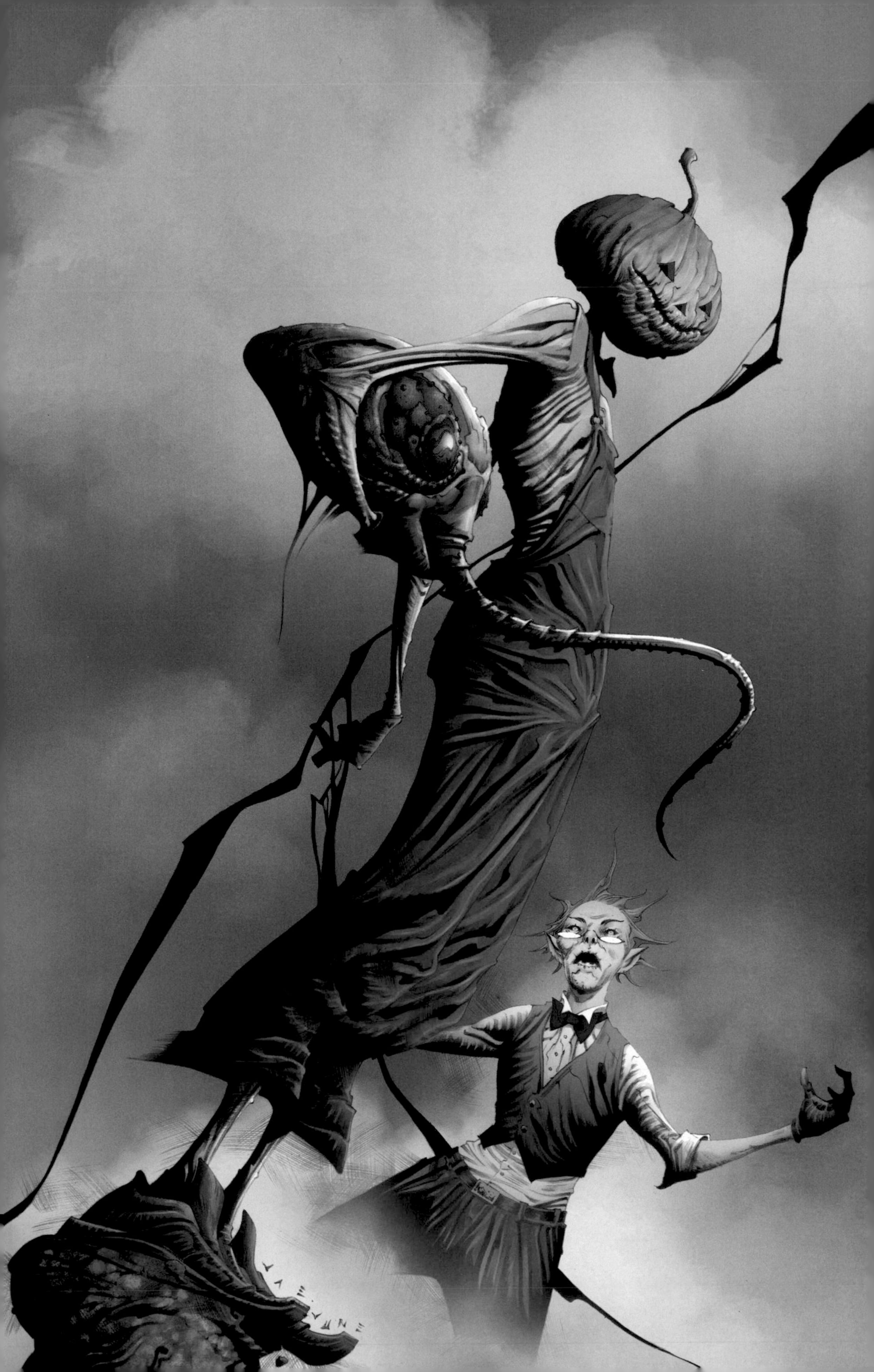

The Dreaming

The Foundation

WRITTEN BY
Simon Spurrier

ILLUSTRATED BY
Bilquis Evely

COLORS BY
Mat Lopes

LETTERS BY
Simon Bowland

COVER ART BY
Jae Lee and *June Chung*

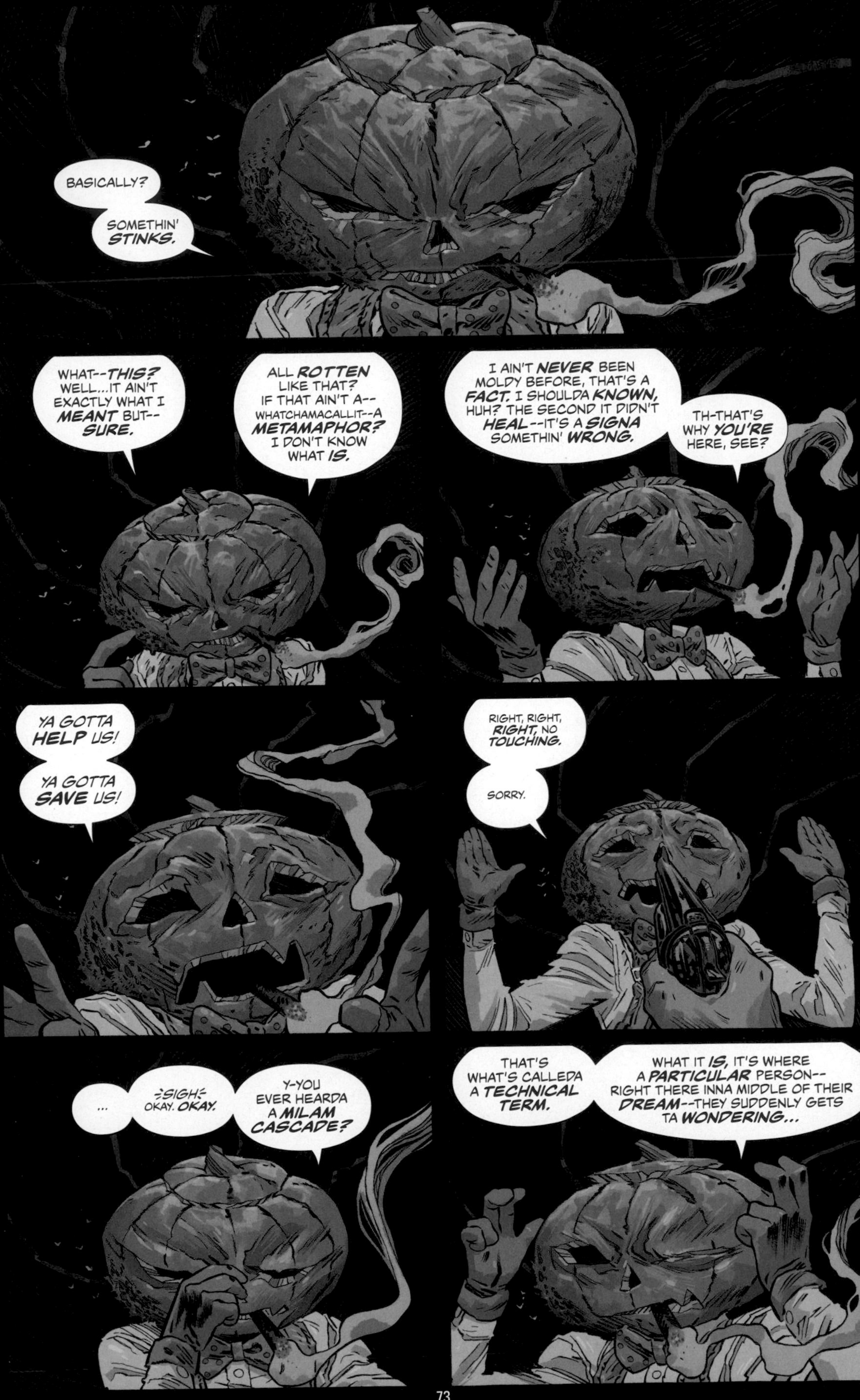
BASICALLY?
SOMETHIN' STINKS.
WHAT--THIS? WELL...IT AIN'T EXACTLY WHAT I MEANT BUT-- SURE.
ALL ROTTEN LIKE THAT? IF THAT AIN'T A-- WHATCHAMACALLIT--A METAMAPHOR? I DON'T KNOW WHAT IS.
I AIN'T NEVER BEEN MOLDY BEFORE, THAT'S A FACT. I SHOULDA KNOWN, HUH? THE SECOND IT DIDN'T HEAL--IT'S A SIGNA SOMETHIN' WRONG.
TH-THAT'S WHY YOU'RE HERE, SEE?
YA GOTTA HELP US!
YA GOTTA SAVE US!
RIGHT, RIGHT, RIGHT, NO TOUCHING.
SORRY.
...
=SIGH= OKAY. OKAY.
Y-YOU EVER HEARDA A MILAM CASCADE?
THAT'S WHAT'S CALLEDA A TECHNICAL TERM.
WHAT IT IS, IT'S WHERE A PARTICULAR PERSON-- RIGHT THERE INNA MIDDLE OF THEIR DREAM--THEY SUDDENLY GETS TA WONDERING...

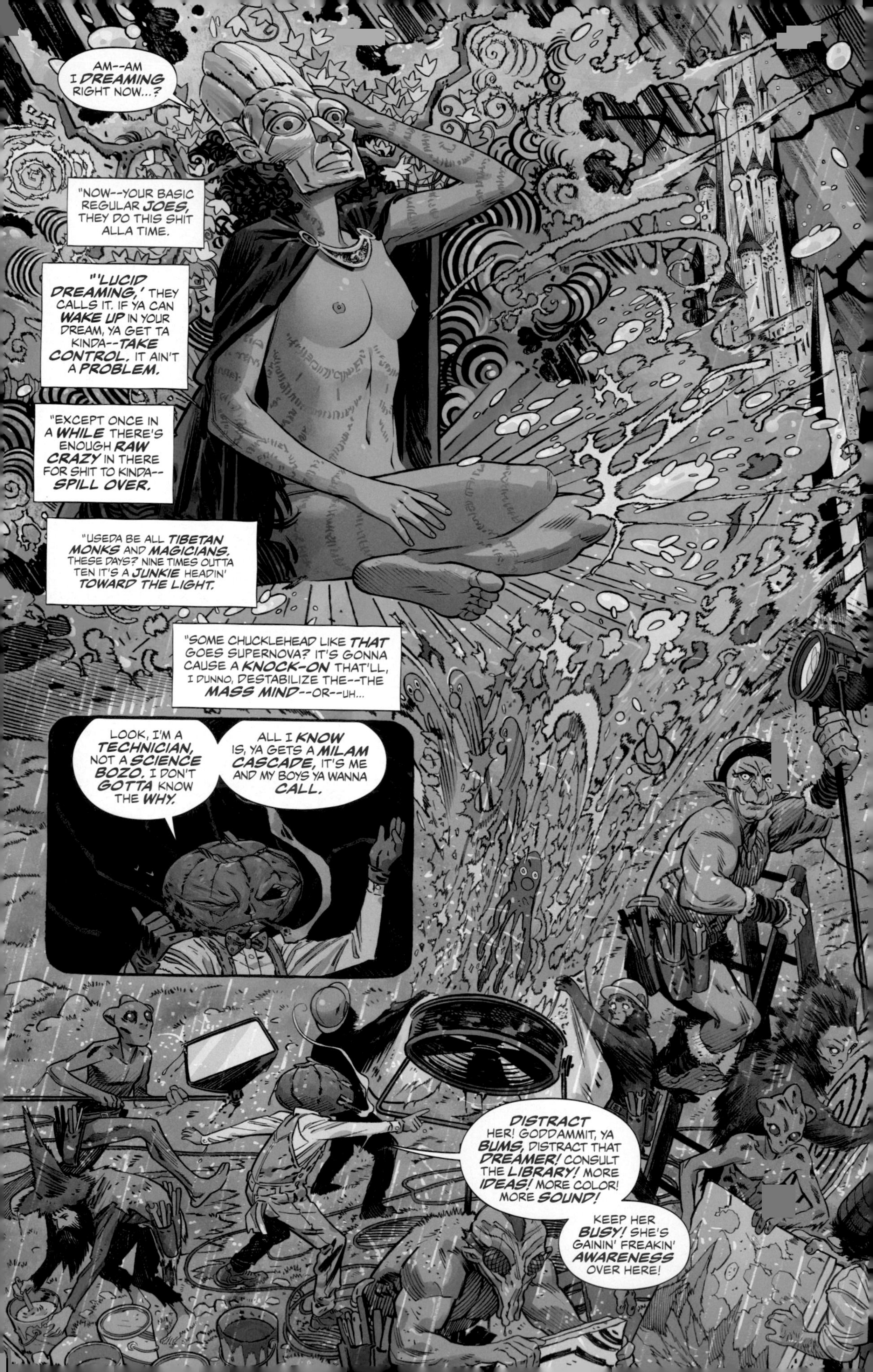
AM--AM I DREAMING RIGHT NOW...?
"NOW--YOUR BASIC REGULAR JOES, THEY DO THIS SHIT ALLA TIME.
"'LUCID DREAMING,' THEY CALLS IT. IF YA CAN WAKE UP IN YOUR DREAM, YA GET TA KINDA--TAKE CONTROL. IT AIN'T A PROBLEM.
"EXCEPT ONCE IN A WHILE THERE'S ENOUGH RAW CRAZY IN THERE FOR SHIT TO KINDA--SPILL OVER.
"USEDA BE ALL TIBETAN MONKS AND MAGICIANS. THESE DAYS? NINE TIMES OUTTA TEN IT'S A JUNKIE HEADIN' TOWARD THE LIGHT.
"SOME CHUCKLEHEAD LIKE THAT GOES SUPERNOVA? IT'S GONNA CAUSE A KNOCK-ON THAT'LL, I DUNNO, DESTABILIZE THE--THE MASS MIND--OR--UH...
LOOK, I'M A TECHNICIAN, NOT A SCIENCE BOZO. I DON'T GOTTA KNOW THE WHY.
ALL I KNOW IS, YA GETS A MILAM CASCADE, IT'S ME AND MY BOYS YA WANNA CALL.
DISTRACT HER! GODDAMMIT, YA BUMS, DISTRACT THAT DREAMER! CONSULT THE LIBRARY! MORE IDEAS! MORE COLOR! MORE SOUND!
KEEP HER BUSY! SHE'S GAININ' FREAKIN' AWARENESS OVER HERE!

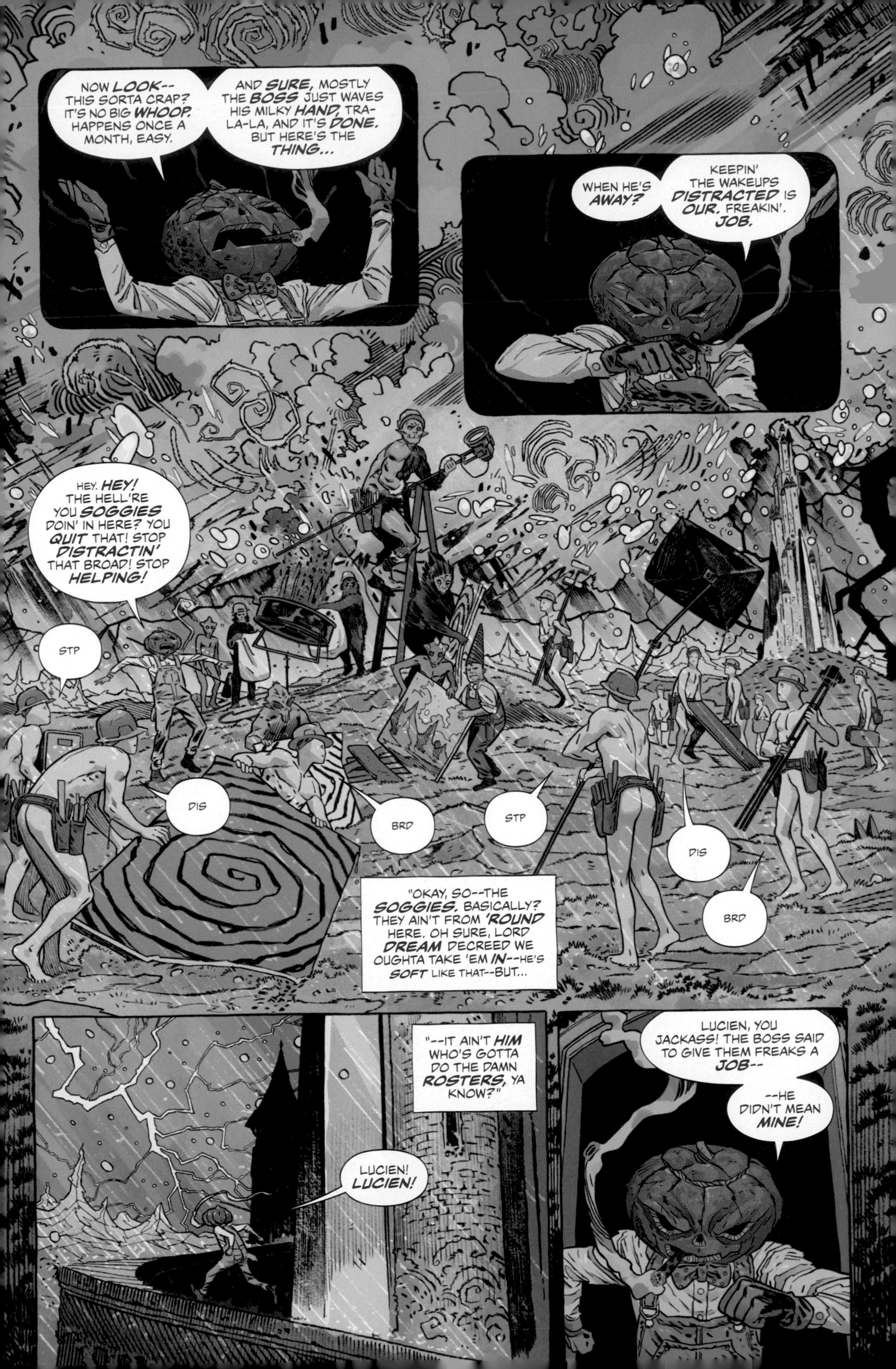
NOW LOOK-- THIS SORTA CRAP? IT'S NO BIG WHOOP. HAPPENS ONCE A MONTH, EASY.
AND SURE, MOSTLY THE BOSS JUST WAVES HIS MILKY HAND, TRA-LA-LA, AND IT'S DONE. BUT HERE'S THE THING...
WHEN HE'S AWAY?
KEEPIN' THE WAKEUPS DISTRACTED IS OUR. FREAKIN'. JOB.
HEY. HEY! THE HELL'RE YOU SOGGIES DOIN' IN HERE? YOU QUIT THAT! STOP DISTRACTIN' THAT BROAD! STOP HELPING!
STP
DIS
BRD
STP
DIS
BRD
"OKAY, SO--THE SOGGIES. BASICALLY? THEY AIN'T FROM 'ROUND HERE. OH SURE, LORD DREAM DECREED WE OUGHTA TAKE 'EM IN--HE'S SOFT LIKE THAT--BUT...
"--IT AIN'T HIM WHO'S GOTTA DO THE DAMN ROSTERS, YA KNOW?"
LUCIEN! LUCIEN!
LUCIEN, YOU JACKASS! THE BOSS SAID TO GIVE THEM FREAKS A JOB--
--HE DIDN'T MEAN MINE!

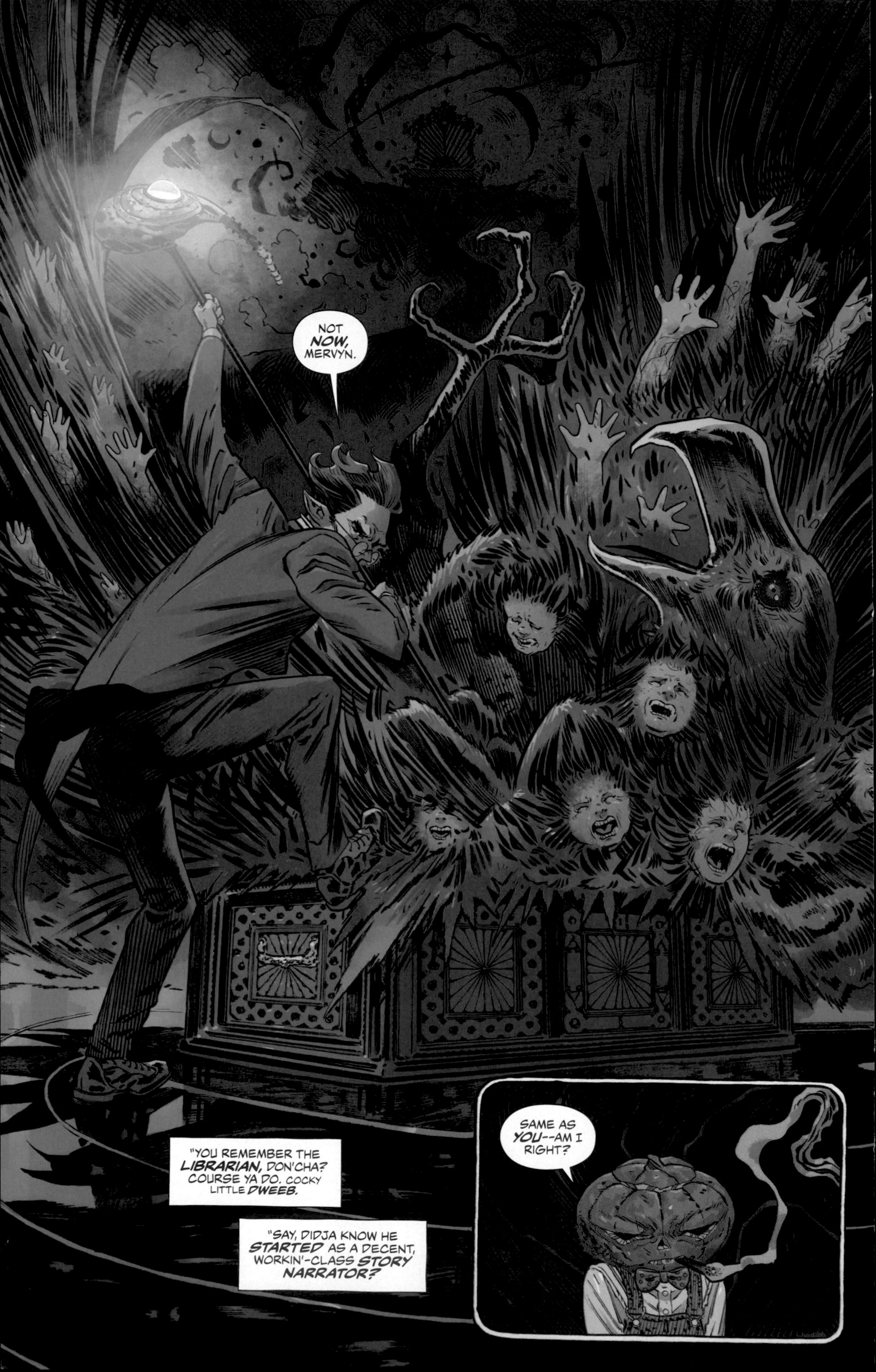
NOT NOW, MERVYN.
"YOU REMEMBER THE LIBRARIAN, DON'CHA? COURSE YA DO. COCKY LITTLE DWEEB.
"SAY, DIDJA KNOW HE STARTED AS A DECENT, WORKIN'-CLASS STORY NARRATOR?
SAME AS YOU--AM I RIGHT?

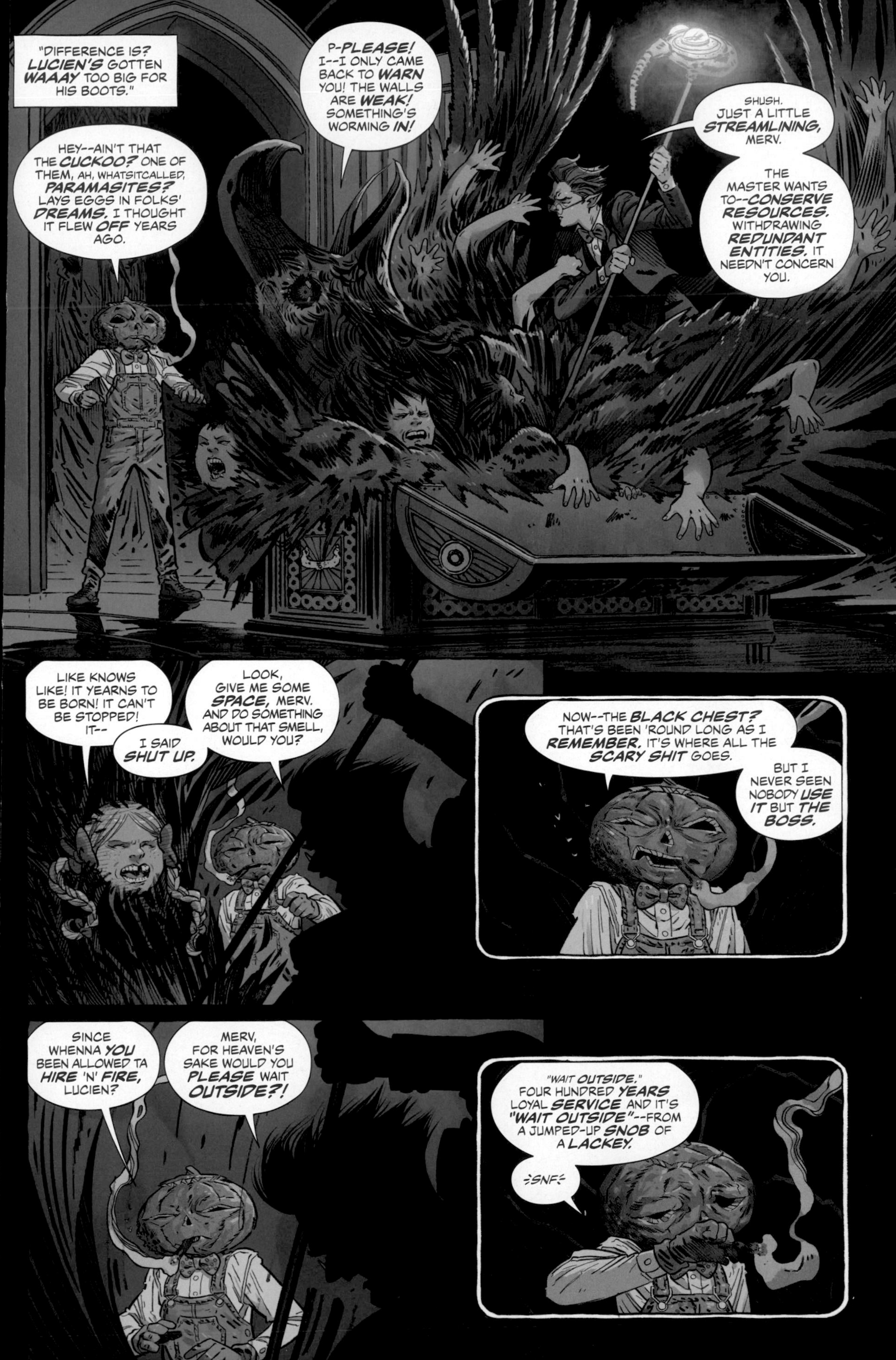
"DIFFERENCE IS? LUCIEN'S GOTTEN WAAAY TOO BIG FOR HIS BOOTS."
HEY--AIN'T THAT THE CUCKOO? ONE OF THEM, AH, WHATSITCALLED, PARAMASITES? LAYS EGGS IN FOLKS' DREAMS. I THOUGHT IT FLEW OFF YEARS AGO.
P-PLEASE! I--I ONLY CAME BACK TO WARN YOU! THE WALLS ARE WEAK! SOMETHING'S WORMING IN!
SHUSH. JUST A LITTLE STREAMLINING, MERV.
THE MASTER WANTS TO--CONSERVE RESOURCES. WITHDRAWING REDUNDANT ENTITIES. IT NEEDN'T CONCERN YOU.
LIKE KNOWS LIKE! IT YEARNS TO BE BORN! IT CAN'T BE STOPPED! IT--
I SAID SHUT UP.
LOOK, GIVE ME SOME SPACE, MERV. AND DO SOMETHING ABOUT THAT SMELL, WOULD YOU?
NOW--THE BLACK CHEST? THAT'S BEEN 'ROUND LONG AS I REMEMBER. IT'S WHERE ALL THE SCARY SHIT GOES.
BUT I NEVER SEEN NOBODY USE IT BUT THE BOSS.
SINCE WHENNA YOU BEEN ALLOWED TA HIRE 'N' FIRE, LUCIEN?
MERV, FOR HEAVEN'S SAKE WOULD YOU PLEASE WAIT OUTSIDE?!
"WAIT OUTSIDE." FOUR HUNDRED YEARS LOYAL SERVICE AND IT'S "WAIT OUTSIDE"--FROM A JUMPED-UP SNOB OF A LACKEY.
SNF

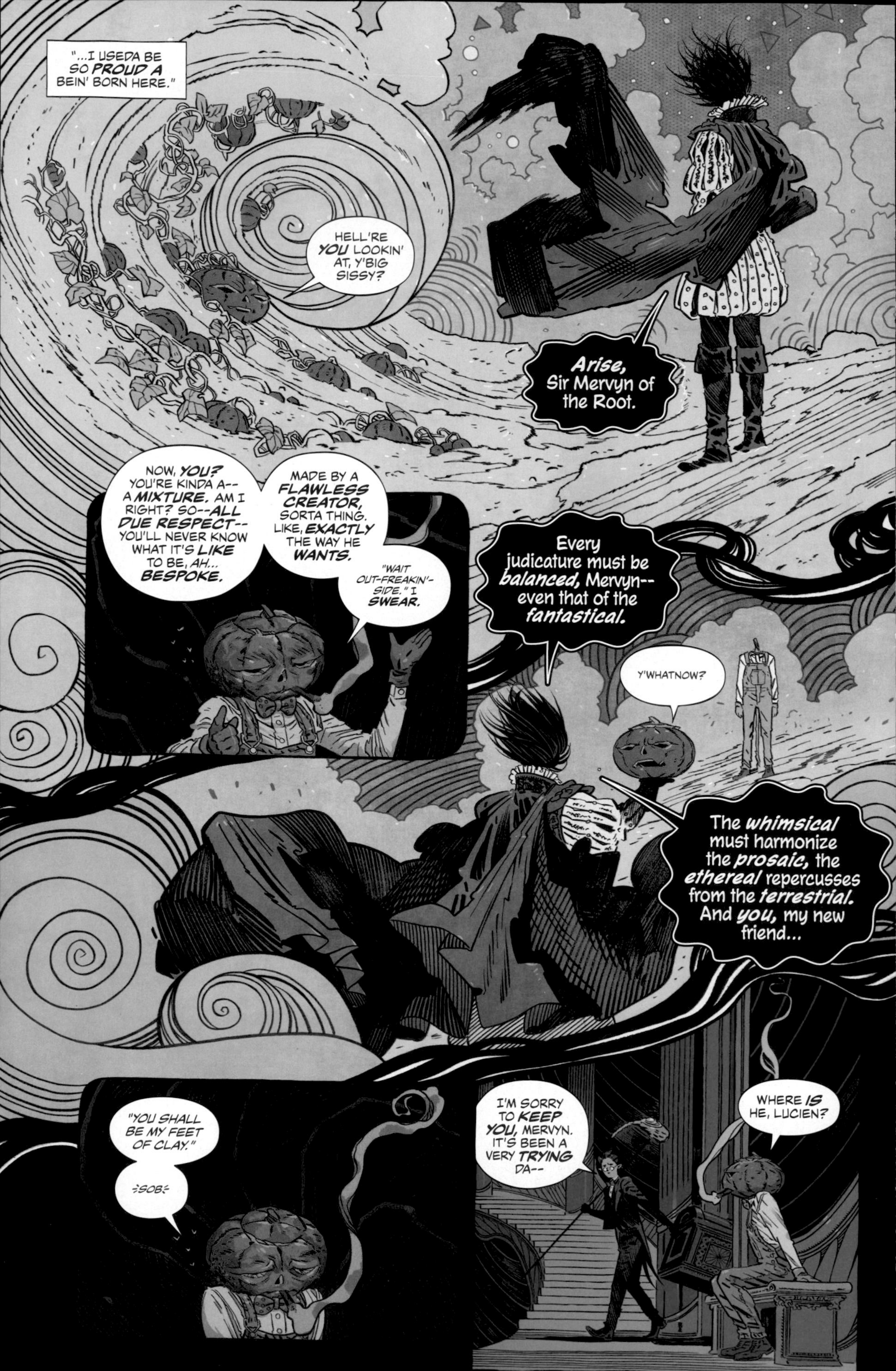
"...I USEDA BE SO PROUD A BEIN' BORN HERE."
HELL'RE YOU LOOKIN' AT, Y'BIG SISSY?
Arise, Sir Mervyn of the Root.
NOW, YOU? YOU'RE KINDA A-- A MIXTURE. AM I RIGHT? SO--ALL DUE RESPECT-- YOU'LL NEVER KNOW WHAT IT'S LIKE TO BE, AH... BESPOKE.
MADE BY A FLAWLESS CREATOR, SORTA THING. LIKE, EXACTLY THE WAY HE WANTS.
"WAIT OUT-FREAKIN'-SIDE." I SWEAR.
Every judicature must be balanced, Mervyn-- even that of the fantastical.
Y'WHATNOW?
The whimsical must harmonize the prosaic, the ethereal repercusses from the terrestrial. And you, my new friend...
"YOU SHALL BE MY FEET OF CLAY."
SOB
I'M SORRY TO KEEP YOU, MERVYN. IT'S BEEN A VERY TRYING DA--
WHERE IS HE, LUCIEN?

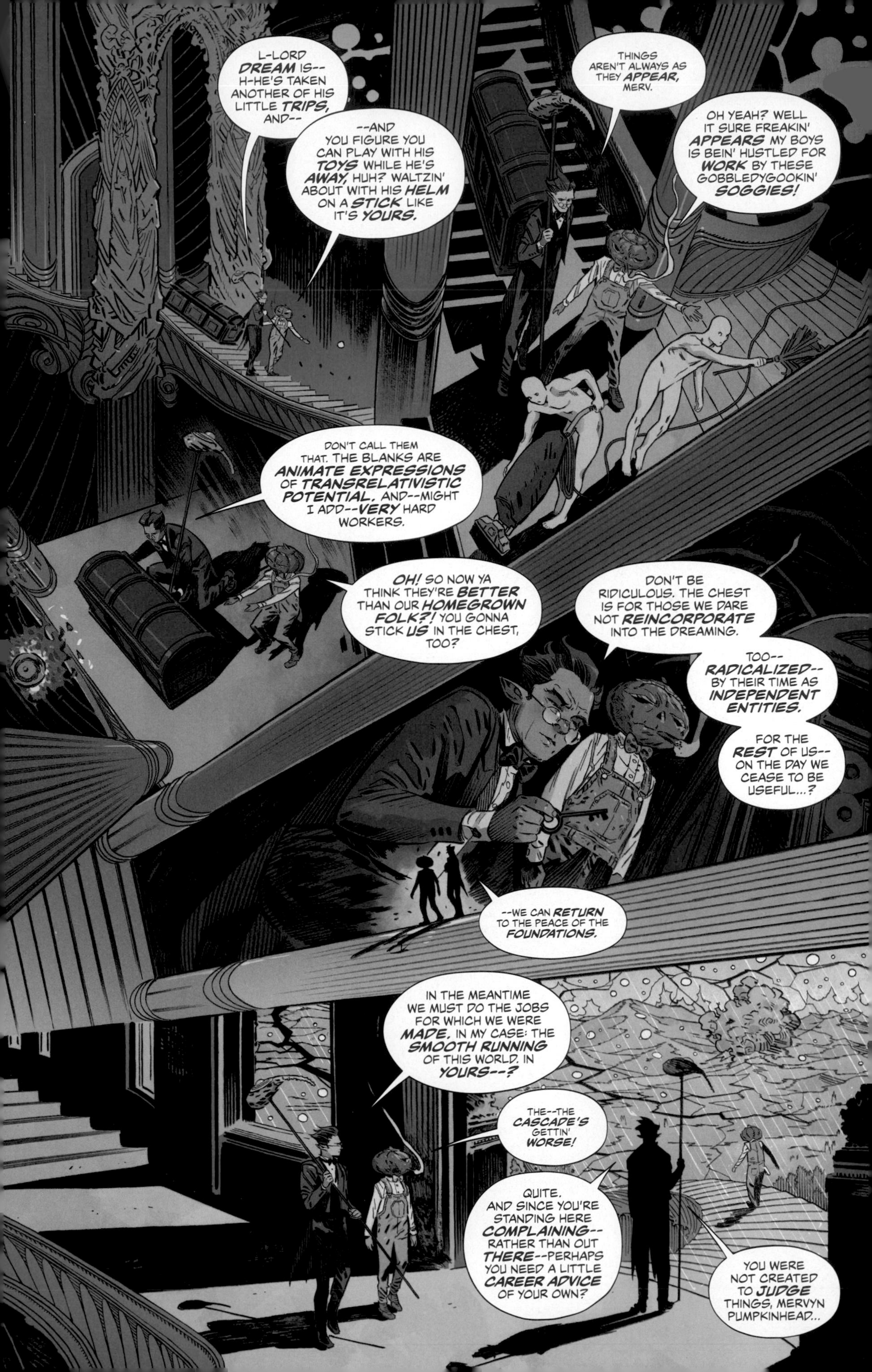
L-LORD DREAM IS-- H-HE'S TAKEN ANOTHER OF HIS LITTLE TRIPS, AND--
--AND YOU FIGURE YOU CAN PLAY WITH HIS TOYS WHILE HE'S AWAY, HUH? WALTZIN' ABOUT WITH HIS HELM ON A STICK LIKE IT'S YOURS.
THINGS AREN'T ALWAYS AS THEY APPEAR, MERV.
OH YEAH? WELL IT SURE FREAKIN' APPEARS MY BOYS IS BEIN' HUSTLED FOR WORK BY THESE GOBBLEDYGOOKIN' SOGGIES!
DON'T CALL THEM THAT. THE BLANKS ARE ANIMATE EXPRESSIONS OF TRANSRELATIVISTIC POTENTIAL, AND--MIGHT I ADD--VERY HARD WORKERS.
OH! SO NOW YA THINK THEY'RE BETTER THAN OUR HOMEGROWN FOLK?! YOU GONNA STICK US IN THE CHEST, TOO?
DON'T BE RIDICULOUS. THE CHEST IS FOR THOSE WE DARE NOT REINCORPORATE INTO THE DREAMING.
TOO-- RADICALIZED-- BY THEIR TIME AS INDEPENDENT ENTITIES.
FOR THE REST OF US-- ON THE DAY WE CEASE TO BE USEFUL...?
--WE CAN RETURN TO THE PEACE OF THE FOUNDATIONS.
IN THE MEANTIME WE MUST DO THE JOBS FOR WHICH WE WERE MADE. IN MY CASE: THE SMOOTH RUNNING OF THIS WORLD. IN YOURS--?
THE--THE CASCADE'S GETTIN' WORSE!
QUITE. AND SINCE YOU'RE STANDING HERE COMPLAINING-- RATHER THAN OUT THERE--PERHAPS YOU NEED A LITTLE CAREER ADVICE OF YOUR OWN?
YOU WERE NOT CREATED TO JUDGE THINGS, MERVYN PUMPKINHEAD...

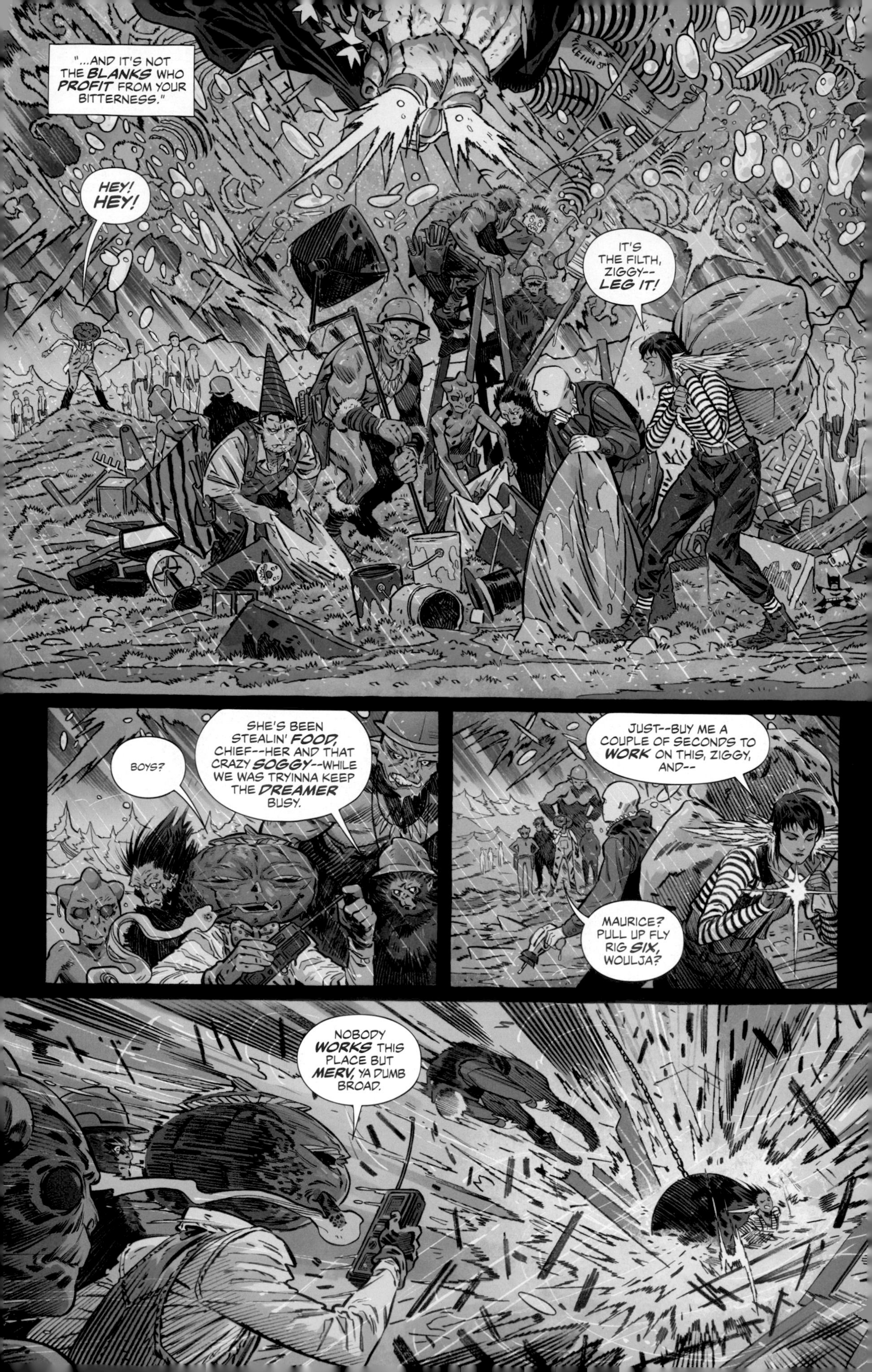
"...AND IT'S NOT THE BLANKS WHO PROFIT FROM YOUR BITTERNESS."
HEY! HEY!
IT'S THE FILTH, ZIGGY-- LEG IT!
BOYS?
SHE'S BEEN STEALIN' FOOD, CHIEF--HER AND THAT CRAZY SOGGY--WHILE WE WAS TRYINNA KEEP THE DREAMER BUSY.
JUST--BUY ME A COUPLE OF SECONDS TO WORK ON THIS, ZIGGY, AND--
MAURICE? PULL UP FLY RIG SIX, WOULJA?
NOBODY WORKS THIS PLACE BUT MERV, YA DUMB BROAD.

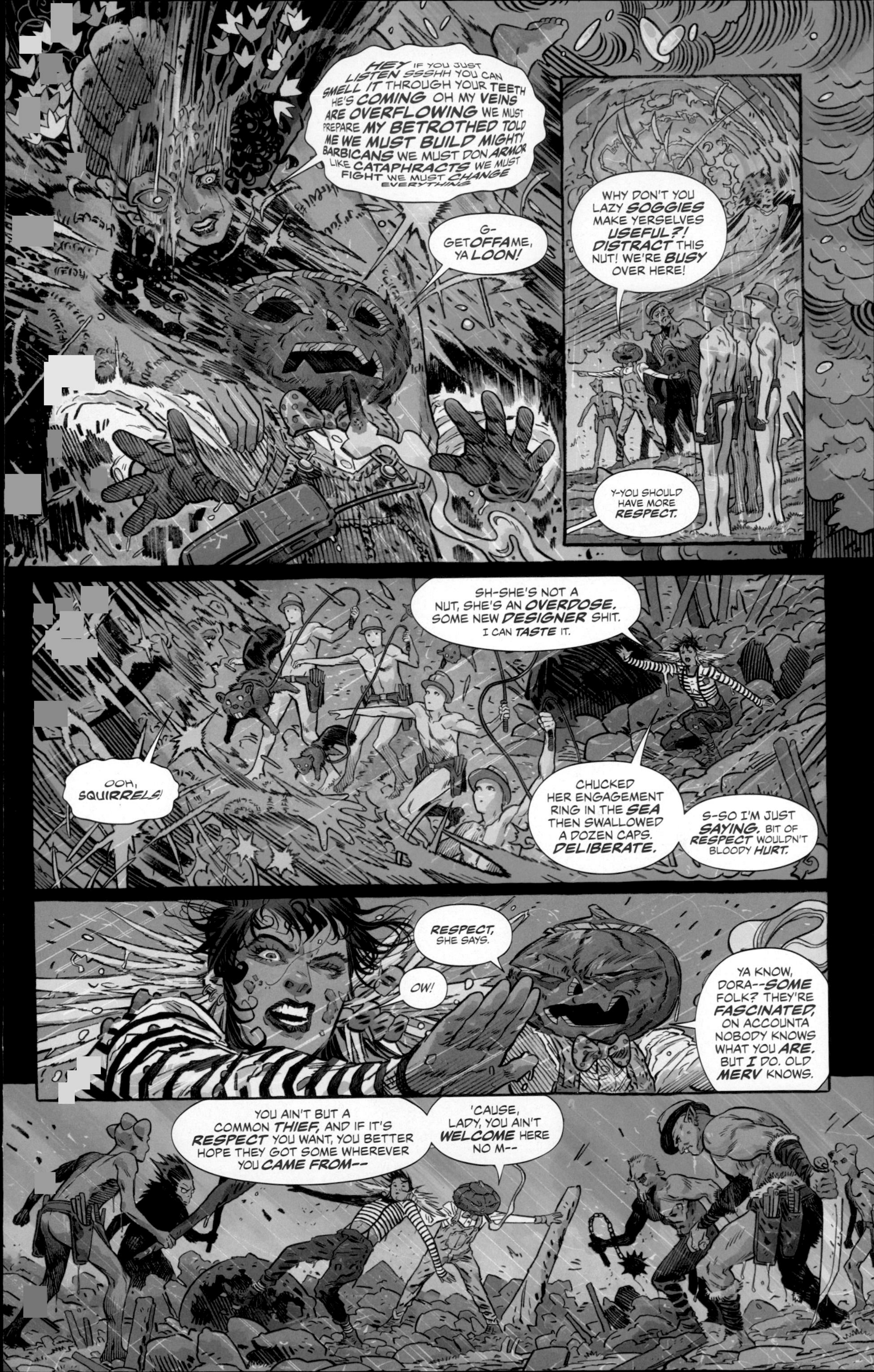
HEY IF YOU JUST LISTEN SSSHH YOU CAN SMELL IT THROUGH YOUR TEETH HE'S COMING OH MY VEINS ARE OVERFLOWING WE MUST PREPARE MY BETROTHED TOLD ME WE MUST BUILD MIGHTY BARBICANS WE MUST DON ARMOR LIKE CATAPHRACTS WE MUST FIGHT WE MUST CHANGE EVERYTHING
G-GETOFFAME, YA LOON!
WHY DON'T YOU LAZY SOGGIES MAKE YERSELVES USEFUL?! DISTRACT THIS NUT! WE'RE BUSY OVER HERE!
Y-YOU SHOULD HAVE MORE RESPECT.
OOH, SQUIRRELS!
SH-SHE'S NOT A NUT, SHE'S AN OVERDOSE. SOME NEW DESIGNER SHIT. I CAN TASTE IT.
CHUCKED HER ENGAGEMENT RING IN THE SEA THEN SWALLOWED A DOZEN CAPS. DELIBERATE.
S-SO I'M JUST SAYING. BIT OF RESPECT WOULDN'T BLOODY HURT.
RESPECT, SHE SAYS.
OW!
YA KNOW, DORA--SOME FOLK? THEY'RE FASCINATED, ON ACCOUNTA NOBODY KNOWS WHAT YOU ARE. BUT I DO. OLD MERV KNOWS.
YOU AIN'T BUT A COMMON THIEF, AND IF IT'S RESPECT YOU WANT, YOU BETTER HOPE THEY GOT SOME WHEREVER YOU CAME FROM--
'CAUSE, LADY, YOU AIN'T WELCOME HERE NO M--

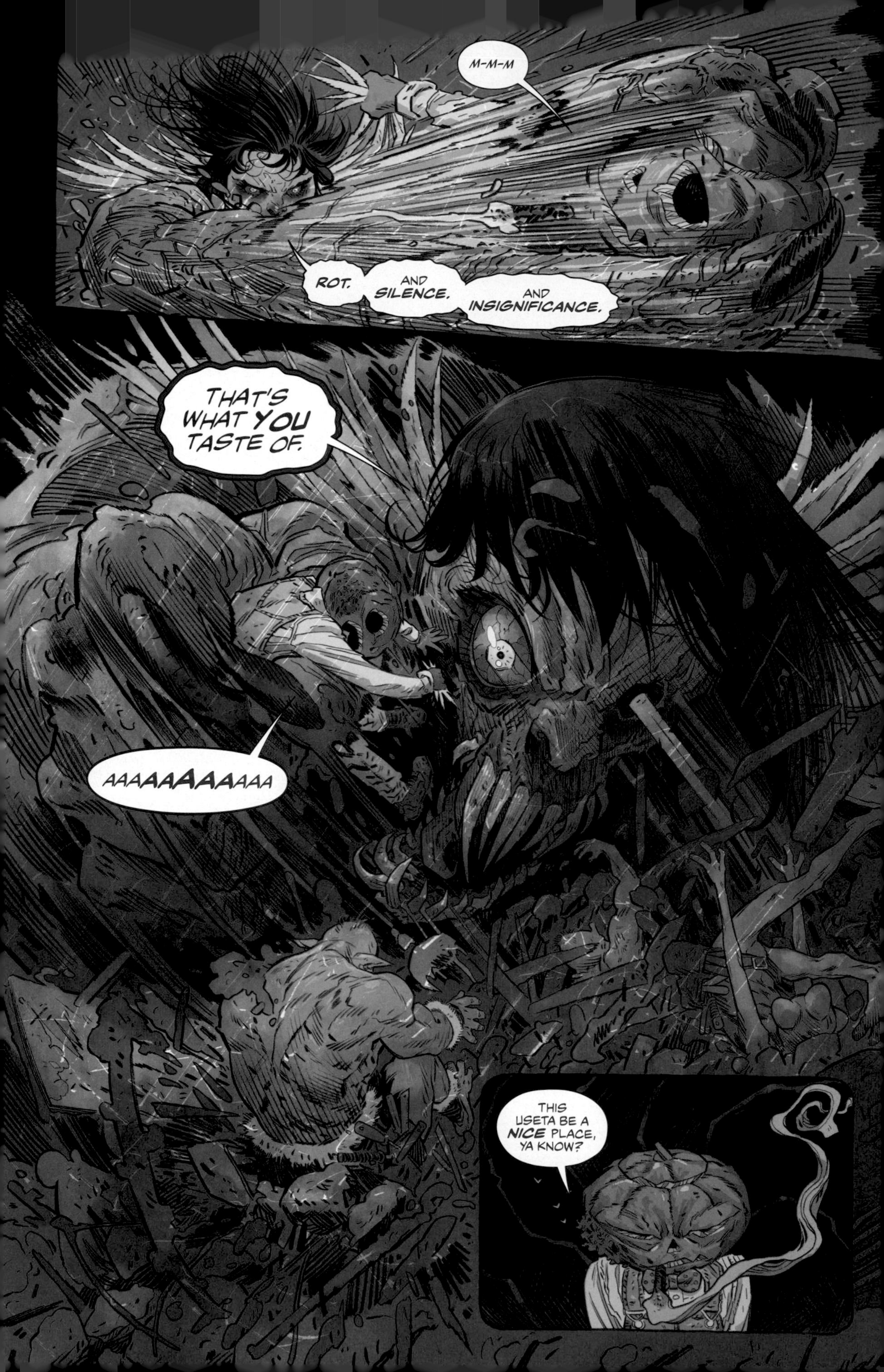
M-M-M
ROT.
AND SILENCE.
AND INSIGNIFICANCE.
THAT'S WHAT YOU TASTE OF.
AAAAAAAAAAAA
THIS USETA BE A NICE PLACE, YA KNOW?

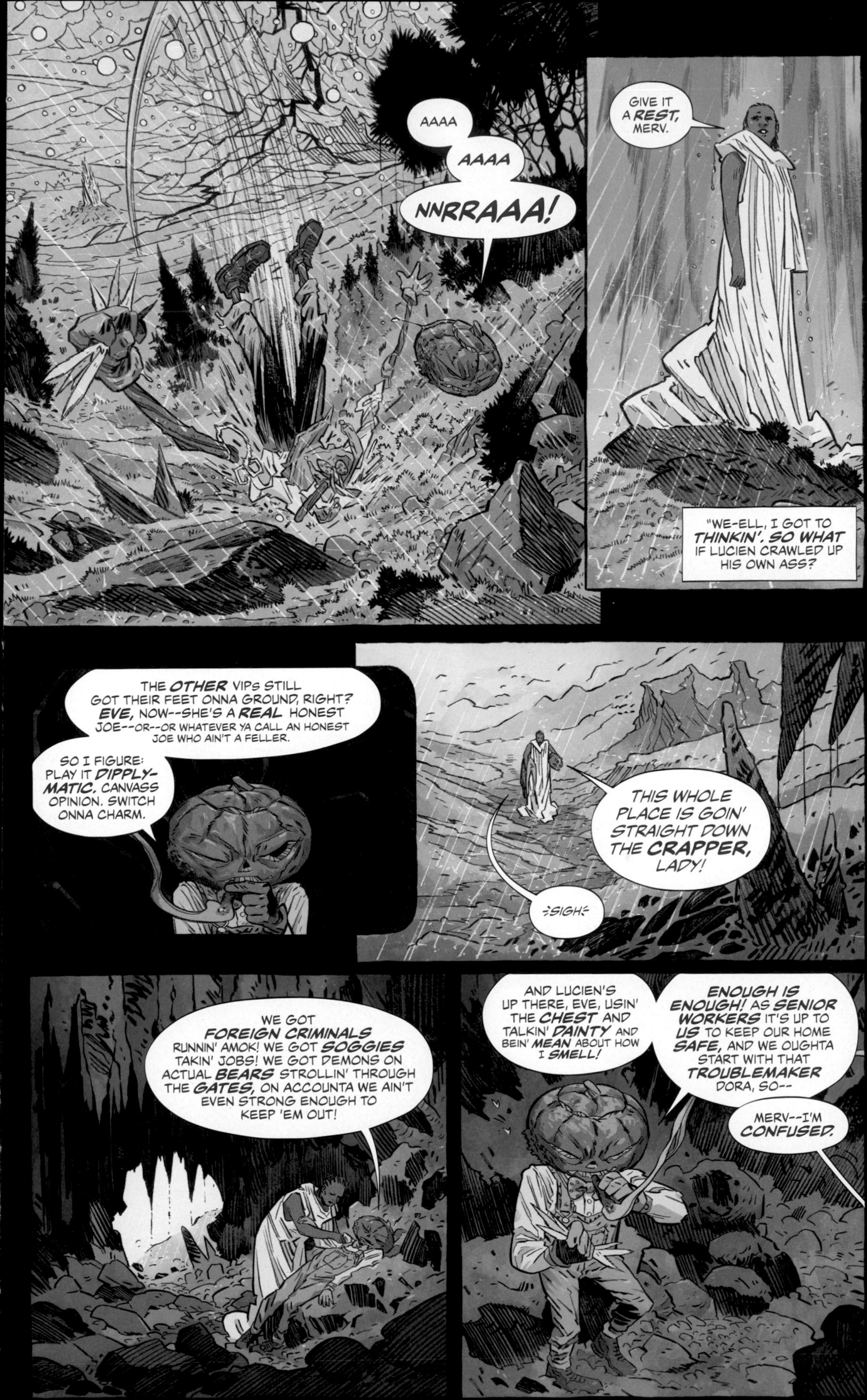
AAAA
AAAA
NNRRAAA!
GIVE IT A REST, MERV.
"WE-ELL, I GOT TO THINKIN'. SO WHAT IF LUCIEN CRAWLED UP HIS OWN ASS?
THE OTHER VIPs STILL GOT THEIR FEET ONNA GROUND, RIGHT? EVE, NOW--SHE'S A REAL HONEST JOE--OR--OR WHATEVER YA CALL AN HONEST JOE WHO AIN'T A FELLER.
SO I FIGURE: PLAY IT DIPPLY-MATIC. CANVASS OPINION. SWITCH ONNA CHARM.
THIS WHOLE PLACE IS GOIN' STRAIGHT DOWN THE CRAPPER, LADY!
SIGH
WE GOT FOREIGN CRIMINALS RUNNIN' AMOK! WE GOT SOGGIES TAKIN' JOBS! WE GOT DEMONS ON ACTUAL BEARS STROLLIN' THROUGH THE GATES, ON ACCOUNTA WE AIN'T EVEN STRONG ENOUGH TO KEEP 'EM OUT!
AND LUCIEN'S UP THERE, EVE, USIN' THE CHEST AND TALKIN' DAINTY AND BEIN' MEAN ABOUT HOW I SMELL!
ENOUGH IS ENOUGH! AS SENIOR WORKERS IT'S UP TO US TO KEEP OUR HOME SAFE, AND WE OUGHTA START WITH THAT TROUBLEMAKER DORA, SO--
MERV--I'M CONFUSED.

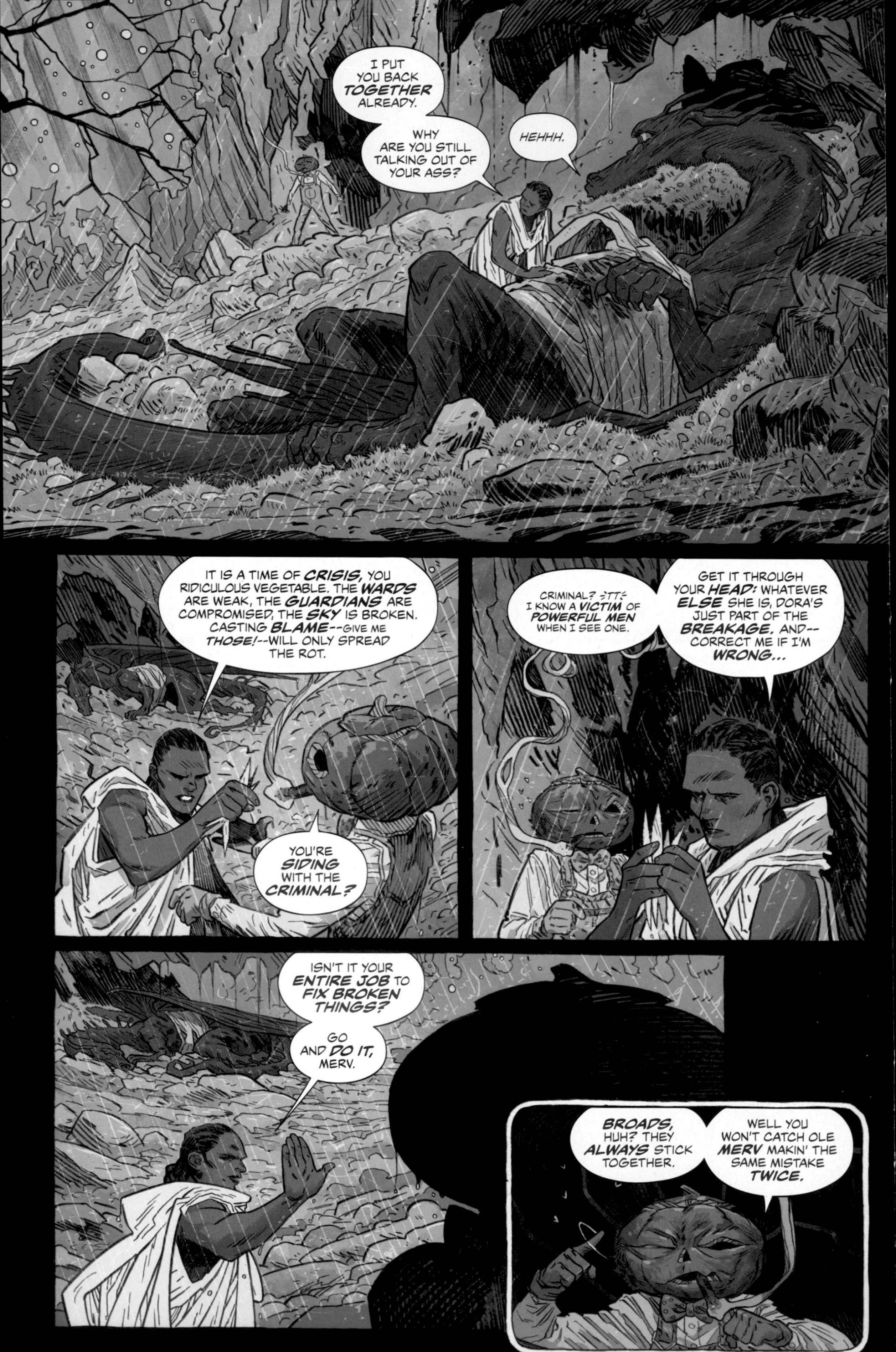
I PUT YOU BACK TOGETHER ALREADY.
WHY ARE YOU STILL TALKING OUT OF YOUR ASS?
HEHHH.
IT IS A TIME OF CRISIS, YOU RIDICULOUS VEGETABLE. THE WARDS ARE WEAK, THE GUARDIANS ARE COMPROMISED, THE SKY IS BROKEN. CASTING BLAME--GIVE ME THOSE!--WILL ONLY SPREAD THE ROT.
YOU'RE SIDING WITH THE CRIMINAL?
CRIMINAL? I KNOW A VICTIM OF POWERFUL MEN WHEN I SEE ONE.
GET IT THROUGH YOUR HEAD: WHATEVER ELSE SHE IS, DORA'S JUST PART OF THE BREAKAGE. AND--CORRECT ME IF I'M WRONG...
ISN'T IT YOUR ENTIRE JOB TO FIX BROKEN THINGS?
GO AND DO IT, MERV.
BROADS, HUH? THEY ALWAYS STICK TOGETHER.
WELL YOU WON'T CATCH OLE MERV MAKIN' THE SAME MISTAKE TWICE.

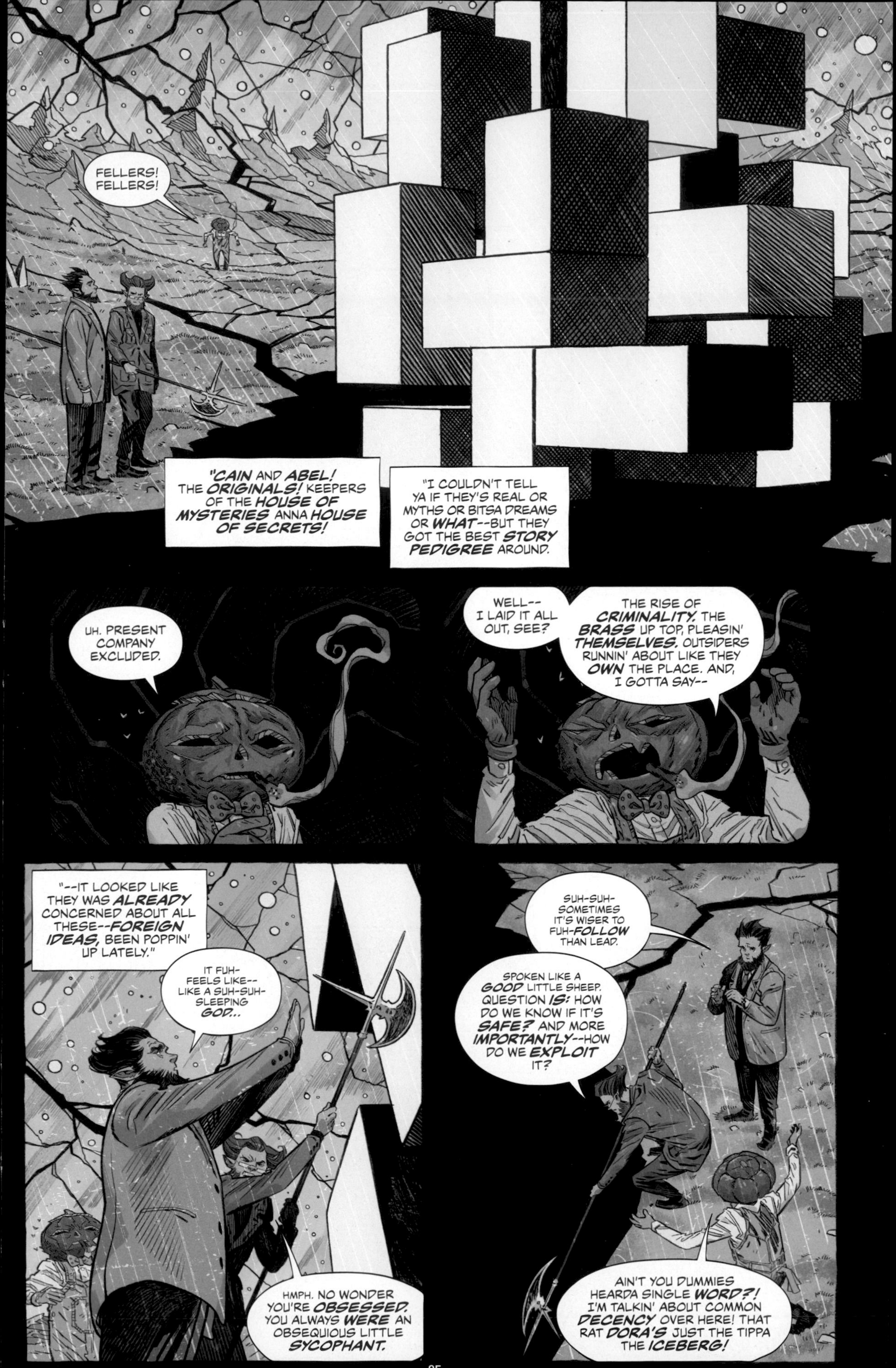
FELLERS! FELLERS!
"CAIN AND ABEL! THE ORIGINALS! KEEPERS OF THE HOUSE OF MYSTERIES ANNA HOUSE OF SECRETS!
"I COULDN'T TELL YA IF THEY'S REAL OR MYTHS OR BITSA DREAMS OR WHAT--BUT THEY GOT THE BEST STORY PEDIGREE AROUND.
UH. PRESENT COMPANY EXCLUDED.
WELL-- I LAID IT ALL OUT, SEE?
THE RISE OF CRIMINALITY. THE BRASS UP TOP, PLEASIN' THEMSELVES. OUTSIDERS RUNNIN' ABOUT LIKE THEY OWN THE PLACE. AND, I GOTTA SAY--
"--IT LOOKED LIKE THEY WAS ALREADY CONCERNED ABOUT ALL THESE--FOREIGN IDEAS, BEEN POPPIN' UP LATELY."
IT FUH-FEELS LIKE--LIKE A SUH-SUH-SLEEPING GOD...
HMPH. NO WONDER YOU'RE OBSESSED. YOU ALWAYS WERE AN OBSEQUIOUS LITTLE SYCOPHANT.
SUH-SUH-SOMETIMES IT'S WISER TO FUH-FOLLOW THAN LEAD.
SPOKEN LIKE A GOOD LITTLE SHEEP. QUESTION IS: HOW DO WE KNOW IF IT'S SAFE? AND MORE IMPORTANTLY--HOW DO WE EXPLOIT IT?
AIN'T YOU DUMMIES HEARDA SINGLE WORD?! I'M TALKIN' ABOUT COMMON DECENCY OVER HERE! THAT RAT DORA'S JUST THE TIPPA THE ICEBERG!

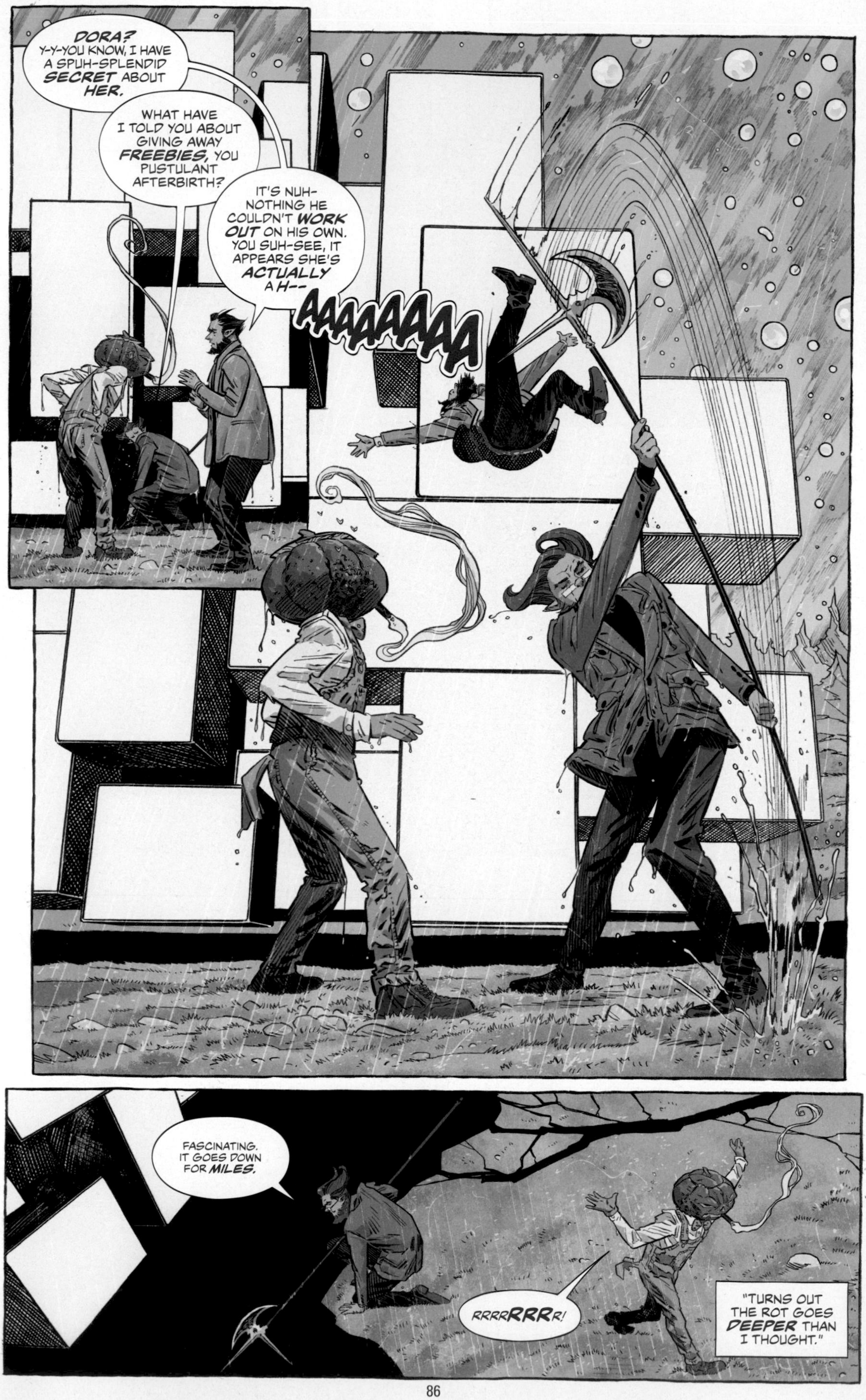
DORA? Y-Y-YOU KNOW, I HAVE A SPUH-SPLENDID SECRET ABOUT HER.
WHAT HAVE I TOLD YOU ABOUT GIVING AWAY FREEBIES, YOU PUSTULANT AFTERBIRTH?
IT'S NUH-NOTHING HE COULDN'T WORK OUT ON HIS OWN. YOU SUH-SEE, IT APPEARS SHE'S ACTUALLY A H--
AAAAAAAA
FASCINATING. IT GOES DOWN FOR MILES.
RRRRRRRR!
"TURNS OUT THE ROT GOES DEEPER THAN I THOUGHT."

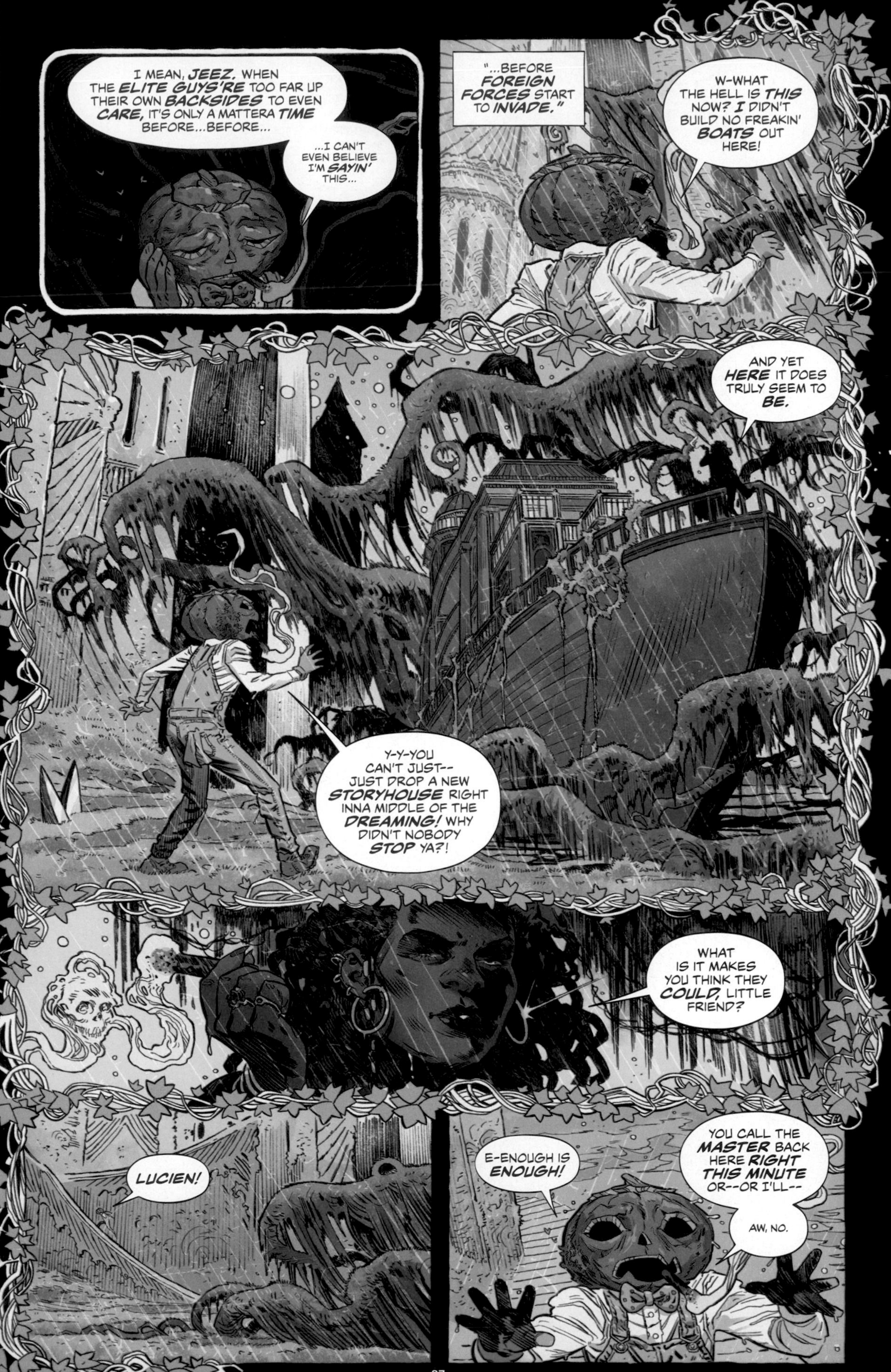
I MEAN, JEEZ. WHEN THE ELITE GUYS'RE TOO FAR UP THEIR OWN BACKSIDES TO EVEN CARE, IT'S ONLY A MATTERA TIME BEFORE...BEFORE...
...I CAN'T EVEN BELIEVE I'M SAYIN' THIS...
"...BEFORE FOREIGN FORCES START TO INVADE."
W-WHAT THE HELL IS THIS NOW? I DIDN'T BUILD NO FREAKIN' BOATS OUT HERE!
AND YET HERE IT DOES TRULY SEEM TO BE.
Y-Y-YOU CAN'T JUST--JUST DROP A NEW STORYHOUSE RIGHT INNA MIDDLE OF THE DREAMING! WHY DIDN'T NOBODY STOP YA?!
WHAT IS IT MAKES YOU THINK THEY COULD, LITTLE FRIEND?
LUCIEN!
E-ENOUGH IS ENOUGH!
YOU CALL THE MASTER BACK HERE RIGHT THIS MINUTE OR--OR I'LL--
AW, NO.

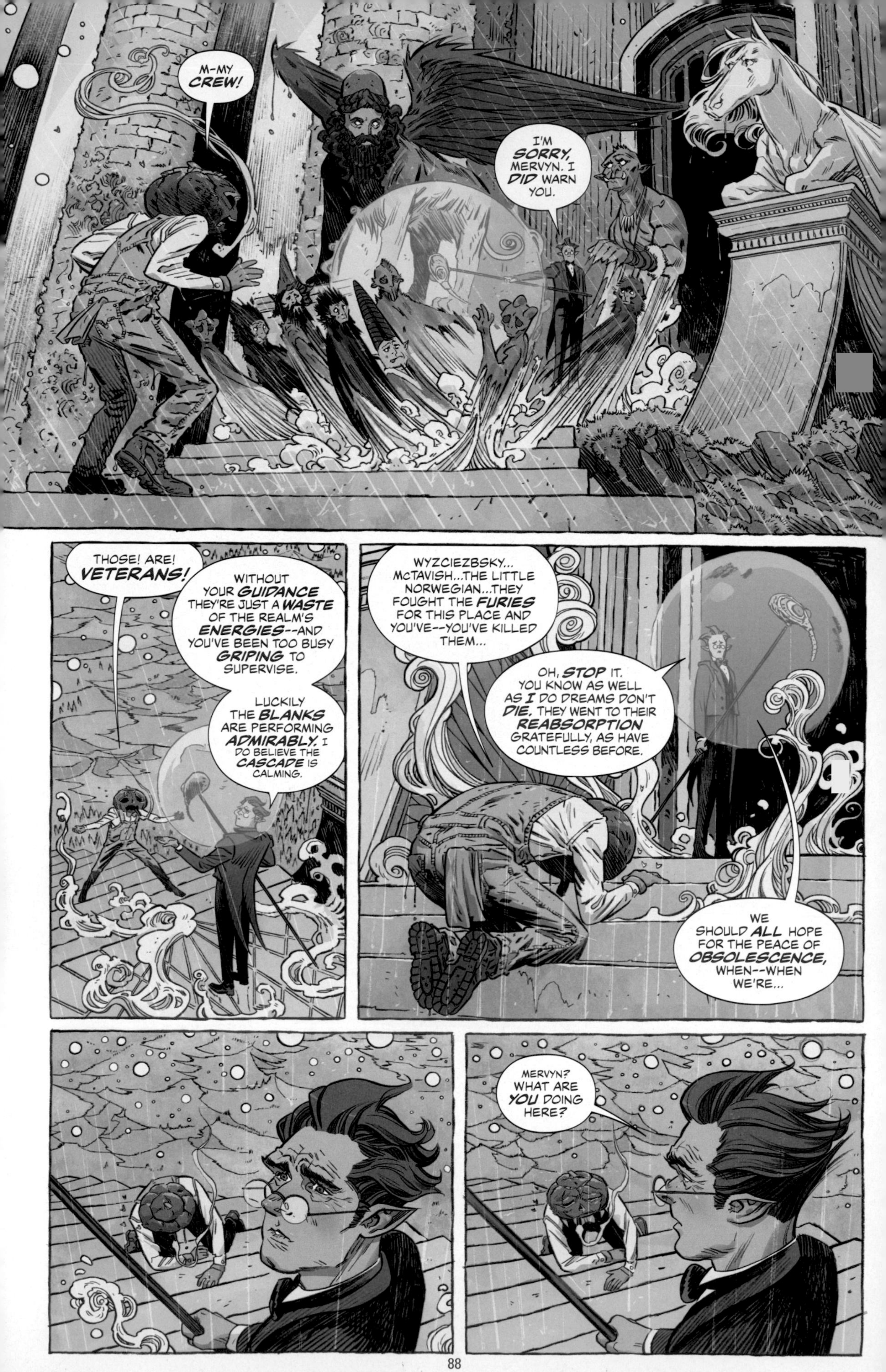
M-MY CREW!
I'M SORRY, MERVYN. I DID WARN YOU.
THOSE! ARE! VETERANS!
WITHOUT YOUR GUIDANCE THEY'RE JUST A WASTE OF THE REALM'S ENERGIES--AND YOU'VE BEEN TOO BUSY GRIPING TO SUPERVISE.
LUCKILY THE BLANKS ARE PERFORMING ADMIRABLY. I DO BELIEVE THE CASCADE IS CALMING.
WYZCIEZBSKY... McTAVISH...THE LITTLE NORWEGIAN...THEY FOUGHT THE FURIES FOR THIS PLACE AND YOU'VE--YOU'VE KILLED THEM...
OH, STOP IT. YOU KNOW AS WELL AS I DO DREAMS DON'T DIE. THEY WENT TO THEIR REABSORPTION GRATEFULLY, AS HAVE COUNTLESS BEFORE.
WE SHOULD ALL HOPE FOR THE PEACE OF OBSOLESCENCE, WHEN--WHEN WE'RE...
MERVYN? WHAT ARE YOU DOING HERE?

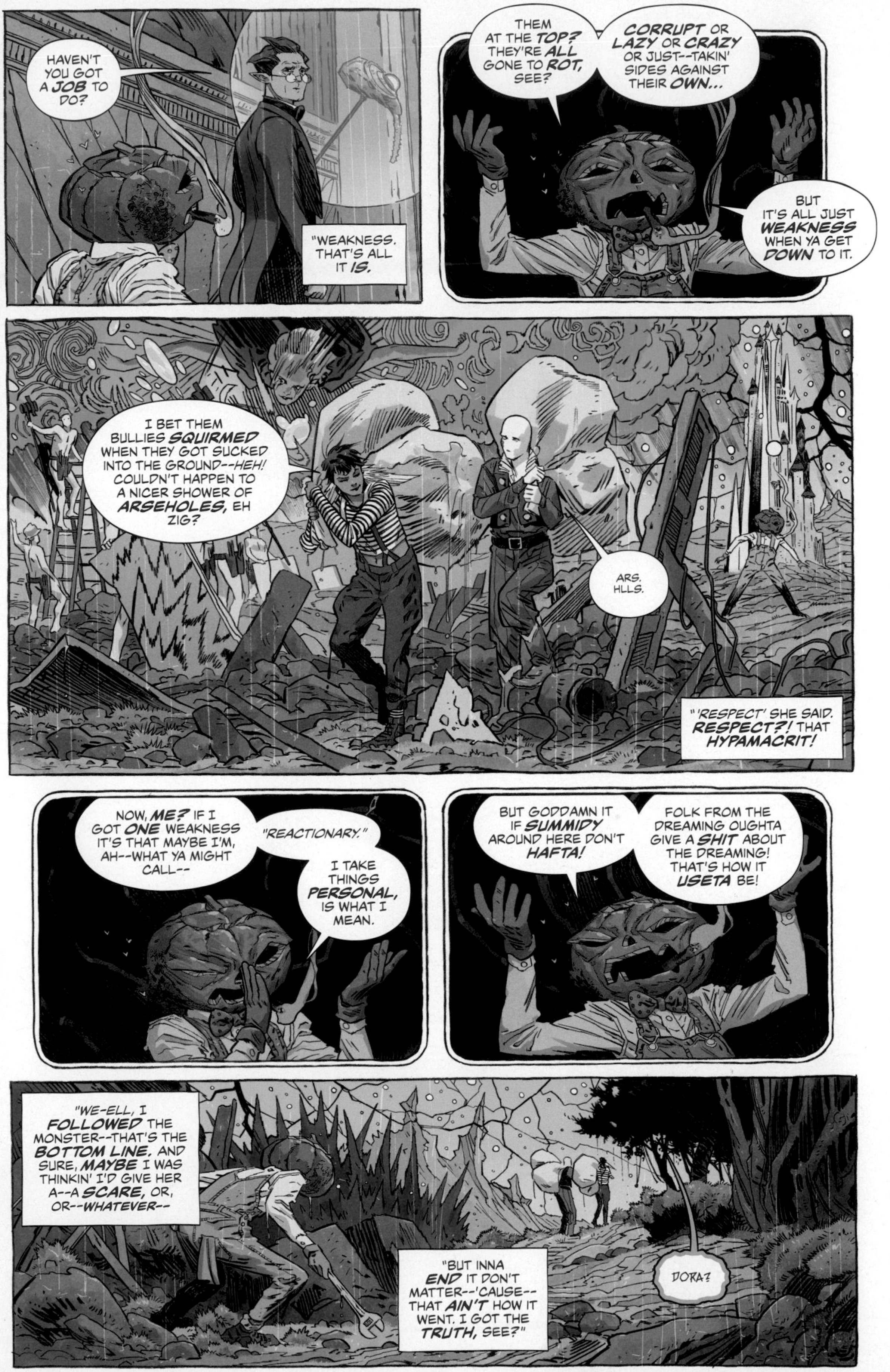
HAVEN'T YOU GOT A JOB TO DO?
"WEAKNESS. THAT'S ALL IT IS.
THEM AT THE TOP? THEY'RE ALL GONE TO ROT, SEE?
CORRUPT OR LAZY OR CRAZY OR JUST--TAKIN' SIDES AGAINST THEIR OWN...
BUT IT'S ALL JUST WEAKNESS WHEN YA GET DOWN TO IT.
I BET THEM BULLIES SQUIRMED WHEN THEY GOT SUCKED INTO THE GROUND--HEH! COULDN'T HAPPEN TO A NICER SHOWER OF ARSEHOLES, EH ZIG?
ARS. HLLS.
"'RESPECT' SHE SAID. RESPECT?! THAT HYPAMACRIT!
NOW, ME? IF I GOT ONE WEAKNESS IT'S THAT MAYBE I'M, AH--WHAT YA MIGHT CALL--
"REACTIONARY."
I TAKE THINGS PERSONAL, IS WHAT I MEAN.
BUT GODDAMN IT IF SUMMIDY AROUND HERE DON'T HAFTA!
FOLK FROM THE DREAMING OUGHTA GIVE A SHIT ABOUT THE DREAMING! THAT'S HOW IT USETA BE!
"WE-ELL, I FOLLOWED THE MONSTER--THAT'S THE BOTTOM LINE. AND SURE, MAYBE I WAS THINKIN' I'D GIVE HER A--A SCARE, OR, OR--WHATEVER--
"BUT INNA END IT DON'T MATTER--'CAUSE--THAT AIN'T HOW IT WENT. I GOT THE TRUTH, SEE?"
DORA?

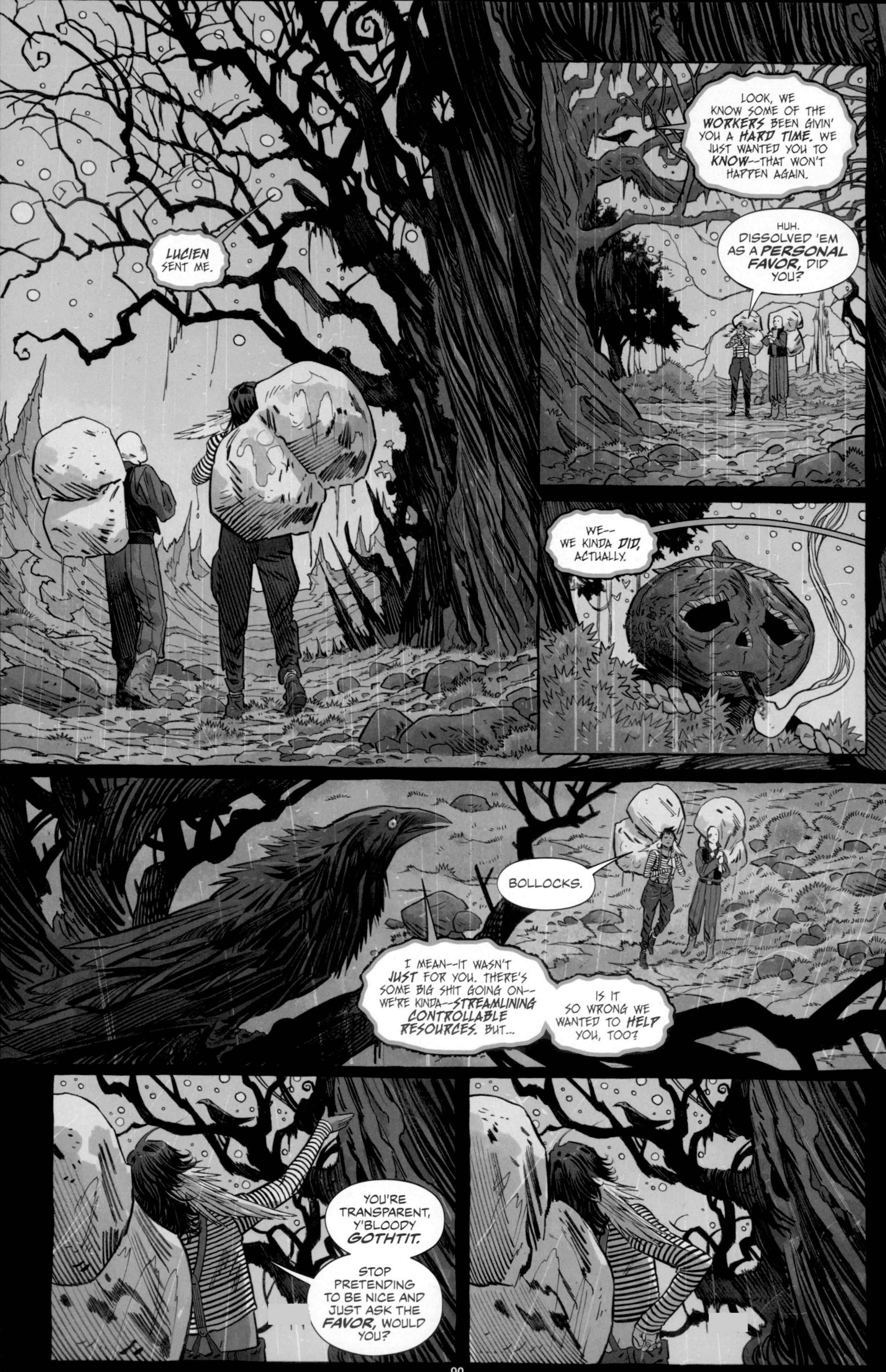
LUCIEN SENT ME.
LOOK, WE KNOW SOME OF THE WORKERS BEEN GIVIN' YOU A HARD TIME. WE JUST WANTED YOU TO KNOW--THAT WON'T HAPPEN AGAIN.
HUH. DISSOLVED 'EM AS A PERSONAL FAVOR, DID YOU?
WE-- WE KINDA DID, ACTUALLY.
BOLLOCKS.
I MEAN--IT WASN'T JUST FOR YOU. THERE'S SOME BIG SHIT GOING ON-- WE'RE KINDA--STREAMLINING CONTROLLABLE RESOURCES. BUT...
IS IT SO WRONG WE WANTED TO HELP YOU, TOO?
YOU'RE TRANSPARENT, Y'BLOODY GOTHTIT.
STOP PRETENDING TO BE NICE AND JUST ASK THE FAVOR, WOULD YOU?

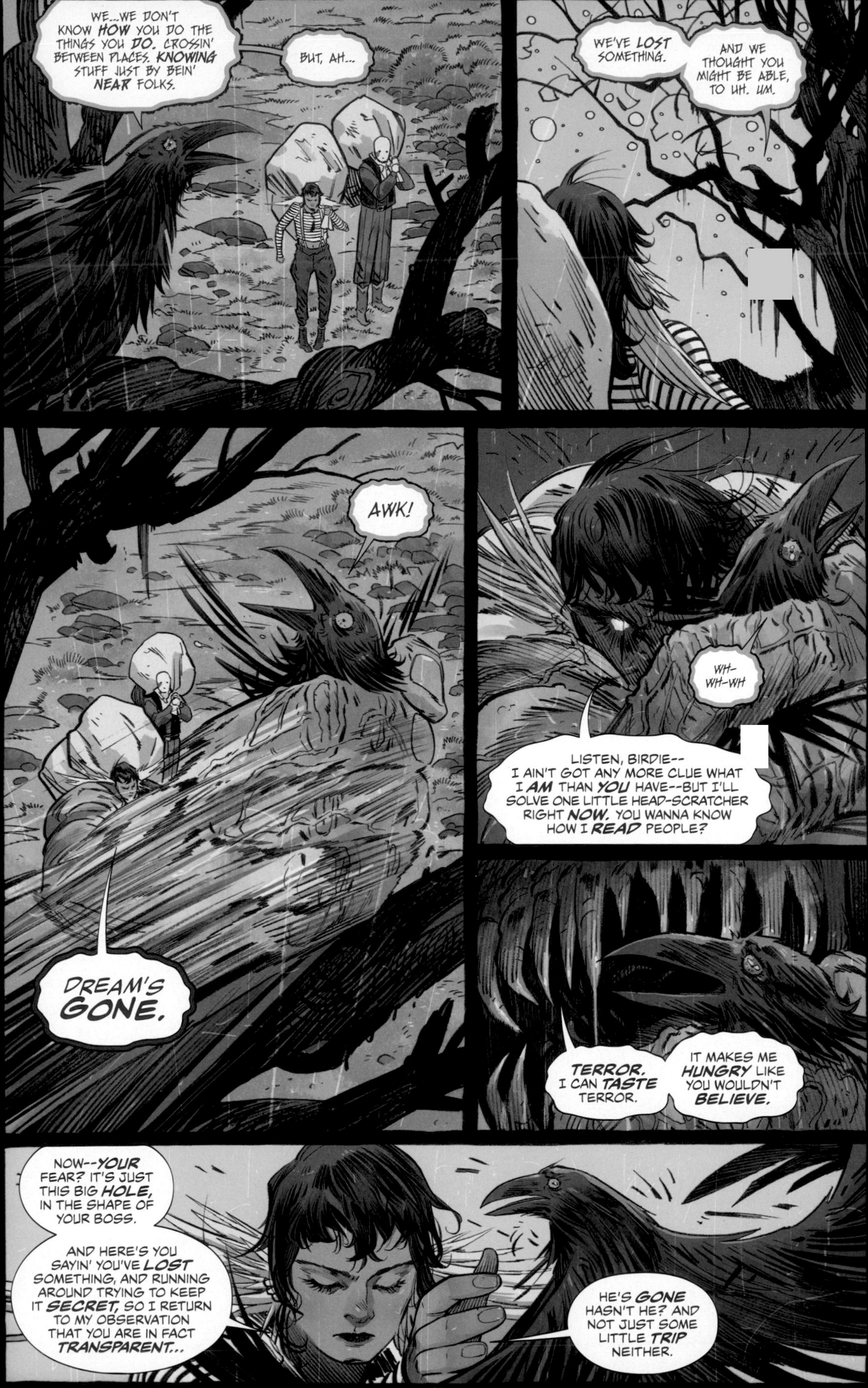
WE...WE DON'T KNOW HOW YOU DO THE THINGS YOU DO. CROSSIN' BETWEEN PLACES. KNOWING STUFF JUST BY BEIN' NEAR FOLKS.
BUT, AH...
WE'VE LOST SOMETHING.
AND WE THOUGHT YOU MIGHT BE ABLE, TO UH. UM.
AWK!
DREAM'S GONE.
WH-WH-WH
LISTEN, BIRDIE-- I AIN'T GOT ANY MORE CLUE WHAT I AM THAN YOU HAVE--BUT I'LL SOLVE ONE LITTLE HEAD-SCRATCHER RIGHT NOW. YOU WANNA KNOW HOW I READ PEOPLE?
TERROR. I CAN TASTE TERROR.
IT MAKES ME HUNGRY LIKE YOU WOULDN'T BELIEVE.
NOW--YOUR FEAR? IT'S JUST THIS BIG HOLE, IN THE SHAPE OF YOUR BOSS.
AND HERE'S YOU SAYIN' YOU'VE LOST SOMETHING, AND RUNNING AROUND TRYING TO KEEP IT SECRET, SO I RETURN TO MY OBSERVATION THAT YOU ARE IN FACT TRANSPARENT...
HE'S GONE HASN'T HE? AND NOT JUST SOME LITTLE TRIP NEITHER.

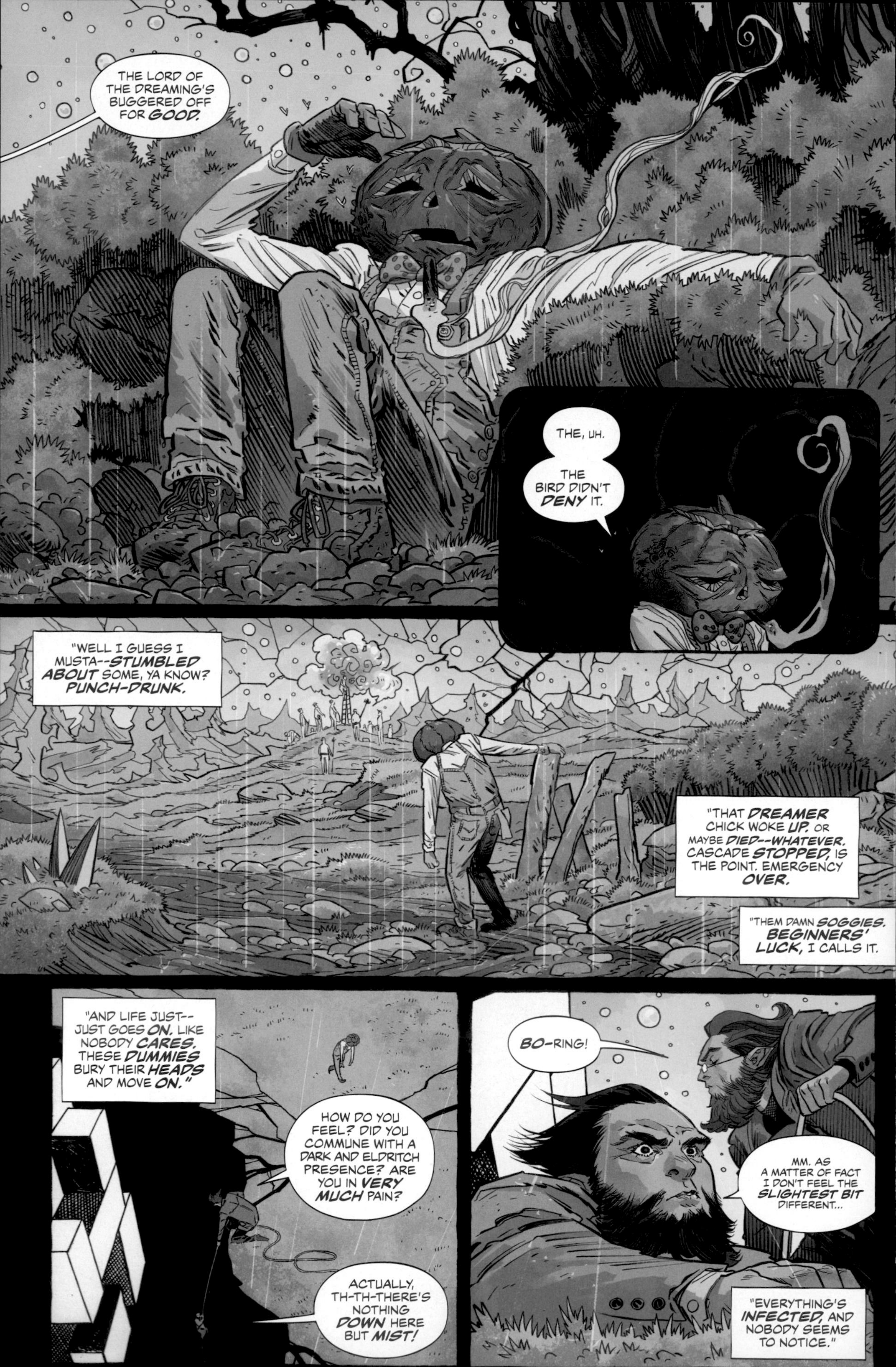
THE LORD OF THE DREAMING'S BUGGERED OFF FOR GOOD.
THE, UH.
THE BIRD DIDN'T DENY IT.
"WELL I GUESS I MUSTA--STUMBLED ABOUT SOME, YA KNOW? PUNCH-DRUNK.
"THAT DREAMER CHICK WOKE UP. OR MAYBE DIED--WHATEVER. CASCADE STOPPED, IS THE POINT. EMERGENCY OVER.
"THEM DAMN SOGGIES. BEGINNERS' LUCK, I CALLS IT.
"AND LIFE JUST--JUST GOES ON. LIKE NOBODY CARES. THESE DUMMIES BURY THEIR HEADS AND MOVE ON."
HOW DO YOU FEEL? DID YOU COMMUNE WITH A DARK AND ELDRITCH PRESENCE? ARE YOU IN VERY MUCH PAIN?
ACTUALLY, TH-TH-THERE'S NOTHING DOWN HERE BUT MIST!
BO-RING!
MM. AS A MATTER OF FACT I DON'T FEEL THE SLIGHTEST BIT DIFFERENT...
"EVERYTHING'S INFECTED, AND NOBODY SEEMS TO NOTICE."

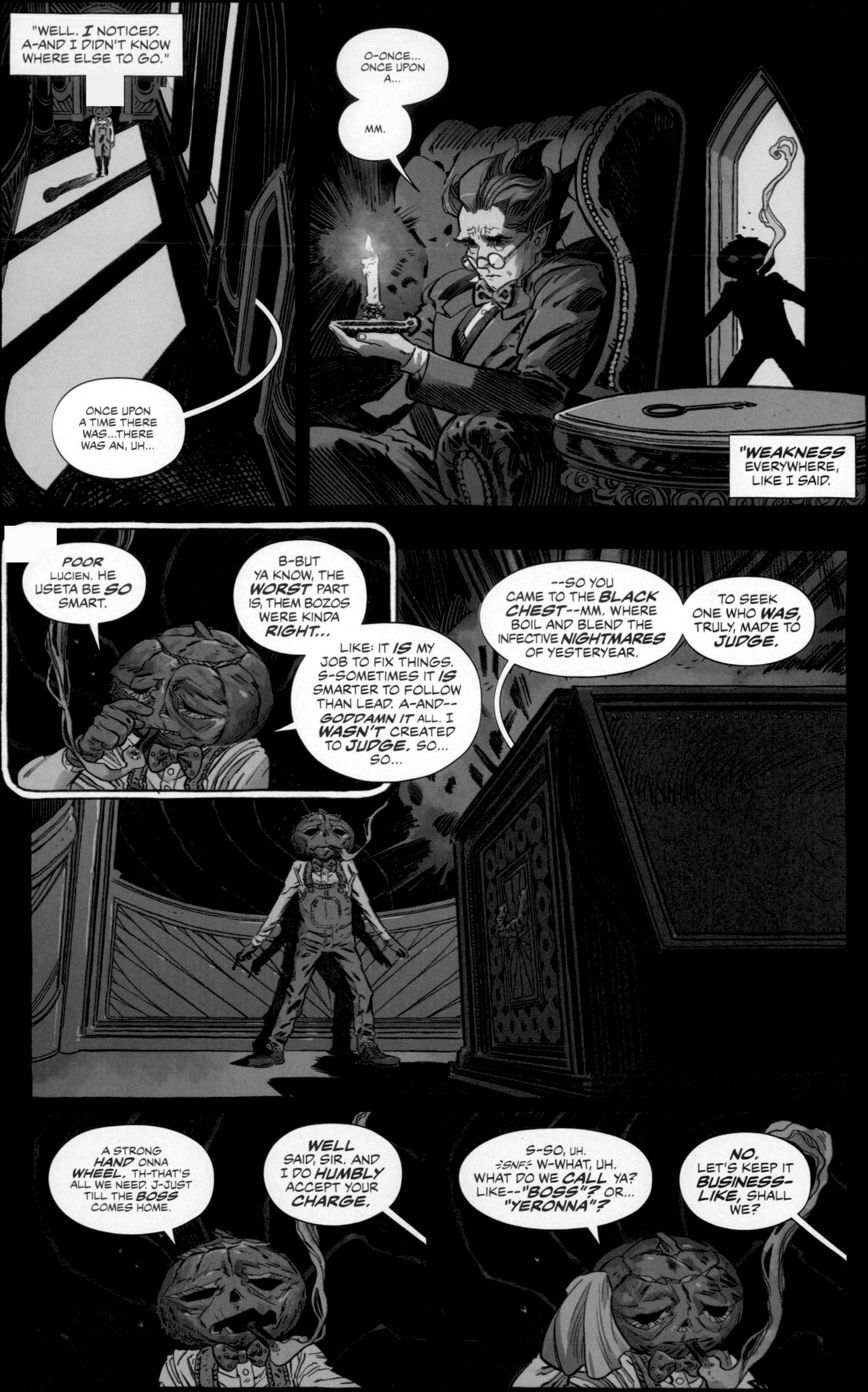

"WELL. I NOTICED. A-AND I DIDN'T KNOW WHERE ELSE TO GO."
ONCE UPON A TIME THERE WAS...THERE WAS AN, UH...
O-ONCE... ONCE UPON A...
MM.
"WEAKNESS EVERYWHERE, LIKE I SAID.
POOR LUCIEN. HE USETA BE SO SMART.
B-BUT YA KNOW, THE WORST PART IS, THEM BOZOS WERE KINDA RIGHT...
LIKE: IT IS MY JOB TO FIX THINGS. S-SOMETIMES IT IS SMARTER TO FOLLOW THAN LEAD. A-AND-- GODDAMN IT ALL. I WASN'T CREATED TO JUDGE. SO... SO...
--SO YOU CAME TO THE BLACK CHEST--MM. WHERE BOIL AND BLEND THE INFECTIVE NIGHTMARES OF YESTERYEAR.
TO SEEK ONE WHO WAS, TRULY, MADE TO JUDGE.
A STRONG HAND ONNA WHEEL. TH-THAT'S ALL WE NEED. J-JUST TILL THE BOSS COMES HOME.
WELL SAID, SIR. AND I DO HUMBLY ACCEPT YOUR CHARGE.
S-SO, UH. SNF W-WHAT, UH. WHAT DO WE CALL YA? LIKE--"BOSS"? OR... "YERONNA"?
NO. LET'S KEEP IT BUSINESS-LIKE, SHALL WE?

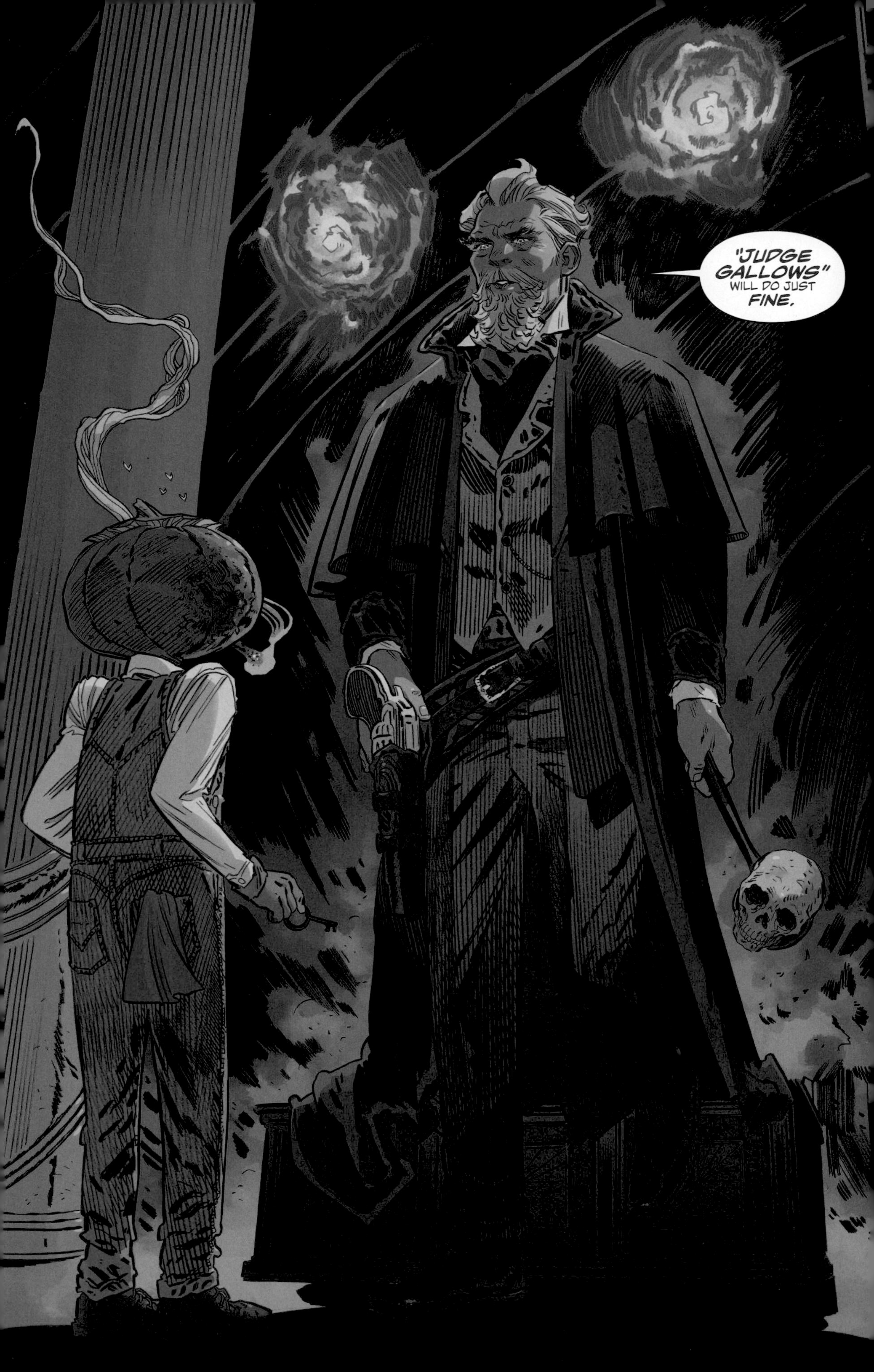
"JUDGE GALLOWS" WILL DO JUST FINE.

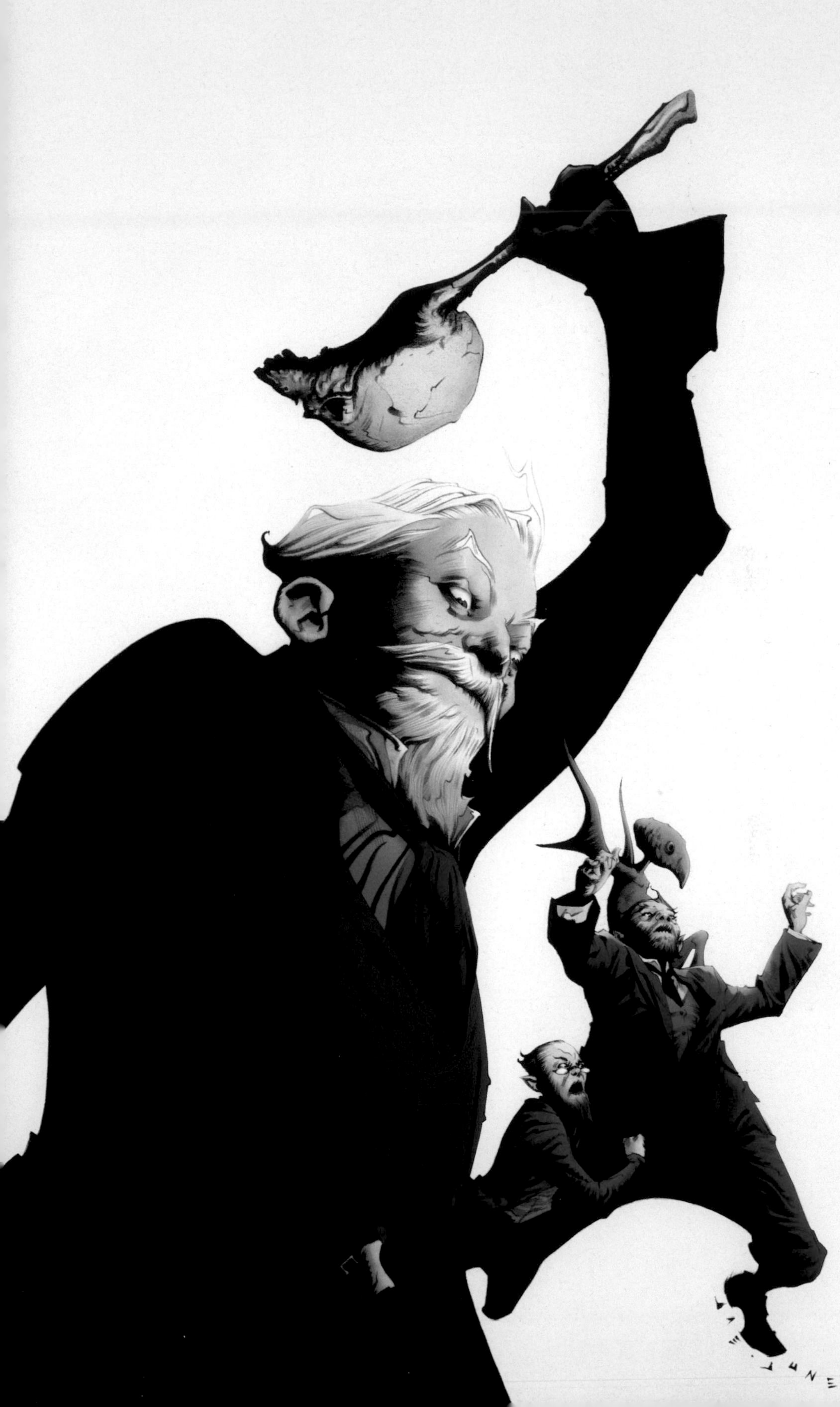

THE DREAMING

The Glory

WRITTEN BY
Simon Spurrier

ILLUSTRATED BY
Bilquis Evely

COLORS BY
Mat Lopes

LETTERS BY
Simon Bowland

COVER ART BY
Jae Lee and *June Chung*

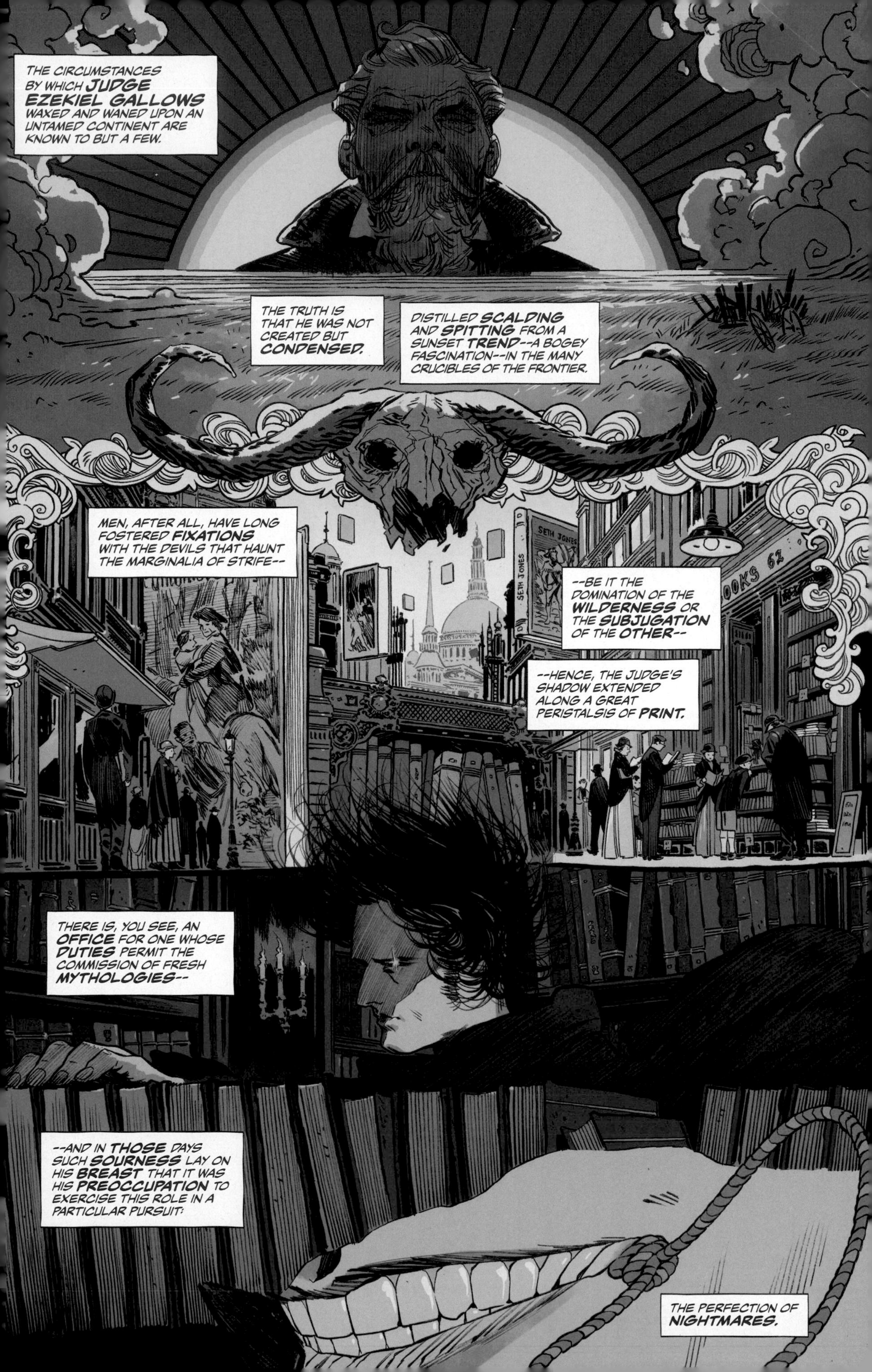
THE CIRCUMSTANCES BY WHICH JUDGE EZEKIEL GALLOWS WAXED AND WANED UPON AN UNTAMED CONTINENT ARE KNOWN TO BUT A FEW.
THE TRUTH IS THAT HE WAS NOT CREATED BUT CONDENSED.
DISTILLED SCALDING AND SPITTING FROM A SUNSET TREND--A BOGEY FASCINATION--IN THE MANY CRUCIBLES OF THE FRONTIER.
MEN, AFTER ALL, HAVE LONG FOSTERED FIXATIONS WITH THE DEVILS THAT HAUNT THE MARGINALIA OF STRIFE--
SETH JONES
SETH JONES
--BE IT THE DOMINATION OF THE WILDERNESS OR THE SUBJUGATION OF THE OTHER--
--HENCE, THE JUDGE'S SHADOW EXTENDED ALONG A GREAT PERISTALSIS OF PRINT.
THERE IS, YOU SEE, AN OFFICE FOR ONE WHOSE DUTIES PERMIT THE COMMISSION OF FRESH MYTHOLOGIES--
--AND IN THOSE DAYS SUCH SOURNESS LAY ON HIS BREAST THAT IT WAS HIS PREOCCUPATION TO EXERCISE THIS ROLE IN A PARTICULAR PURSUIT:
THE PERFECTION OF NIGHTMARES.

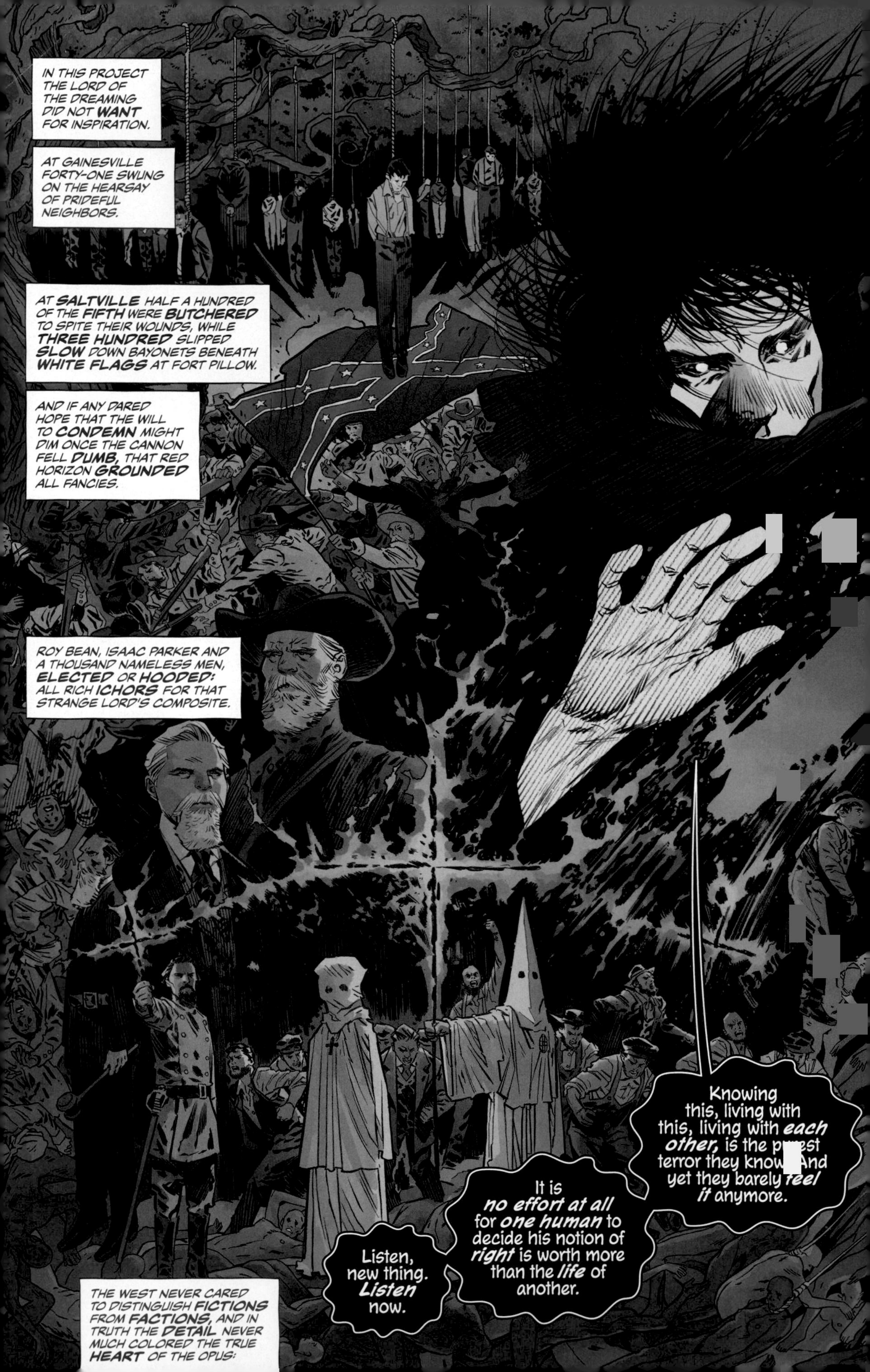
IN THIS PROJECT THE LORD OF THE DREAMING DID NOT WANT FOR INSPIRATION.
AT GAINESVILLE FORTY-ONE SWUNG ON THE HEARSAY OF PRIDEFUL NEIGHBORS.
AT SALTVILLE HALF A HUNDRED OF THE FIFTH WERE BUTCHERED TO SPITE THEIR WOUNDS, WHILE THREE HUNDRED SLIPPED SLOW DOWN BAYONETS BENEATH WHITE FLAGS AT FORT PILLOW.
AND IF ANY DARED HOPE THAT THE WILL TO CONDEMN MIGHT DIM ONCE THE CANNON FELL DUMB, THAT RED HORIZON GROUNDED ALL FANCIES.
ROY BEAN, ISAAC PARKER AND A THOUSAND NAMELESS MEN, ELECTED OR HOODED: ALL RICH ICHORS FOR THAT STRANGE LORD'S COMPOSITE.
Knowing this, living with this, living with each other, is the p rest terror they know And yet they barely feel it anymore.
It is no effort at all for one human to decide his notion of right is worth more than the life of another.
Listen, new thing. Listen now.
THE WEST NEVER CARED TO DISTINGUISH FICTIONS FROM FACTIONS, AND IN TRUTH THE DETAIL NEVER MUCH COLORED THE TRUE HEART OF THE OPUS:

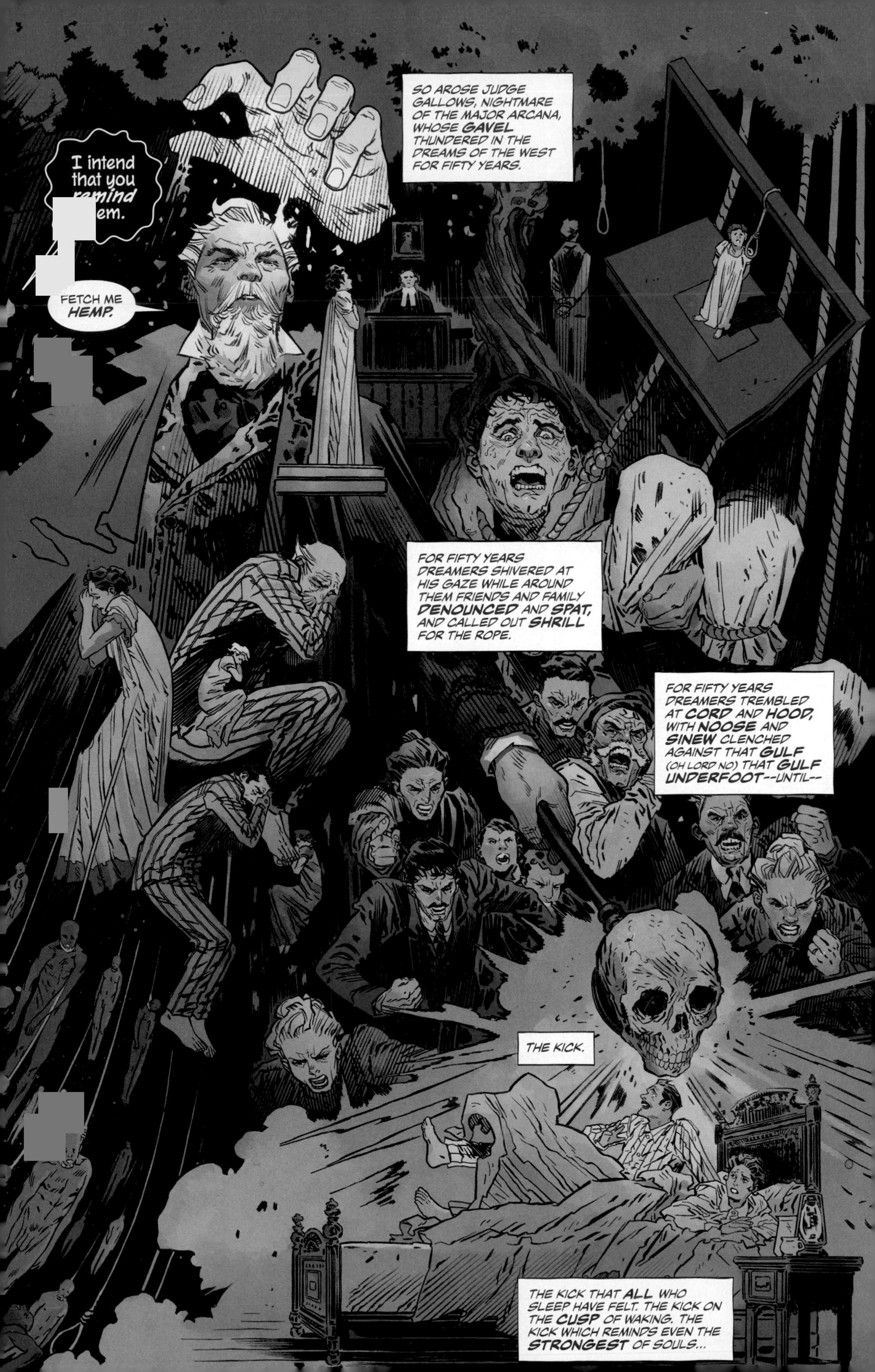

I intend that you remind em.
FETCH ME HEMP.
SO AROSE JUDGE GALLOWS, NIGHTMARE OF THE MAJOR ARCANA, WHOSE GAVEL THUNDERED IN THE DREAMS OF THE WEST FOR FIFTY YEARS.
FOR FIFTY YEARS DREAMERS SHIVERED AT HIS GAZE WHILE AROUND THEM FRIENDS AND FAMILY DENOUNCED AND SPAT, AND CALLED OUT SHRILL FOR THE ROPE.
FOR FIFTY YEARS DREAMERS TREMBLED AT CORD AND HOOD, WITH NOOSE AND SINEW CLENCHED AGAINST THAT GULF (OH LORD NO) THAT GULF UNDERFOOT--UNTIL--
THE KICK.
THE KICK THAT ALL WHO SLEEP HAVE FELT. THE KICK ON THE CUSP OF WAKING. THE KICK WHICH REMINDS EVEN THE STRONGEST OF SOULS...

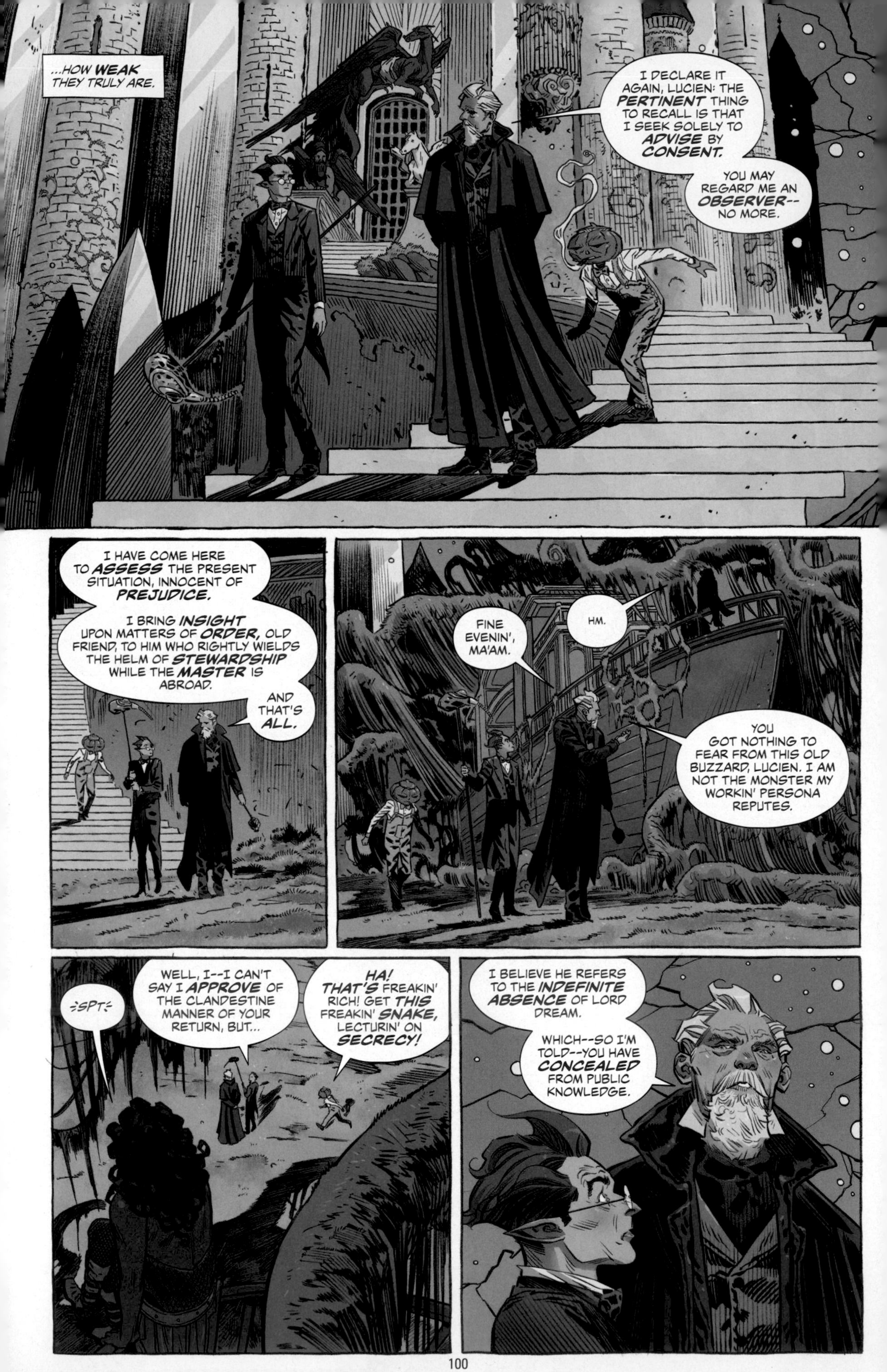
...HOW WEAK THEY TRULY ARE.
I DECLARE IT AGAIN, LUCIEN: THE PERTINENT THING TO RECALL IS THAT I SEEK SOLELY TO ADVISE BY CONSENT.
YOU MAY REGARD ME AN OBSERVER-- NO MORE.
I HAVE COME HERE TO ASSESS THE PRESENT SITUATION, INNOCENT OF PREJUDICE.
I BRING INSIGHT UPON MATTERS OF ORDER, OLD FRIEND, TO HIM WHO RIGHTLY WIELDS THE HELM OF STEWARDSHIP WHILE THE MASTER IS ABROAD.
AND THAT'S ALL.
FINE EVENIN', MA'AM.
HM.
YOU GOT NOTHING TO FEAR FROM THIS OLD BUZZARD, LUCIEN. I AM NOT THE MONSTER MY WORKIN' PERSONA REPUTES.
SPT
WELL, I--I CAN'T SAY I APPROVE OF THE CLANDESTINE MANNER OF YOUR RETURN, BUT...
HA! THAT'S FREAKIN' RICH! GET THIS FREAKIN' SNAKE, LECTURIN' ON SECRECY!
I BELIEVE HE REFERS TO THE INDEFINITE ABSENCE OF LORD DREAM.
WHICH--SO I'M TOLD--YOU HAVE CONCEALED FROM PUBLIC KNOWLEDGE.

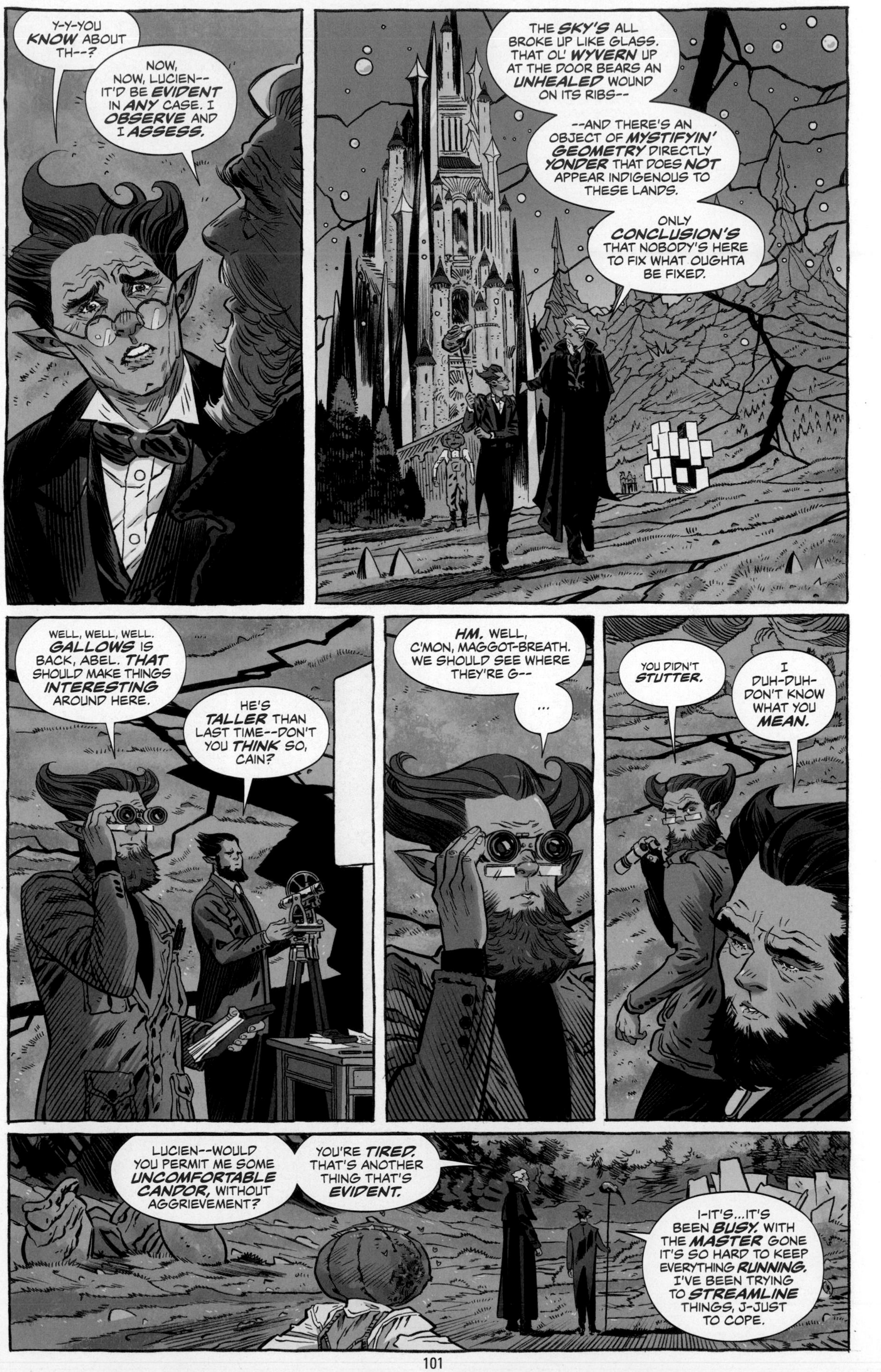

Y-Y-YOU KNOW ABOUT TH--?
NOW, NOW, LUCIEN--IT'D BE EVIDENT IN ANY CASE. I OBSERVE AND I ASSESS.
THE SKY'S ALL BROKE UP LIKE GLASS. THAT OL' WYVERN UP AT THE DOOR BEARS AN UNHEALED WOUND ON ITS RIBS--
--AND THERE'S AN OBJECT OF MYSTIFYIN' GEOMETRY DIRECTLY YONDER THAT DOES NOT APPEAR INDIGENOUS TO THESE LANDS.
ONLY CONCLUSION'S THAT NOBODY'S HERE TO FIX WHAT OUGHTA BE FIXED.
WELL, WELL, WELL. GALLOWS IS BACK, ABEL. THAT SHOULD MAKE THINGS INTERESTING AROUND HERE.
HE'S TALLER THAN LAST TIME--DON'T YOU THINK SO, CAIN?
HM. WELL, C'MON, MAGGOT-BREATH. WE SHOULD SEE WHERE THEY'RE G--
...
YOU DIDN'T STUTTER.
I DUH-DUH-DON'T KNOW WHAT YOU MEAN.
LUCIEN--WOULD YOU PERMIT ME SOME UNCOMFORTABLE CANDOR, WITHOUT AGGRIEVEMENT?
YOU'RE TIRED. THAT'S ANOTHER THING THAT'S EVIDENT.
I-IT'S...IT'S BEEN BUSY. WITH THE MASTER GONE IT'S SO HARD TO KEEP EVERYTHING RUNNING. I'VE BEEN TRYING TO STREAMLINE THINGS, J-JUST TO COPE.

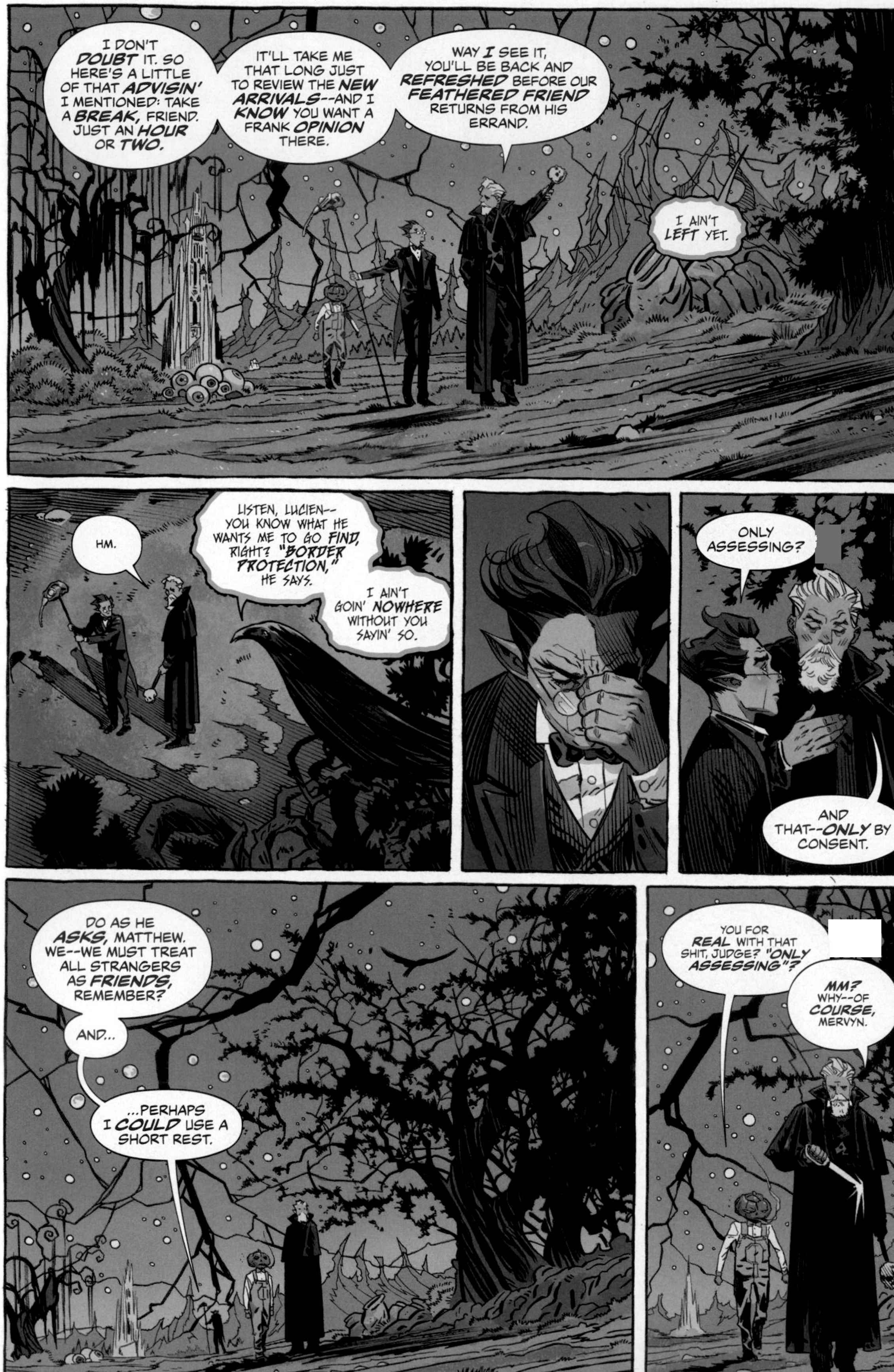
I DON'T DOUBT IT. SO HERE'S A LITTLE OF THAT ADVISIN' I MENTIONED: TAKE A BREAK, FRIEND. JUST AN HOUR OR TWO.
IT'LL TAKE ME THAT LONG JUST TO REVIEW THE NEW ARRIVALS--AND I KNOW YOU WANT A FRANK OPINION THERE.
WAY I SEE IT, YOU'LL BE BACK AND REFRESHED BEFORE OUR FEATHERED FRIEND RETURNS FROM HIS ERRAND.
I AIN'T LEFT YET.
HM.
LISTEN, LUCIEN--YOU KNOW WHAT HE WANTS ME TO GO FIND, RIGHT? "BORDER PROTECTION," HE SAYS.
I AIN'T GOIN' NOWHERE WITHOUT YOU SAYIN' SO.
ONLY ASSESSING?
AND THAT--ONLY BY CONSENT.
DO AS HE ASKS, MATTHEW. WE--WE MUST TREAT ALL STRANGERS AS FRIENDS, REMEMBER?
AND...
...PERHAPS I COULD USE A SHORT REST.
YOU FOR REAL WITH THAT SHIT, JUDGE? "ONLY ASSESSING"?
MM? WHY--OF COURSE, MERVYN.

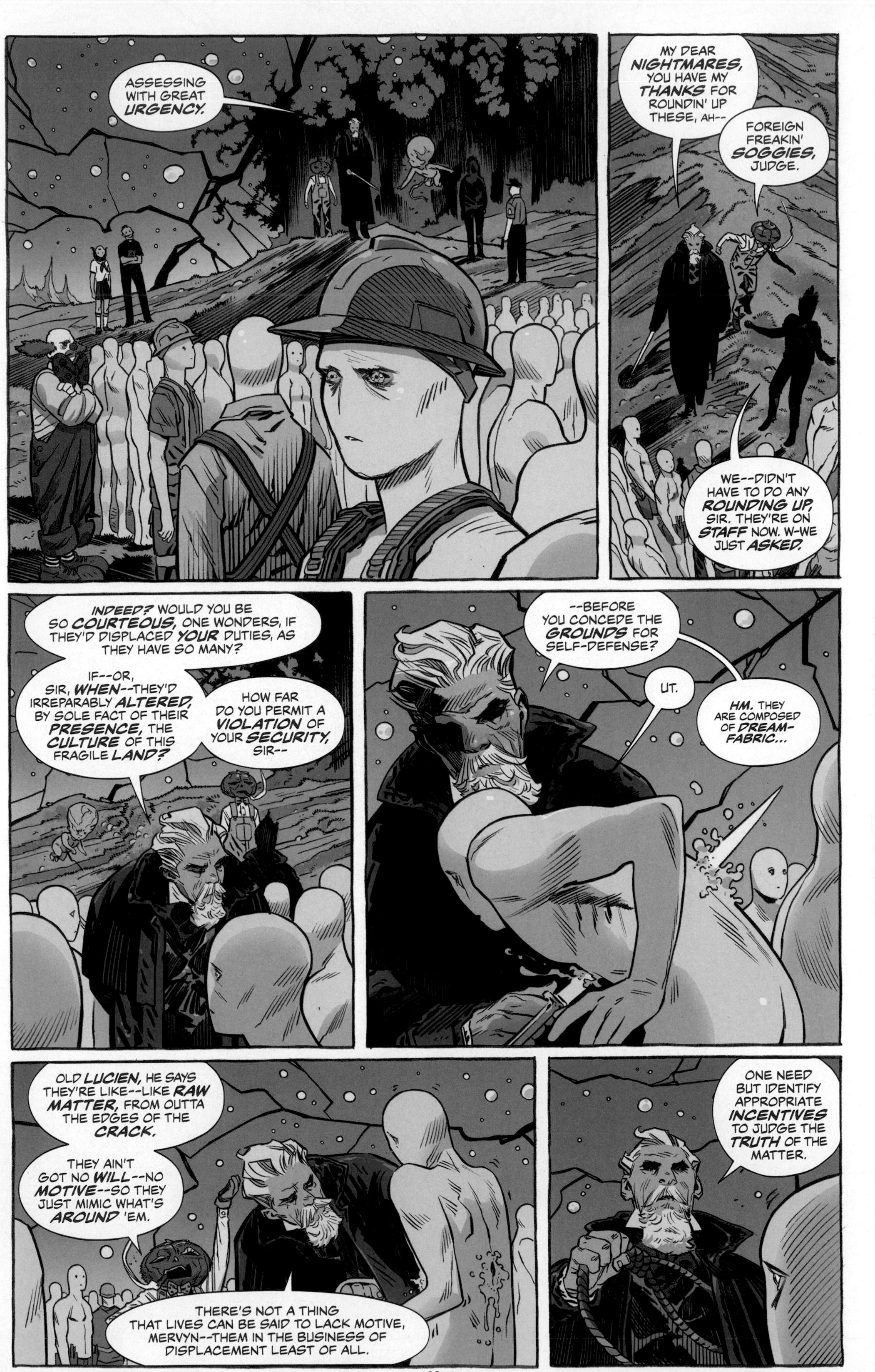
ASSESSING WITH GREAT URGENCY.
MY DEAR NIGHTMARES, YOU HAVE MY THANKS FOR ROUNDIN' UP THESE, AH--
FOREIGN FREAKIN' SOGGIES, JUDGE.
WE--DIDN'T HAVE TO DO ANY ROUNDING UP, SIR. THEY'RE ON STAFF NOW. W-WE JUST ASKED.
INDEED? WOULD YOU BE SO COURTEOUS, ONE WONDERS, IF THEY'D DISPLACED YOUR DUTIES, AS THEY HAVE SO MANY?
IF--OR, SIR, WHEN--THEY'D IRREPARABLY ALTERED, BY SOLE FACT OF THEIR PRESENCE, THE CULTURE OF THIS FRAGILE LAND?
HOW FAR DO YOU PERMIT A VIOLATION OF YOUR SECURITY, SIR--
--BEFORE YOU CONCEDE THE GROUNDS FOR SELF-DEFENSE?
UT.
HM. THEY ARE COMPOSED OF DREAM-FABRIC...
OLD LUCIEN, HE SAYS THEY'RE LIKE--LIKE RAW MATTER, FROM OUTTA THE EDGES OF THE CRACK.
THEY AIN'T GOT NO WILL--NO MOTIVE--SO THEY JUST MIMIC WHAT'S AROUND 'EM.
THERE'S NOT A THING THAT LIVES CAN BE SAID TO LACK MOTIVE, MERVYN--THEM IN THE BUSINESS OF DISPLACEMENT LEAST OF ALL.
ONE NEED BUT IDENTIFY APPROPRIATE INCENTIVES TO JUDGE THE TRUTH OF THE MATTER.

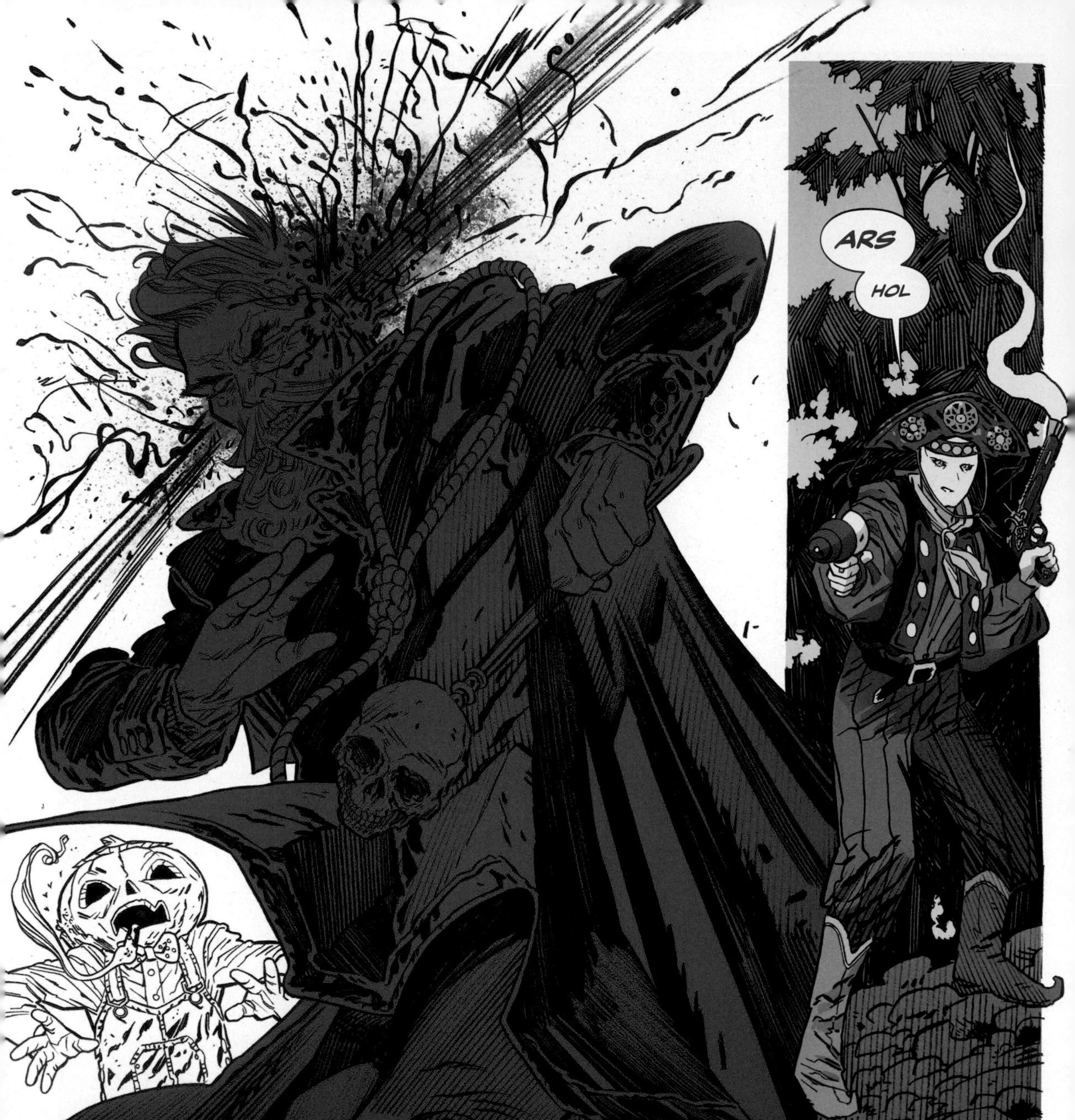
ARS
HOL
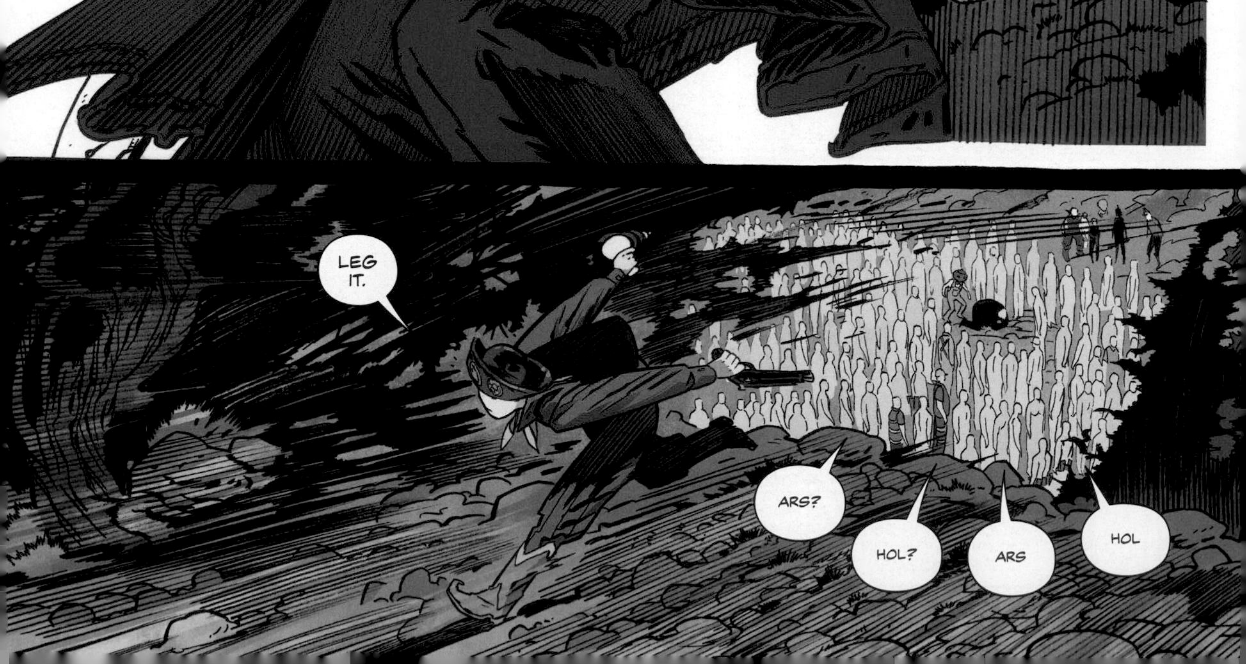
LEG IT.
ARS?
HOL?
ARS
HOL

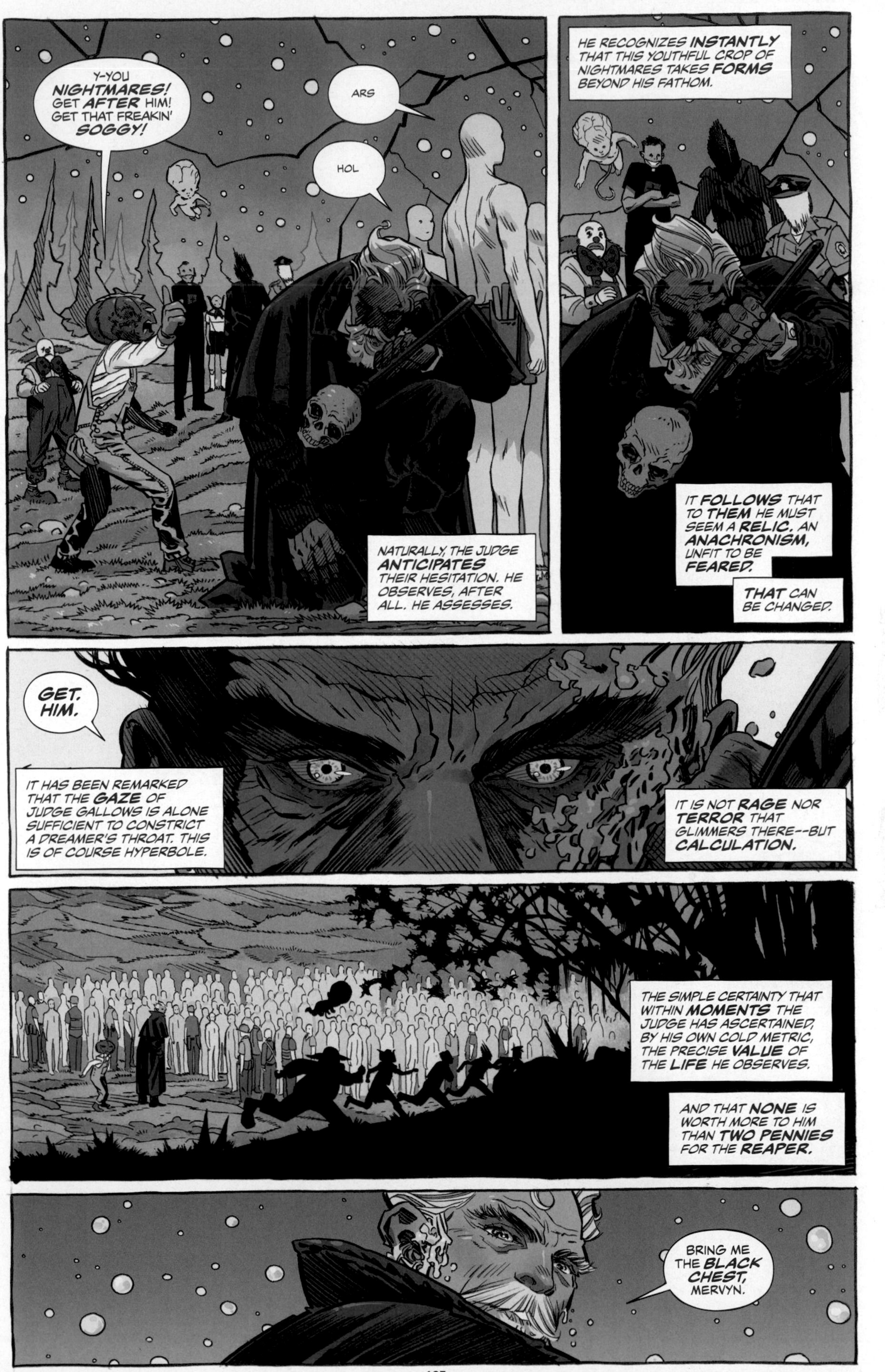
Y-YOU NIGHTMARES! GET AFTER HIM! GET THAT FREAKIN' SOGGY!
ARS
HOL
NATURALLY, THE JUDGE ANTICIPATES THEIR HESITATION. HE OBSERVES, AFTER ALL. HE ASSESSES.
HE RECOGNIZES INSTANTLY THAT THIS YOUTHFUL CROP OF NIGHTMARES TAKES FORMS BEYOND HIS FATHOM.
IT FOLLOWS THAT TO THEM HE MUST SEEM A RELIC. AN ANACHRONISM, UNFIT TO BE FEARED.
THAT CAN BE CHANGED.
GET. HIM.
IT HAS BEEN REMARKED THAT THE GAZE OF JUDGE GALLOWS IS ALONE SUFFICIENT TO CONSTRICT A DREAMER'S THROAT. THIS IS OF COURSE HYPERBOLE.
IT IS NOT RAGE NOR TERROR THAT GLIMMERS THERE--BUT CALCULATION.
THE SIMPLE CERTAINTY THAT WITHIN MOMENTS THE JUDGE HAS ASCERTAINED, BY HIS OWN COLD METRIC, THE PRECISE VALUE OF THE LIFE HE OBSERVES.
AND THAT NONE IS WORTH MORE TO HIM THAN TWO PENNIES FOR THE REAPER.
BRING ME THE BLACK CHEST, MERVYN.

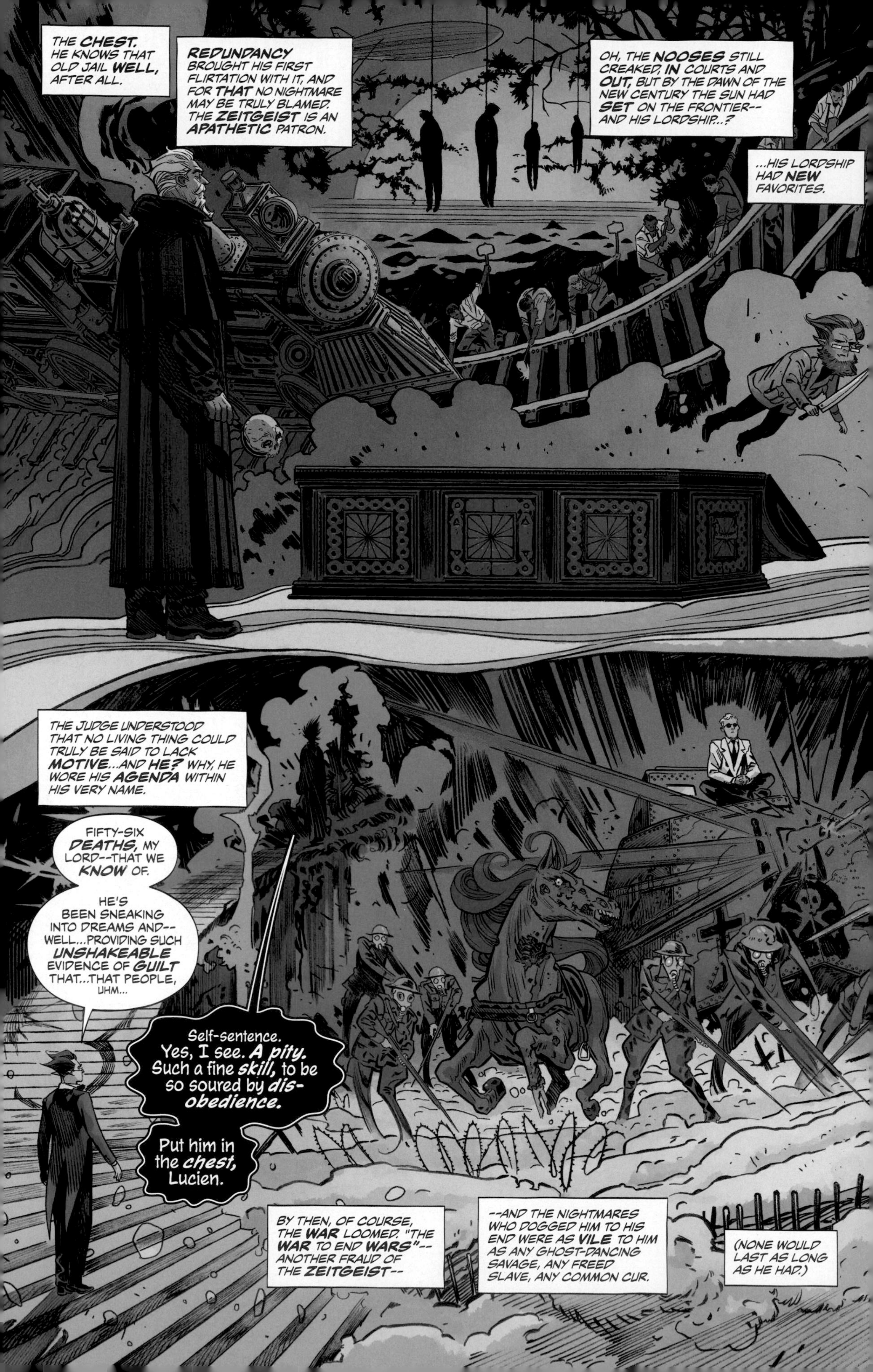
THE CHEST. HE KNOWS THAT OLD JAIL WELL, AFTER ALL.
REDUNDANCY BROUGHT HIS FIRST FLIRTATION WITH IT, AND FOR THAT NO NIGHTMARE MAY BE TRULY BLAMED. THE ZEITGEIST IS AN APATHETIC PATRON.
OH, THE NOOSES STILL CREAKED, IN COURTS AND OUT, BUT BY THE DAWN OF THE NEW CENTURY THE SUN HAD SET ON THE FRONTIER-- AND HIS LORDSHIP...?
...HIS LORDSHIP HAD NEW FAVORITES.
THE JUDGE UNDERSTOOD THAT NO LIVING THING COULD TRULY BE SAID TO LACK MOTIVE...AND HE? WHY, HE WORE HIS AGENDA WITHIN HIS VERY NAME.
FIFTY-SIX DEATHS, MY LORD--THAT WE KNOW OF.
HE'S BEEN SNEAKING INTO DREAMS AND--WELL...PROVIDING SUCH UNSHAKEABLE EVIDENCE OF GUILT THAT...THAT PEOPLE, UHM...
Self-sentence. Yes, I see. A pity. Such a fine skill, to be so soured by dis-obedience.
Put him in the chest, Lucien.
BY THEN, OF COURSE, THE WAR LOOMED. "THE WAR TO END WARS"-- ANOTHER FRAUD OF THE ZEITGEIST--
--AND THE NIGHTMARES WHO DOGGED HIM TO HIS END WERE AS VILE TO HIM AS ANY GHOST-DANCING SAVAGE, ANY FREED SLAVE, ANY COMMON CUR.
(NONE WOULD LAST AS LONG AS HE HAD.)

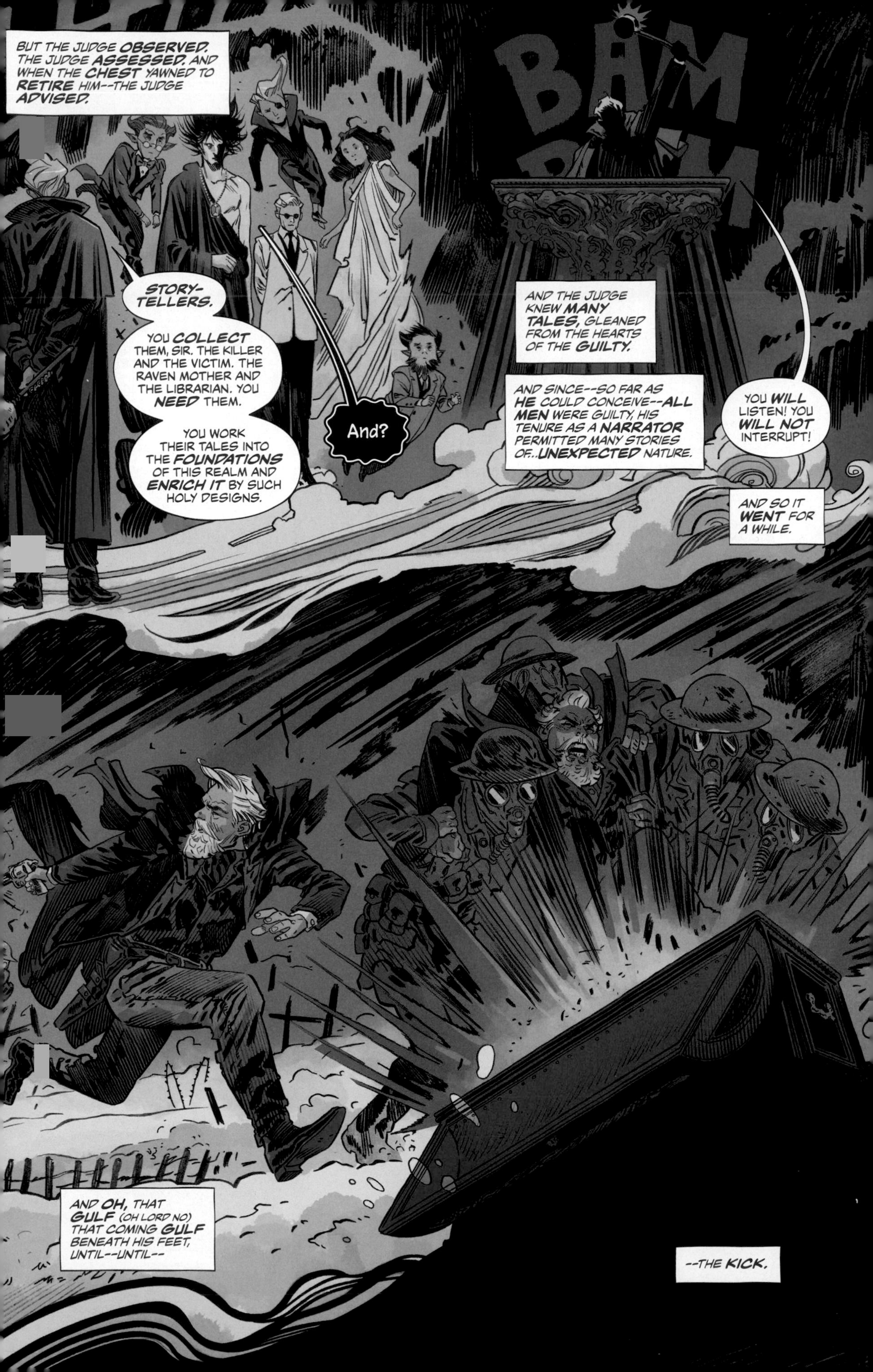
BUT THE JUDGE OBSERVED. THE JUDGE ASSESSED. AND WHEN THE CHEST YAWNED TO RETIRE HIM--THE JUDGE ADVISED.
BAM
STORY-TELLERS.
YOU COLLECT THEM, SIR. THE KILLER AND THE VICTIM. THE RAVEN MOTHER AND THE LIBRARIAN. YOU NEED THEM.
YOU WORK THEIR TALES INTO THE FOUNDATIONS OF THIS REALM AND ENRICH IT BY SUCH HOLY DESIGNS.
And?
AND THE JUDGE KNEW MANY TALES, GLEANED FROM THE HEARTS OF THE GUILTY.
AND SINCE--SO FAR AS HE COULD CONCEIVE--ALL MEN WERE GUILTY, HIS TENURE AS A NARRATOR PERMITTED MANY STORIES OF..UNEXPECTED NATURE.
YOU WILL LISTEN! YOU WILL NOT INTERRUPT!
AND SO IT WENT FOR A WHILE.
AND OH, THAT GULF (OH LORD NO) THAT COMING GULF BENEATH HIS FEET, UNTIL--UNTIL--
--THE KICK.

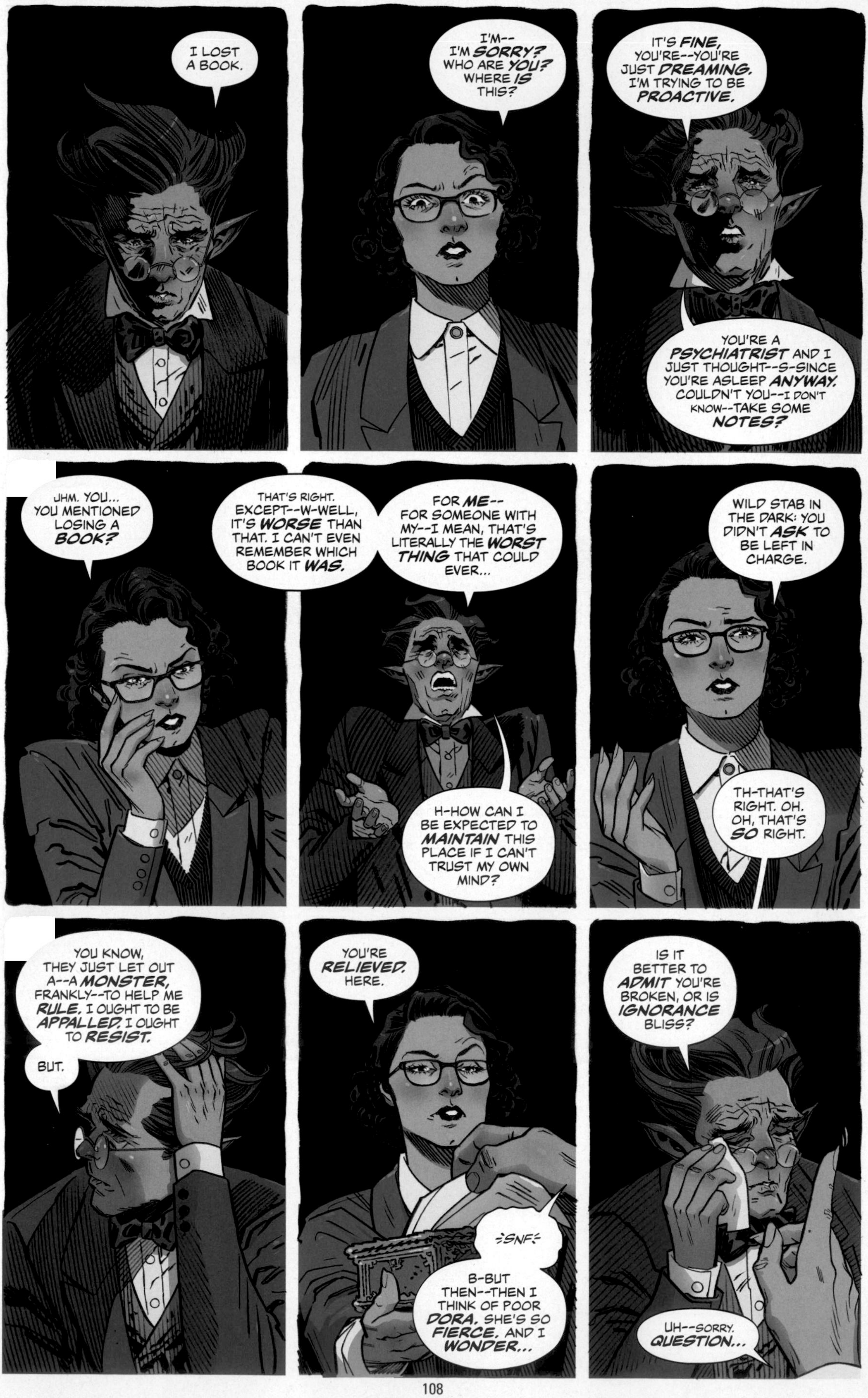

I LOST A BOOK.
I'M-- I'M SORRY? WHO ARE YOU? WHERE IS THIS?
IT'S FINE, YOU'RE--YOU'RE JUST DREAMING. I'M TRYING TO BE PROACTIVE.
YOU'RE A PSYCHIATRIST AND I JUST THOUGHT--S-SINCE YOU'RE ASLEEP ANYWAY. COULDN'T YOU--I DON'T KNOW--TAKE SOME NOTES?
UHM. YOU... YOU MENTIONED LOSING A BOOK?
THAT'S RIGHT. EXCEPT--W-WELL, IT'S WORSE THAN THAT. I CAN'T EVEN REMEMBER WHICH BOOK IT WAS.
FOR ME-- FOR SOMEONE WITH MY--I MEAN, THAT'S LITERALLY THE WORST THING THAT COULD EVER...
H-HOW CAN I BE EXPECTED TO MAINTAIN THIS PLACE IF I CAN'T TRUST MY OWN MIND?
WILD STAB IN THE DARK: YOU DIDN'T ASK TO BE LEFT IN CHARGE.
TH-THAT'S RIGHT. OH. OH, THAT'S SO RIGHT.
YOU KNOW, THEY JUST LET OUT A--A MONSTER, FRANKLY--TO HELP ME RULE. I OUGHT TO BE APPALLED. I OUGHT TO RESIST.
BUT.
YOU'RE RELIEVED. HERE.
SNF
B-BUT THEN--THEN I THINK OF POOR DORA. SHE'S SO FIERCE. AND I WONDER...
IS IT BETTER TO ADMIT YOU'RE BROKEN, OR IS IGNORANCE BLISS?
UH--SORRY. QUESTION...

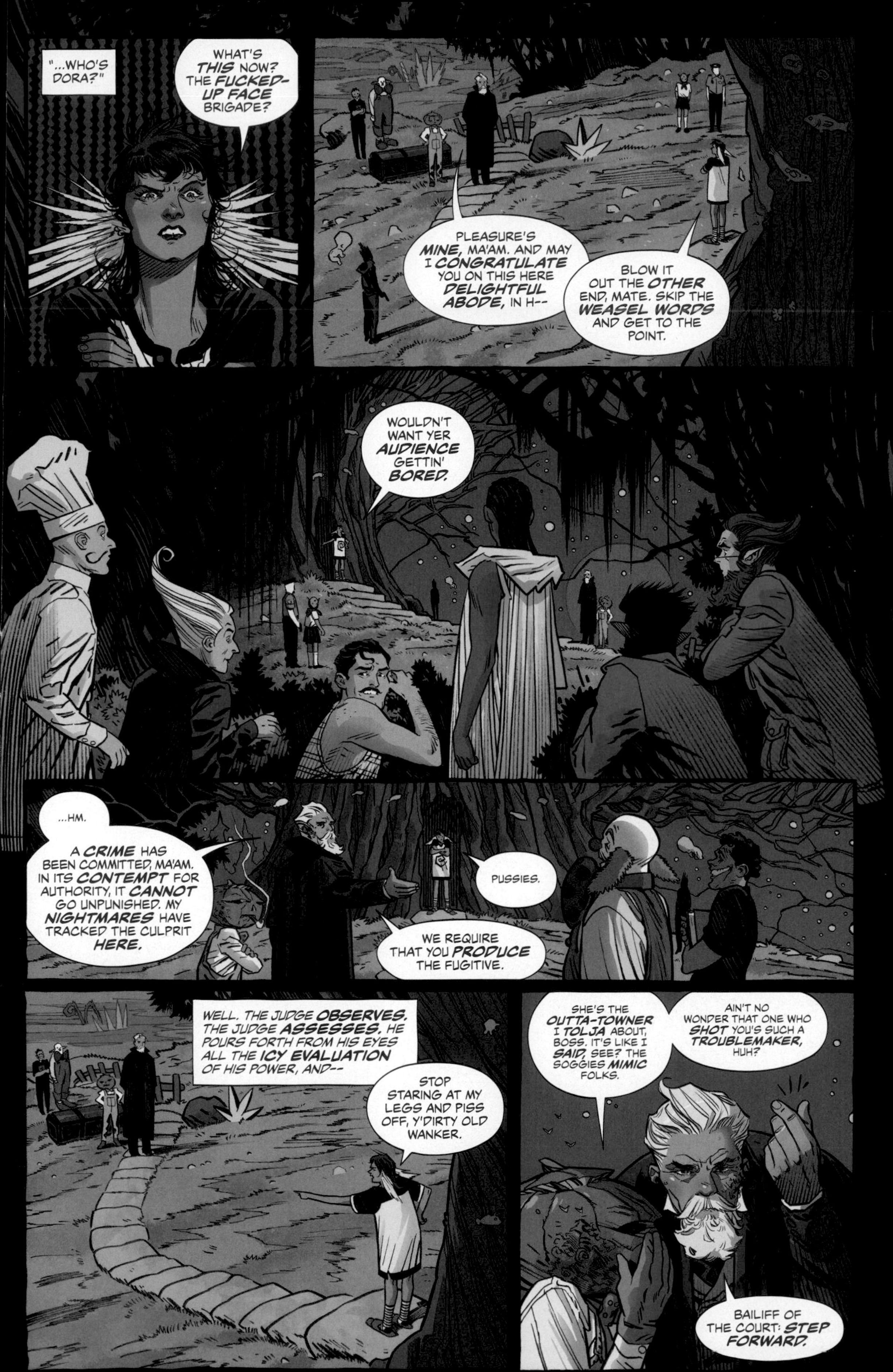

"...WHO'S DORA?"
WHAT'S THIS NOW? THE FUCKED-UP FACE BRIGADE?
PLEASURE'S MINE, MA'AM. AND MAY I CONGRATULATE YOU ON THIS HERE DELIGHTFUL ABODE, IN H--
BLOW IT OUT THE OTHER END, MATE. SKIP THE WEASEL WORDS AND GET TO THE POINT.
WOULDN'T WANT YER AUDIENCE GETTIN' BORED.
...HM.
A CRIME HAS BEEN COMMITTED, MA'AM. IN ITS CONTEMPT FOR AUTHORITY, IT CANNOT GO UNPUNISHED. MY NIGHTMARES HAVE TRACKED THE CULPRIT HERE.
PUSSIES.
WE REQUIRE THAT YOU PRODUCE THE FUGITIVE.
WELL. THE JUDGE OBSERVES. THE JUDGE ASSESSES. HE POURS FORTH FROM HIS EYES ALL THE ICY EVALUATION OF HIS POWER, AND--
STOP STARING AT MY LEGS AND PISS OFF, Y'DIRTY OLD WANKER.
SHE'S THE OUTTA-TOWNER I TOLJA ABOUT, BOSS. IT'S LIKE I SAID, SEE? THE SOGGIES MIMIC FOLKS.
AIN'T NO WONDER THAT ONE WHO SHOT YOU'S SUCH A TROUBLEMAKER, HUH?
BAILIFF OF THE COURT: STEP FORWARD.

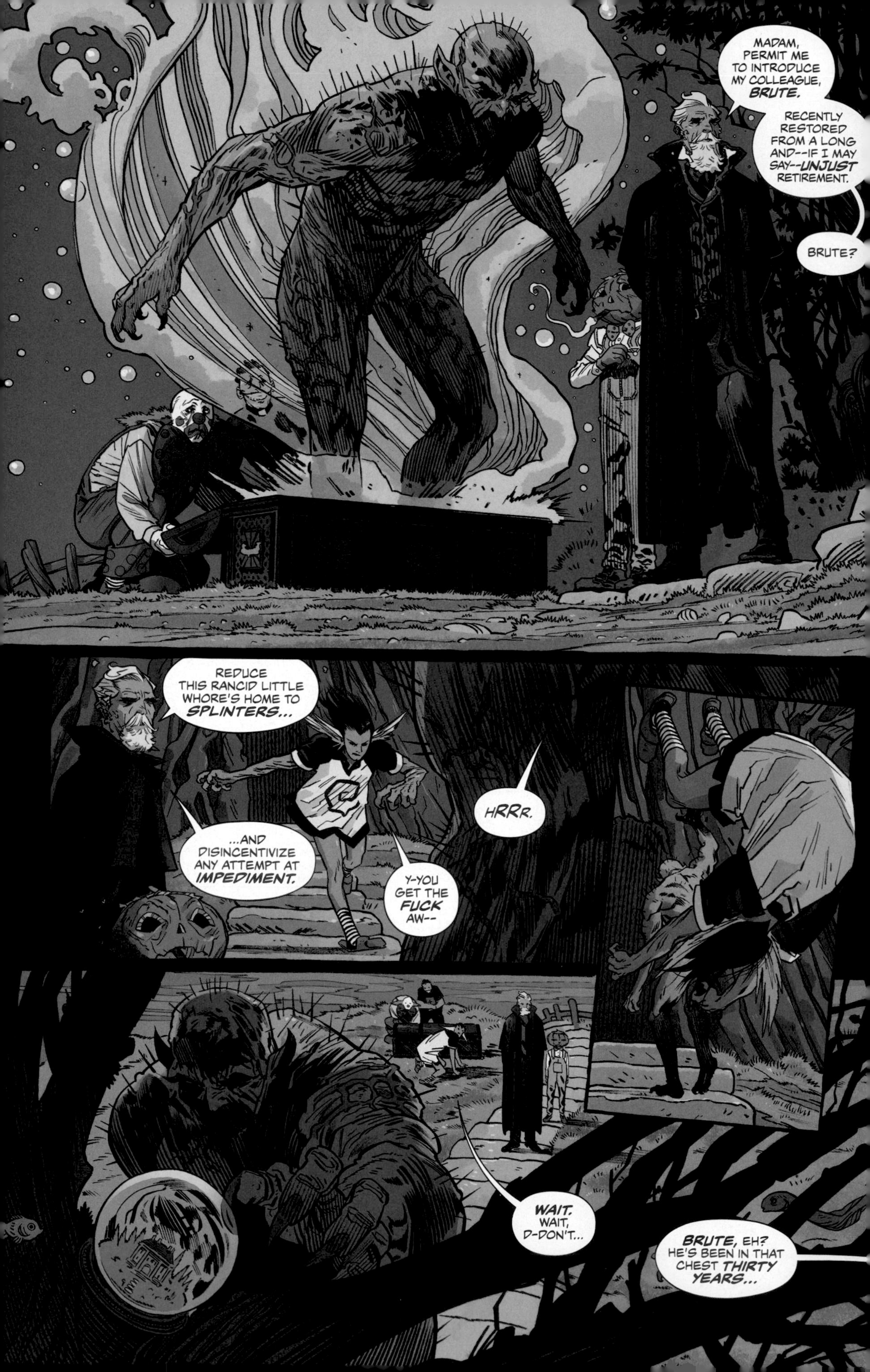
MADAM, PERMIT ME TO INTRODUCE MY COLLEAGUE, BRUTE.
RECENTLY RESTORED FROM A LONG AND--IF I MAY SAY--UNJUST RETIREMENT.
BRUTE?
REDUCE THIS RANCID LITTLE WHORE'S HOME TO SPLINTERS...
...AND DISINCENTIVIZE ANY ATTEMPT AT IMPEDIMENT.
Y-YOU GET THE FUCK AW--
HRRR.
WAIT. WAIT, D-DON'T...
BRUTE, EH? HE'S BEEN IN THAT CHEST THIRTY YEARS...

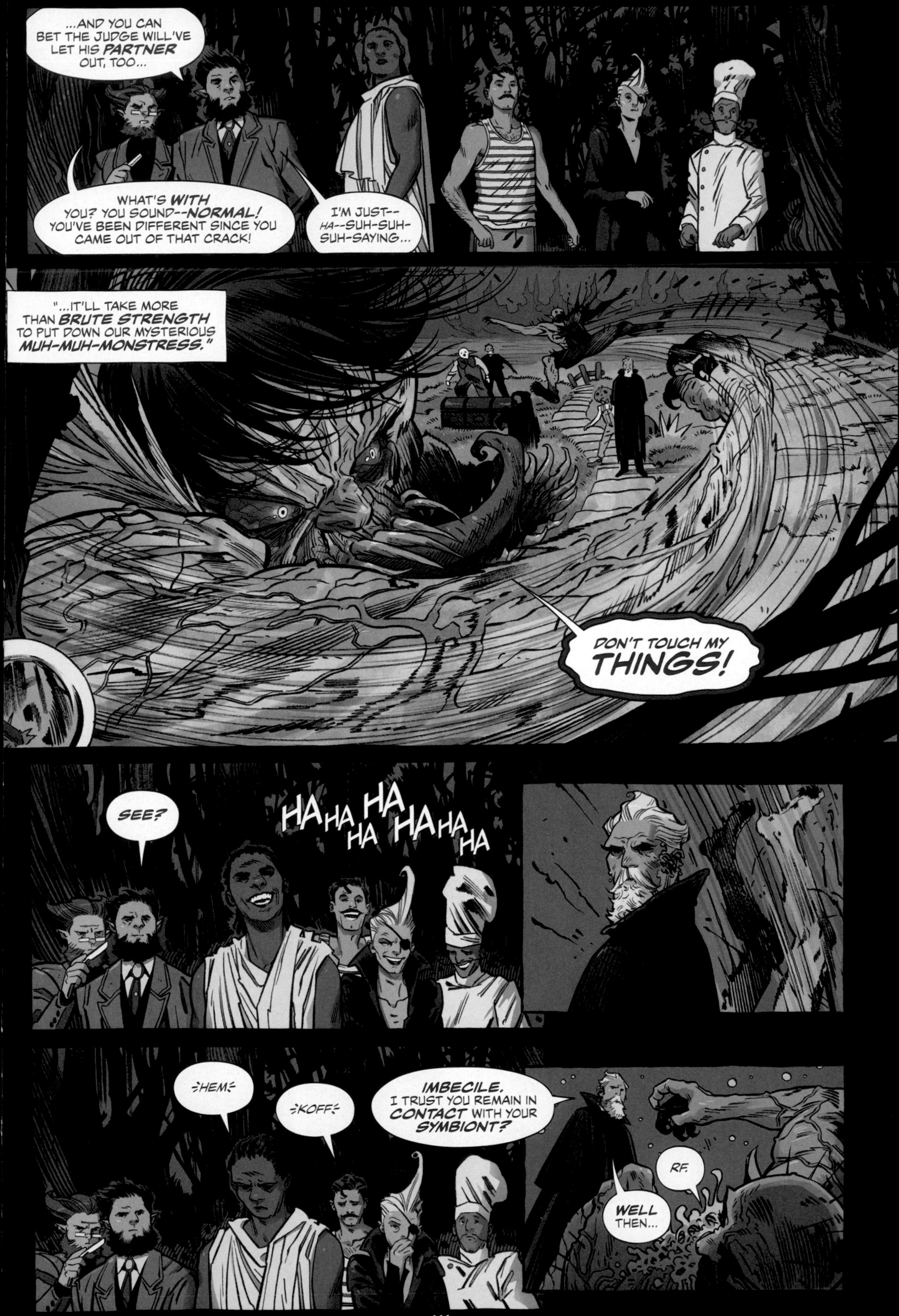

...AND YOU CAN BET THE JUDGE WILL'VE LET HIS PARTNER OUT, TOO...
WHAT'S WITH YOU? YOU SOUND--NORMAL! YOU'VE BEEN DIFFERENT SINCE YOU CAME OUT OF THAT CRACK!
I'M JUST-- HA--SUH-SUH-SUH-SAYING...
"...IT'LL TAKE MORE THAN BRUTE STRENGTH TO PUT DOWN OUR MYSTERIOUS MUH-MUH-MONSTRESS."
DON'T TOUCH MY THINGS!
SEE?
HAHAHA HA HAHAHA HA
:HEM:
:KOFF:
IMBECILE. I TRUST YOU REMAIN IN CONTACT WITH YOUR SYMBIONT?
RF.
WELL THEN...

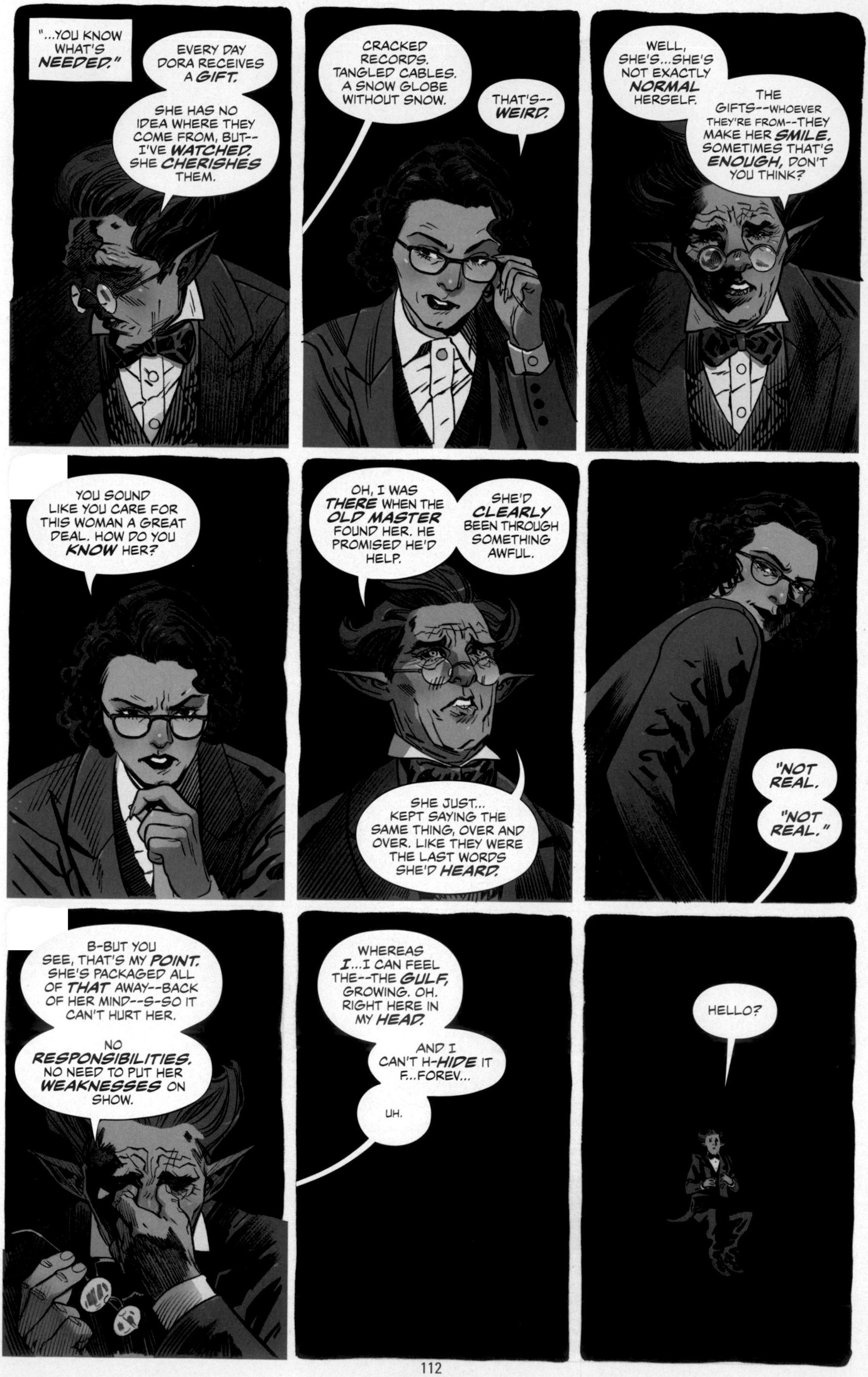
"...YOU KNOW WHAT'S NEEDED."
EVERY DAY DORA RECEIVES A GIFT.
SHE HAS NO IDEA WHERE THEY COME FROM, BUT-- I'VE WATCHED. SHE CHERISHES THEM.
CRACKED RECORDS. TANGLED CABLES. A SNOW GLOBE WITHOUT SNOW.
THAT'S-- WEIRD.
WELL, SHE'S...SHE'S NOT EXACTLY NORMAL HERSELF.
THE GIFTS--WHOEVER THEY'RE FROM--THEY MAKE HER SMILE. SOMETIMES THAT'S ENOUGH, DON'T YOU THINK?
YOU SOUND LIKE YOU CARE FOR THIS WOMAN A GREAT DEAL. HOW DO YOU KNOW HER?
OH, I WAS THERE WHEN THE OLD MASTER FOUND HER. HE PROMISED HE'D HELP.
SHE'D CLEARLY BEEN THROUGH SOMETHING AWFUL.
SHE JUST... KEPT SAYING THE SAME THING, OVER AND OVER. LIKE THEY WERE THE LAST WORDS SHE'D HEARD.
"NOT REAL.
"NOT REAL."
B-BUT YOU SEE, THAT'S MY POINT. SHE'S PACKAGED ALL OF THAT AWAY--BACK OF HER MIND--S-SO IT CAN'T HURT HER.
NO RESPONSIBILITIES. NO NEED TO PUT HER WEAKNESSES ON SHOW.
WHEREAS I...I CAN FEEL THE--THE GULF, GROWING. OH. RIGHT HERE IN MY HEAD.
AND I CAN'T H-HIDE IT F...FOREV...
UH.
HELLO?

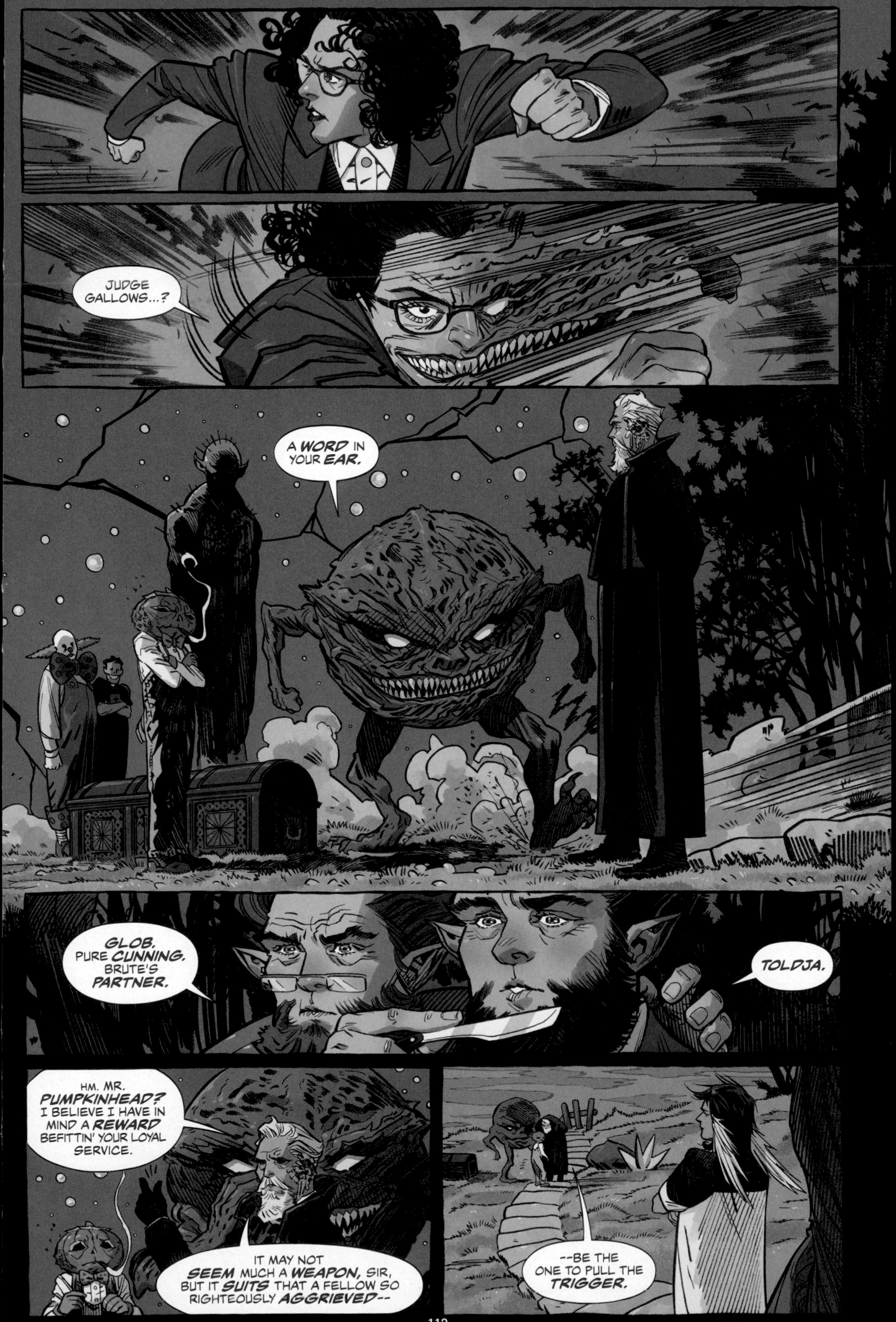
JUDGE GALLOWS...?
A WORD IN YOUR EAR.
GLOB. PURE CUNNING. BRUTE'S PARTNER.
TOLDJA.
HM. MR. PUMPKINHEAD? I BELIEVE I HAVE IN MIND A REWARD BEFITTIN' YOUR LOYAL SERVICE.
IT MAY NOT SEEM MUCH A WEAPON, SIR, BUT IT SUITS THAT A FELLOW SO RIGHTEOUSLY AGGRIEVED--
--BE THE ONE TO PULL THE TRIGGER.

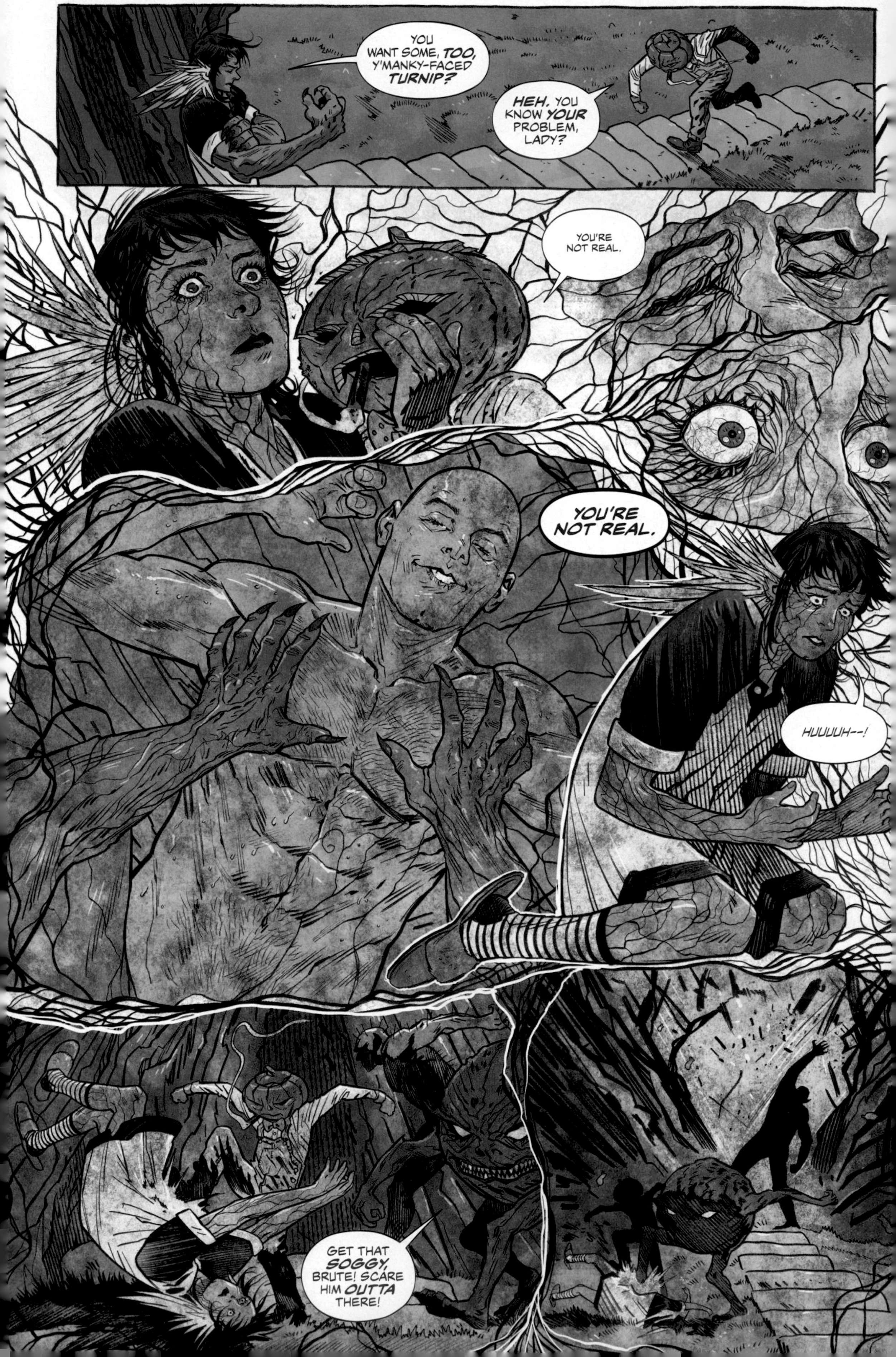
YOU WANT SOME, TOO, Y'MANKY-FACED TURNIP?
HEH. YOU KNOW YOUR PROBLEM, LADY?
YOU'RE NOT REAL.
YOU'RE NOT REAL.
HUUUUH--!
GET THAT SOGGY, BRUTE! SCARE HIM OUTTA THERE!

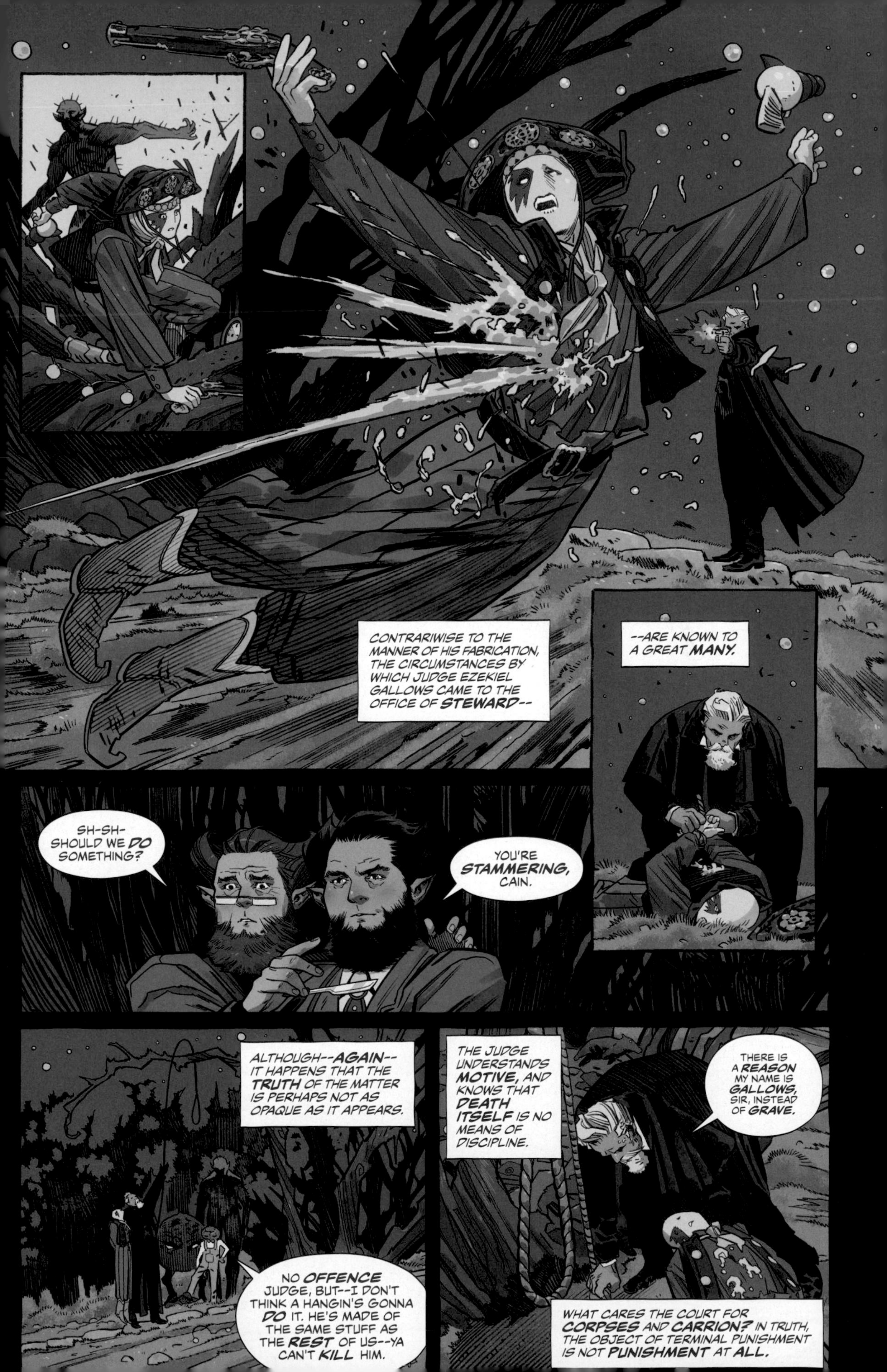
CONTRARIWISE TO THE MANNER OF HIS FABRICATION, THE CIRCUMSTANCES BY WHICH JUDGE EZEKIEL GALLOWS CAME TO THE OFFICE OF STEWARD--
--ARE KNOWN TO A GREAT MANY.
SH-SH-SHOULD WE DO SOMETHING?
YOU'RE STAMMERING, CAIN.
ALTHOUGH--AGAIN--IT HAPPENS THAT THE TRUTH OF THE MATTER IS PERHAPS NOT AS OPAQUE AS IT APPEARS.
NO OFFENCE JUDGE, BUT--I DON'T THINK A HANGIN'S GONNA DO IT. HE'S MADE OF THE SAME STUFF AS THE REST OF US--YA CAN'T KILL HIM.
THE JUDGE UNDERSTANDS MOTIVE, AND KNOWS THAT DEATH ITSELF IS NO MEANS OF DISCIPLINE.
THERE IS A REASON MY NAME IS GALLOWS, SIR, INSTEAD OF GRAVE.
WHAT CARES THE COURT FOR CORPSES AND CARRION? IN TRUTH, THE OBJECT OF TERMINAL PUNISHMENT IS NOT PUNISHMENT AT ALL.

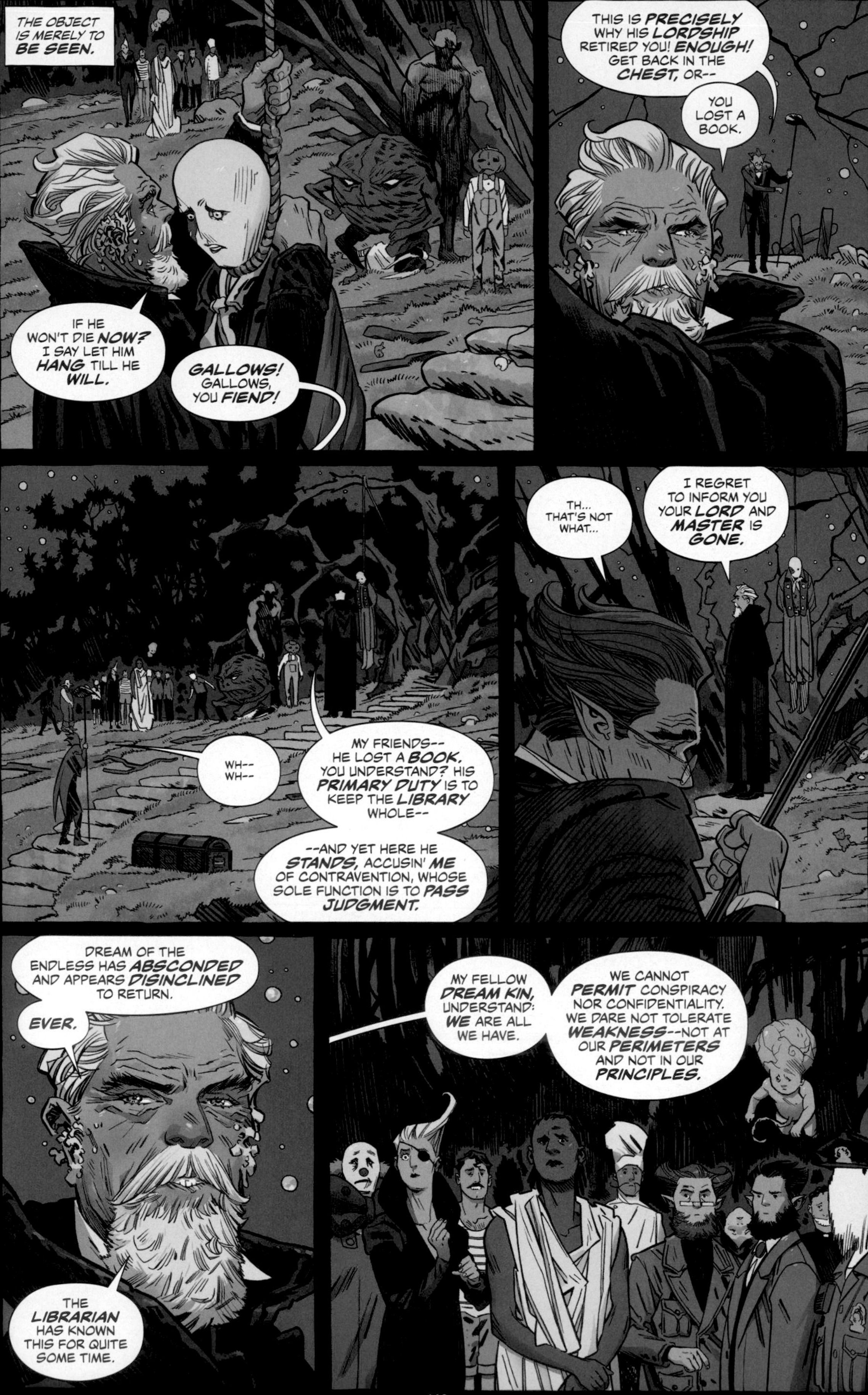
THE OBJECT IS MERELY TO BE SEEN.
IF HE WON'T DIE NOW? I SAY LET HIM HANG TILL HE WILL.
GALLOWS! GALLOWS, YOU FIEND!
THIS IS PRECISELY WHY HIS LORDSHIP RETIRED YOU! ENOUGH! GET BACK IN THE CHEST, OR--
YOU LOST A BOOK.
WH-- WH--
MY FRIENDS-- HE LOST A BOOK. YOU UNDERSTAND? HIS PRIMARY DUTY IS TO KEEP THE LIBRARY WHOLE--
--AND YET HERE HE STANDS, ACCUSIN' ME OF CONTRAVENTION, WHOSE SOLE FUNCTION IS TO PASS JUDGMENT.
TH... THAT'S NOT WHAT...
I REGRET TO INFORM YOU YOUR LORD AND MASTER IS GONE.
DREAM OF THE ENDLESS HAS ABSCONDED AND APPEARS DISINCLINED TO RETURN.
EVER.
THE LIBRARIAN HAS KNOWN THIS FOR QUITE SOME TIME.
MY FELLOW DREAM KIN, UNDERSTAND: WE ARE ALL WE HAVE.
WE CANNOT PERMIT CONSPIRACY NOR CONFIDENTIALITY. WE DARE NOT TOLERATE WEAKNESS--NOT AT OUR PERIMETERS AND NOT IN OUR PRINCIPLES.

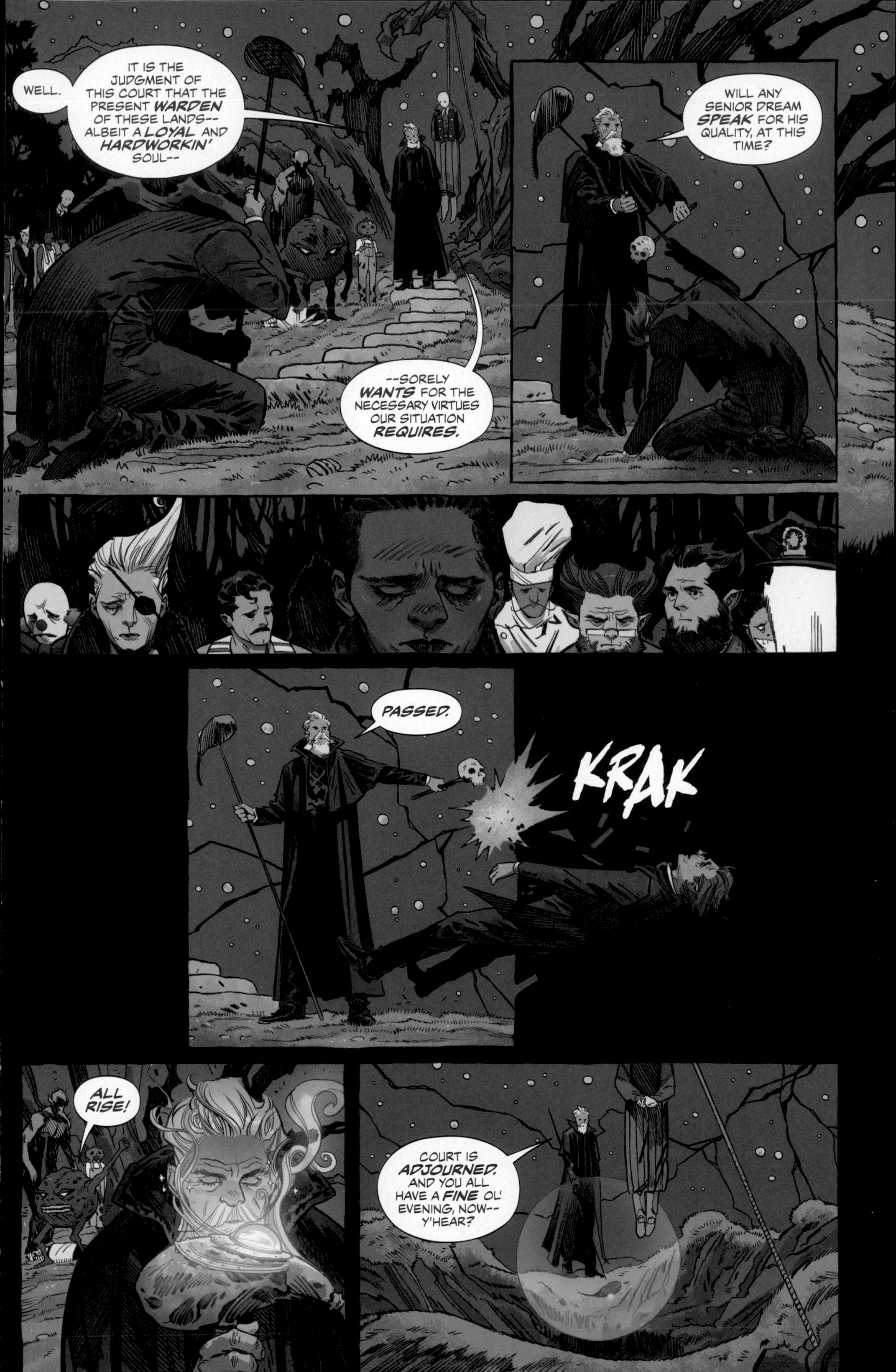
WELL.
IT IS THE JUDGMENT OF THIS COURT THAT THE PRESENT WARDEN OF THESE LANDS-- ALBEIT A LOYAL AND HARDWORKIN' SOUL--
--SORELY WANTS FOR THE NECESSARY VIRTUES OUR SITUATION REQUIRES.
WILL ANY SENIOR DREAM SPEAK FOR HIS QUALITY, AT THIS TIME?
PASSED.
KRAK
ALL RISE!
COURT IS ADJOURNED. AND YOU ALL HAVE A FINE OL' EVENING, NOW-- Y'HEAR?

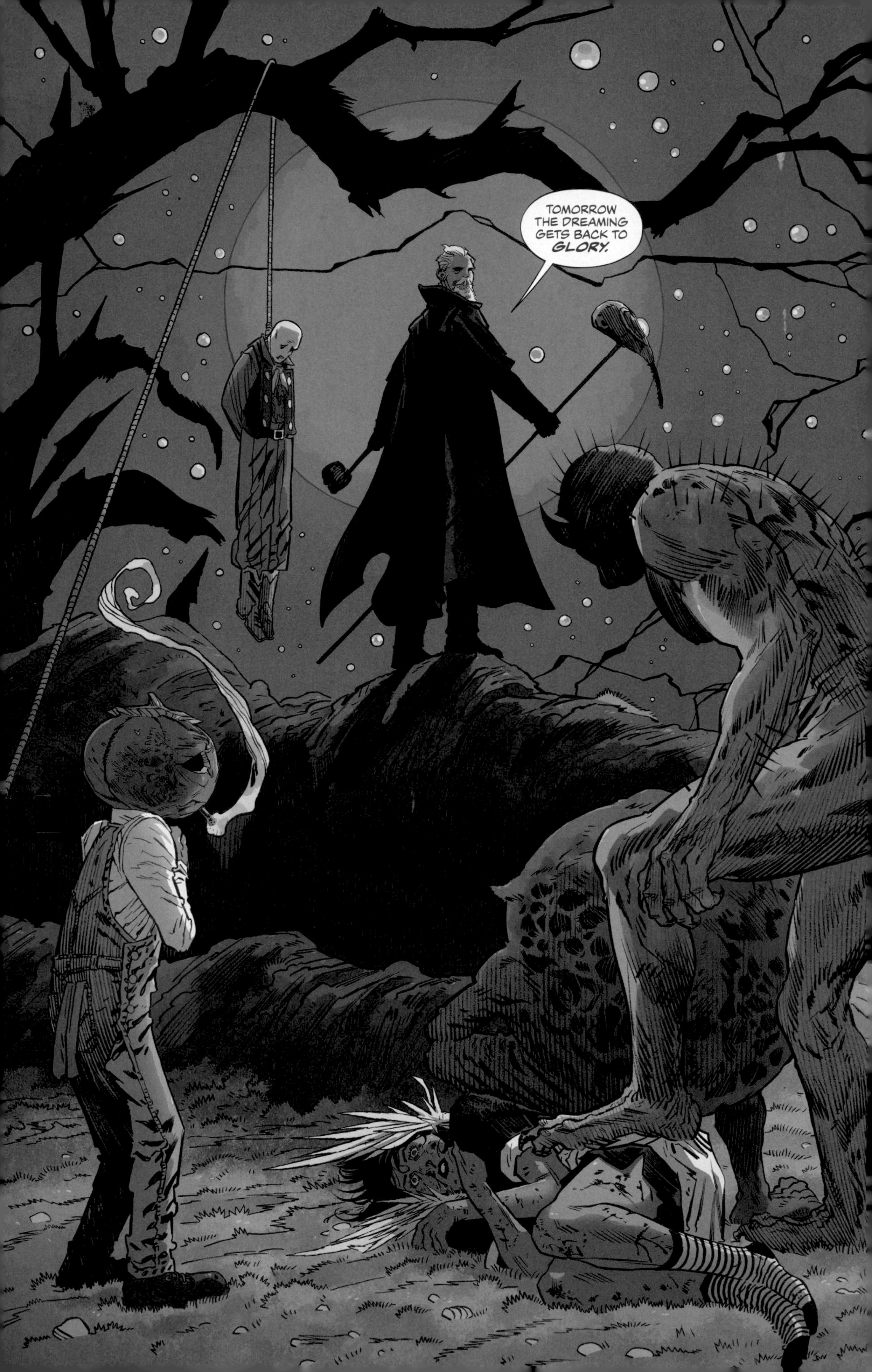
TOMORROW THE DREAMING GETS BACK TO GLORY.

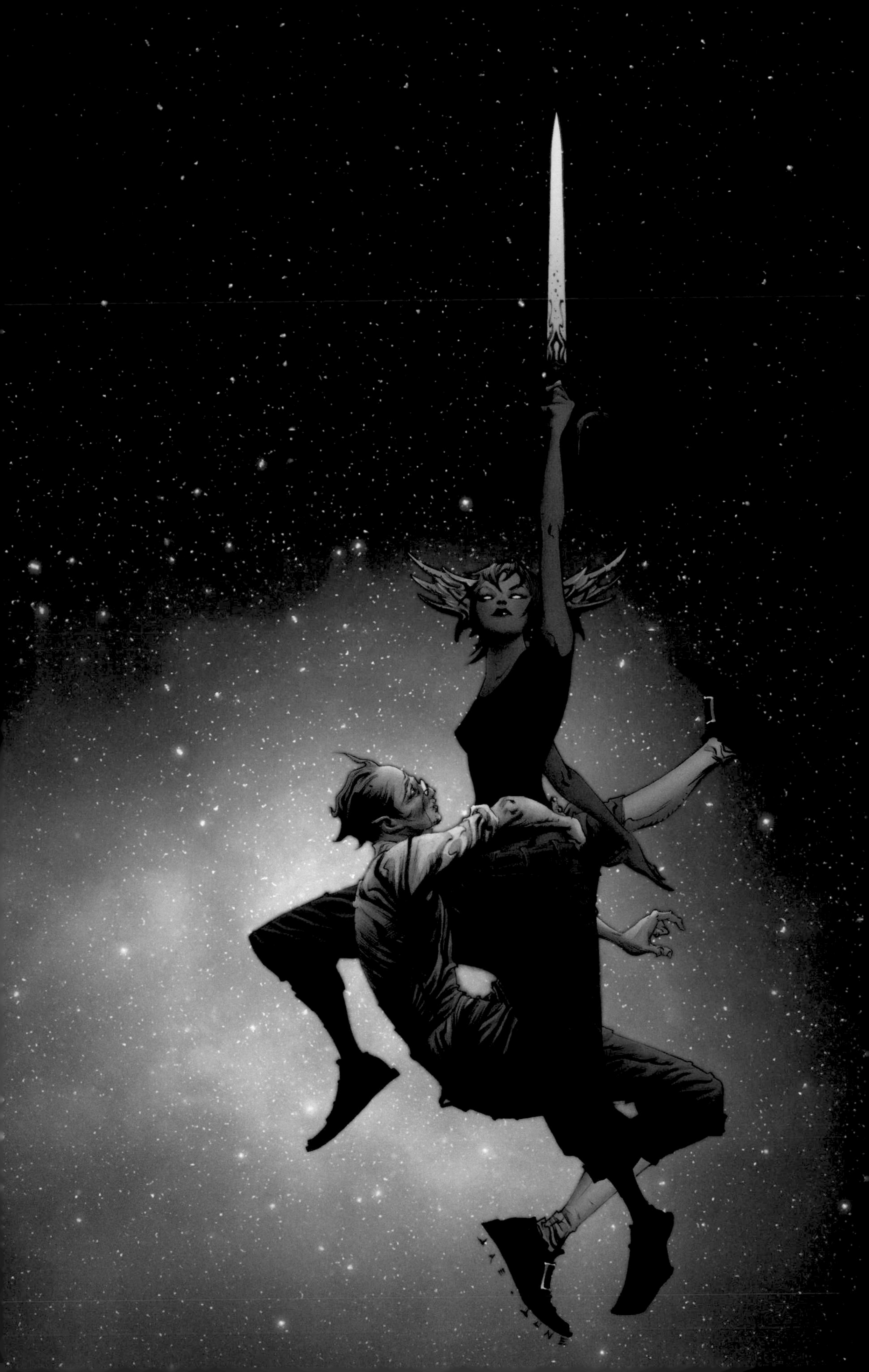

The Dreaming

Eternity

WRITTEN BY
Simon Spurrier

ILLUSTRATED BY
Bilquis Evely

COLORS BY
Mat Lopes

LETTERS BY
Simon Bowland

COVER ART BY
Jae Lee and *June Chung*

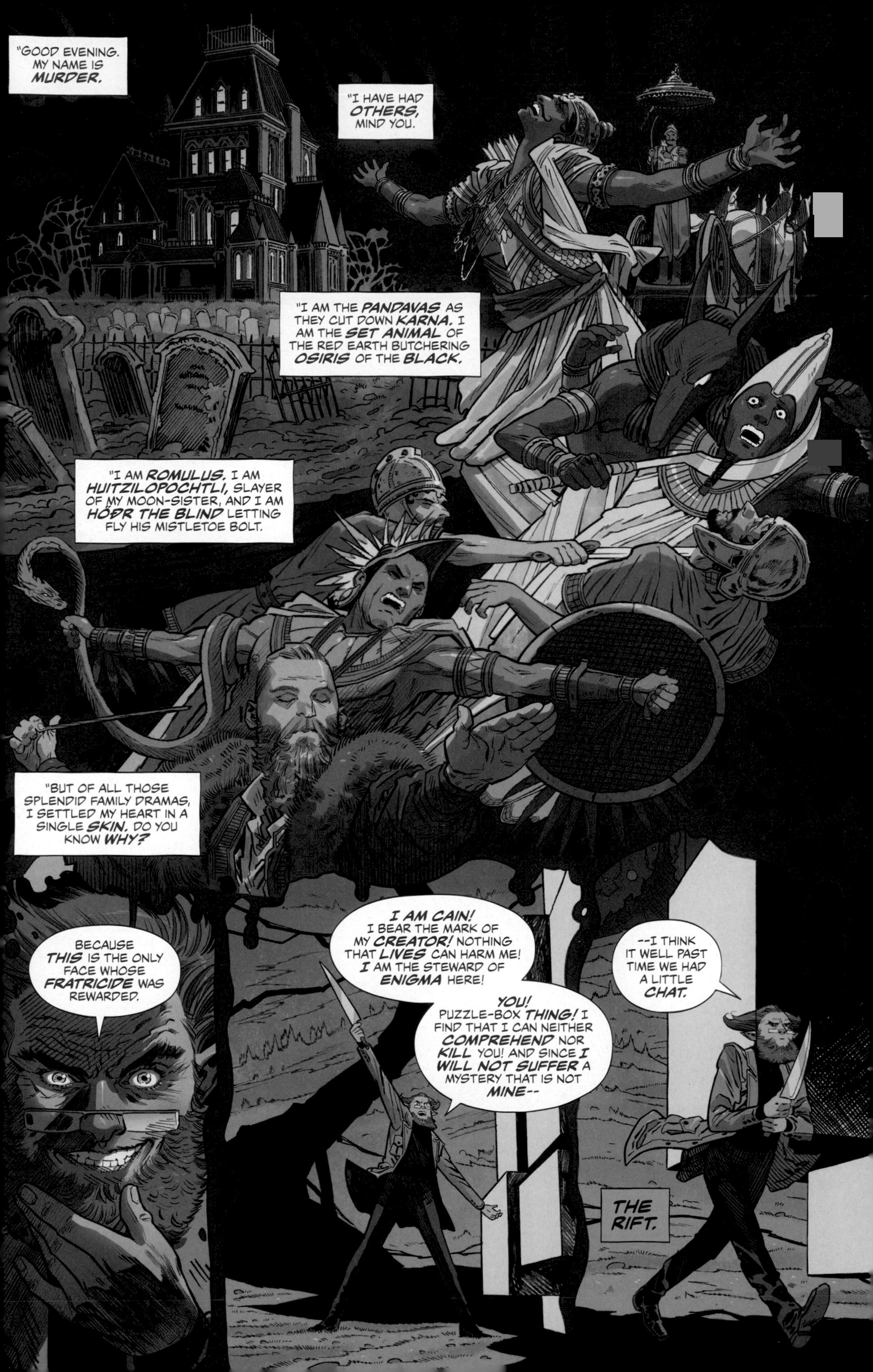
"GOOD EVENING. MY NAME IS MURDER.
"I HAVE HAD OTHERS, MIND YOU.
"I AM THE PANDAVAS AS THEY CUT DOWN KARNA. I AM THE SET ANIMAL OF THE RED EARTH BUTCHERING OSIRIS OF THE BLACK.
"I AM ROMULUS. I AM HUITZILOPOCHTLI, SLAYER OF MY MOON-SISTER, AND I AM HÖDR THE BLIND LETTING FLY HIS MISTLETOE BOLT.
"BUT OF ALL THOSE SPLENDID FAMILY DRAMAS, I SETTLED MY HEART IN A SINGLE SKIN. DO YOU KNOW WHY?
BECAUSE THIS IS THE ONLY FACE WHOSE FRATRICIDE WAS REWARDED.
I AM CAIN! I BEAR THE MARK OF MY CREATOR! NOTHING THAT LIVES CAN HARM ME! I AM THE STEWARD OF ENIGMA HERE!
YOU! PUZZLE-BOX THING! I FIND THAT I CAN NEITHER COMPREHEND NOR KILL YOU! AND SINCE I WILL NOT SUFFER A MYSTERY THAT IS NOT MINE--
--I THINK IT WELL PAST TIME WE HAD A LITTLE CHAT.
THE RIFT.

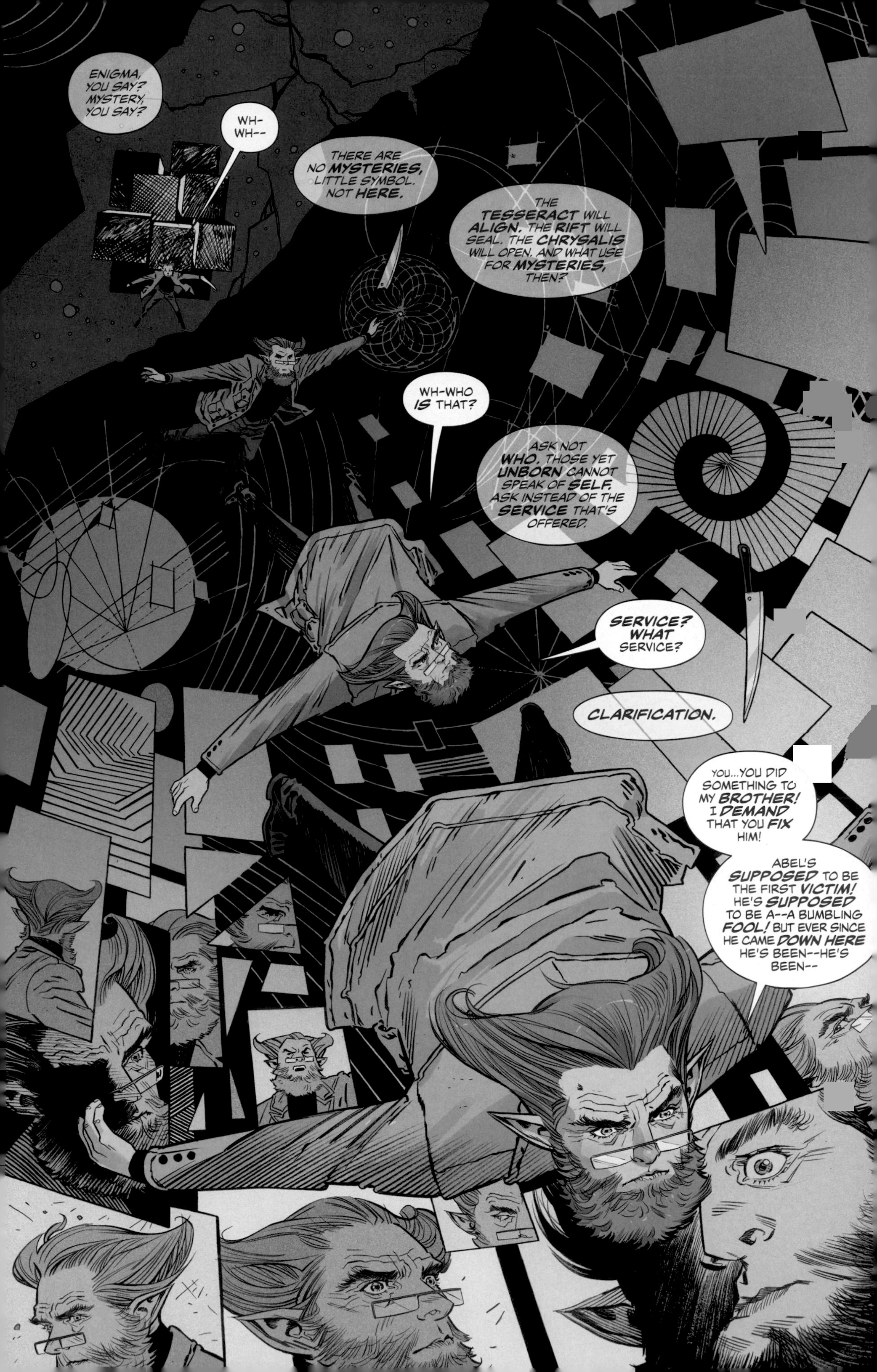
ENIGMA, YOU SAY? MYSTERY, YOU SAY?
WH- WH--
THERE ARE NO MYSTERIES, LITTLE SYMBOL. NOT HERE.
THE TESSERACT WILL ALIGN. THE RIFT WILL SEAL. THE CHRYSALIS WILL OPEN. AND WHAT USE FOR MYSTERIES, THEN?
WH-WHO IS THAT?
ASK NOT WHO. THOSE YET UNBORN CANNOT SPEAK OF SELF. ASK INSTEAD OF THE SERVICE THAT'S OFFERED.
SERVICE? WHAT SERVICE?
CLARIFICATION.
YOU...YOU DID SOMETHING TO MY BROTHER! I DEMAND THAT YOU FIX HIM!
ABEL'S SUPPOSED TO BE THE FIRST VICTIM! HE'S SUPPOSED TO BE A--A BUMBLING FOOL! BUT EVER SINCE HE CAME DOWN HERE HE'S BEEN--HE'S BEEN--

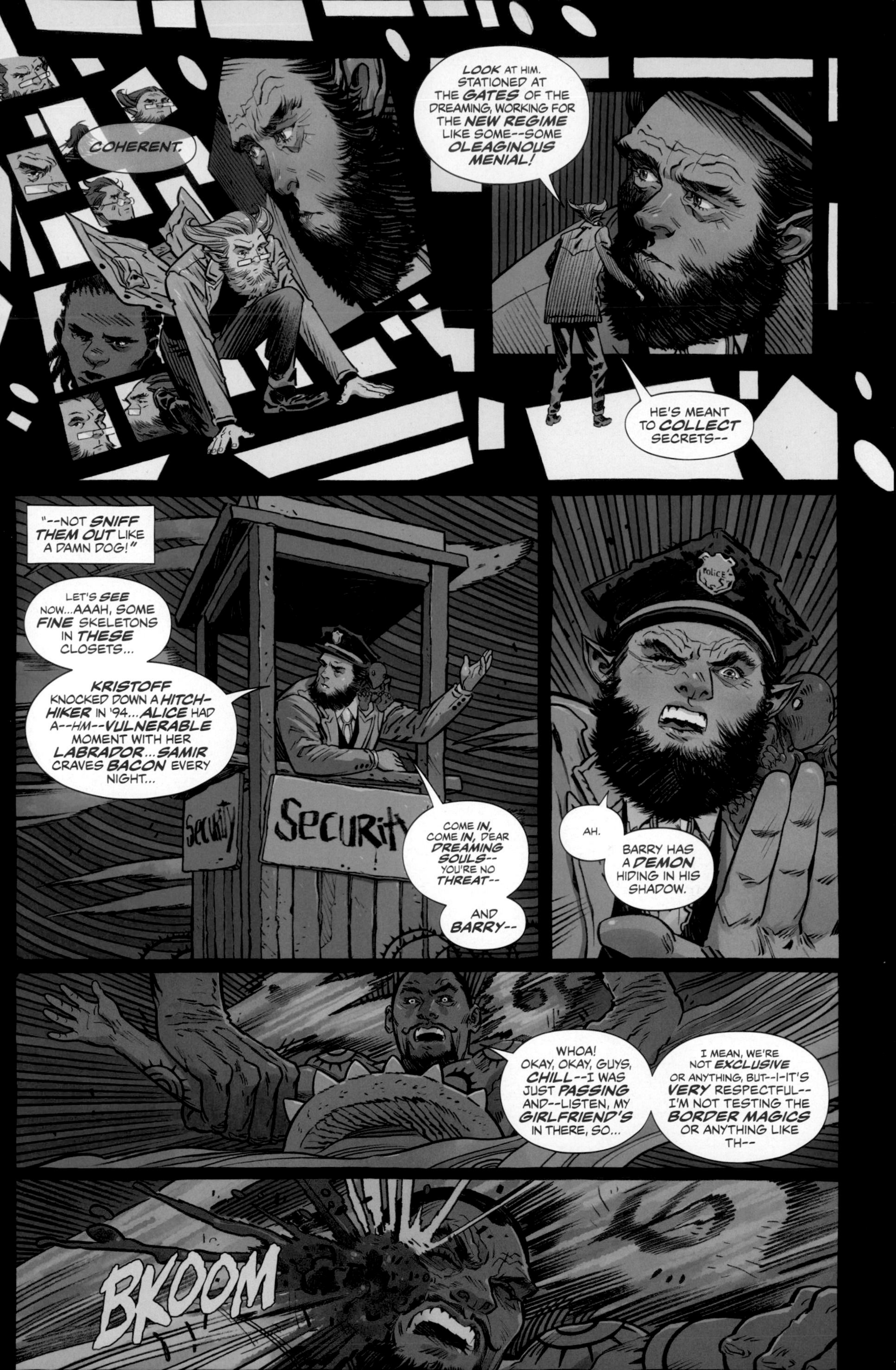
COHERENT.
LOOK AT HIM. STATIONED AT THE GATES OF THE DREAMING, WORKING FOR THE NEW REGIME LIKE SOME--SOME OLEAGINOUS MENIAL!
HE'S MEANT TO COLLECT SECRETS--
"--NOT SNIFF THEM OUT LIKE A DAMN DOG!"
LET'S SEE NOW...AAAH, SOME FINE SKELETONS IN THESE CLOSETS...
KRISTOFF KNOCKED DOWN A HITCH-HIKER IN '94...ALICE HAD A--HM--VULNERABLE MOMENT WITH HER LABRADOR...SAMIR CRAVES BACON EVERY NIGHT...
Security
Security
COME IN, COME IN, DEAR DREAMING SOULS--YOU'RE NO THREAT--
AND BARRY--
POLICE
AH.
BARRY HAS A DEMON HIDING IN HIS SHADOW.
WHOA! OKAY, OKAY, GUYS, CHILL--I WAS JUST PASSING AND--LISTEN, MY GIRLFRIEND'S IN THERE, SO...
I MEAN, WE'RE NOT EXCLUSIVE OR ANYTHING, BUT--I-IT'S VERY RESPECTFUL--I'M NOT TESTING THE BORDER MAGICS OR ANYTHING LIKE TH--
BKOOM

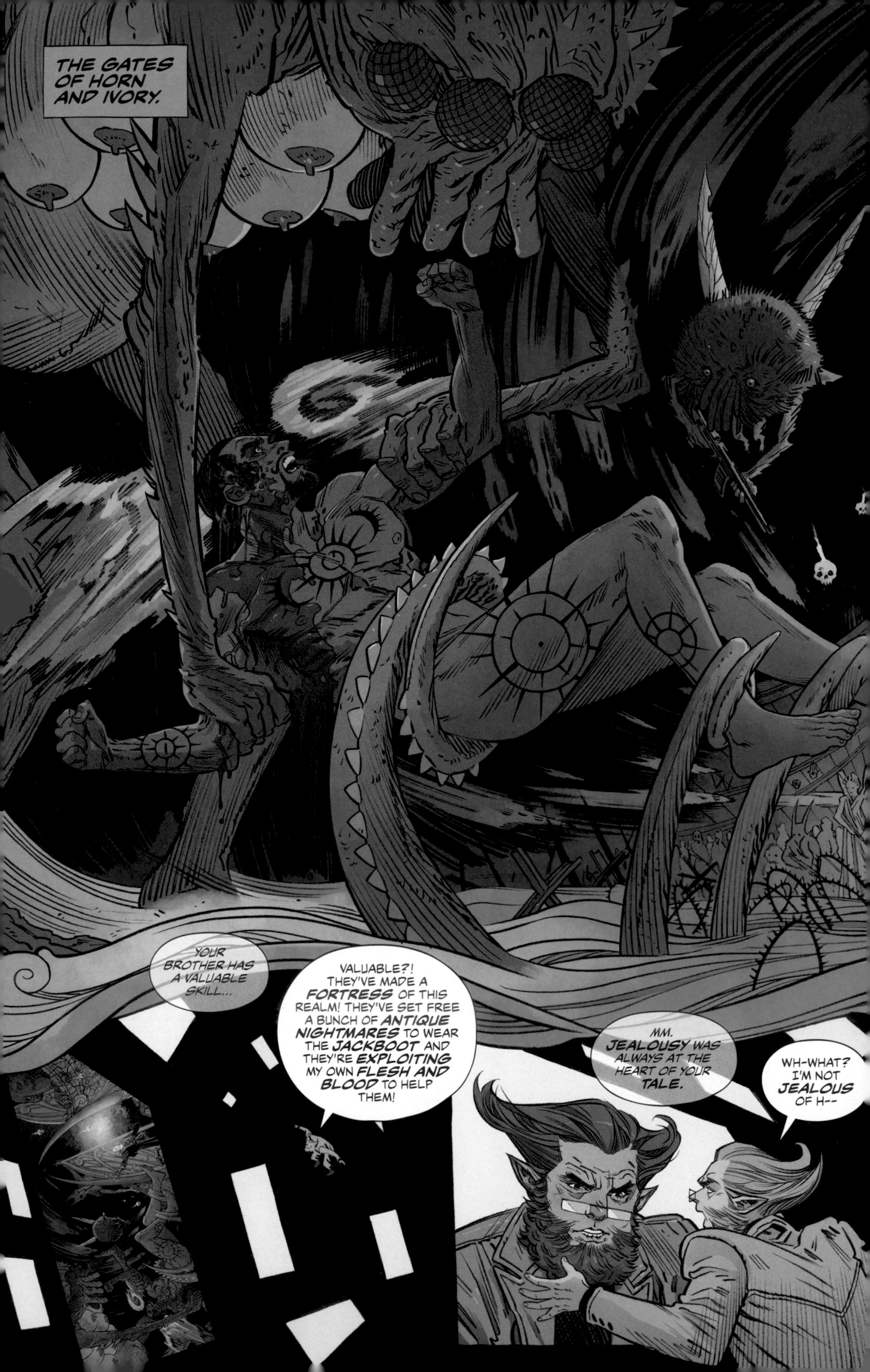
THE GATES OF HORN AND IVORY.
YOUR BROTHER HAS A VALUABLE SKILL...
VALUABLE?! THEY'VE MADE A FORTRESS OF THIS REALM! THEY'VE SET FREE A BUNCH OF ANTIQUE NIGHTMARES TO WEAR THE JACKBOOT AND THEY'RE EXPLOITING MY OWN FLESH AND BLOOD TO HELP THEM!
MM. JEALOUSY WAS ALWAYS AT THE HEART OF YOUR TALE.
WH-WHAT? I'M NOT JEALOUS OF H--

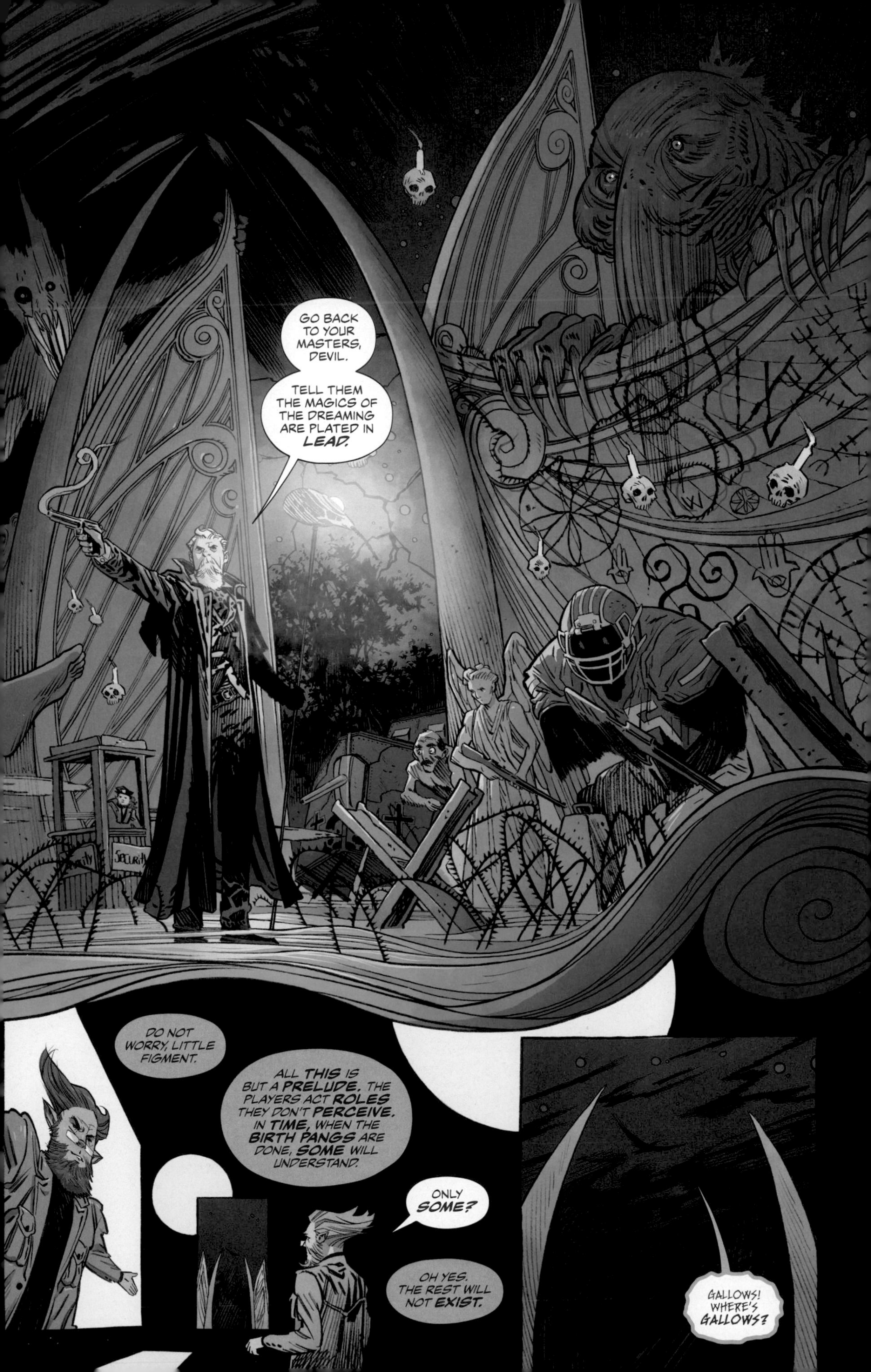
GO BACK TO YOUR MASTERS, DEVIL.
TELL THEM THE MAGICS OF THE DREAMING ARE PLATED IN **LEAD.**
Security
DO NOT WORRY, LITTLE FIGMENT.
ALL **THIS** IS BUT A **PRELUDE.** THE PLAYERS ACT **ROLES** THEY DON'T **PERCEIVE.** IN **TIME,** WHEN THE **BIRTH PANGS** ARE DONE, **SOME** WILL UNDERSTAND.
ONLY **SOME?**
OH YES. THE REST WILL NOT **EXIST.**
GALLOWS! WHERE'S **GALLOWS?**

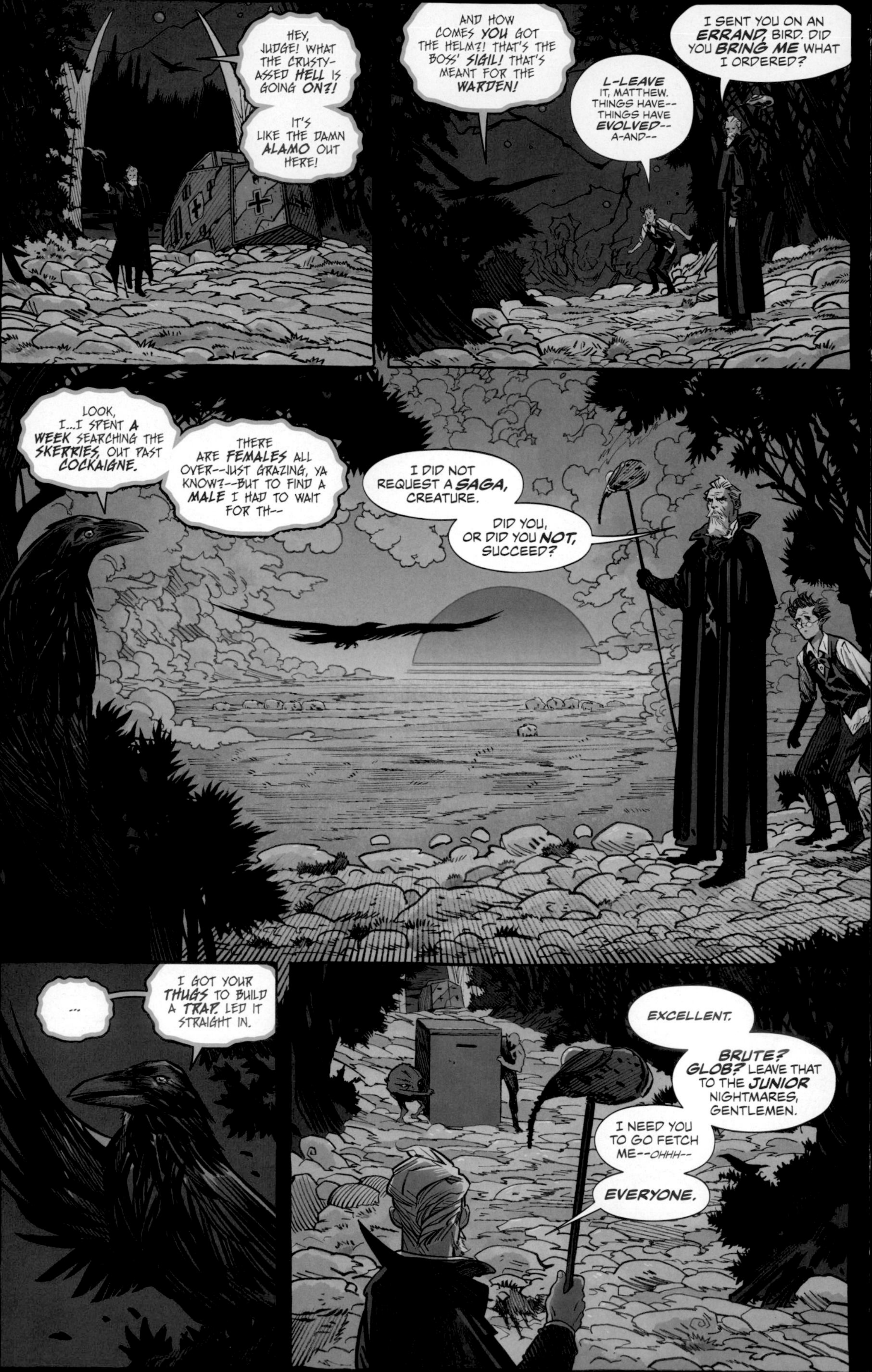
HEY, JUDGE! WHAT THE CRUSTY-ASSED HELL IS GOING ON?!
IT'S LIKE THE DAMN ALAMO OUT HERE!
AND HOW COMES YOU GOT THE HELM?! THAT'S THE BOSS' SIGIL! THAT'S MEANT FOR THE WARDEN!
L-LEAVE IT, MATTHEW. THINGS HAVE-- THINGS HAVE EVOLVED-- A-AND--
I SENT YOU ON AN ERRAND, BIRD. DID YOU BRING ME WHAT I ORDERED?
LOOK, I...I SPENT A WEEK SEARCHING THE SKERRIES, OUT PAST COCKAIGNE.
THERE ARE FEMALES ALL OVER--JUST GRAZING, YA KNOW?--BUT TO FIND A MALE I HAD TO WAIT FOR TH--
I DID NOT REQUEST A SAGA, CREATURE.
DID YOU, OR DID YOU NOT, SUCCEED?
...
I GOT YOUR THUGS TO BUILD A TRAP. LED IT STRAIGHT IN.
EXCELLENT.
BRUTE? GLOB? LEAVE THAT TO THE JUNIOR NIGHTMARES, GENTLEMEN.
I NEED YOU TO GO FETCH ME--OHHH--
EVERYONE.

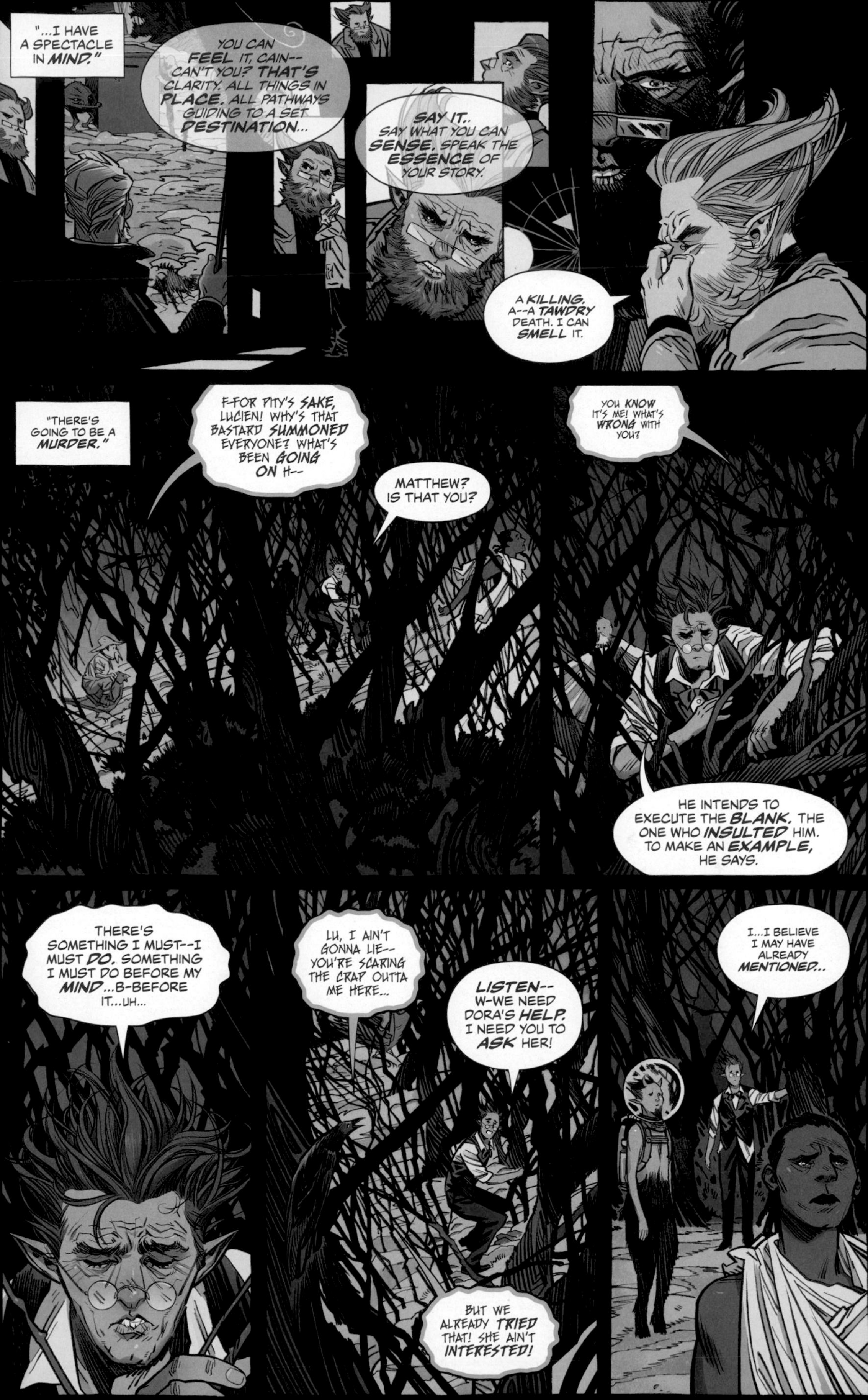
"...I HAVE A SPECTACLE IN MIND."
YOU CAN FEEL IT, CAIN-- CAN'T YOU? THAT'S CLARITY. ALL THINGS IN PLACE. ALL PATHWAYS GUIDING TO A SET DESTINATION...
SAY IT.. SAY WHAT YOU CAN SENSE. SPEAK THE ESSENCE OF YOUR STORY.
A KILLING. A--A TAWDRY DEATH. I CAN SMELL IT.
"THERE'S GOING TO BE A MURDER."
F-FOR PITY'S SAKE, LUCIEN! WHY'S THAT BASTARD SUMMONED EVERYONE? WHAT'S BEEN GOING ON H--
MATTHEW? IS THAT YOU?
YOU KNOW IT'S ME! WHAT'S WRONG WITH YOU?
HE INTENDS TO EXECUTE THE BLANK, THE ONE WHO INSULTED HIM. TO MAKE AN EXAMPLE, HE SAYS.
THERE'S SOMETHING I MUST--I MUST DO. SOMETHING I MUST DO BEFORE MY MIND...B-BEFORE IT...UH...
LU, I AIN'T GONNA LIE-- YOU'RE SCARING THE CRAP OUTTA ME HERE...
LISTEN-- W-WE NEED DORA'S HELP. I NEED YOU TO ASK HER!
BUT WE ALREADY TRIED THAT! SHE AIN'T INTERESTED!
I...I BELIEVE I MAY HAVE ALREADY MENTIONED...

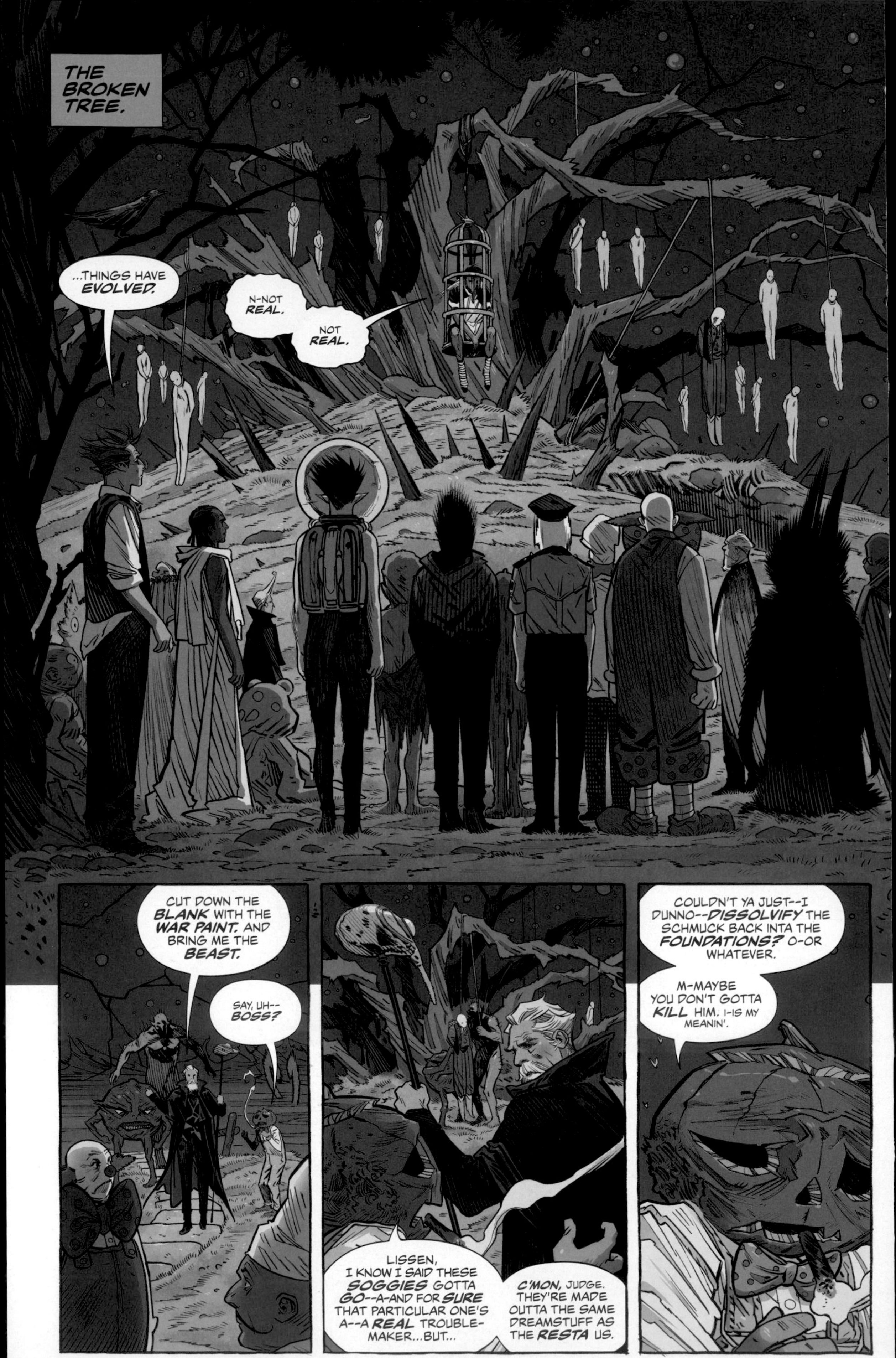
THE BROKEN TREE.
...THINGS HAVE EVOLVED.
N-NOT REAL.
NOT REAL.
CUT DOWN THE BLANK WITH THE WAR PAINT. AND BRING ME THE BEAST.
SAY, UH-- BOSS?
LISSEN, I KNOW I SAID THESE SOGGIES GOTTA GO--A-AND FOR SURE THAT PARTICULAR ONE'S A--A REAL TROUBLE-MAKER...BUT...
C'MON, JUDGE. THEY'RE MADE OUTTA THE SAME DREAMSTUFF AS THE RESTA US.
COULDN'T YA JUST--I DUNNO--DISSOLVIFY THE SCHMUCK BACK INTA THE FOUNDATIONS? O-OR WHATEVER.
M-MAYBE YOU DON'T GOTTA KILL HIM. I-IS MY MEANIN'.

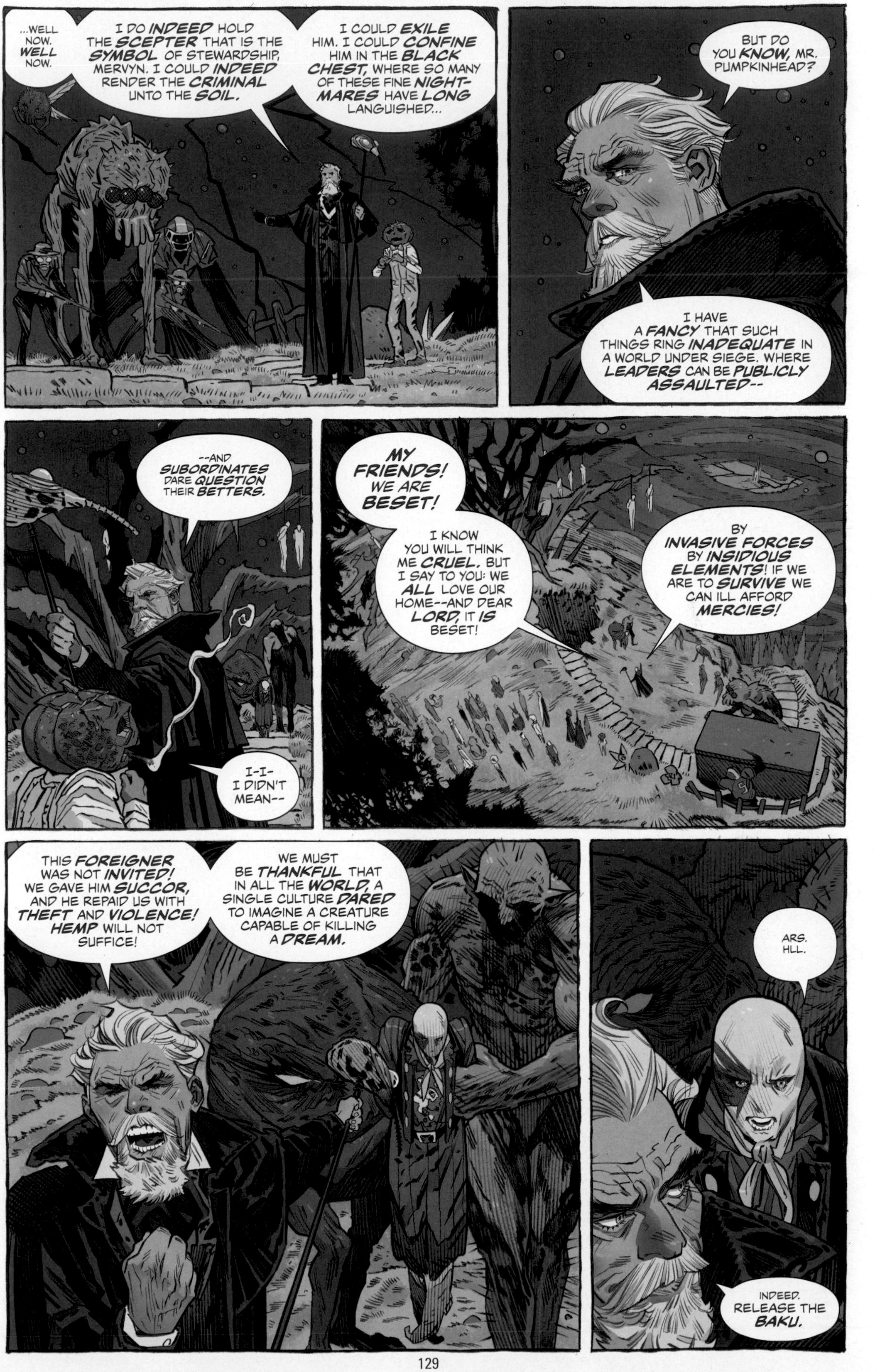
...WELL NOW. WELL NOW.
I DO INDEED HOLD THE SCEPTER THAT IS THE SYMBOL OF STEWARDSHIP, MERVYN. I COULD INDEED RENDER THE CRIMINAL UNTO THE SOIL.
I COULD EXILE HIM. I COULD CONFINE HIM IN THE BLACK CHEST, WHERE SO MANY OF THESE FINE NIGHT-MARES HAVE LONG LANGUISHED...
BUT DO YOU KNOW, MR. PUMPKINHEAD?
I HAVE A FANCY THAT SUCH THINGS RING INADEQUATE IN A WORLD UNDER SIEGE. WHERE LEADERS CAN BE PUBLICLY ASSAULTED--
--AND SUBORDINATES DARE QUESTION THEIR BETTERS.
I-I- I DIDN'T MEAN--
MY FRIENDS! WE ARE BESET!
I KNOW YOU WILL THINK ME CRUEL. BUT I SAY TO YOU: WE ALL LOVE OUR HOME--AND DEAR LORD, IT IS BESET!
BY INVASIVE FORCES BY INSIDIOUS ELEMENTS! IF WE ARE TO SURVIVE WE CAN ILL AFFORD MERCIES!
THIS FOREIGNER WAS NOT INVITED! WE GAVE HIM SUCCOR, AND HE REPAID US WITH THEFT AND VIOLENCE! HEMP WILL NOT SUFFICE!
WE MUST BE THANKFUL THAT IN ALL THE WORLD, A SINGLE CULTURE DARED TO IMAGINE A CREATURE CAPABLE OF KILLING A DREAM.
ARS. HLL.
INDEED. RELEASE THE BAKU.

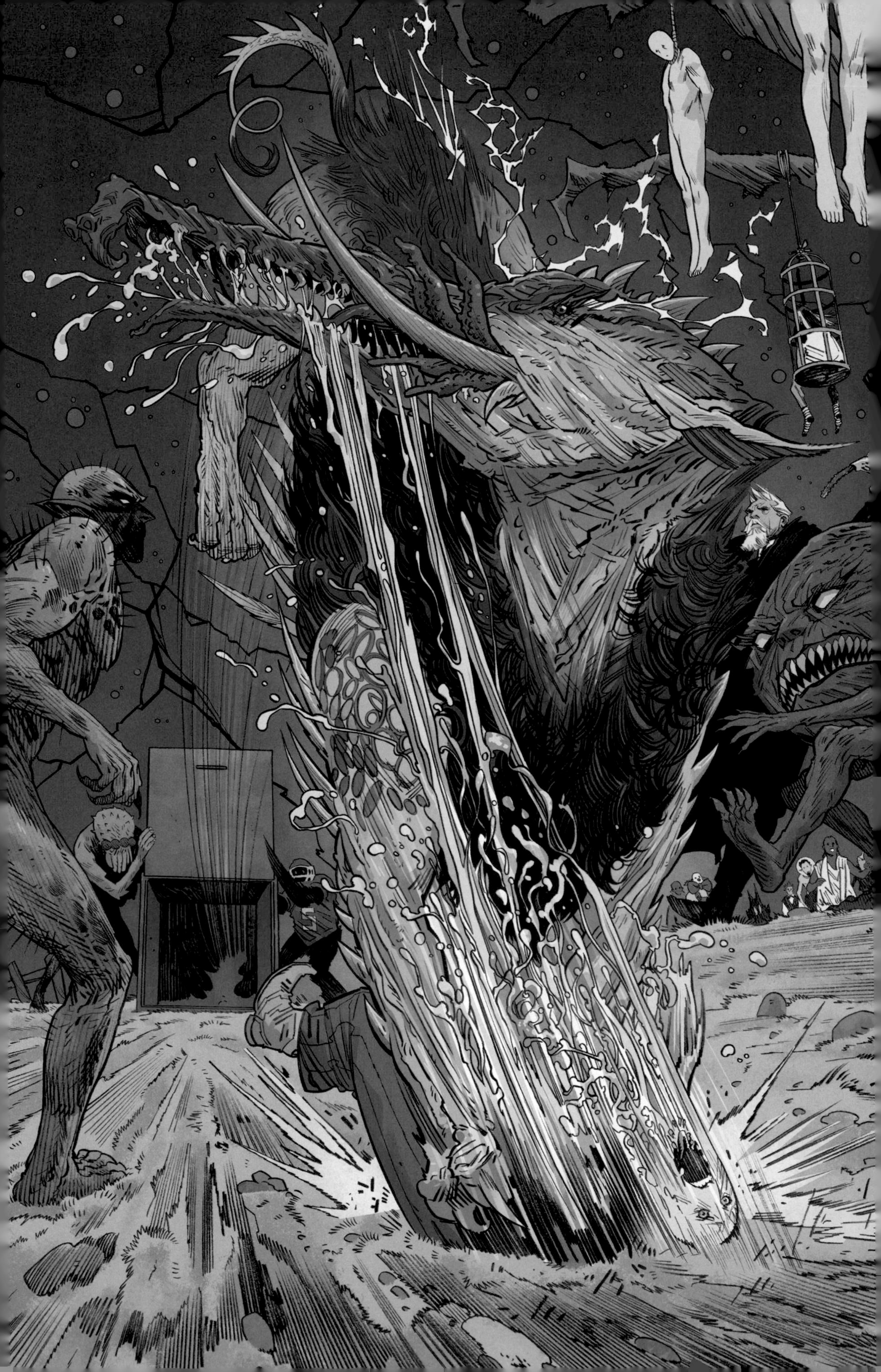

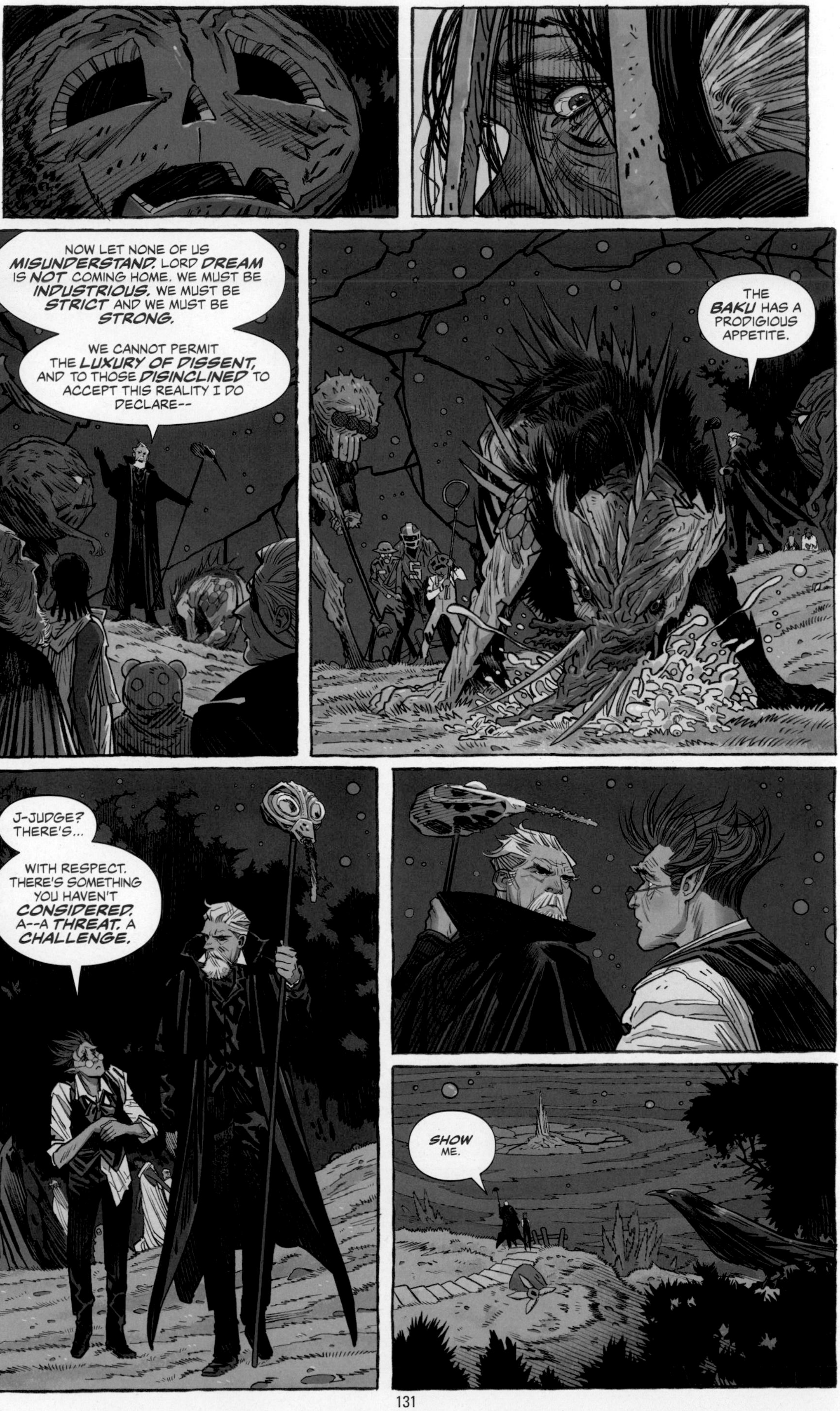
NOW LET NONE OF US MISUNDERSTAND. LORD DREAM IS NOT COMING HOME. WE MUST BE INDUSTRIOUS. WE MUST BE STRICT AND WE MUST BE STRONG.
WE CANNOT PERMIT THE LUXURY OF DISSENT, AND TO THOSE DISINCLINED TO ACCEPT THIS REALITY I DO DECLARE--
THE BAKU HAS A PRODIGIOUS APPETITE.
J-JUDGE? THERE'S...
WITH RESPECT. THERE'S SOMETHING YOU HAVEN'T CONSIDERED. A--A THREAT. A CHALLENGE.
SHOW ME.

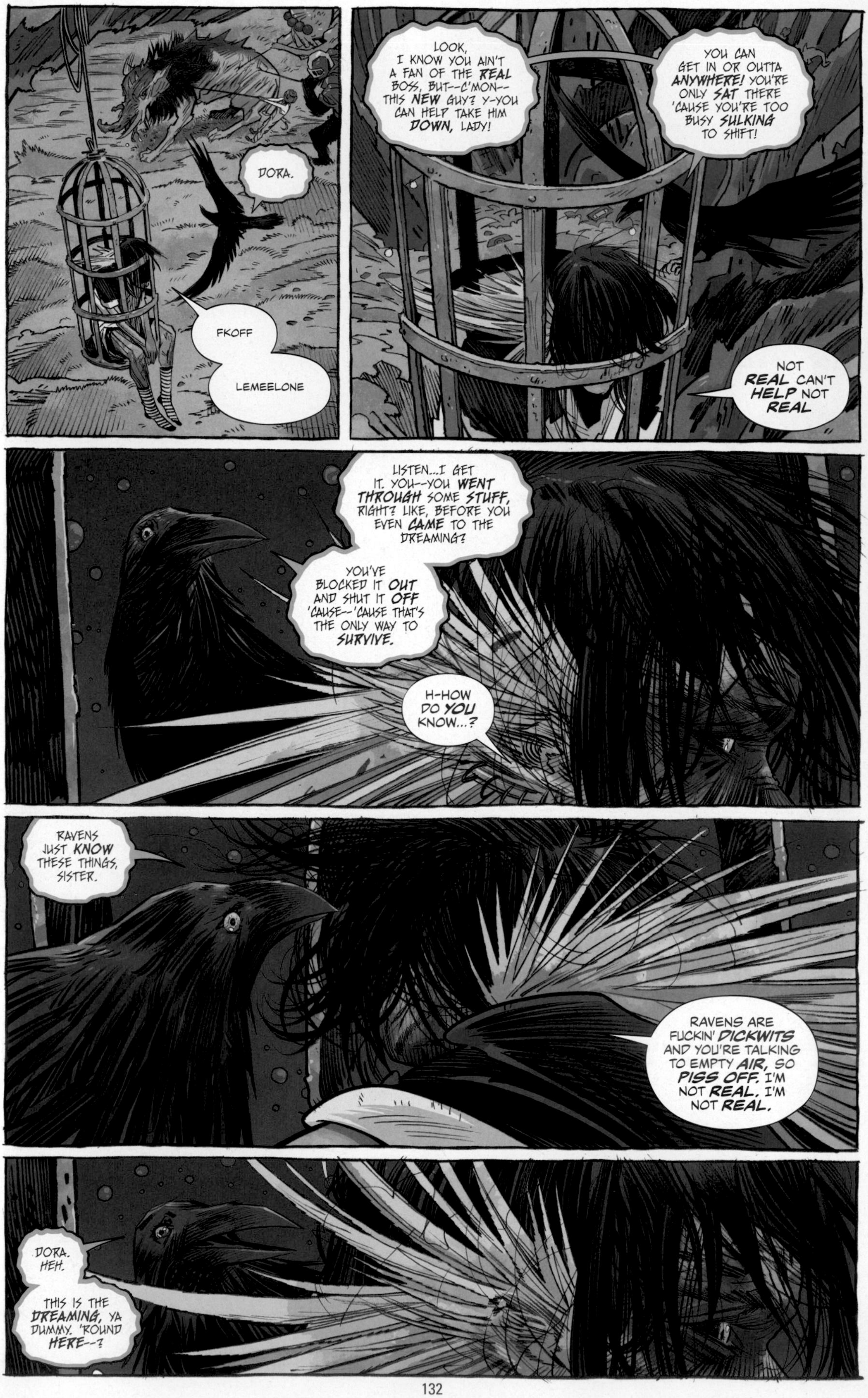
DORA.
FKOFF
LEMEELONE
LOOK, I KNOW YOU AIN'T A FAN OF THE REAL BOSS, BUT--C'MON--THIS NEW GUY? Y-YOU CAN HELP TAKE HIM DOWN, LADY!
YOU CAN GET IN OR OUTTA ANYWHERE! YOU'RE ONLY SAT THERE 'CAUSE YOU'RE TOO BUSY SULKING TO SHIFT!
NOT REAL CAN'T HELP NOT REAL
LISTEN...I GET IT. YOU--YOU WENT THROUGH SOME STUFF, RIGHT? LIKE, BEFORE YOU EVEN CAME TO THE DREAMING?
YOU'VE BLOCKED IT OUT AND SHUT IT OFF 'CAUSE--'CAUSE THAT'S THE ONLY WAY TO SURVIVE.
H-HOW DO YOU KNOW...?
RAVENS JUST KNOW THESE THINGS, SISTER.
RAVENS ARE FUCKIN' DICKWITS AND YOU'RE TALKING TO EMPTY AIR, SO PISS OFF. I'M NOT REAL. I'M NOT REAL.
DORA. HEH.
THIS IS THE DREAMING, YA DUMMY. 'ROUND HERE--?

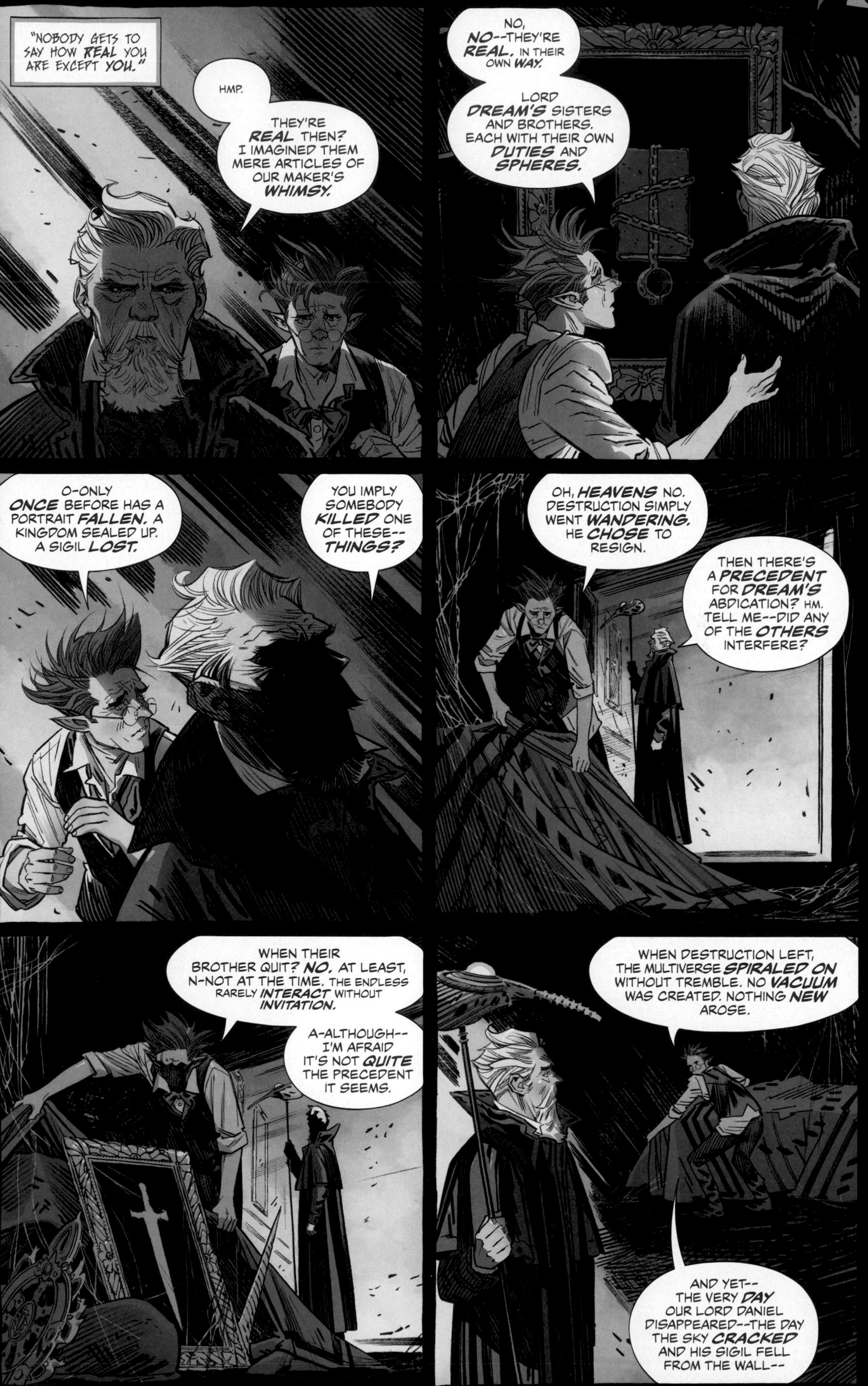
"NOBODY GETS TO SAY HOW REAL YOU ARE EXCEPT YOU."
HMP.
THEY'RE REAL THEN? I IMAGINED THEM MERE ARTICLES OF OUR MAKER'S WHIMSY.
NO, NO--THEY'RE REAL. IN THEIR OWN WAY.
LORD DREAM'S SISTERS AND BROTHERS. EACH WITH THEIR OWN DUTIES AND SPHERES.
O-ONLY ONCE BEFORE HAS A PORTRAIT FALLEN. A KINGDOM SEALED UP. A SIGIL LOST.
YOU IMPLY SOMEBODY KILLED ONE OF THESE--THINGS?
OH, HEAVENS NO. DESTRUCTION SIMPLY WENT WANDERING. HE CHOSE TO RESIGN.
THEN THERE'S A PRECEDENT FOR DREAM'S ABDICATION? HM. TELL ME--DID ANY OF THE OTHERS INTERFERE?
WHEN THEIR BROTHER QUIT? NO. AT LEAST, N-NOT AT THE TIME. THE ENDLESS RARELY INTERACT WITHOUT INVITATION.
A-ALTHOUGH--I'M AFRAID IT'S NOT QUITE THE PRECEDENT IT SEEMS.
WHEN DESTRUCTION LEFT, THE MULTIVERSE SPIRALED ON WITHOUT TREMBLE. NO VACUUM WAS CREATED. NOTHING NEW AROSE.
AND YET--THE VERY DAY OUR LORD DANIEL DISAPPEARED--THE DAY THE SKY CRACKED AND HIS SIGIL FELL FROM THE WALL--

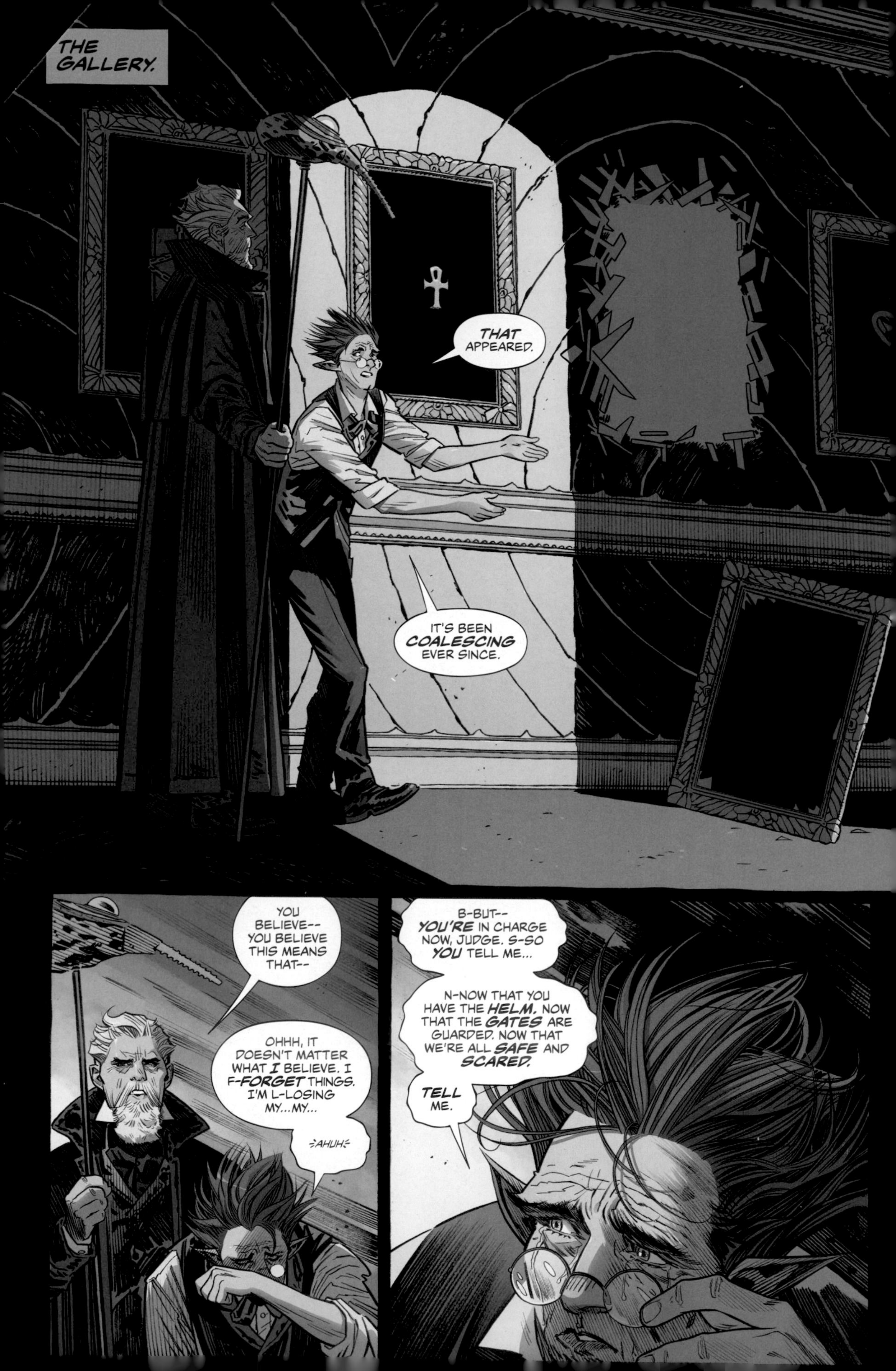
THE GALLERY.
THAT APPEARED.
IT'S BEEN COALESCING EVER SINCE.
YOU BELIEVE-- YOU BELIEVE THIS MEANS THAT--
OHHH, IT DOESN'T MATTER WHAT I BELIEVE. I F-FORGET THINGS. I'M L-LOSING MY...MY...
AHUH
B-BUT-- YOU'RE IN CHARGE NOW, JUDGE. S-SO YOU TELL ME...
N-NOW THAT YOU HAVE THE HELM. NOW THAT THE GATES ARE GUARDED. NOW THAT WE'RE ALL SAFE AND SCARED.
TELL ME.

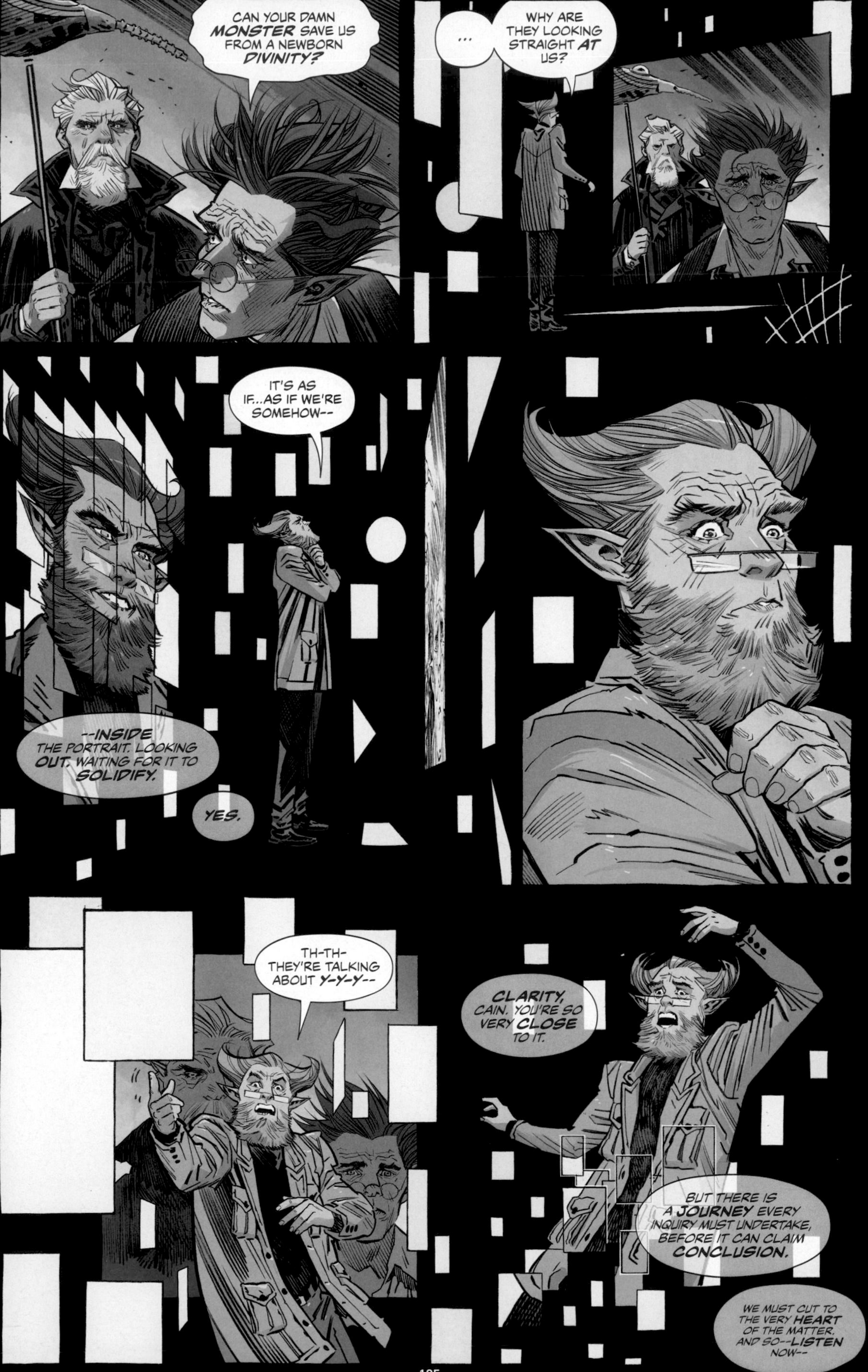

CAN YOUR DAMN MONSTER SAVE US FROM A NEWBORN DIVINITY?
...
WHY ARE THEY LOOKING STRAIGHT AT US?
IT'S AS IF...AS IF WE'RE SOMEHOW--
--INSIDE THE PORTRAIT. LOOKING OUT. WAITING FOR IT TO SOLIDIFY.
YES.
TH-TH- THEY'RE TALKING ABOUT Y-Y-Y--
CLARITY, CAIN. YOU'RE SO VERY CLOSE TO IT.
BUT THERE IS A JOURNEY EVERY INQUIRY MUST UNDERTAKE, BEFORE IT CAN CLAIM CONCLUSION.
WE MUST CUT TO THE VERY HEART OF THE MATTER. AND SO--LISTEN NOW--

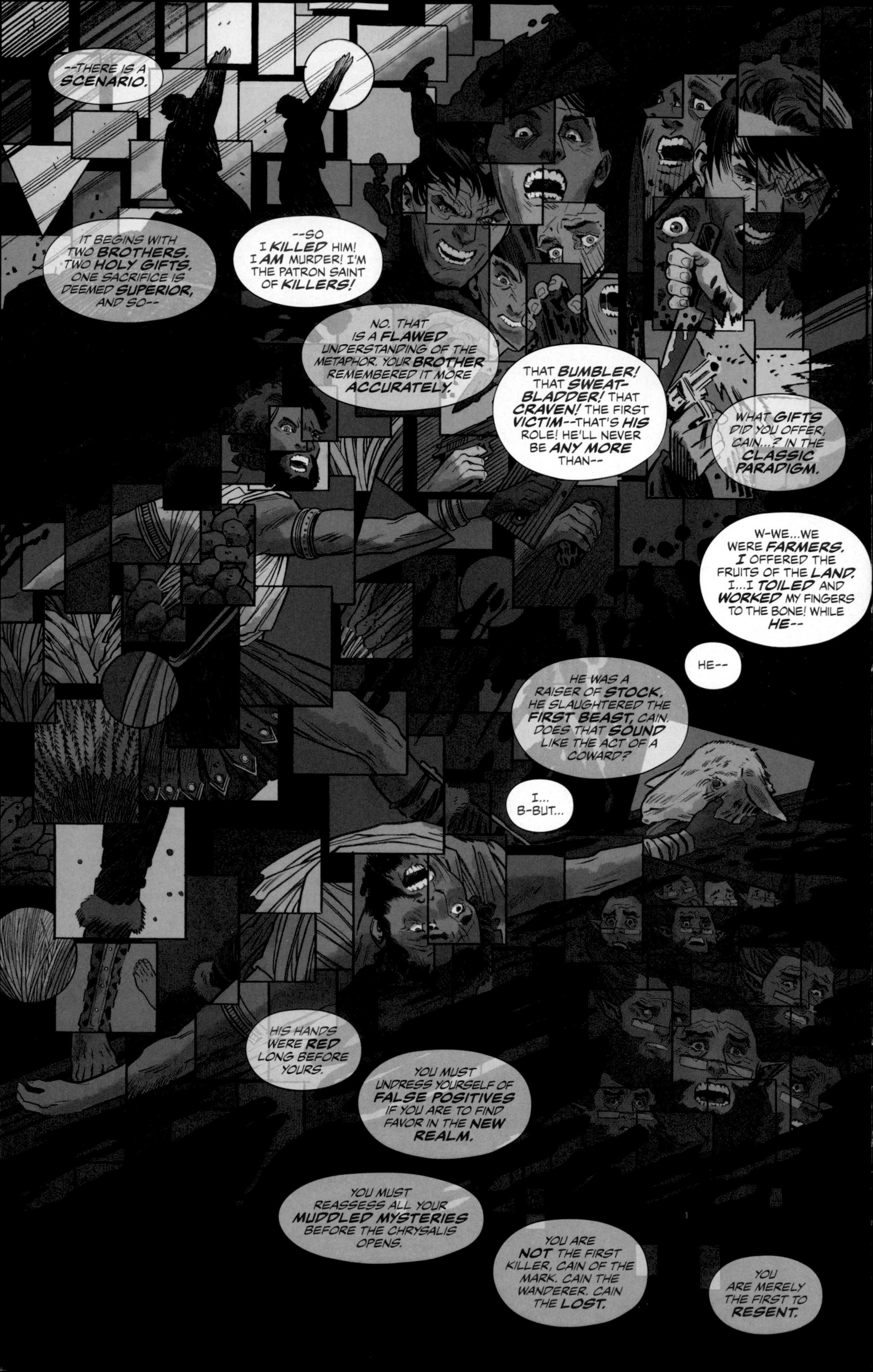
--THERE IS A SCENARIO.
IT BEGINS WITH TWO BROTHERS. TWO HOLY GIFTS. ONE SACRIFICE IS DEEMED SUPERIOR, AND SO--
--SO I KILLED HIM! I AM MURDER! I'M THE PATRON SAINT OF KILLERS!
NO. THAT IS A FLAWED UNDERSTANDING OF THE METAPHOR. YOUR BROTHER REMEMBERED IT MORE ACCURATELY.
THAT BUMBLER! THAT SWEAT-BLADDER! THAT CRAVEN! THE FIRST VICTIM--THAT'S HIS ROLE! HE'LL NEVER BE ANY MORE THAN--
WHAT GIFTS DID YOU OFFER, CAIN...? IN THE CLASSIC PARADIGM.
W-WE...WE WERE FARMERS. I OFFERED THE FRUITS OF THE LAND. I...I TOILED AND WORKED MY FINGERS TO THE BONE! WHILE HE--
HE--
HE WAS A RAISER OF STOCK. HE SLAUGHTERED THE FIRST BEAST, CAIN. DOES THAT SOUND LIKE THE ACT OF A COWARD?
I... B-BUT...
HIS HANDS WERE RED LONG BEFORE YOURS.
YOU MUST UNDRESS YOURSELF OF FALSE POSITIVES IF YOU ARE TO FIND FAVOR IN THE NEW REALM.
YOU MUST REASSESS ALL YOUR MUDDLED MYSTERIES BEFORE THE CHRYSALIS OPENS.
YOU ARE NOT THE FIRST KILLER, CAIN OF THE MARK. CAIN THE WANDERER. CAIN THE LOST.
YOU ARE MERELY THE FIRST TO RESENT.

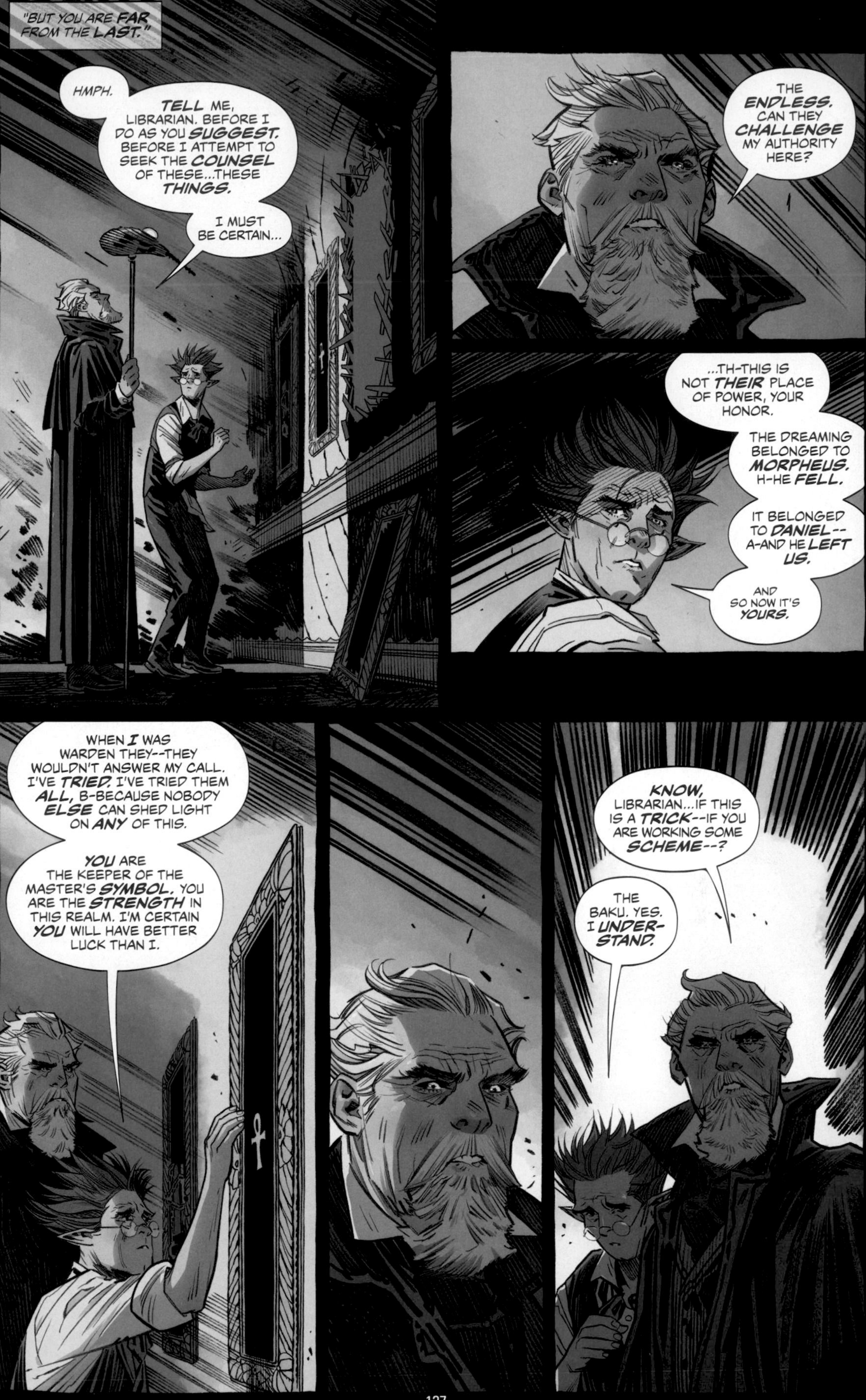

"BUT YOU ARE FAR FROM THE LAST."
HMPH.
TELL ME, LIBRARIAN. BEFORE I DO AS YOU SUGGEST. BEFORE I ATTEMPT TO SEEK THE COUNSEL OF THESE...THESE THINGS.
I MUST BE CERTAIN...
THE ENDLESS. CAN THEY CHALLENGE MY AUTHORITY HERE?
...TH-THIS IS NOT THEIR PLACE OF POWER, YOUR HONOR.
THE DREAMING BELONGED TO MORPHEUS. H-HE FELL.
IT BELONGED TO DANIEL-- A-AND HE LEFT US.
AND SO NOW IT'S YOURS.
WHEN I WAS WARDEN THEY--THEY WOULDN'T ANSWER MY CALL. I'VE TRIED. I'VE TRIED THEM ALL, B-BECAUSE NOBODY ELSE CAN SHED LIGHT ON ANY OF THIS.
YOU ARE THE KEEPER OF THE MASTER'S SYMBOL. YOU ARE THE STRENGTH IN THIS REALM. I'M CERTAIN YOU WILL HAVE BETTER LUCK THAN I.
KNOW, LIBRARIAN...IF THIS IS A TRICK--IF YOU ARE WORKING SOME SCHEME--?
THE BAKU. YES. I UNDER-STAND.

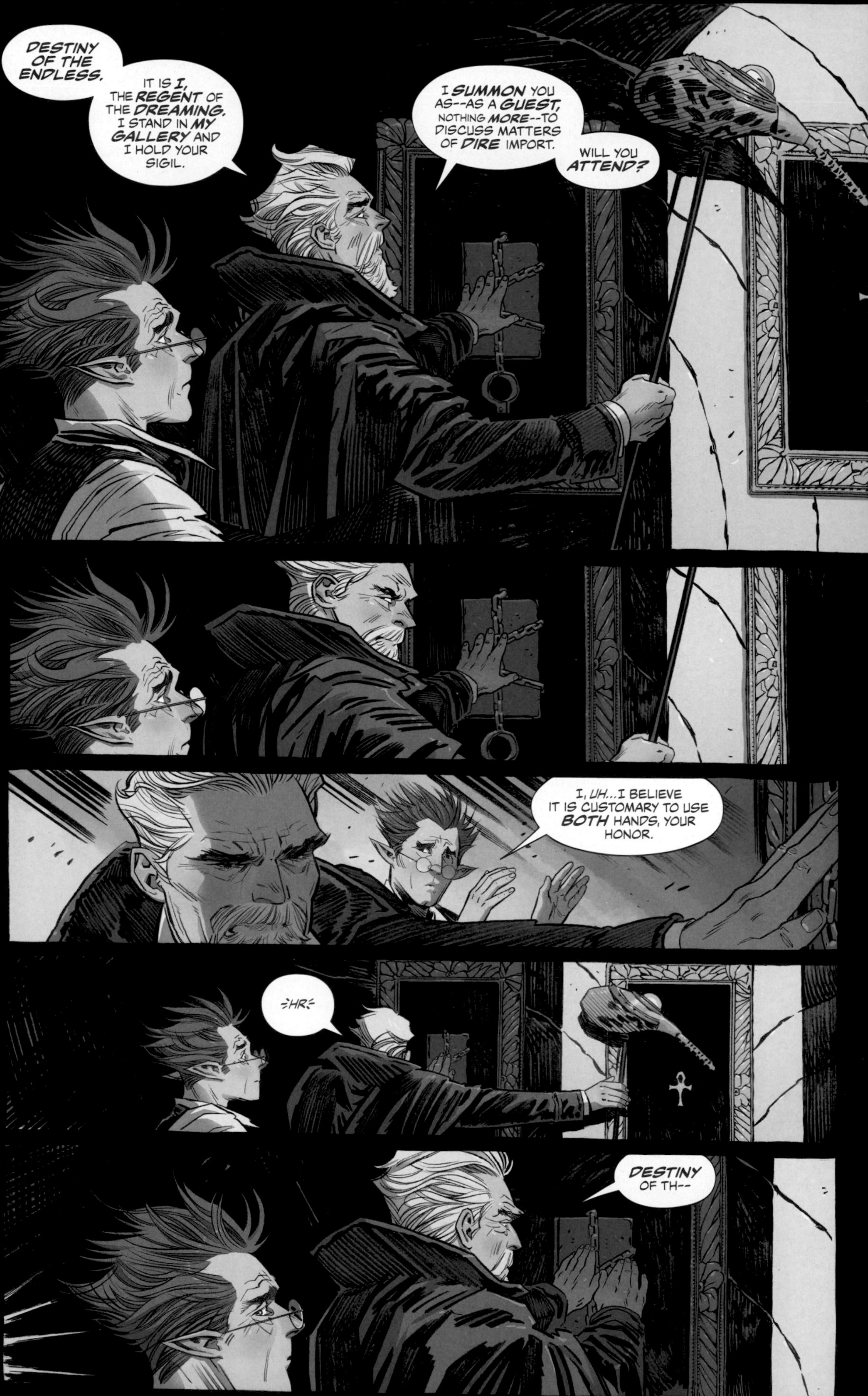
DESTINY OF THE ENDLESS.
IT IS I, THE REGENT OF THE DREAMING. I STAND IN MY GALLERY AND I HOLD YOUR SIGIL.
I SUMMON YOU AS--AS A GUEST, NOTHING MORE--TO DISCUSS MATTERS OF DIRE IMPORT.
WILL YOU ATTEND?
I, UH...I BELIEVE IT IS CUSTOMARY TO USE BOTH HANDS, YOUR HONOR.
HR
DESTINY OF TH--

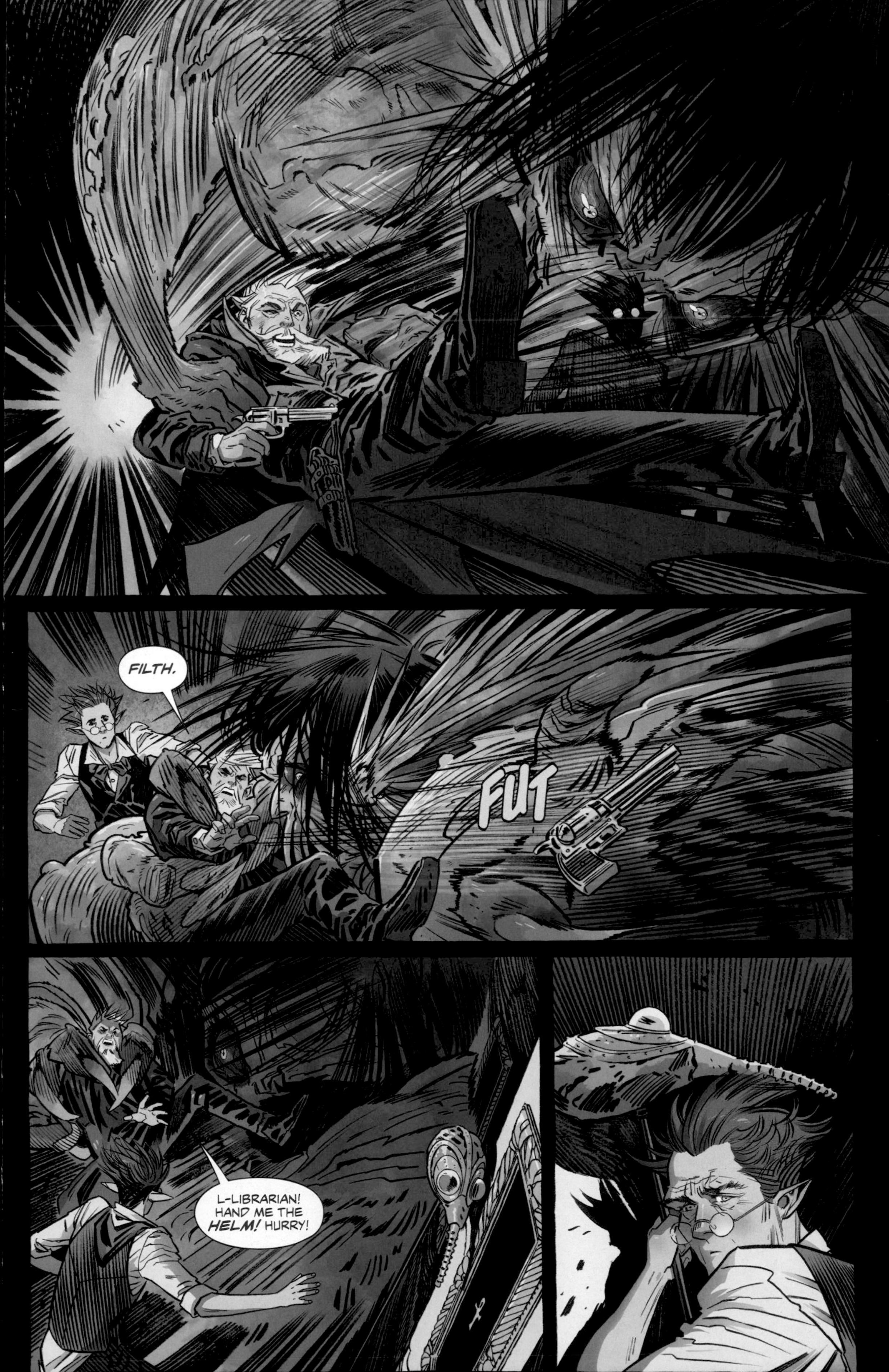
FILTH.
FUT
L-LIBRARIAN! HAND ME THE HELM! HURRY!

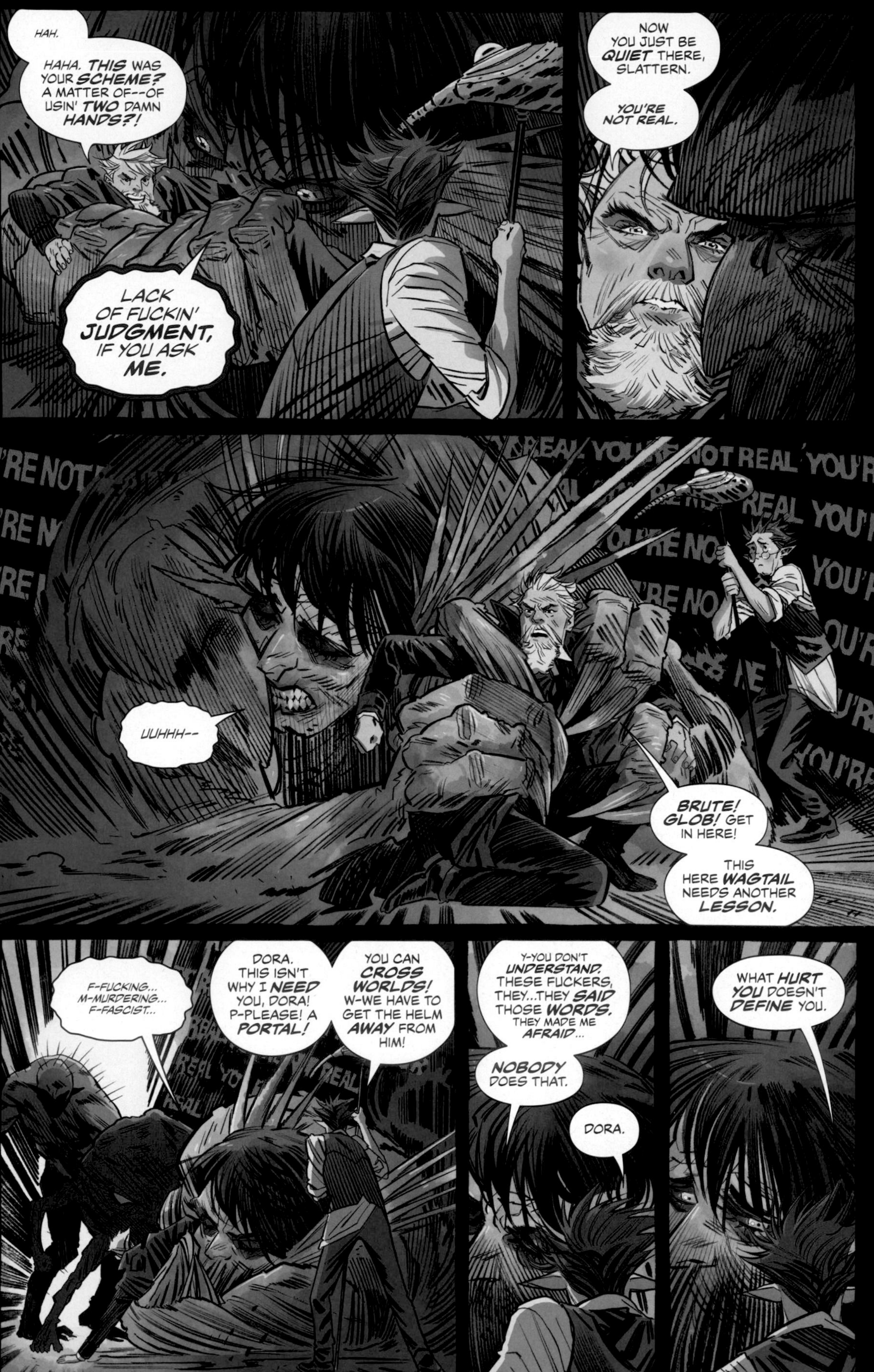
HAH.
HAHA. THIS WAS YOUR SCHEME? A MATTER OF--OF USIN' TWO DAMN HANDS?!
LACK OF FUCKIN' JUDGMENT, IF YOU ASK ME.
NOW YOU JUST BE QUIET THERE, SLATTERN.
YOU'RE NOT REAL.
YOU'RE NOT REAL YOU'RE NOT REAL YOU'RE
UUHHH--
BRUTE! GLOB! GET IN HERE!
THIS HERE WAGTAIL NEEDS ANOTHER LESSON.
F-FUCKING... M-MURDERING... F-FASCIST...
DORA. THIS ISN'T WHY I NEED YOU, DORA! P-PLEASE! A PORTAL!
YOU CAN CROSS WORLDS! W-WE HAVE TO GET THE HELM AWAY FROM HIM!
Y-YOU DON'T UNDERSTAND. THESE FUCKERS, THEY...THEY SAID THOSE WORDS. THEY MADE ME AFRAID...
NOBODY DOES THAT.
DORA.
WHAT HURT YOU DOESN'T DEFINE YOU.

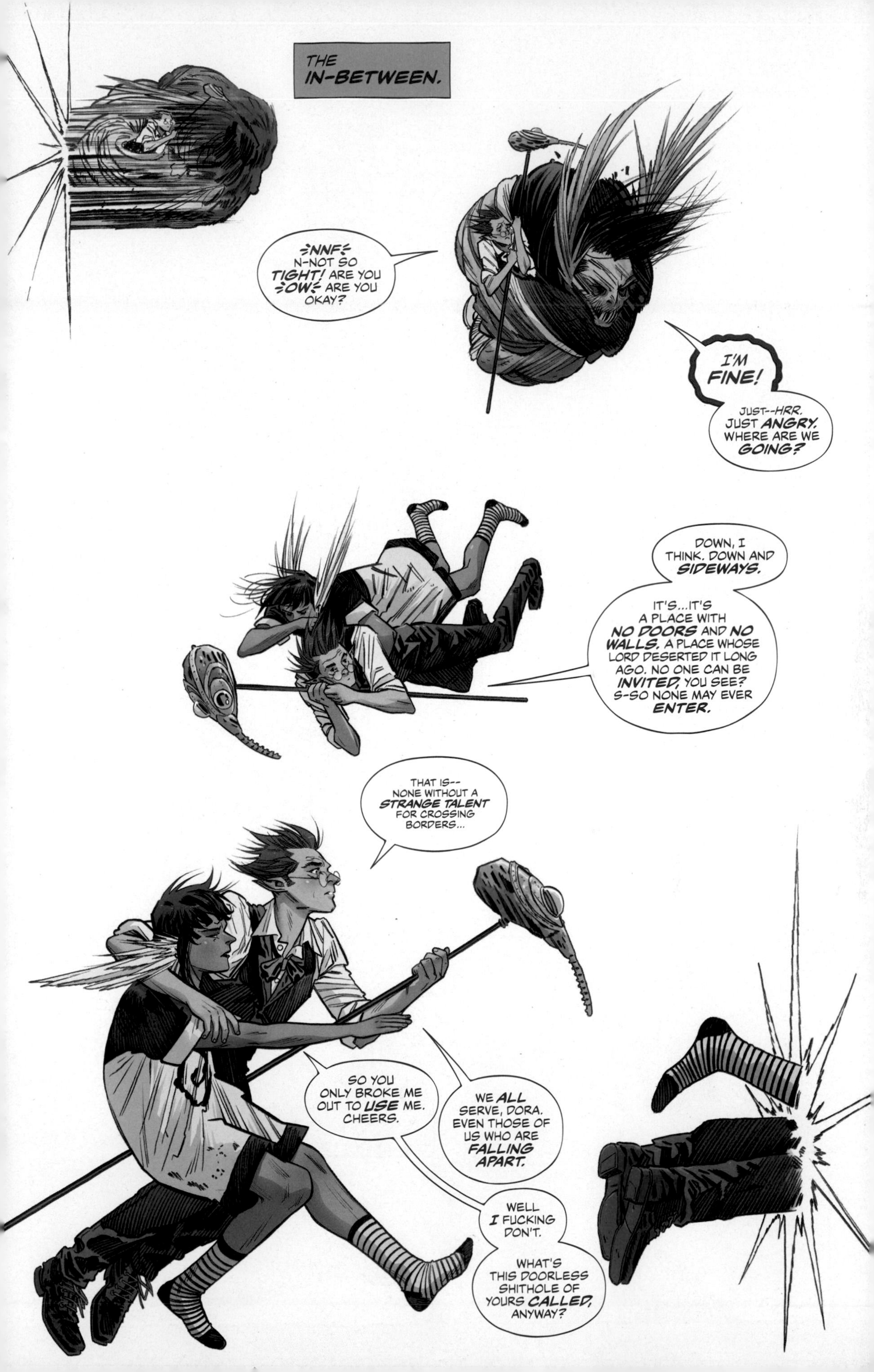
THE IN-BETWEEN.
NNF N-NOT SO TIGHT! ARE YOU OW ARE YOU OKAY?
I'M FINE!
JUST--HRR. JUST ANGRY. WHERE ARE WE GOING?
DOWN, I THINK. DOWN AND SIDEWAYS.
IT'S...IT'S A PLACE WITH NO DOORS AND NO WALLS. A PLACE WHOSE LORD DESERTED IT LONG AGO. NO ONE CAN BE INVITED, YOU SEE? S-SO NONE MAY EVER ENTER.
THAT IS-- NONE WITHOUT A STRANGE TALENT FOR CROSSING BORDERS...
SO YOU ONLY BROKE ME OUT TO USE ME. CHEERS.
WE ALL SERVE, DORA. EVEN THOSE OF US WHO ARE FALLING APART.
WELL I FUCKING DON'T.
WHAT'S THIS DOORLESS SHITHOLE OF YOURS CALLED, ANYWAY?

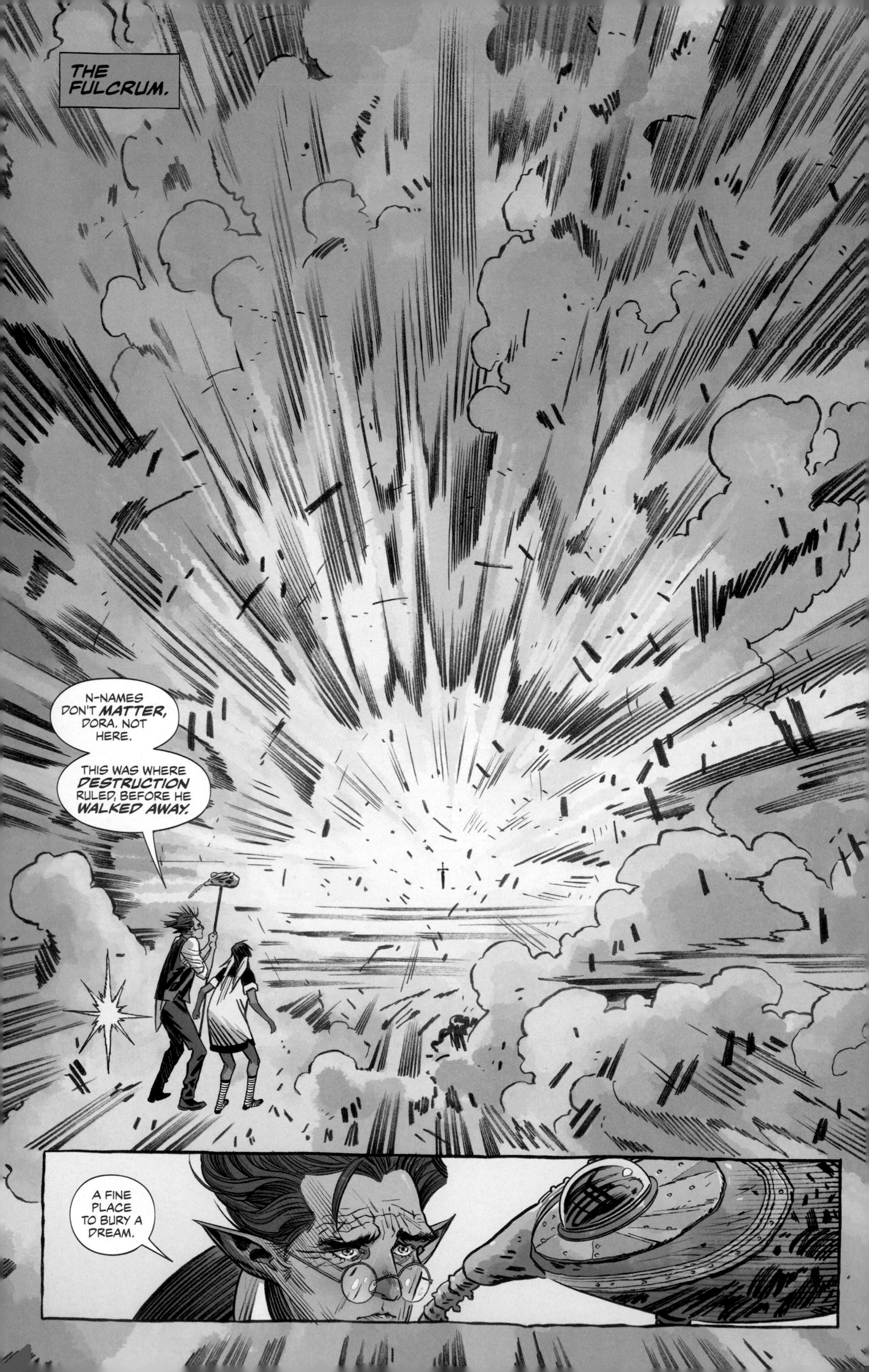
THE FULCRUM.
N-NAMES DON'T MATTER, DORA. NOT HERE.
THIS WAS WHERE DESTRUCTION RULED, BEFORE HE WALKED AWAY.
A FINE PLACE TO BURY A DREAM.

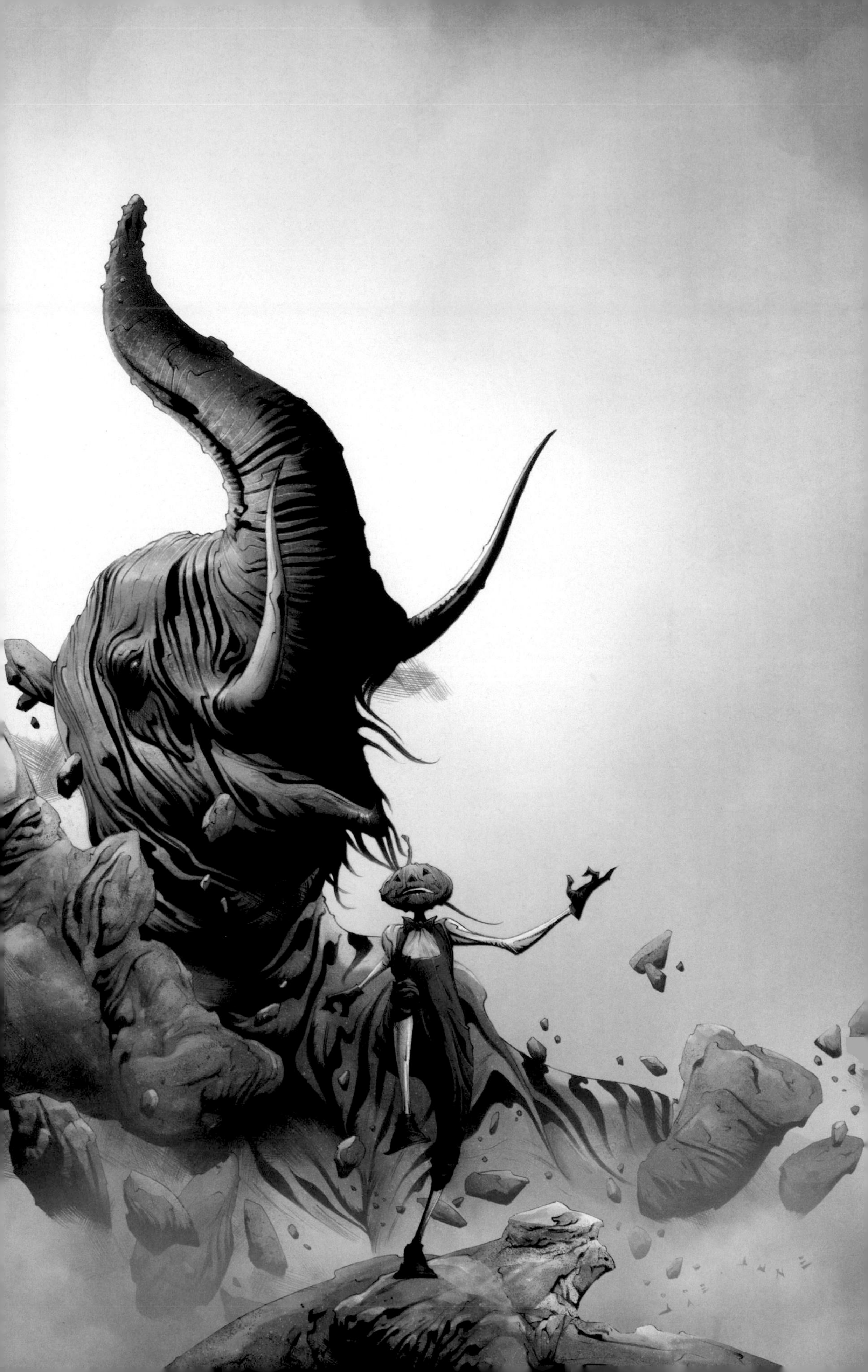

THE DREAMING

The Balance

WRITTEN BY
Simon Spurrier

ILLUSTRATED BY
Bilquis Evely
Abigail Larson

COLORS BY
Mat Lopes
Quinton Winter

LETTERS BY
Simon Bowland

COVER ART BY
Jae Lee and *June Chung*

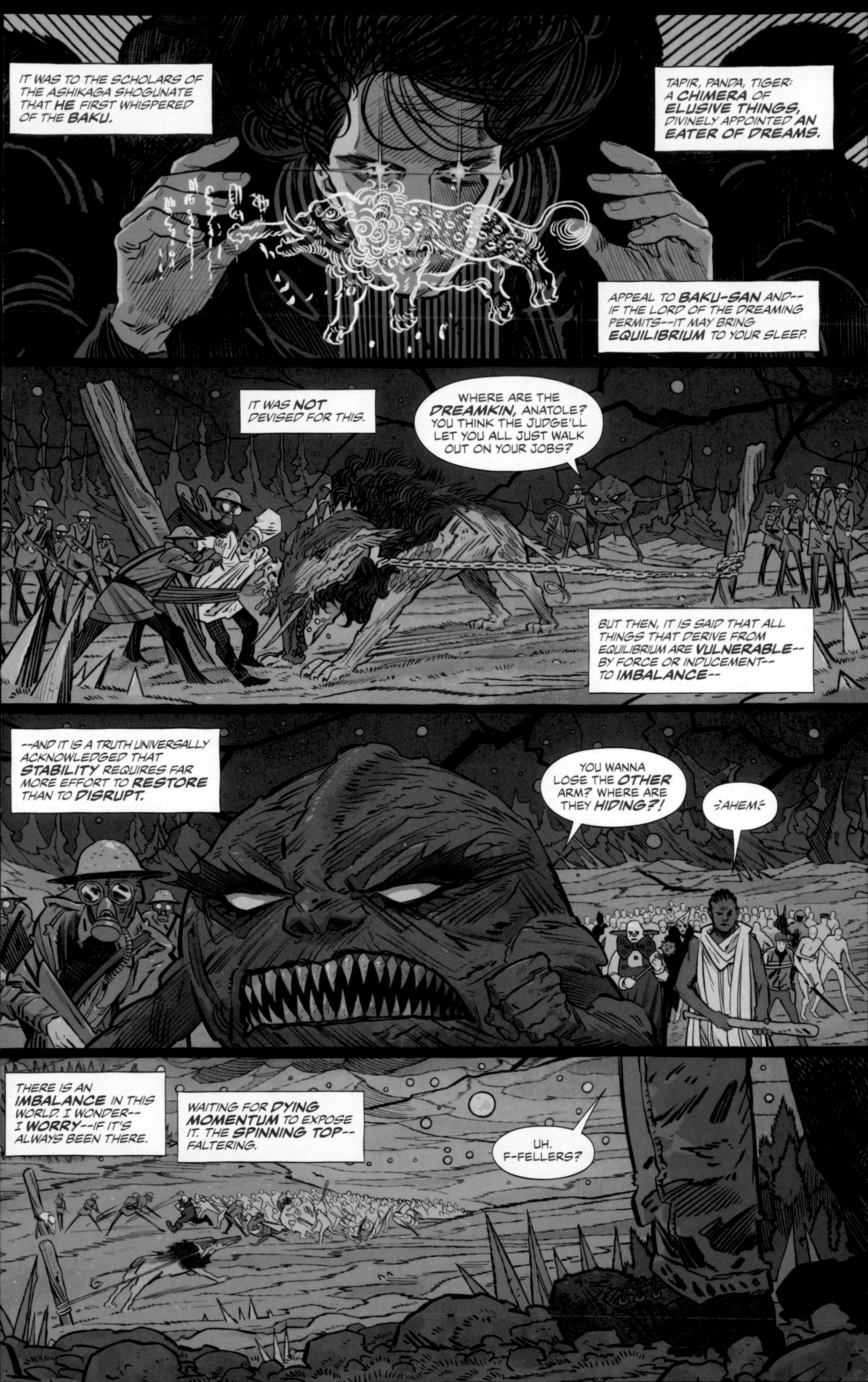
IT WAS TO THE SCHOLARS OF THE ASHIKAGA SHOGUNATE THAT HE FIRST WHISPERED OF THE BAKU.
TAPIR, PANDA, TIGER: A CHIMERA OF ELUSIVE THINGS, DIVINELY APPOINTED AN EATER OF DREAMS.
APPEAL TO BAKU-SAN AND--IF THE LORD OF THE DREAMING PERMITS--IT MAY BRING EQUILIBRIUM TO YOUR SLEEP.
IT WAS NOT DEVISED FOR THIS.
WHERE ARE THE DREAMKIN, ANATOLE? YOU THINK THE JUDGE'LL LET YOU ALL JUST WALK OUT ON YOUR JOBS?
BUT THEN, IT IS SAID THAT ALL THINGS THAT DERIVE FROM EQUILIBRIUM ARE VULNERABLE--BY FORCE OR INDUCEMENT--TO IMBALANCE--
--AND IT IS A TRUTH UNIVERSALLY ACKNOWLEDGED THAT STABILITY REQUIRES FAR MORE EFFORT TO RESTORE THAN TO DISRUPT.
YOU WANNA LOSE THE OTHER ARM? WHERE ARE THEY HIDING?!
AHEM
THERE IS AN IMBALANCE IN THIS WORLD. I WONDER--I WORRY--IF IT'S ALWAYS BEEN THERE.
WAITING FOR DYING MOMENTUM TO EXPOSE IT. THE SPINNING TOP--FALTERING.
UH. F-FELLERS?

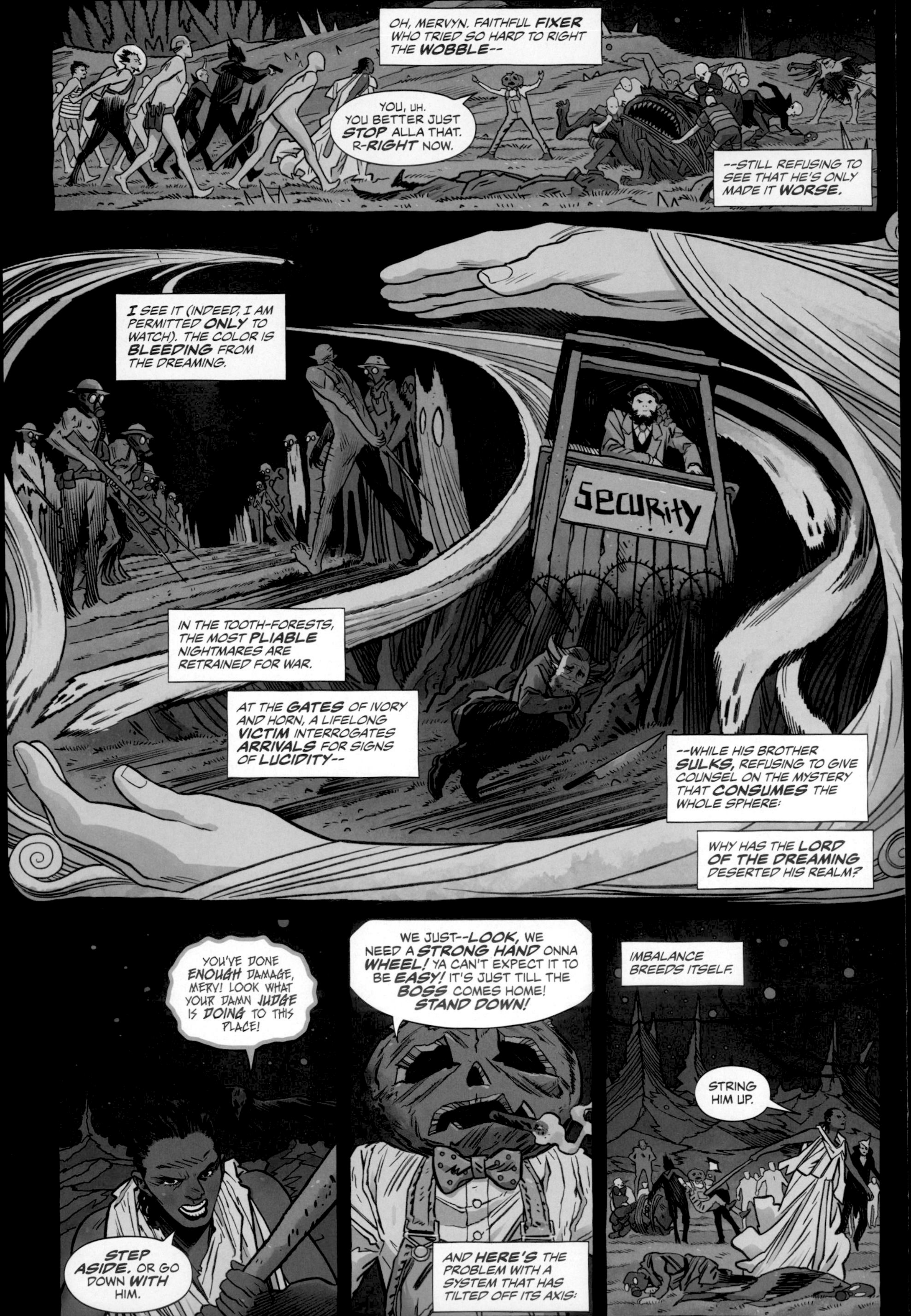
OH, MERVYN. FAITHFUL FIXER WHO TRIED SO HARD TO RIGHT THE WOBBLE--
YOU, UH. YOU BETTER JUST STOP ALLA THAT. R-RIGHT NOW.
--STILL REFUSING TO SEE THAT HE'S ONLY MADE IT WORSE.
I SEE IT (INDEED, I AM PERMITTED ONLY TO WATCH). THE COLOR IS BLEEDING FROM THE DREAMING.
SECURITY
IN THE TOOTH-FORESTS, THE MOST PLIABLE NIGHTMARES ARE RETRAINED FOR WAR.
AT THE GATES OF IVORY AND HORN, A LIFELONG VICTIM INTERROGATES ARRIVALS FOR SIGNS OF LUCIDITY--
--WHILE HIS BROTHER SULKS, REFUSING TO GIVE COUNSEL ON THE MYSTERY THAT CONSUMES THE WHOLE SPHERE:
WHY HAS THE LORD OF THE DREAMING DESERTED HIS REALM?
YOU'VE DONE ENOUGH DAMAGE, MERV! LOOK WHAT YOUR DAMN JUDGE IS DOING TO THIS PLACE!
STEP ASIDE. OR GO DOWN WITH HIM.
WE JUST--LOOK, WE NEED A STRONG HAND ONNA WHEEL! YA CAN'T EXPECT IT TO BE EASY! IT'S JUST TILL THE BOSS COMES HOME! STAND DOWN!
AND HERE'S THE PROBLEM WITH A SYSTEM THAT HAS TILTED OFF ITS AXIS:
IMBALANCE BREEDS ITSELF.
STRING HIM UP.

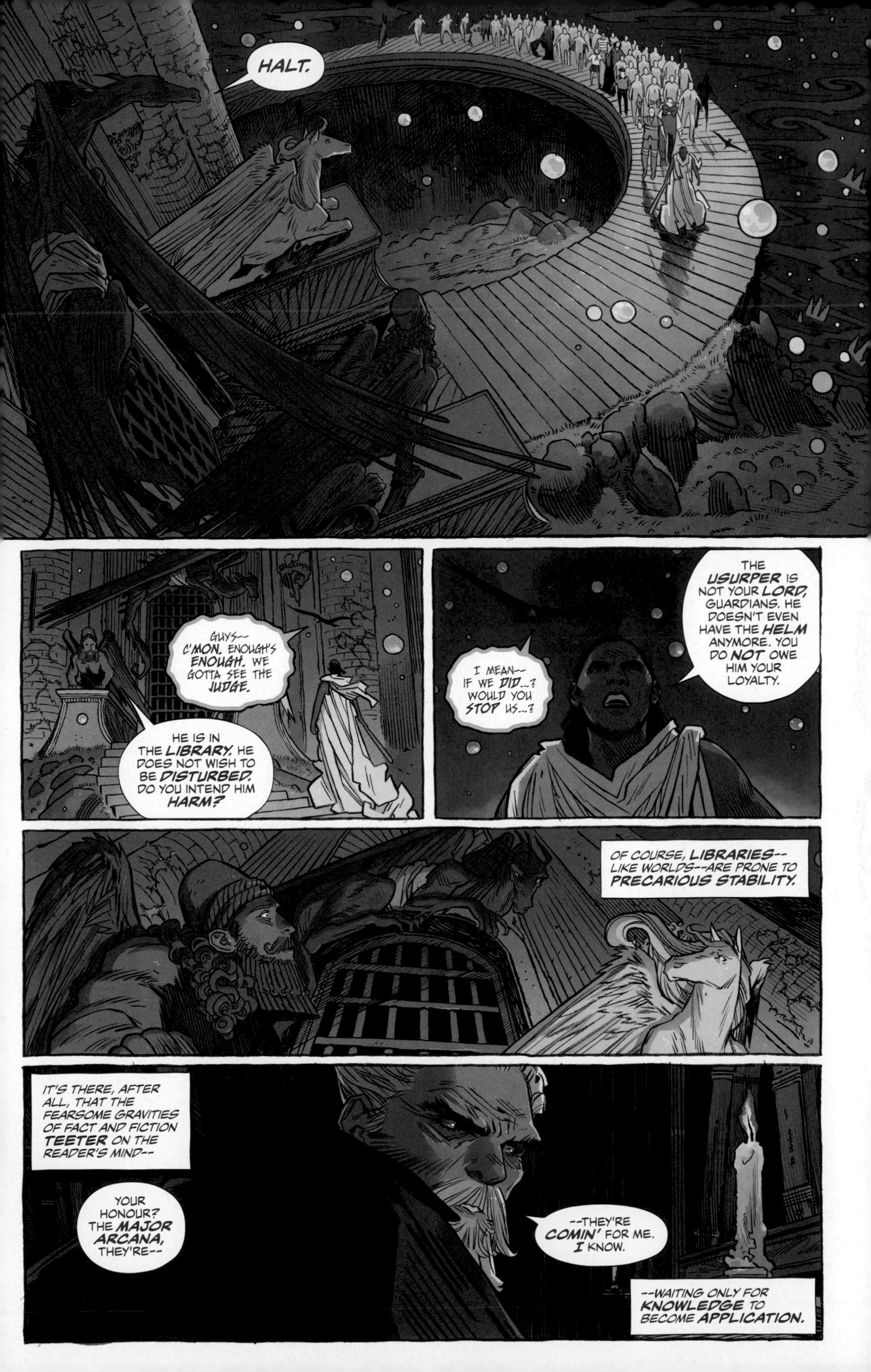
HALT.
GUYS-- C'MON. ENOUGH'S ENOUGH. WE GOTTA SEE THE JUDGE.
HE IS IN THE LIBRARY. HE DOES NOT WISH TO BE DISTURBED. DO YOU INTEND HIM HARM?
I MEAN-- IF WE DID...? WOULD YOU STOP US...?
THE USURPER IS NOT YOUR LORD, GUARDIANS. HE DOESN'T EVEN HAVE THE HELM ANYMORE. YOU DO NOT OWE HIM YOUR LOYALTY.
OF COURSE, LIBRARIES-- LIKE WORLDS--ARE PRONE TO PRECARIOUS STABILITY.
IT'S THERE, AFTER ALL, THAT THE FEARSOME GRAVITIES OF FACT AND FICTION TEETER ON THE READER'S MIND--
YOUR HONOUR? THE MAJOR ARCANA, THEY'RE--
--THEY'RE COMIN' FOR ME. I KNOW.
--WAITING ONLY FOR KNOWLEDGE TO BECOME APPLICATION.

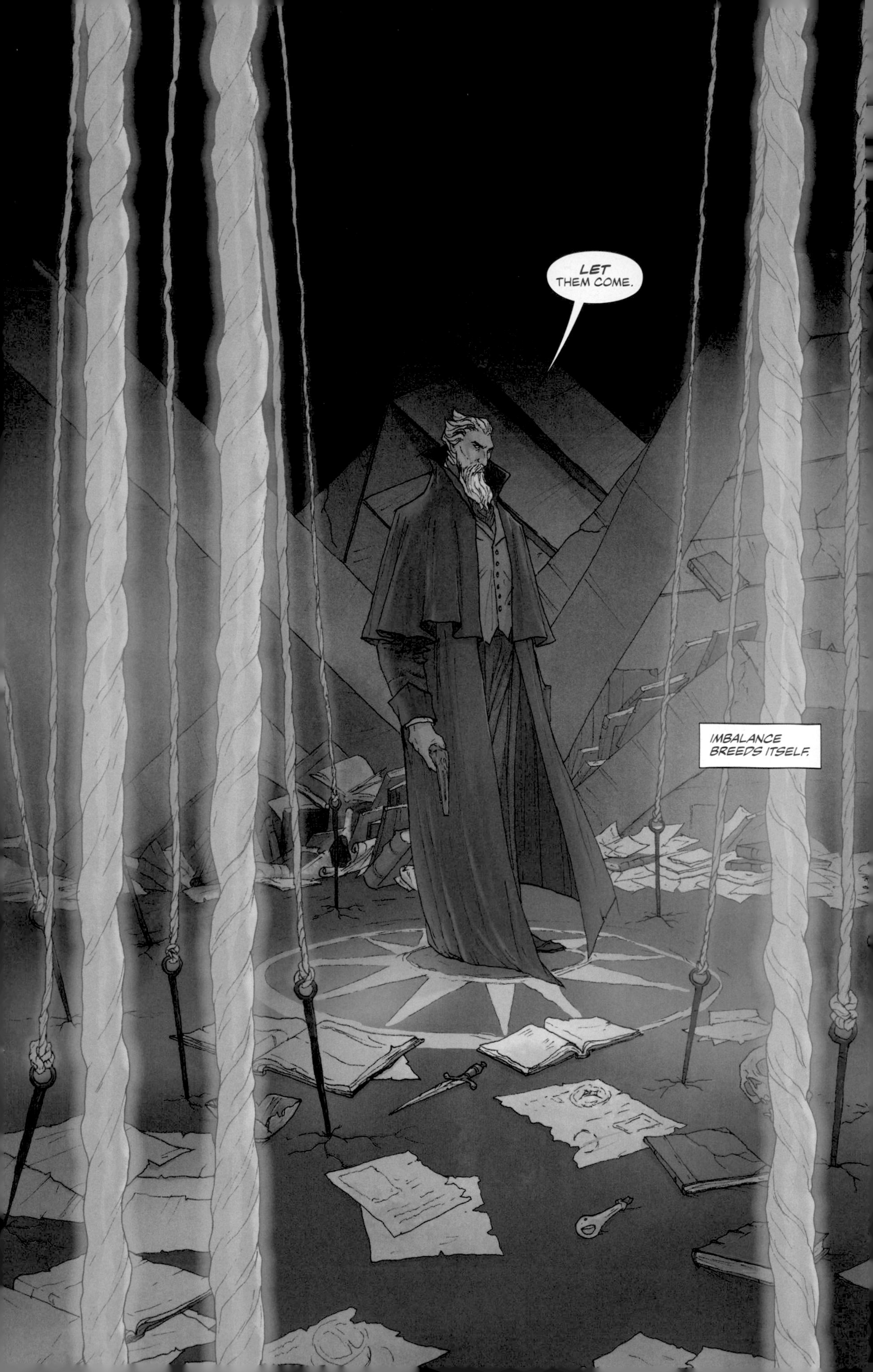
LET THEM COME.
IMBALANCE BREEDS ITSELF.

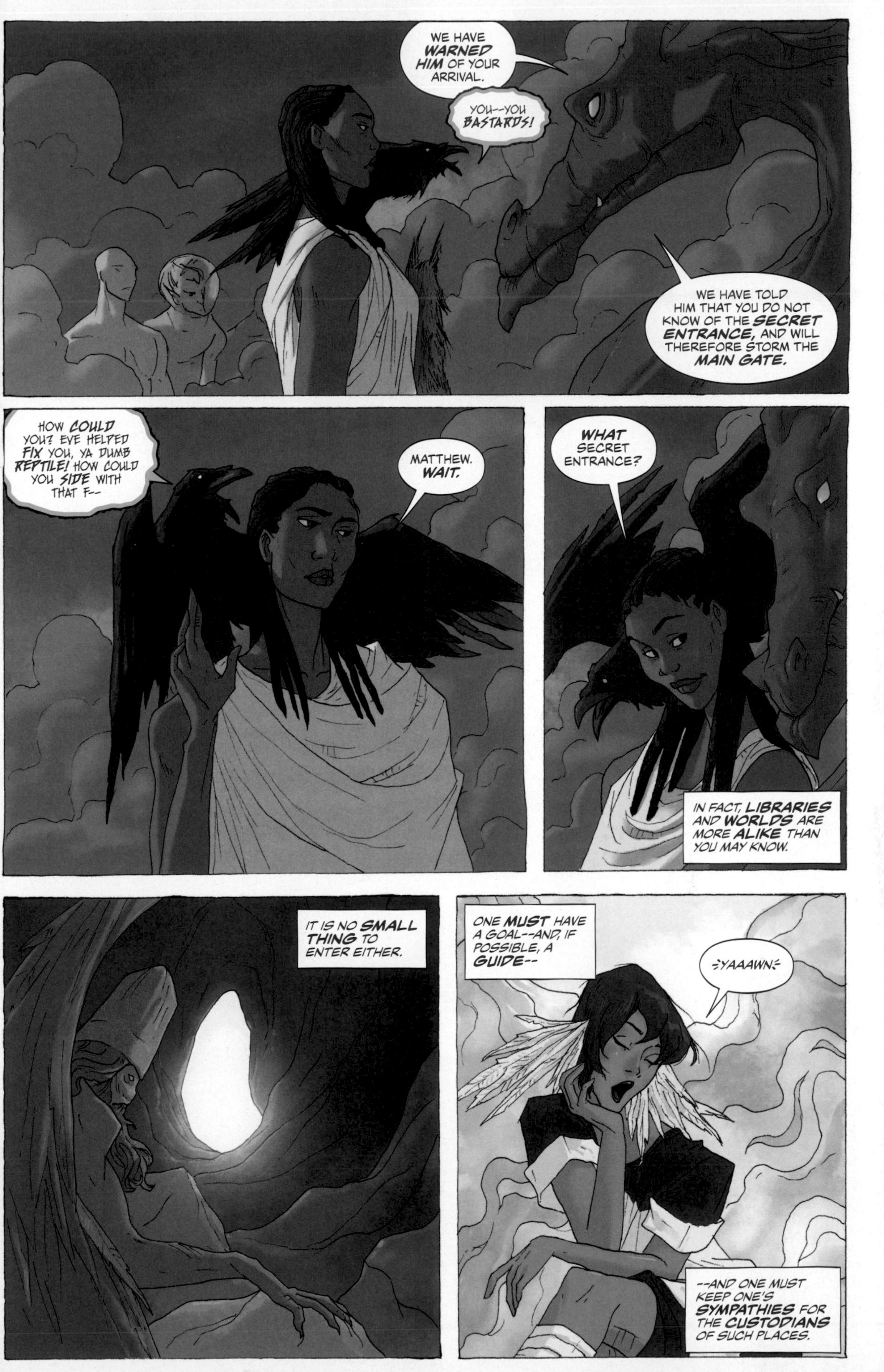
WE HAVE WARNED HIM OF YOUR ARRIVAL.
YOU--YOU BASTARDS!
WE HAVE TOLD HIM THAT YOU DO NOT KNOW OF THE SECRET ENTRANCE, AND WILL THEREFORE STORM THE MAIN GATE.
HOW COULD YOU? EVE HELPED FIX YOU, YA DUMB REPTILE! HOW COULD YOU SIDE WITH THAT F--
MATTHEW. WAIT.
WHAT SECRET ENTRANCE?
IN FACT, LIBRARIES AND WORLDS ARE MORE ALIKE THAN YOU MAY KNOW.
IT IS NO SMALL THING TO ENTER EITHER.
ONE MUST HAVE A GOAL--AND, IF POSSIBLE, A GUIDE--
YAAAWN
--AND ONE MUST KEEP ONE'S SYMPATHIES FOR THE CUSTODIANS OF SUCH PLACES.

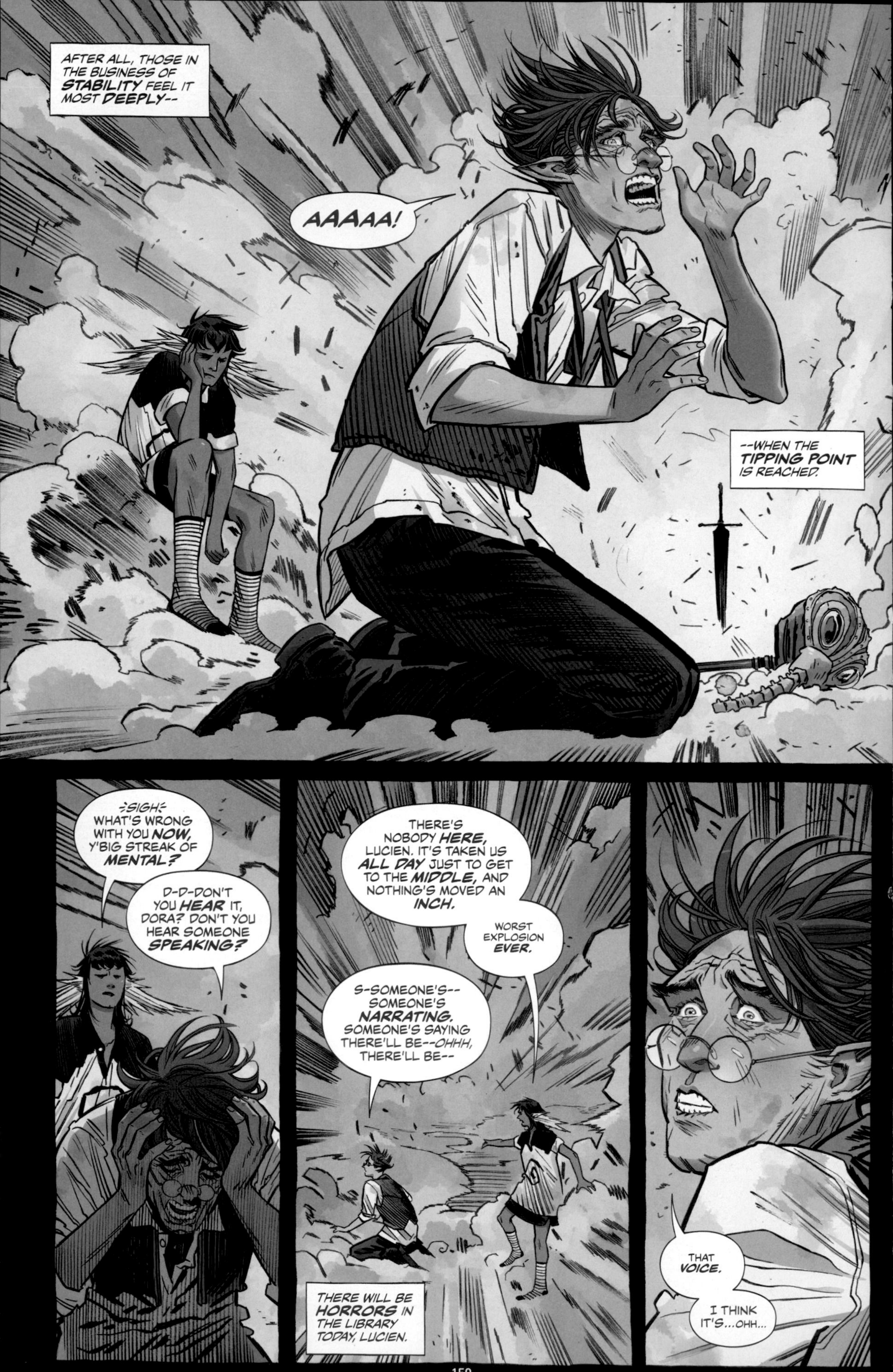
AFTER ALL, THOSE IN THE BUSINESS OF STABILITY FEEL IT MOST DEEPLY--
AAAAA!
--WHEN THE TIPPING POINT IS REACHED.
-SIGH- WHAT'S WRONG WITH YOU NOW, Y'BIG STREAK OF MENTAL?
D-D-DON'T YOU HEAR IT, DORA? DON'T YOU HEAR SOMEONE SPEAKING?
THERE'S NOBODY HERE, LUCIEN. IT'S TAKEN US ALL DAY JUST TO GET TO THE MIDDLE, AND NOTHING'S MOVED AN INCH.
WORST EXPLOSION EVER.
S-SOMEONE'S-- SOMEONE'S NARRATING. SOMEONE'S SAYING THERE'LL BE--OHHH, THERE'LL BE--
THERE WILL BE HORRORS IN THE LIBRARY TODAY, LUCIEN.
THAT VOICE.
I THINK IT'S...OHH...

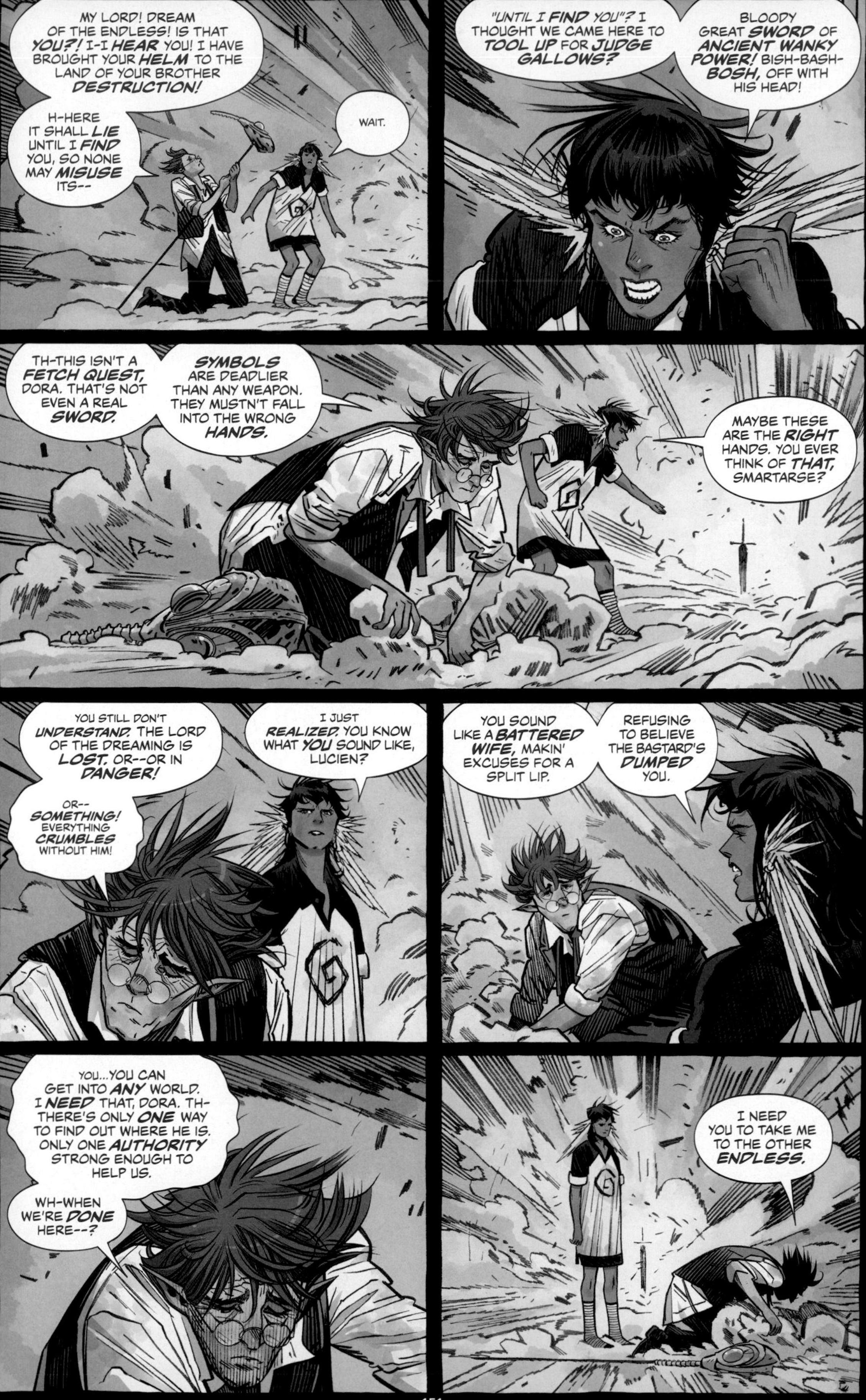
MY LORD! DREAM OF THE ENDLESS! IS THAT YOU?! I-I HEAR YOU! I HAVE BROUGHT YOUR HELM TO THE LAND OF YOUR BROTHER DESTRUCTION!
H-HERE IT SHALL LIE UNTIL I FIND YOU, SO NONE MAY MISUSE ITS--
WAIT.
"UNTIL I FIND YOU"? I THOUGHT WE CAME HERE TO TOOL UP FOR JUDGE GALLOWS?
BLOODY GREAT SWORD OF ANCIENT WANKY POWER! BISH-BASH-BOSH, OFF WITH HIS HEAD!
TH-THIS ISN'T A FETCH QUEST, DORA. THAT'S NOT EVEN A REAL SWORD.
SYMBOLS ARE DEADLIER THAN ANY WEAPON. THEY MUSTN'T FALL INTO THE WRONG HANDS.
MAYBE THESE ARE THE RIGHT HANDS. YOU EVER THINK OF THAT, SMARTARSE?
YOU STILL DON'T UNDERSTAND. THE LORD OF THE DREAMING IS LOST. OR--OR IN DANGER!
OR-- SOMETHING! EVERYTHING CRUMBLES WITHOUT HIM!
I JUST REALIZED. YOU KNOW WHAT YOU SOUND LIKE, LUCIEN?
YOU SOUND LIKE A BATTERED WIFE, MAKIN' EXCUSES FOR A SPLIT LIP.
REFUSING TO BELIEVE THE BASTARD'S DUMPED YOU.
YOU...YOU CAN GET INTO ANY WORLD. I NEED THAT, DORA. TH-THERE'S ONLY ONE WAY TO FIND OUT WHERE HE IS. ONLY ONE AUTHORITY STRONG ENOUGH TO HELP US.
WH-WHEN WE'RE DONE HERE--?
I NEED YOU TO TAKE ME TO THE OTHER ENDLESS.

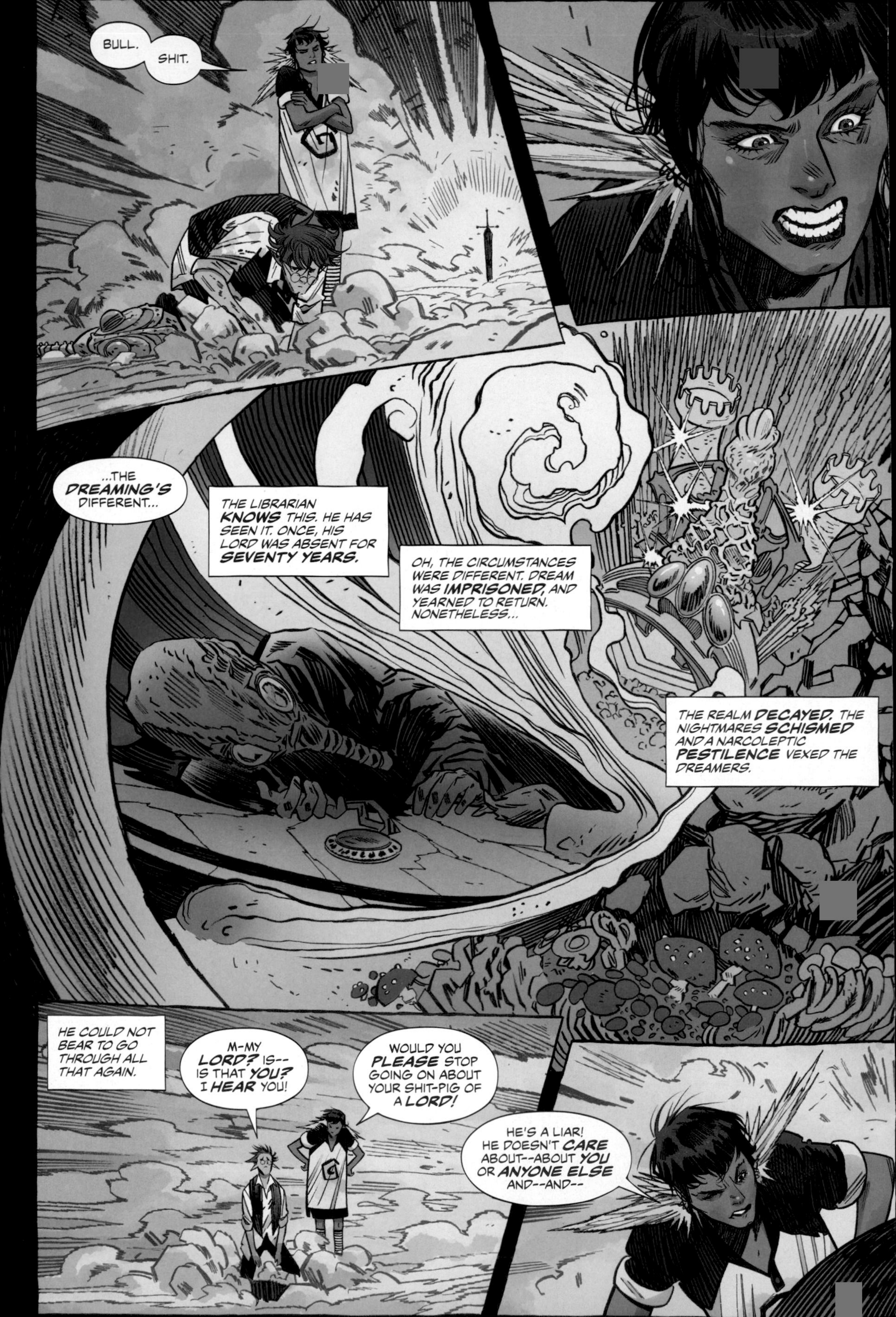
BULL.
SHIT.
...THE DREAMING'S DIFFERENT...
THE LIBRARIAN KNOWS THIS. HE HAS SEEN IT. ONCE, HIS LORD WAS ABSENT FOR SEVENTY YEARS.
OH, THE CIRCUMSTANCES WERE DIFFERENT. DREAM WAS IMPRISONED, AND YEARNED TO RETURN. NONETHELESS...
THE REALM DECAYED, THE NIGHTMARES SCHISMED AND A NARCOLEPTIC PESTILENCE VEXED THE DREAMERS.
HE COULD NOT BEAR TO GO THROUGH ALL THAT AGAIN.
M-MY LORD? IS-- IS THAT YOU? I HEAR YOU!
WOULD YOU PLEASE STOP GOING ON ABOUT YOUR SHIT-PIG OF A LORD!
HE'S A LIAR! HE DOESN'T CARE ABOUT--ABOUT YOU OR ANYONE ELSE AND--AND--

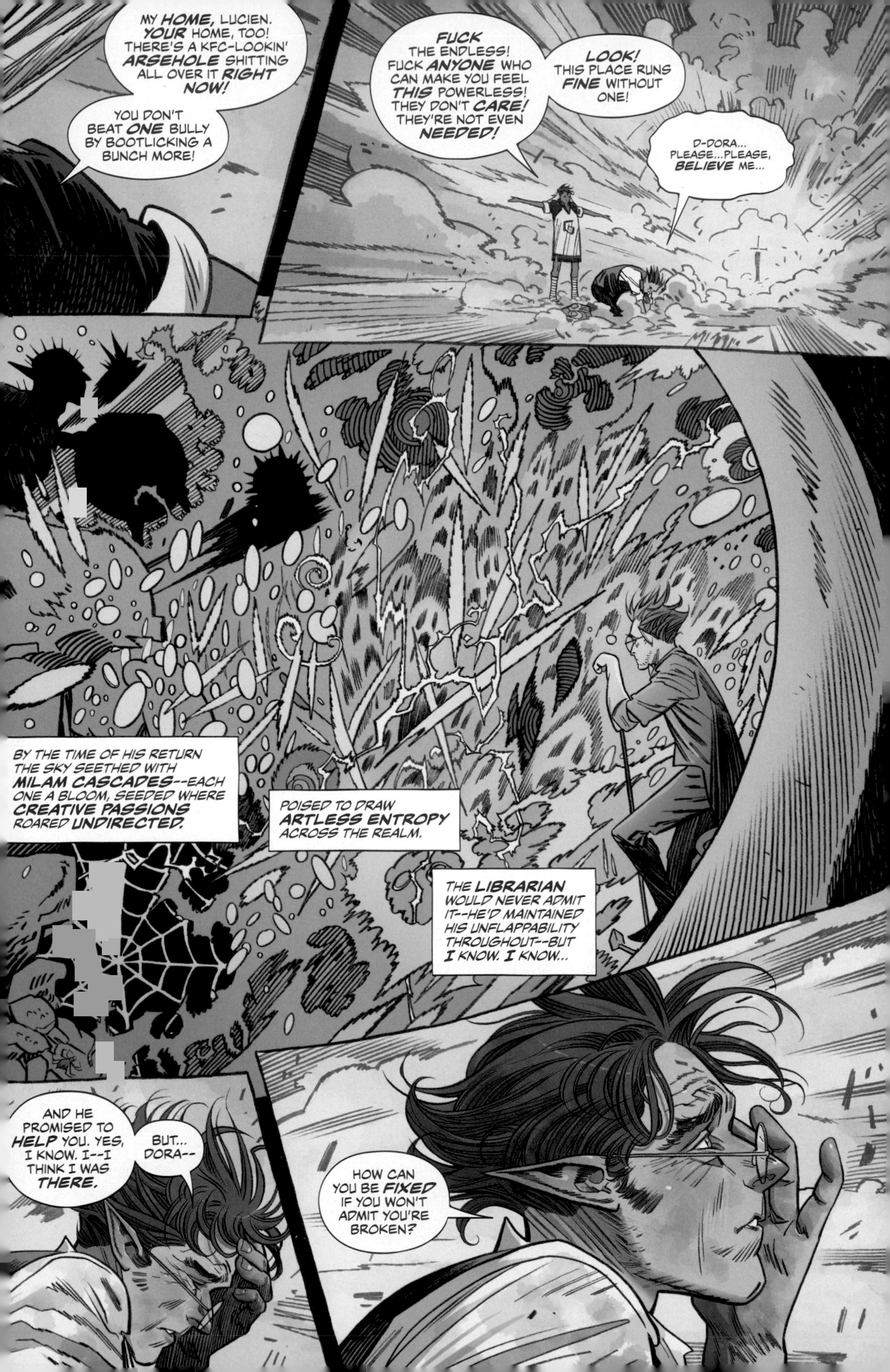

MY HOME, LUCIEN. YOUR HOME, TOO! THERE'S A KFC-LOOKIN' ARSEHOLE SHITTING ALL OVER IT RIGHT NOW!
YOU DON'T BEAT ONE BULLY BY BOOTLICKING A BUNCH MORE!
FUCK THE ENDLESS! FUCK ANYONE WHO CAN MAKE YOU FEEL THIS POWERLESS! THEY DON'T CARE! THEY'RE NOT EVEN NEEDED!
LOOK! THIS PLACE RUNS FINE WITHOUT ONE!
D-DORA... PLEASE...PLEASE, BELIEVE ME...
BY THE TIME OF HIS RETURN THE SKY SEETHED WITH MILAM CASCADES--EACH ONE A BLOOM, SEEDED WHERE CREATIVE PASSIONS ROARED UNDIRECTED.
POISED TO DRAW ARTLESS ENTROPY ACROSS THE REALM.
THE LIBRARIAN WOULD NEVER ADMIT IT--HE'D MAINTAINED HIS UNFLAPPABILITY THROUGHOUT--BUT I KNOW. I KNOW...
AND HE PROMISED TO HELP YOU. YES, I KNOW. I--I THINK I WAS THERE.
BUT... DORA--
HOW CAN YOU BE FIXED IF YOU WON'T ADMIT YOU'RE BROKEN?

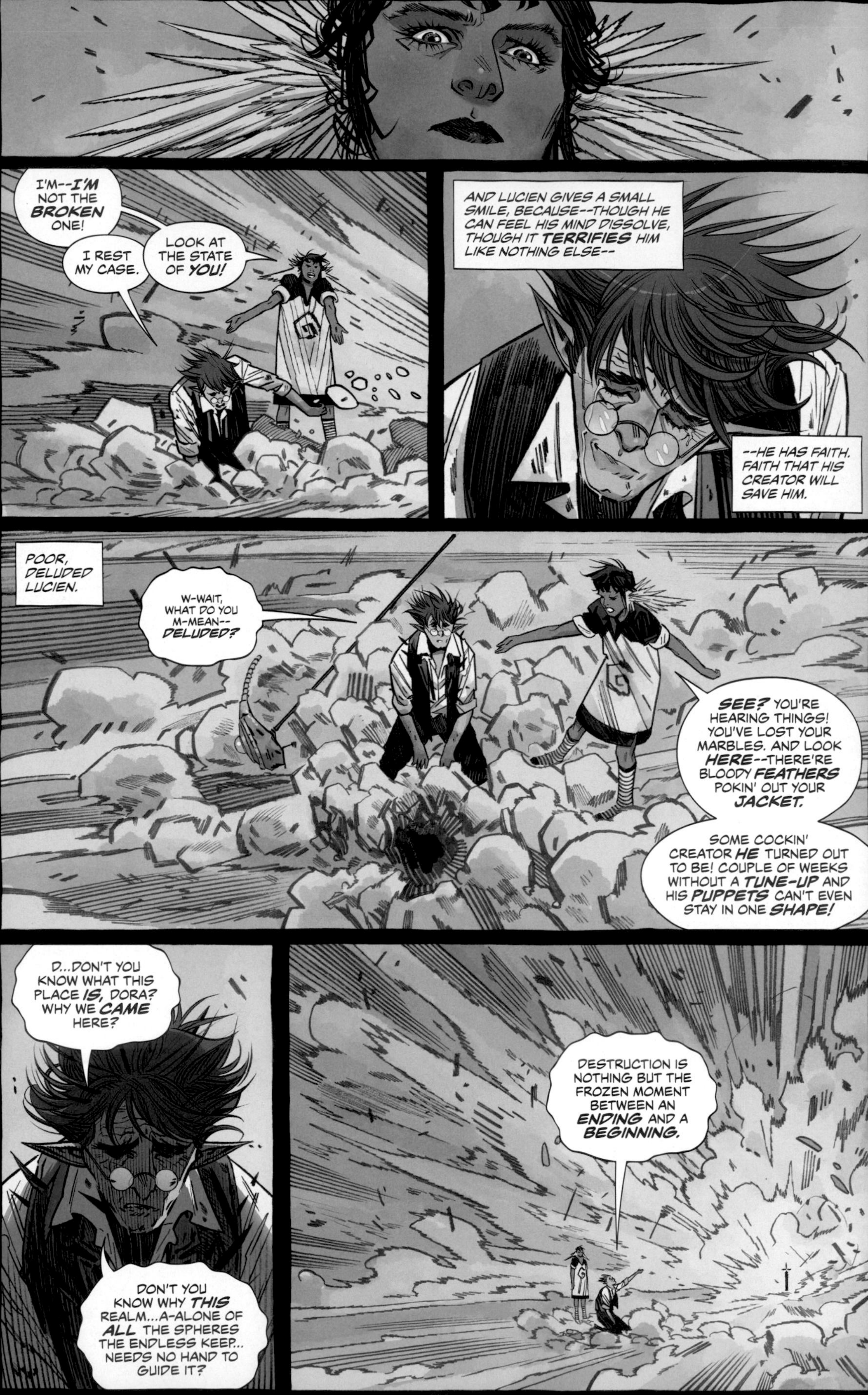
I'M--I'M NOT THE BROKEN ONE!
I REST MY CASE.
LOOK AT THE STATE OF YOU!
AND LUCIEN GIVES A SMALL SMILE, BECAUSE--THOUGH HE CAN FEEL HIS MIND DISSOLVE, THOUGH IT TERRIFIES HIM LIKE NOTHING ELSE--
--HE HAS FAITH. FAITH THAT HIS CREATOR WILL SAVE HIM.
POOR, DELUDED LUCIEN.
W-WAIT, WHAT DO YOU M-MEAN--DELUDED?
SEE? YOU'RE HEARING THINGS! YOU'VE LOST YOUR MARBLES. AND LOOK HERE--THERE'RE BLOODY FEATHERS POKIN' OUT YOUR JACKET.
SOME COCKIN' CREATOR HE TURNED OUT TO BE! COUPLE OF WEEKS WITHOUT A TUNE-UP AND HIS PUPPETS CAN'T EVEN STAY IN ONE SHAPE!
D...DON'T YOU KNOW WHAT THIS PLACE IS, DORA? WHY WE CAME HERE?
DON'T YOU KNOW WHY THIS REALM...A-ALONE OF ALL THE SPHERES THE ENDLESS KEEP... NEEDS NO HAND TO GUIDE IT?
DESTRUCTION IS NOTHING BUT THE FROZEN MOMENT BETWEEN AN ENDING AND A BEGINNING.

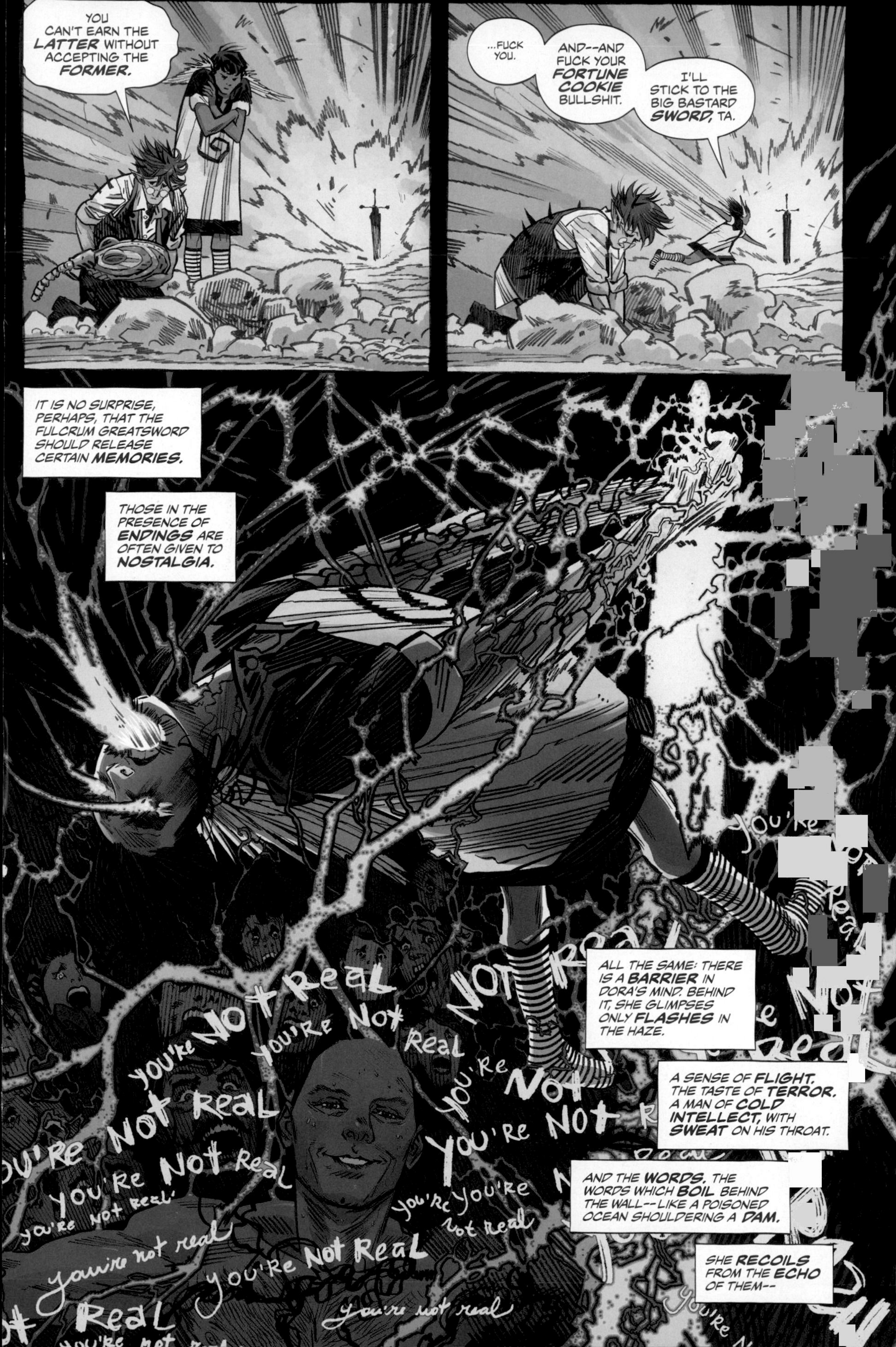
YOU CAN'T EARN THE **LATTER** WITHOUT ACCEPTING THE **FORMER.**
...FUCK YOU.
AND--AND FUCK YOUR **FORTUNE COOKIE** BULLSHIT.
I'LL STICK TO THE BIG BASTARD **SWORD,** TA.
IT IS NO SURPRISE, PERHAPS, THAT THE FULCRUM GREATSWORD SHOULD RELEASE CERTAIN **MEMORIES.**
THOSE IN THE PRESENCE OF **ENDINGS** ARE OFTEN GIVEN TO **NOSTALGIA.**
ALL THE SAME: THERE IS A **BARRIER** IN DORA'S MIND. BEHIND IT, SHE GLIMPSES ONLY **FLASHES** IN THE HAZE.
A SENSE OF **FLIGHT.** THE TASTE OF **TERROR.** A MAN OF **COLD INTELLECT,** WITH **SWEAT** ON HIS THROAT.
AND THE **WORDS.** THE WORDS WHICH **BOIL** BEHIND THE WALL--LIKE A POISONED OCEAN SHOULDERING A **DAM.**
SHE **RECOILS** FROM THE **ECHO** OF THEM--
YOU'RE NOT REAL
YOU'RE NOT REAL
YOU'RE NOT REAL
YOU'RE NOT REAL
YOU'RE NOT REAL
you're not real
you're not real

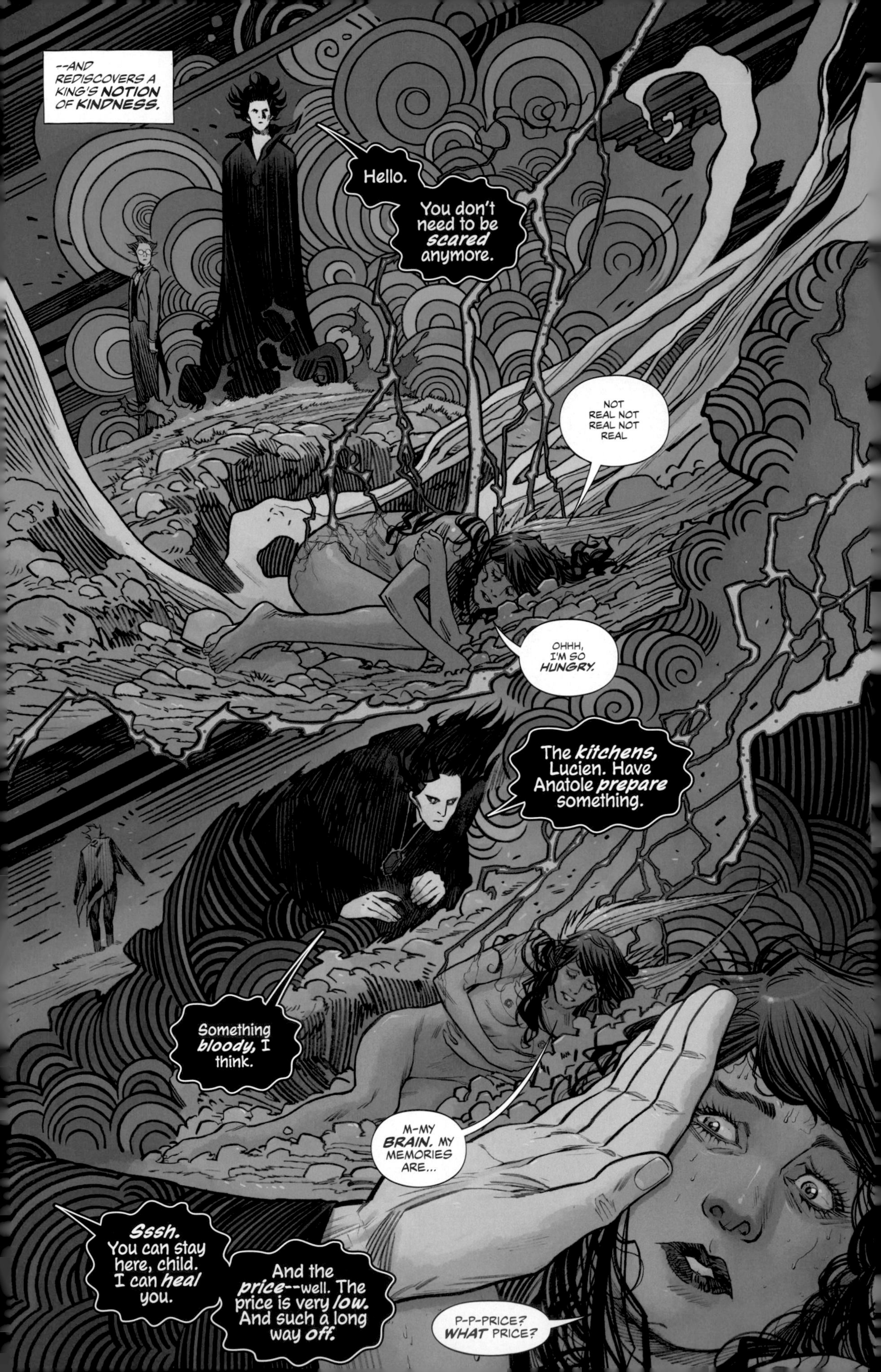
--AND REDISCOVERS A KING'S NOTION OF KINDNESS.
Hello.
You don't need to be scared anymore.
NOT REAL NOT REAL NOT REAL
OHHH, I'M SO HUNGRY.
The kitchens, Lucien. Have Anatole prepare something.
Something bloody, I think.
M-MY BRAIN. MY MEMORIES ARE...
Sssh. You can stay here, child. I can heal you.
And the price--well. The price is very low. And such a long way off.
P-P-PRICE? WHAT PRICE?

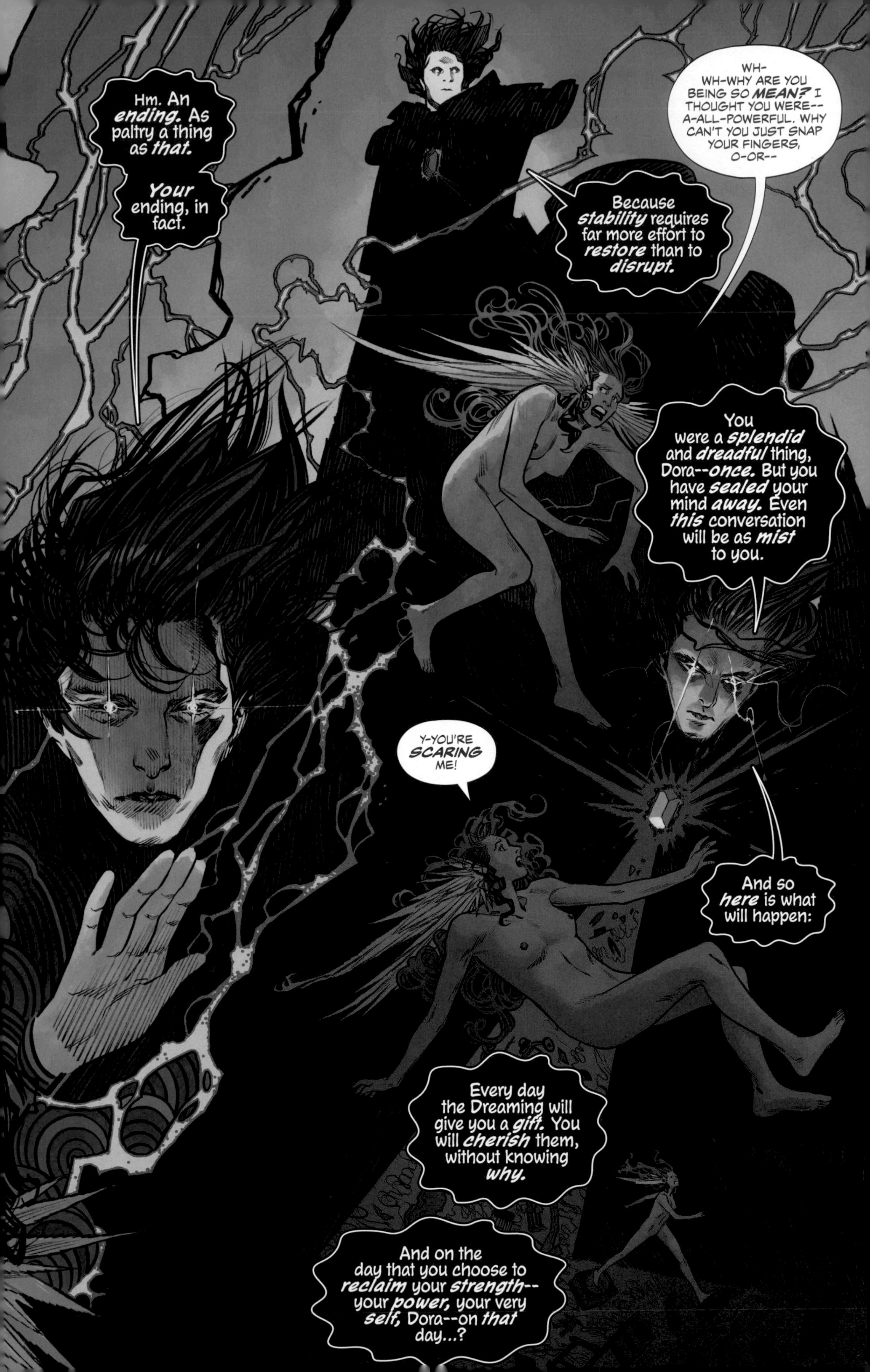
Hm. An *ending.* As paltry a thing as *that.*
Your ending, in fact.
WH-WH-WHY ARE YOU BEING SO *MEAN?* I THOUGHT YOU WERE--A-ALL-POWERFUL. WHY CAN'T YOU JUST SNAP YOUR FINGERS, O-OR--
Because *stability* requires far more effort to *restore* than to *disrupt.*
You were a *splendid* and *dreadful* thing, Dora--*once.* But you have *sealed* your mind *away.* Even *this* conversation will be as *mist* to you.
Y-YOU'RE *SCARING* ME!
And so *here* is what will happen:
Every day the Dreaming will give you a *gift.* You will *cherish* them, without knowing *why.*
And on the day that you choose to *reclaim* your *strength*--your *power,* your very *self,* Dora--on *that* day...?

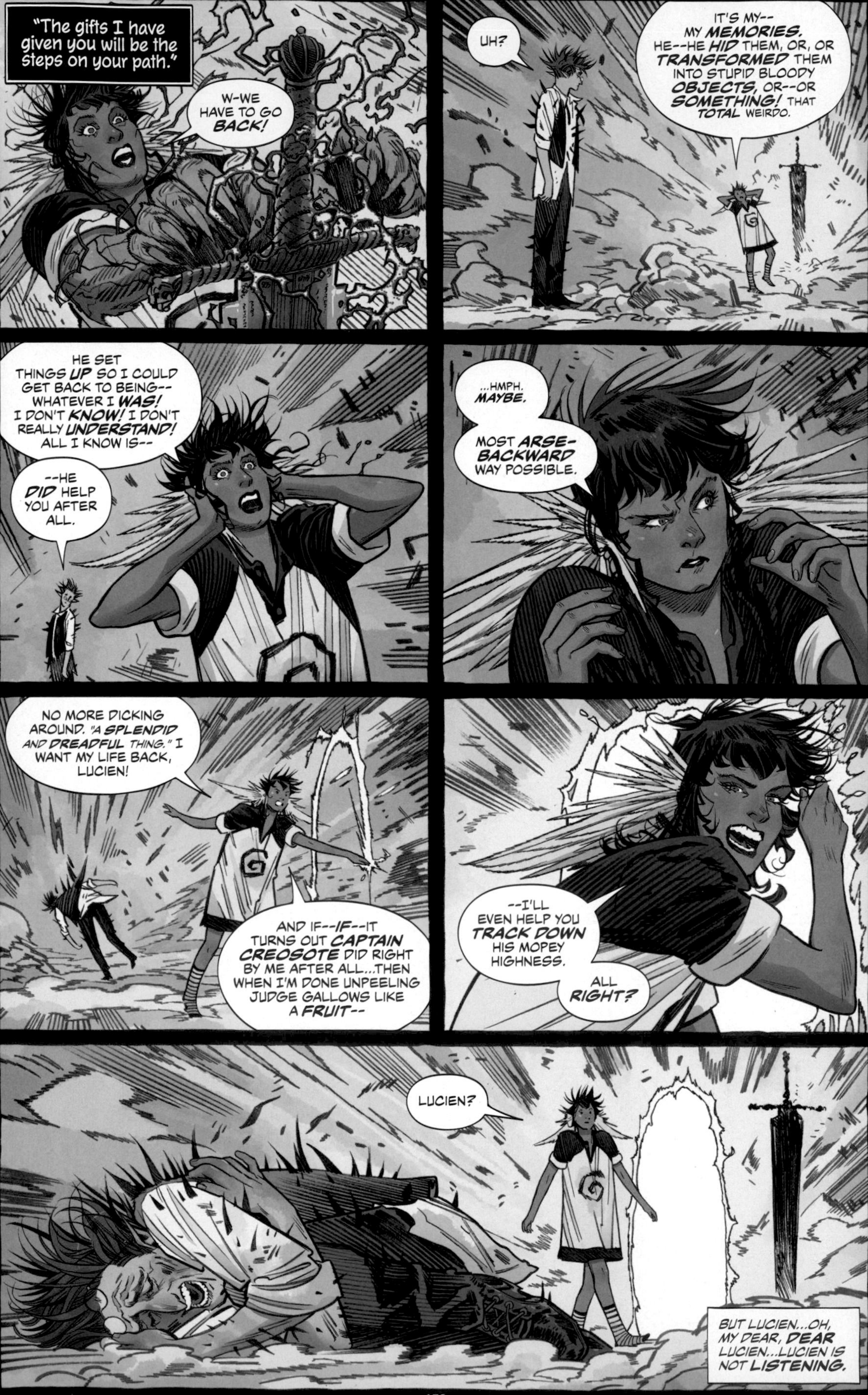
"The gifts I have given you will be the steps on your path."
W-WE HAVE TO GO BACK!
UH?
IT'S MY-- MY MEMORIES. HE--HE HID THEM, OR, OR TRANSFORMED THEM INTO STUPID BLOODY OBJECTS, OR--OR SOMETHING! THAT TOTAL WEIRDO.
HE SET THINGS UP SO I COULD GET BACK TO BEING-- WHATEVER I WAS! I DON'T KNOW! I DON'T REALLY UNDERSTAND! ALL I KNOW IS--
--HE DID HELP YOU AFTER ALL.
...HMPH. MAYBE.
MOST ARSE-BACKWARD WAY POSSIBLE.
NO MORE DICKING AROUND. "A SPLENDID AND DREADFUL THING." I WANT MY LIFE BACK, LUCIEN!
AND IF--IF--IT TURNS OUT CAPTAIN CREOSOTE DID RIGHT BY ME AFTER ALL...THEN WHEN I'M DONE UNPEELING JUDGE GALLOWS LIKE A FRUIT--
--I'LL EVEN HELP YOU TRACK DOWN HIS MOPEY HIGHNESS.
ALL RIGHT?
LUCIEN?
BUT LUCIEN...OH, MY DEAR, DEAR LUCIEN...LUCIEN IS NOT LISTENING.

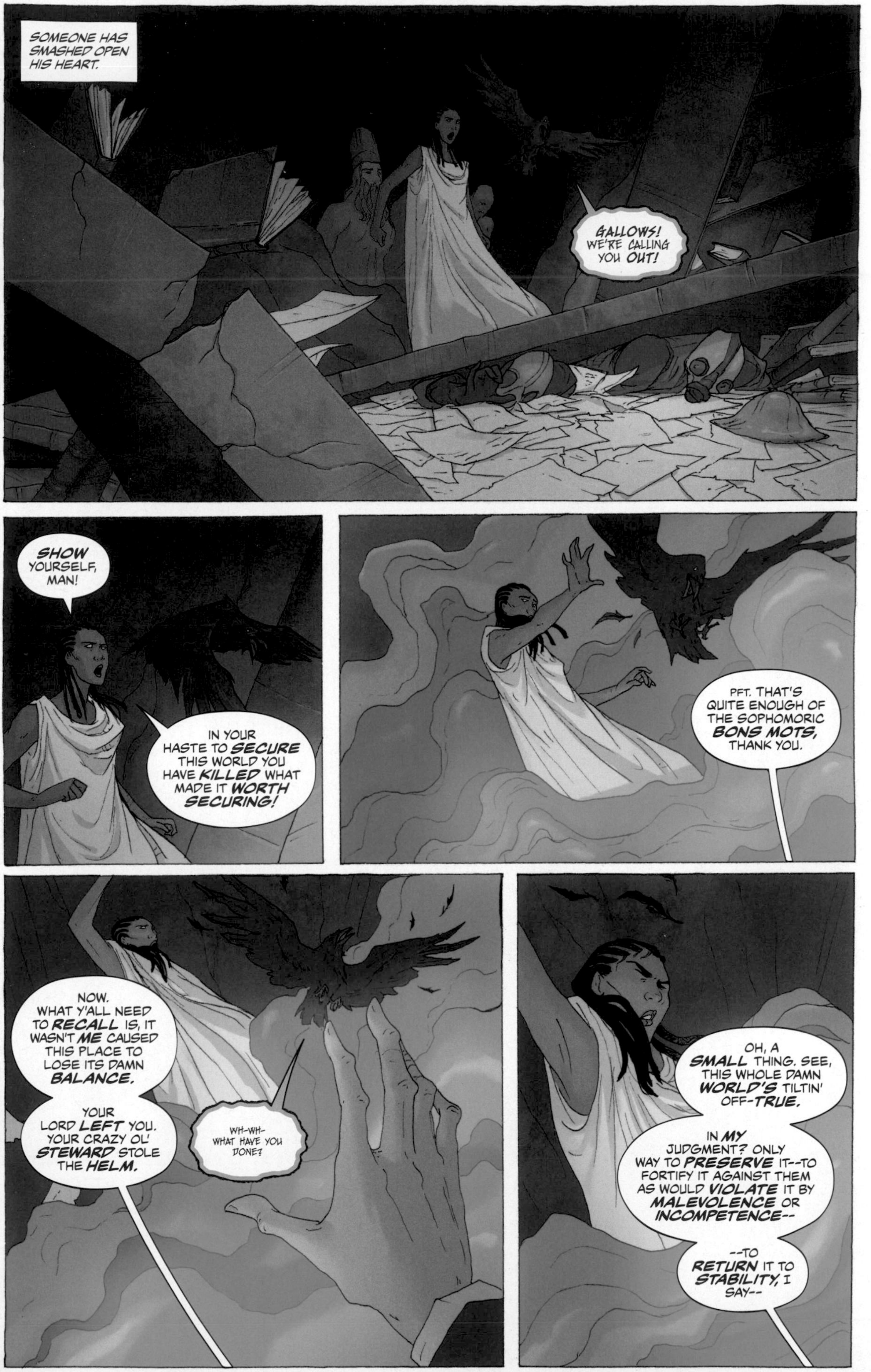
SOMEONE HAS SMASHED OPEN HIS HEART.
GALLOWS! WE'RE CALLING YOU OUT!
SHOW YOURSELF, MAN!
IN YOUR HASTE TO SECURE THIS WORLD YOU HAVE KILLED WHAT MADE IT WORTH SECURING!
PFT. THAT'S QUITE ENOUGH OF THE SOPHOMORIC BONS MOTS, THANK YOU.
NOW. WHAT Y'ALL NEED TO RECALL IS, IT WASN'T ME CAUSED THIS PLACE TO LOSE ITS DAMN BALANCE.
YOUR LORD LEFT YOU. YOUR CRAZY OL' STEWARD STOLE THE HELM.
WH-WH- WHAT HAVE YOU DONE?
OH, A SMALL THING. SEE, THIS WHOLE DAMN WORLD'S TILTIN' OFF-TRUE.
IN MY JUDGMENT? ONLY WAY TO PRESERVE IT--TO FORTIFY IT AGAINST THEM AS WOULD VIOLATE IT BY MALEVOLENCE OR INCOMPETENCE--
--TO RETURN IT TO STABILITY, I SAY--

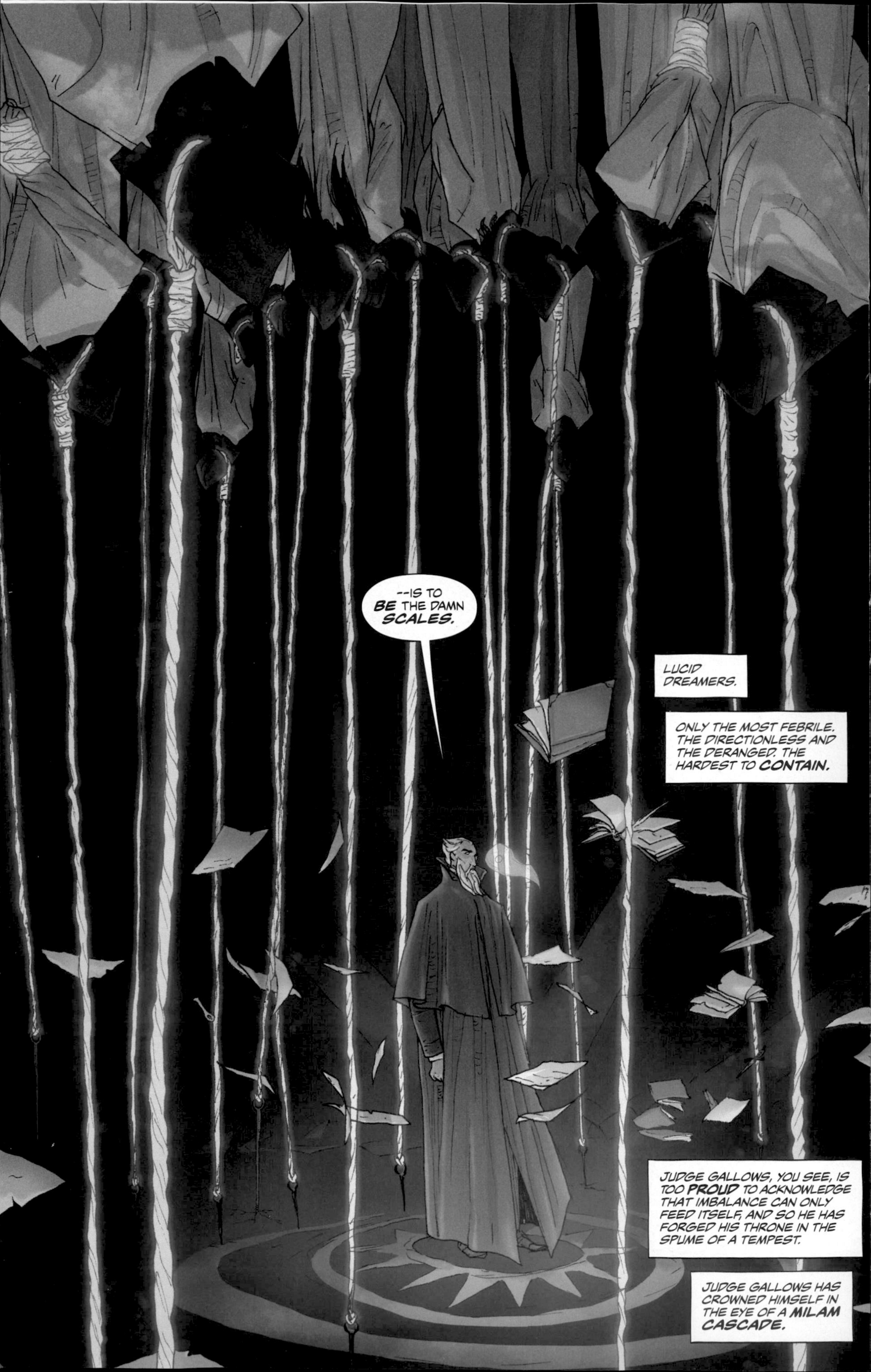
--IS TO BE THE DAMN SCALES.
LUCID DREAMERS.
ONLY THE MOST FEBRILE. THE DIRECTIONLESS AND THE DERANGED. THE HARDEST TO CONTAIN.
JUDGE GALLOWS, YOU SEE, IS TOO PROUD TO ACKNOWLEDGE THAT IMBALANCE CAN ONLY FEED ITSELF, AND SO HE HAS FORGED HIS THRONE IN THE SPUME OF A TEMPEST.
JUDGE GALLOWS HAS CROWNED HIMSELF IN THE EYE OF A MILAM CASCADE.

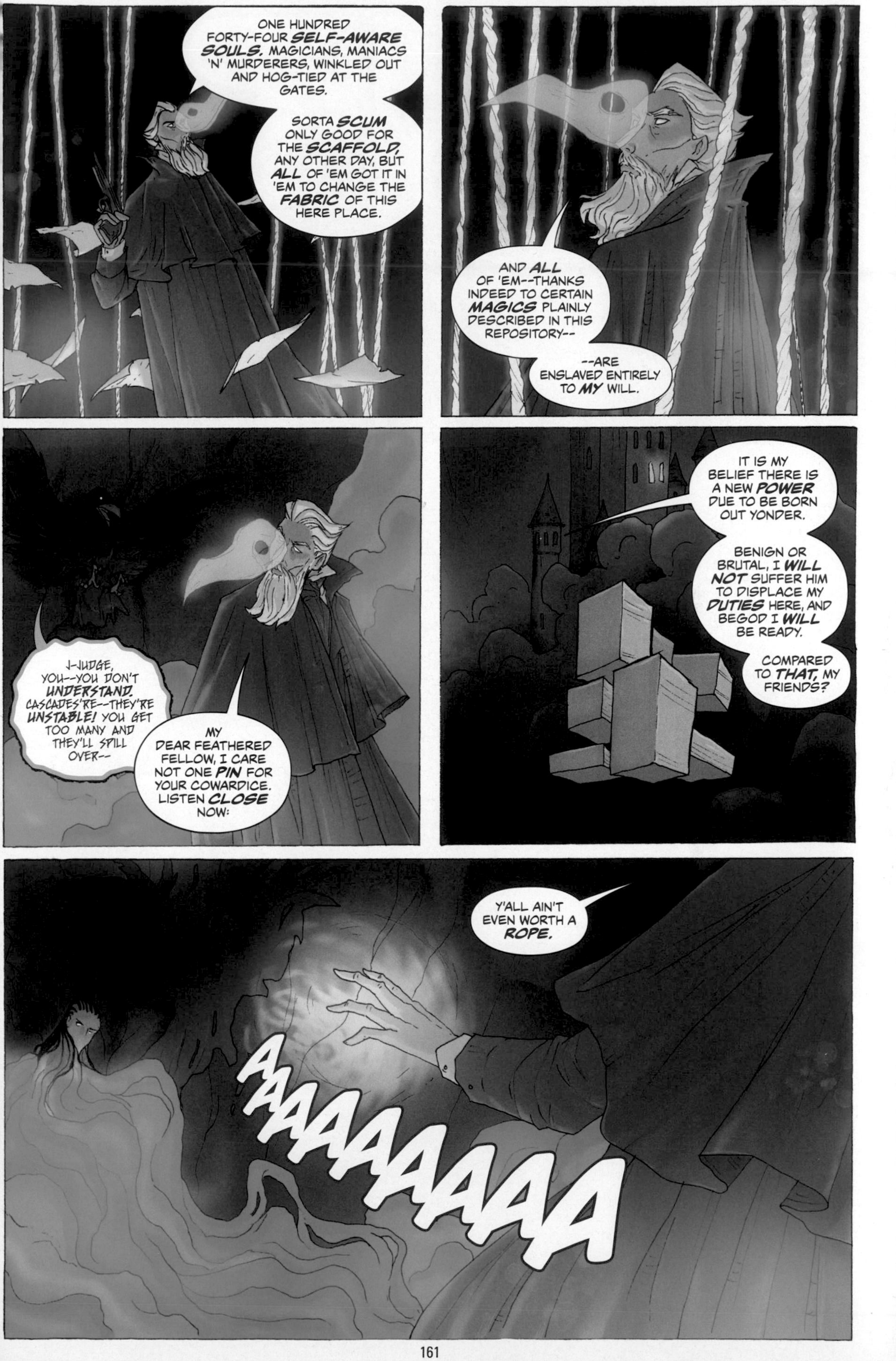
ONE HUNDRED FORTY-FOUR SELF-AWARE SOULS. MAGICIANS, MANIACS 'N' MURDERERS, WINKLED OUT AND HOG-TIED AT THE GATES.
SORTA SCUM ONLY GOOD FOR THE SCAFFOLD, ANY OTHER DAY, BUT ALL OF 'EM GOT IT IN 'EM TO CHANGE THE FABRIC OF THIS HERE PLACE.
AND ALL OF 'EM--THANKS INDEED TO CERTAIN MAGICS PLAINLY DESCRIBED IN THIS REPOSITORY--
--ARE ENSLAVED ENTIRELY TO MY WILL.
J-JUDGE, YOU--YOU DON'T UNDERSTAND. CASCADES'RE--THEY'RE UNSTABLE! YOU GET TOO MANY AND THEY'LL SPILL OVER--
MY DEAR FEATHERED FELLOW, I CARE NOT ONE PIN FOR YOUR COWARDICE. LISTEN CLOSE NOW:
IT IS MY BELIEF THERE IS A NEW POWER DUE TO BE BORN OUT YONDER.
BENIGN OR BRUTAL, I WILL NOT SUFFER HIM TO DISPLACE MY DUTIES HERE, AND BEGOD I WILL BE READY.
COMPARED TO THAT, MY FRIENDS?
Y'ALL AIN'T EVEN WORTH A ROPE.
AAAAAAAAAAAA

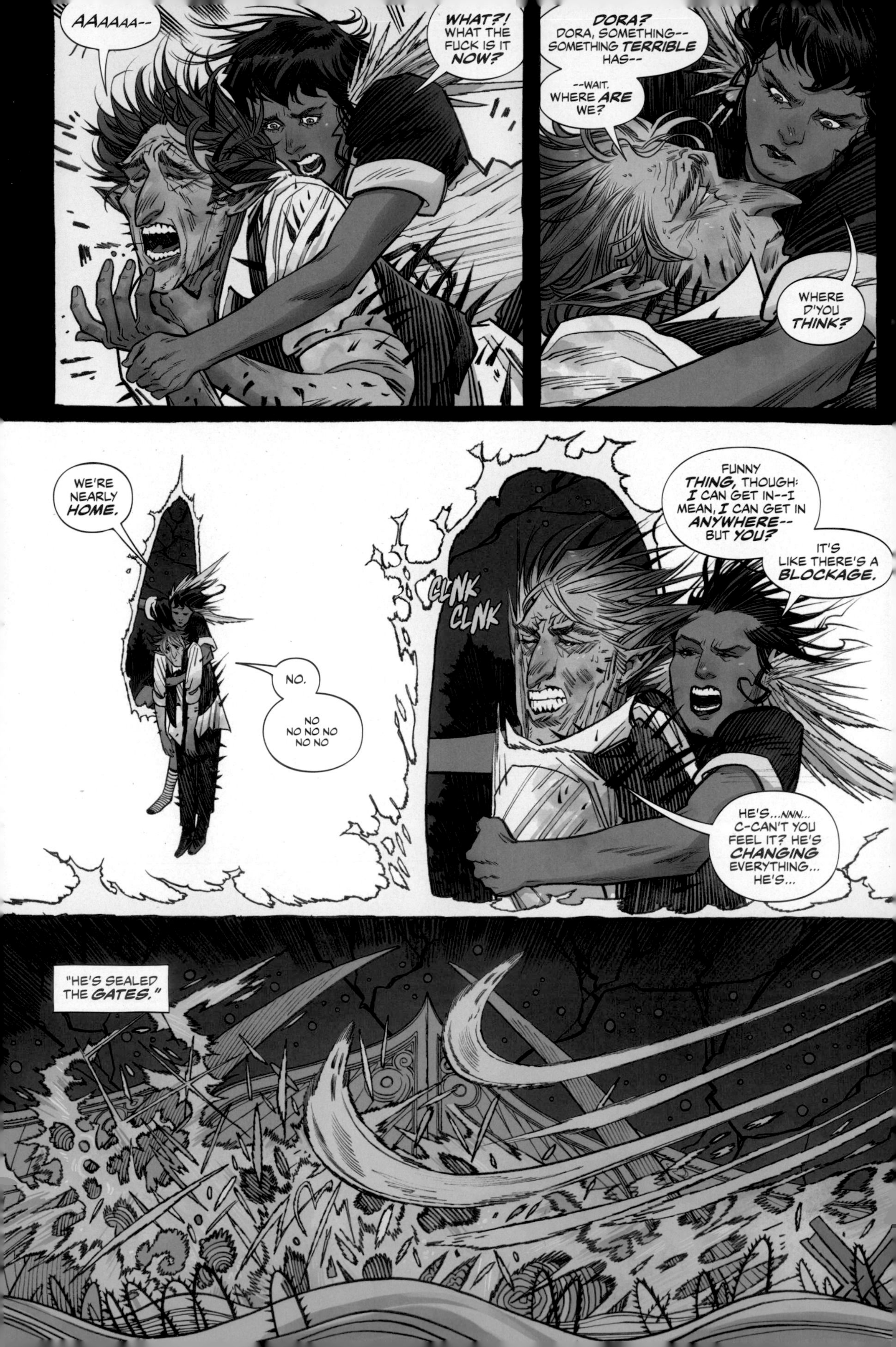
AAAAAA--
WHAT?! WHAT THE FUCK IS IT NOW?
DORA? DORA, SOMETHING-- SOMETHING TERRIBLE HAS--
--WAIT. WHERE ARE WE?
WHERE D'YOU THINK?
WE'RE NEARLY HOME.
NO.
NO NO NO NO NO NO
FUNNY THING, THOUGH: I CAN GET IN--I MEAN, I CAN GET IN ANYWHERE-- BUT YOU?
IT'S LIKE THERE'S A BLOCKAGE.
CLNK CLNK
HE'S...NNN... C-CAN'T YOU FEEL IT? HE'S CHANGING EVERYTHING... HE'S...
"HE'S SEALED THE GATES."

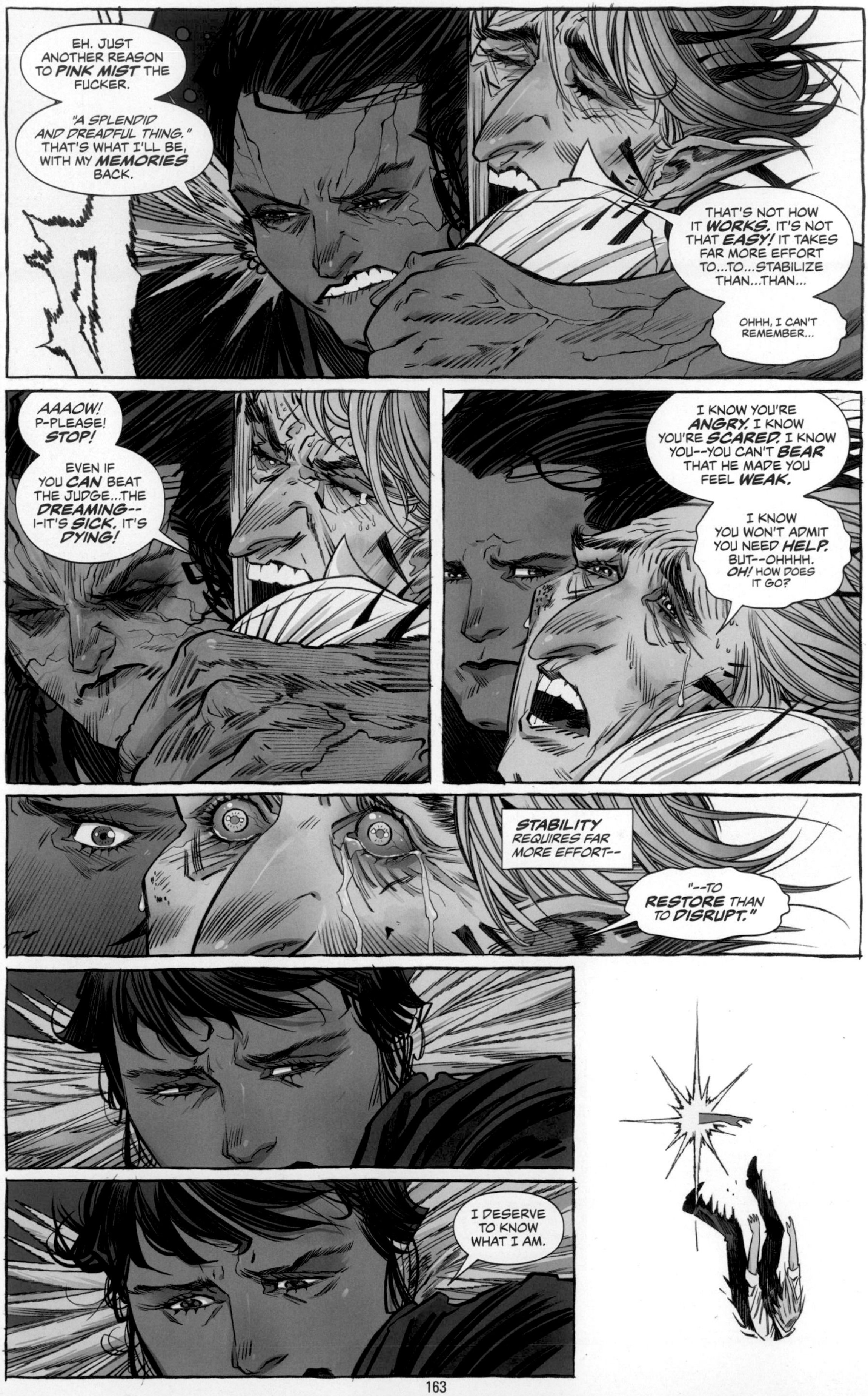
EH. JUST ANOTHER REASON TO PINK MIST THE FUCKER.
"A SPLENDID AND DREADFUL THING." THAT'S WHAT I'LL BE, WITH MY MEMORIES BACK.
THAT'S NOT HOW IT WORKS. IT'S NOT THAT EASY! IT TAKES FAR MORE EFFORT TO...TO...STABILIZE THAN...THAN...
OHHH, I CAN'T REMEMBER...
AAAOW! P-PLEASE! STOP!
EVEN IF YOU CAN BEAT THE JUDGE...THE DREAMING-- I-IT'S SICK. IT'S DYING!
I KNOW YOU'RE ANGRY. I KNOW YOU'RE SCARED. I KNOW YOU--YOU CAN'T BEAR THAT HE MADE YOU FEEL WEAK.
I KNOW YOU WON'T ADMIT YOU NEED HELP. BUT--OHHHH. OH! HOW DOES IT GO?
STABILITY REQUIRES FAR MORE EFFORT--
"--TO RESTORE THAN TO DISRUPT."
I DESERVE TO KNOW WHAT I AM.

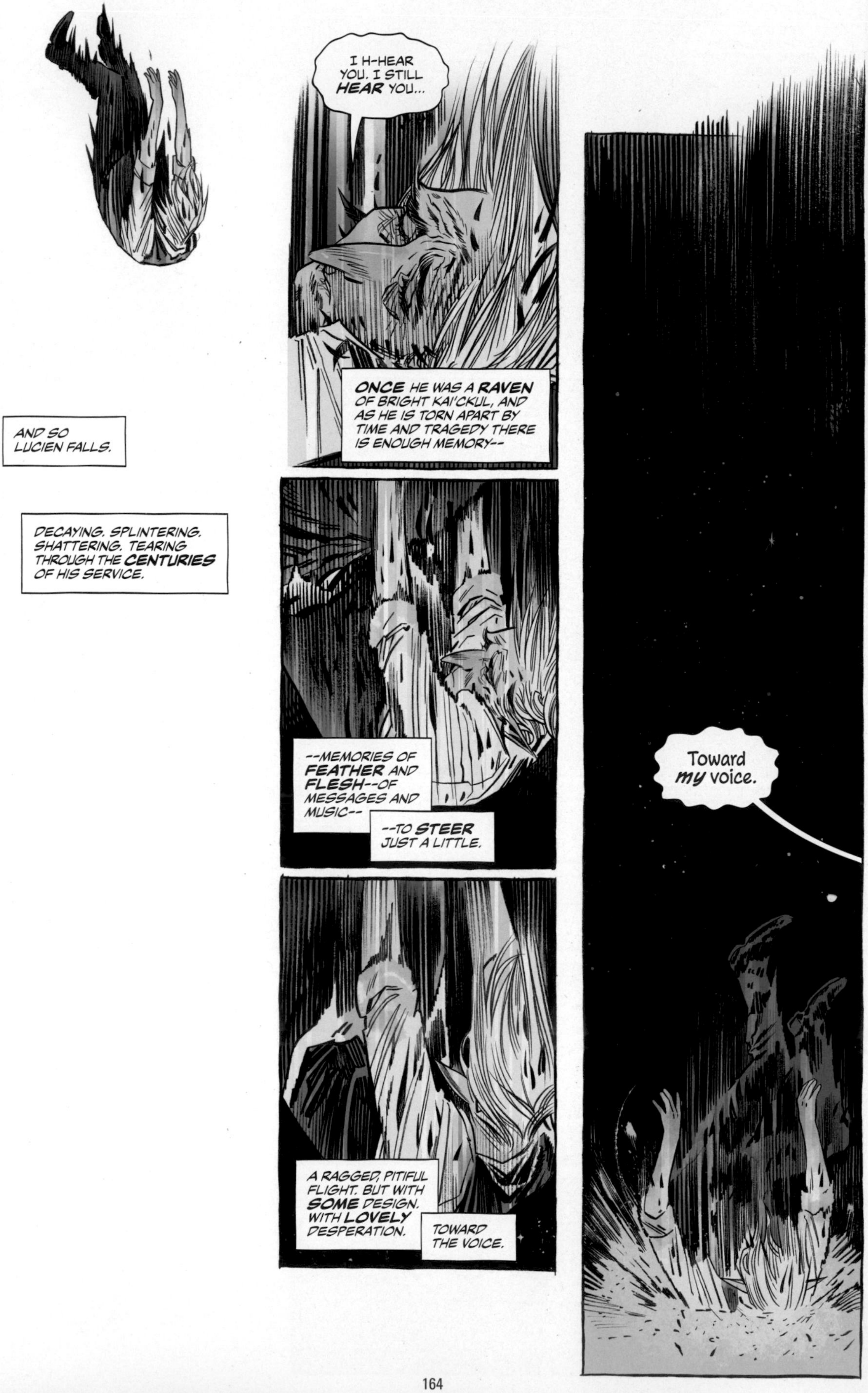
AND SO LUCIEN FALLS.
DECAYING. SPLINTERING. SHATTERING. TEARING THROUGH THE CENTURIES OF HIS SERVICE.
I H-HEAR YOU. I STILL HEAR YOU...
ONCE HE WAS A RAVEN OF BRIGHT KAI'CKUL, AND AS HE IS TORN APART BY TIME AND TRAGEDY THERE IS ENOUGH MEMORY--
--MEMORIES OF FEATHER AND FLESH--OF MESSAGES AND MUSIC--
--TO STEER JUST A LITTLE.
A RAGGED, PITIFUL FLIGHT. BUT WITH SOME DESIGN. WITH LOVELY DESPERATION.
TOWARD THE VOICE.
Toward my voice.

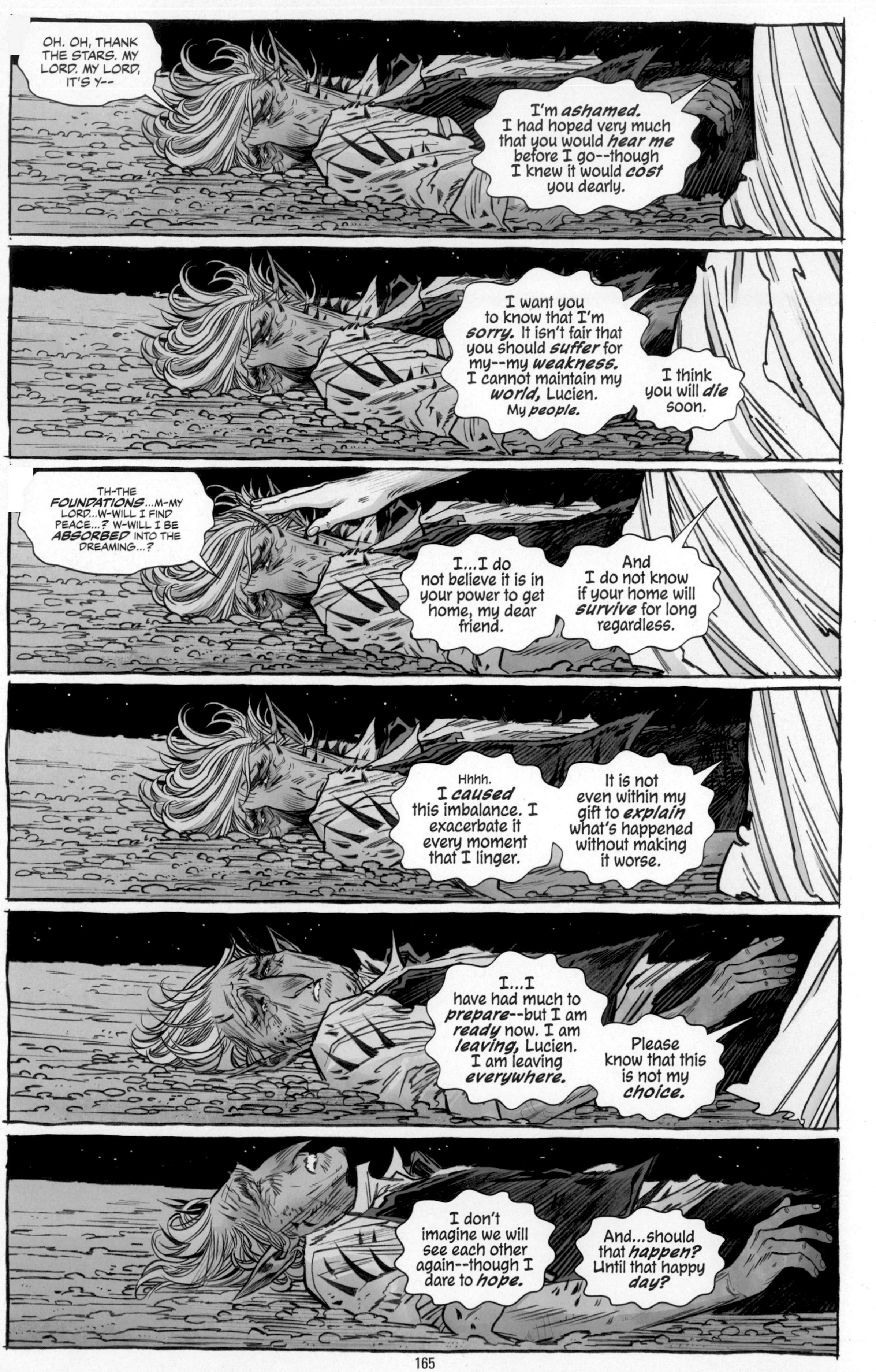
OH. OH, THANK THE STARS. MY LORD. MY LORD, IT'S Y--
I'm *ashamed.* I had hoped very much that you would *hear me* before I go--though I knew it would *cost* you dearly.
I want you to know that I'm *sorry.* It isn't fair that you should *suffer* for my--my *weakness.* I cannot maintain my *world,* Lucien. My *people.*
I think you will *die* soon.
TH-THE *FOUNDATIONS*...M-MY LORD...W-WILL I FIND PEACE...? W-WILL I BE *ABSORBED* INTO THE DREAMING...?
I...I do not believe it is in your power to get home, my dear friend.
And I do not know if your home will *survive* for long regardless.
Hhhh. I *caused* this imbalance. I exacerbate it every moment that I linger.
It is not even within my gift to *explain* what's happened without making it worse.
I...I have had much to *prepare*--but I am *ready* now. I am *leaving,* Lucien. I am leaving *everywhere.*
Please know that this is not my *choice.*
I don't imagine we will see each other again--though I dare to *hope.*
And...should that *happen?* Until that happy *day?*

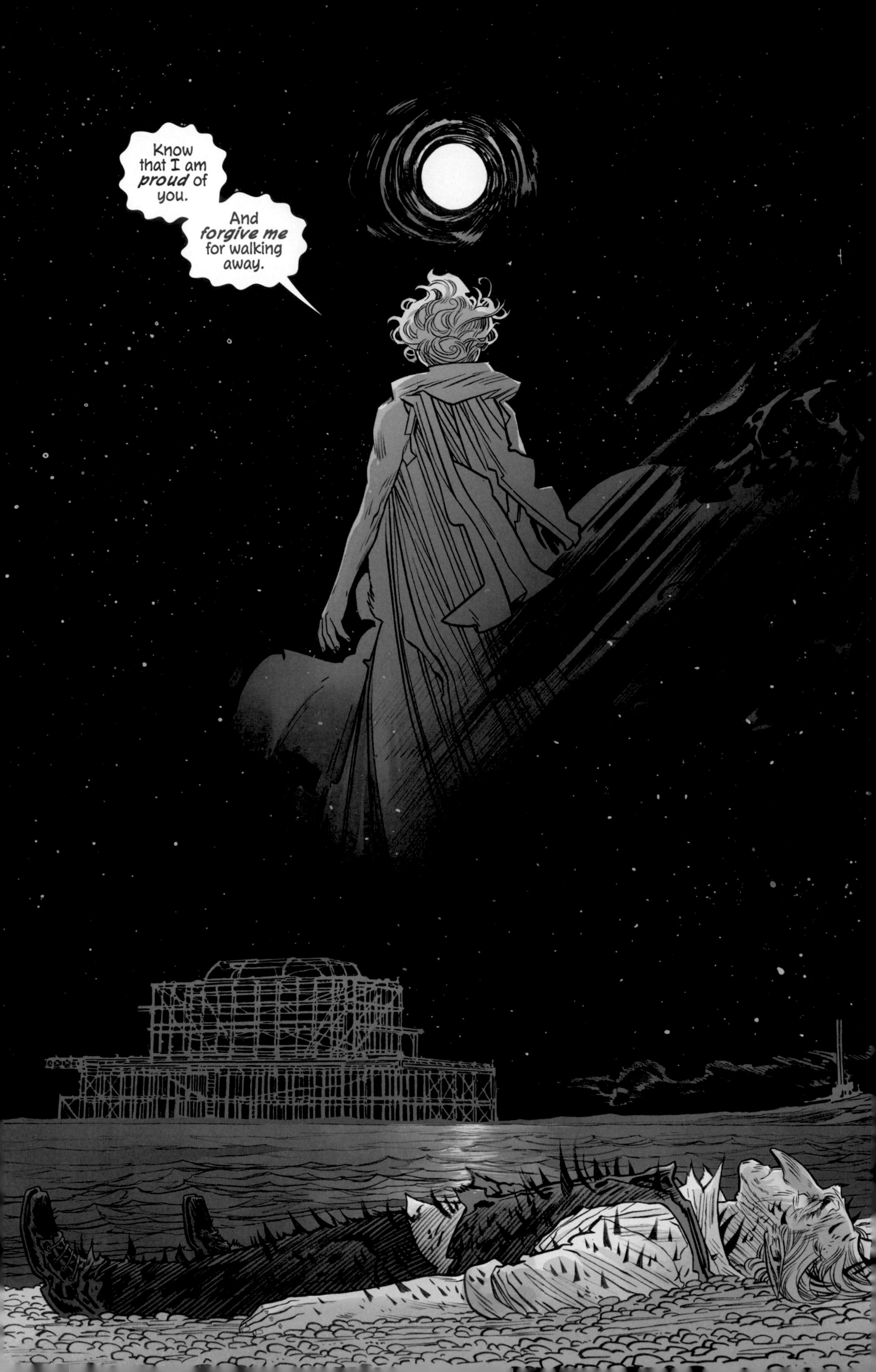
Know that I am *proud* of you.
And *forgive me* for walking away.

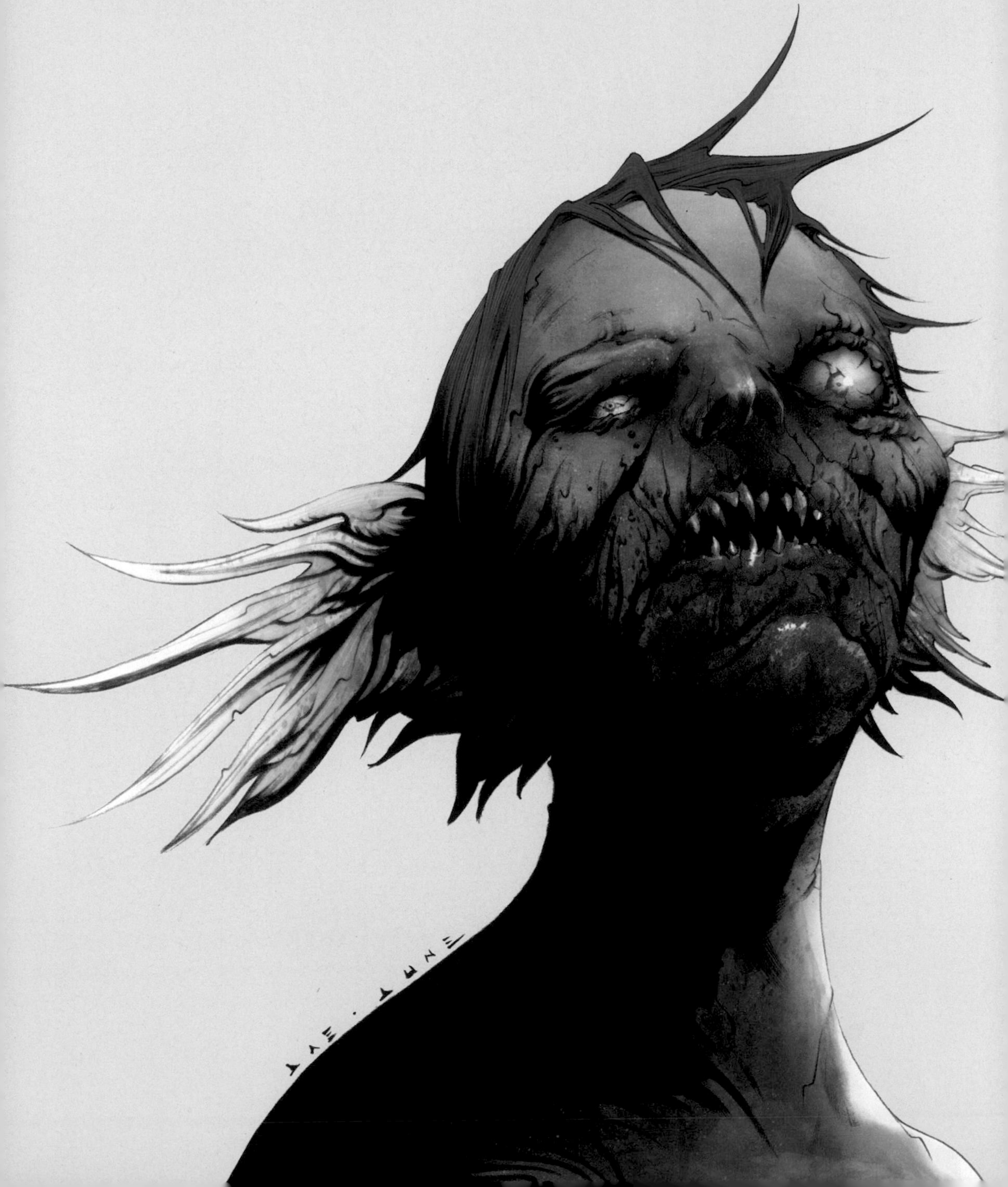

THE DREAMING

Judgment

WRITTEN BY
Simon Spurrier

ILLUSTRATED BY
Bilquis Evely

COLORS BY
Mat Lopes

LETTERS BY
Simon Bowland

COVER ART BY
Jae Lee and *June Chung*

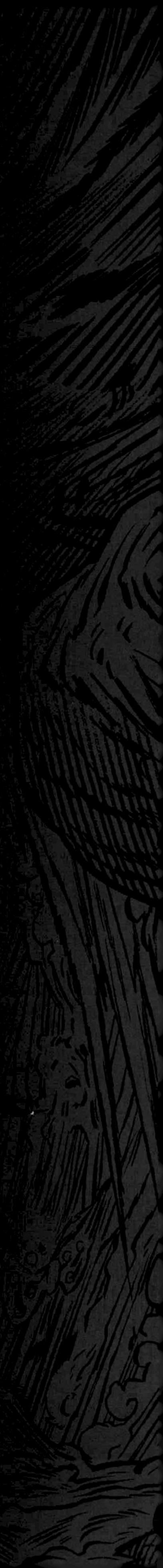

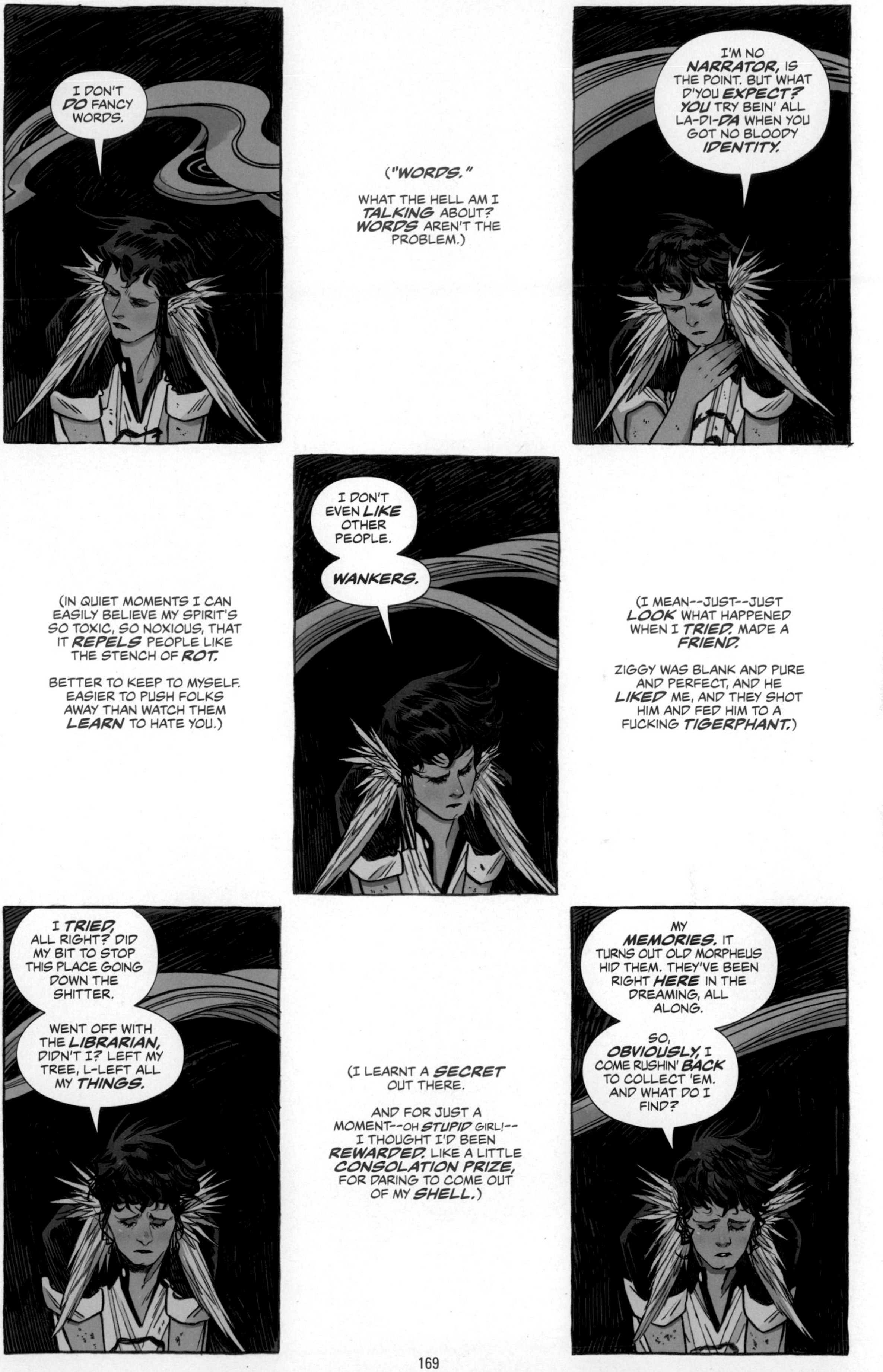
I DON'T DO FANCY WORDS.
("WORDS."
WHAT THE HELL AM I TALKING ABOUT? WORDS AREN'T THE PROBLEM.)
I'M NO NARRATOR, IS THE POINT. BUT WHAT D'YOU EXPECT? YOU TRY BEIN' ALL LA-DI-DA WHEN YOU GOT NO BLOODY IDENTITY.
(IN QUIET MOMENTS I CAN EASILY BELIEVE MY SPIRIT'S SO TOXIC, SO NOXIOUS, THAT IT REPELS PEOPLE LIKE THE STENCH OF ROT.
BETTER TO KEEP TO MYSELF. EASIER TO PUSH FOLKS AWAY THAN WATCH THEM LEARN TO HATE YOU.)
I DON'T EVEN LIKE OTHER PEOPLE.
WANKERS.
(I MEAN--JUST--JUST LOOK WHAT HAPPENED WHEN I TRIED. MADE A FRIEND.
ZIGGY WAS BLANK AND PURE AND PERFECT, AND HE LIKED ME, AND THEY SHOT HIM AND FED HIM TO A FUCKING TIGERPHANT.)
I TRIED, ALL RIGHT? DID MY BIT TO STOP THIS PLACE GOING DOWN THE SHITTER.
WENT OFF WITH THE LIBRARIAN, DIDN'T I? LEFT MY TREE, L-LEFT ALL MY THINGS.
(I LEARNT A SECRET OUT THERE.
AND FOR JUST A MOMENT--OH STUPID GIRL!--I THOUGHT I'D BEEN REWARDED. LIKE A LITTLE CONSOLATION PRIZE, FOR DARING TO COME OUT OF MY SHELL.)
MY MEMORIES. IT TURNS OUT OLD MORPHEUS HID THEM. THEY'VE BEEN RIGHT HERE IN THE DREAMING, ALL ALONG.
SO, OBVIOUSLY, I COME RUSHIN' BACK TO COLLECT 'EM. AND WHAT DO I FIND?

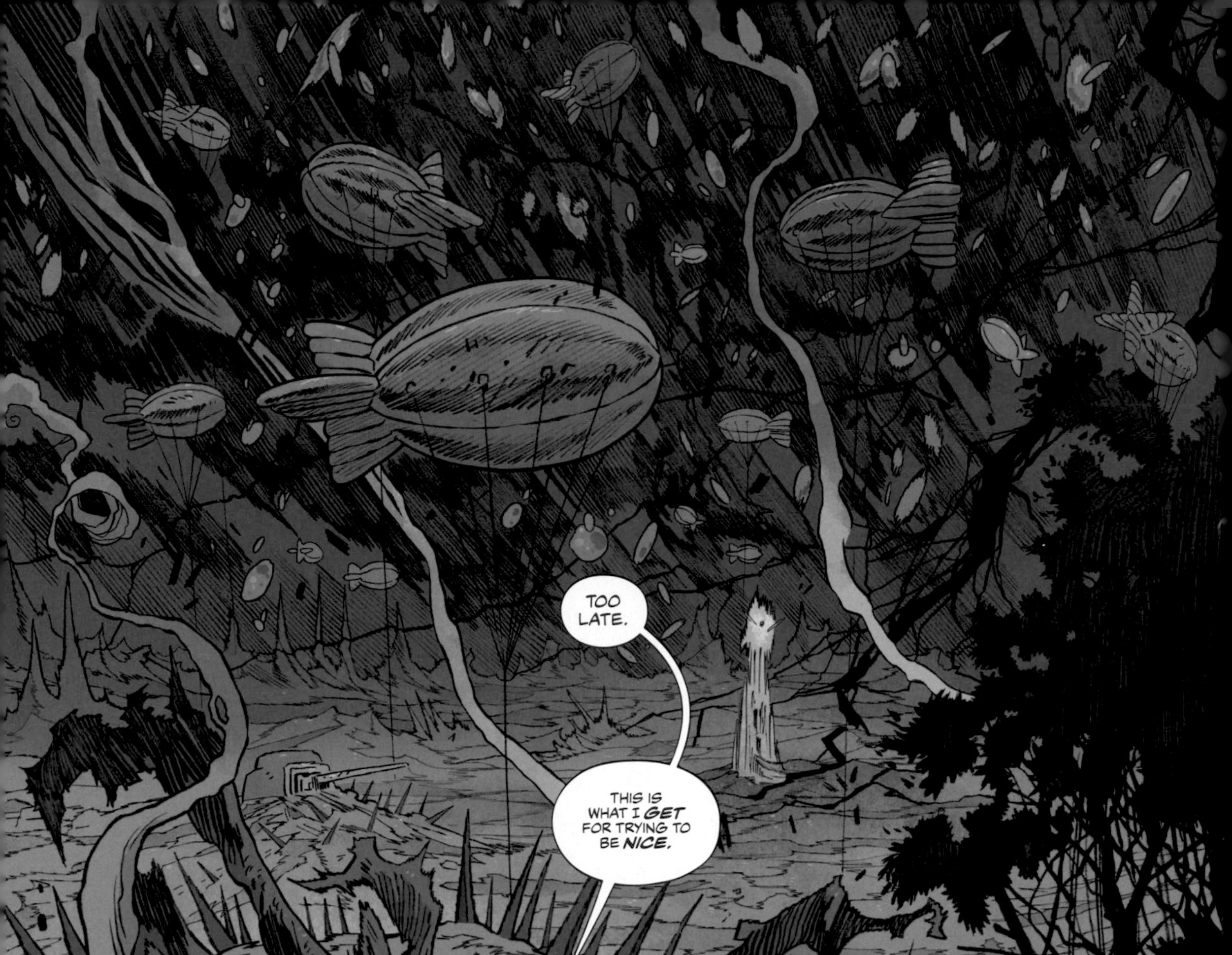
TOO LATE.
THIS IS WHAT I GET FOR TRYING TO BE NICE.

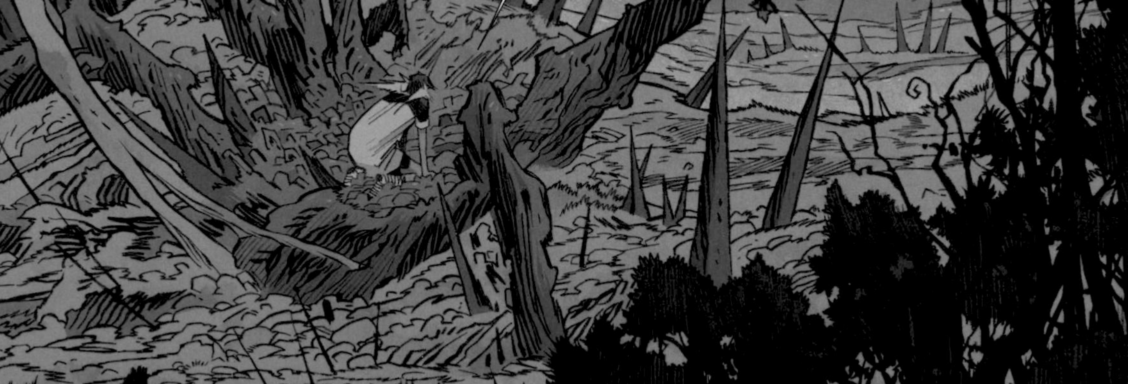
MM. OUR JUMPED-UP JUDGE IS CERTAINLY MAKING SOME CHANGES. HE SAYS THE DREAMING'S EASIER TO DEFEND LIKE THIS.
I'M GOING TO KILL HIM.
I'M GOING TO SPLIT HIS THROAT AND POP HIS JOINTS AND TWIST HIS THUMBS AND BREAK HIS TEETH AND--AND--AND...

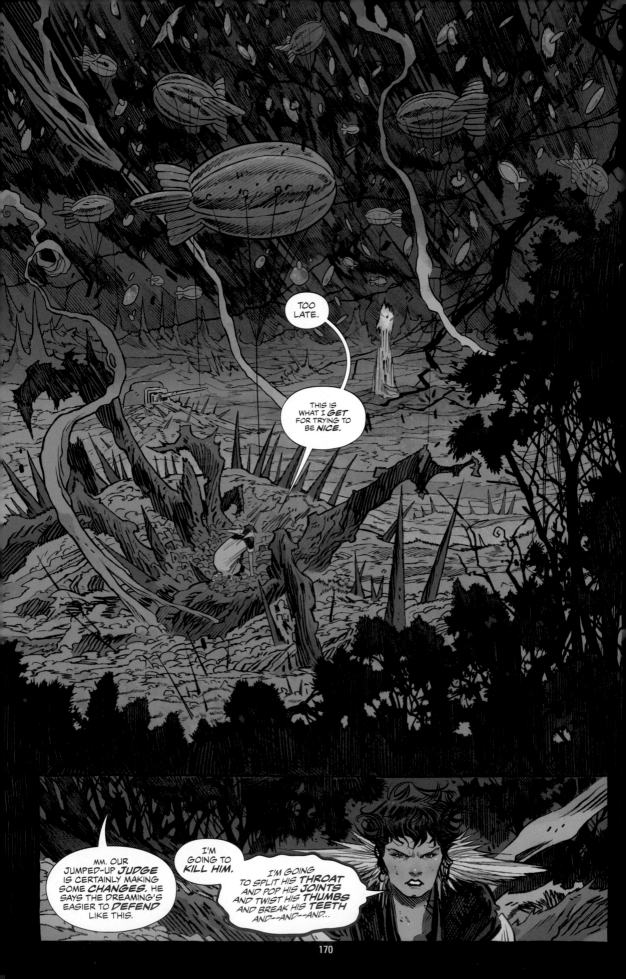

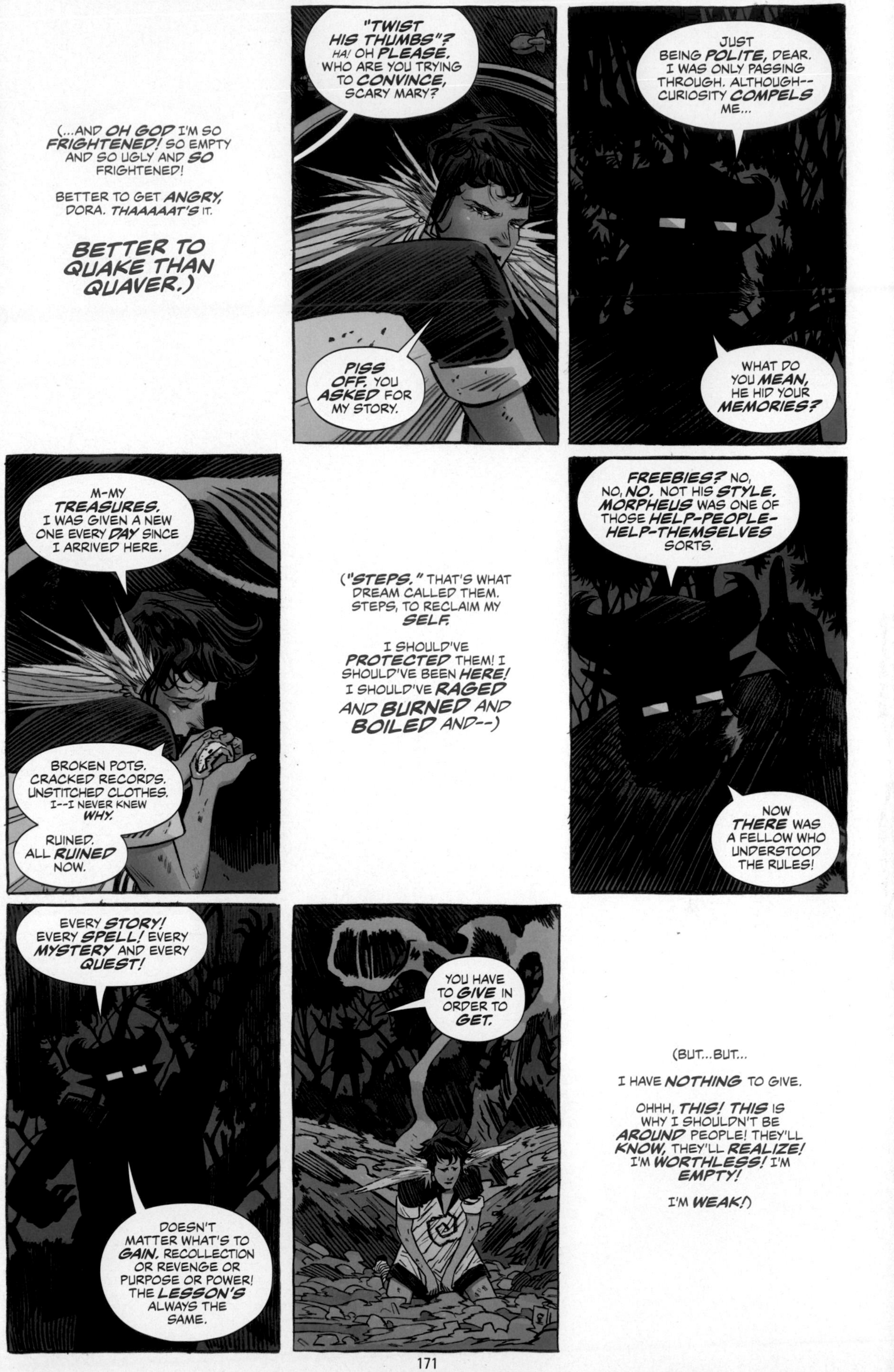
(...AND OH GOD I'M SO FRIGHTENED! SO EMPTY AND SO UGLY AND SO FRIGHTENED!
BETTER TO GET ANGRY, DORA. THAAAAAT'S IT.
BETTER TO QUAKE THAN QUAVER.)
"TWIST HIS THUMBS"? HA! OH PLEASE. WHO ARE YOU TRYING TO CONVINCE, SCARY MARY?
PISS OFF. YOU ASKED FOR MY STORY.
JUST BEING POLITE, DEAR. I WAS ONLY PASSING THROUGH. ALTHOUGH-- CURIOSITY COMPELS ME...
WHAT DO YOU MEAN, HE HID YOUR MEMORIES?
M-MY TREASURES. I WAS GIVEN A NEW ONE EVERY DAY SINCE I ARRIVED HERE.
BROKEN POTS. CRACKED RECORDS. UNSTITCHED CLOTHES. I--I NEVER KNEW WHY.
RUINED. ALL RUINED NOW.
("STEPS." THAT'S WHAT DREAM CALLED THEM. STEPS, TO RECLAIM MY SELF.
I SHOULD'VE PROTECTED THEM! I SHOULD'VE BEEN HERE! I SHOULD'VE RAGED AND BURNED AND BOILED AND--)
FREEBIES? NO, NO, NO. NOT HIS STYLE. MORPHEUS WAS ONE OF THOSE HELP-PEOPLE-HELP-THEMSELVES SORTS.
NOW THERE WAS A FELLOW WHO UNDERSTOOD THE RULES!
EVERY STORY! EVERY SPELL! EVERY MYSTERY AND EVERY QUEST!
DOESN'T MATTER WHAT'S TO GAIN. RECOLLECTION OR REVENGE OR PURPOSE OR POWER! THE LESSON'S ALWAYS THE SAME.
YOU HAVE TO GIVE IN ORDER TO GET.
(BUT...BUT...
I HAVE NOTHING TO GIVE.
OHHH, THIS! THIS IS WHY I SHOULDN'T BE AROUND PEOPLE! THEY'LL KNOW, THEY'LL REALIZE! I'M WORTHLESS! I'M EMPTY!
I'M WEAK!)

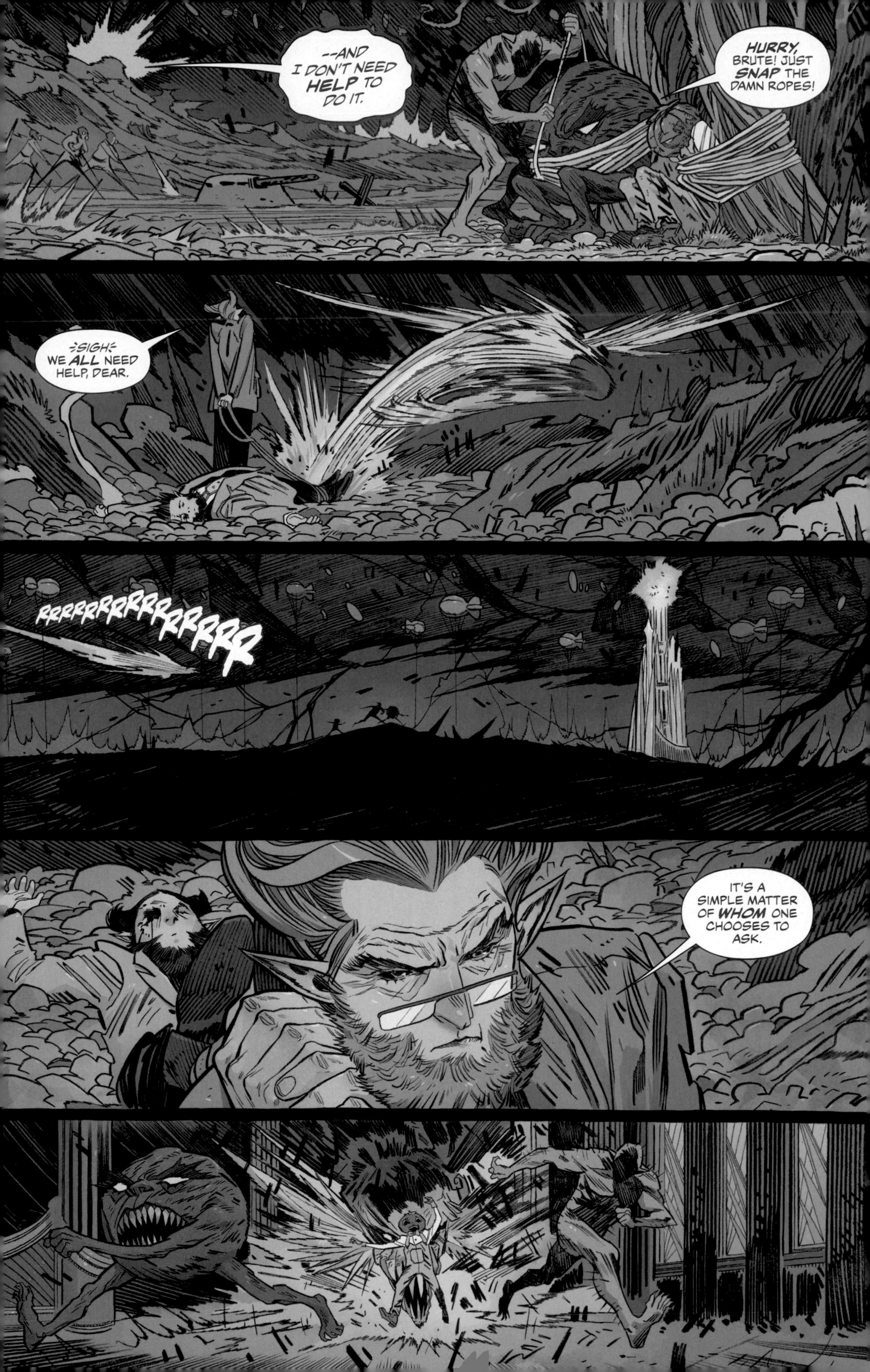
--AND I DON'T NEED **HELP** TO DO IT.
HURRY, BRUTE! JUST ***SNAP*** THE DAMN ROPES!
SIGH
WE ***ALL*** NEED HELP, DEAR.
RRRRRRRRRRRRRRRR
IT'S A SIMPLE MATTER OF ***WHOM*** ONE CHOOSES TO ASK.

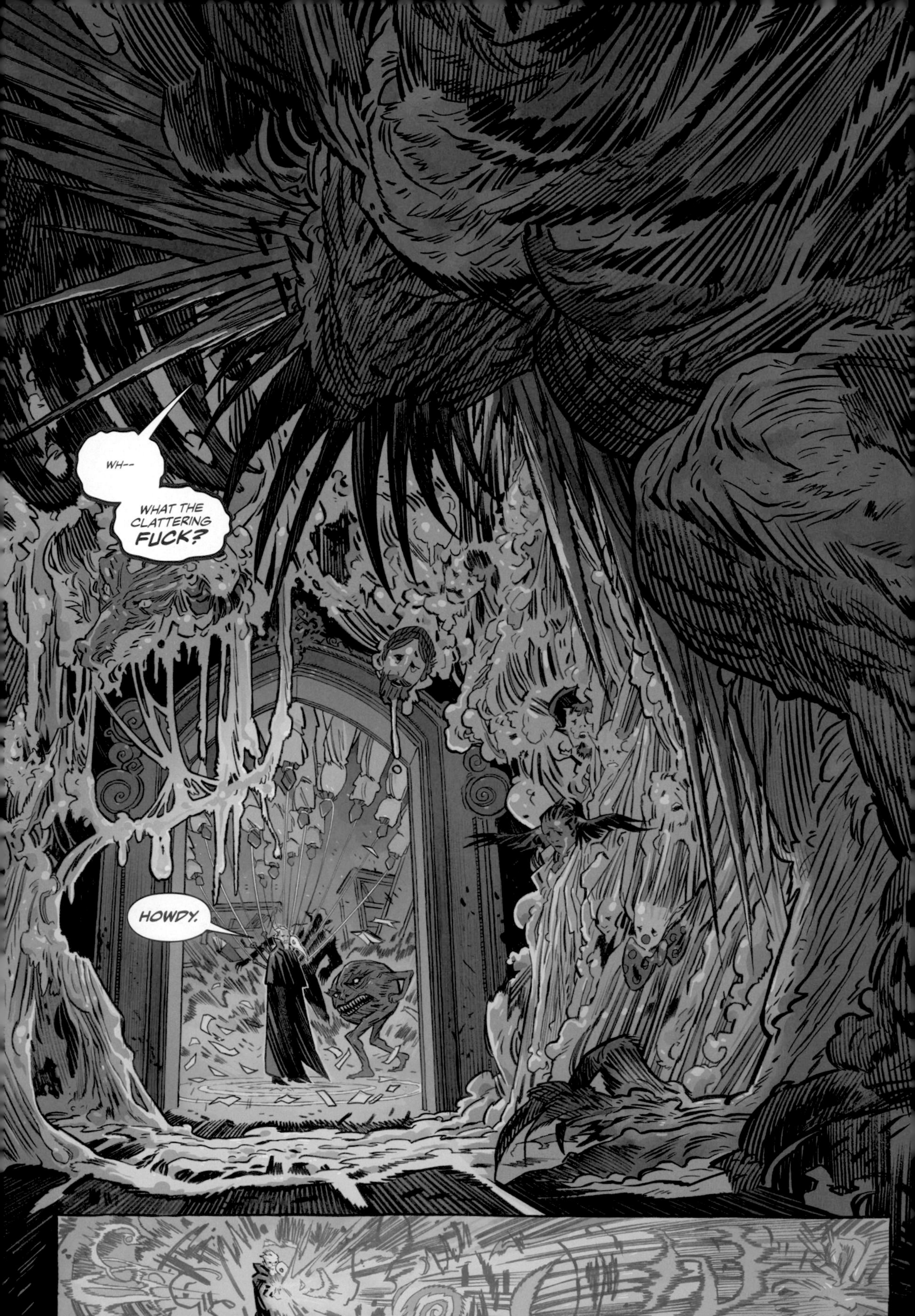
WH--
WHAT THE CLATTERING FUCK?
HOWDY.
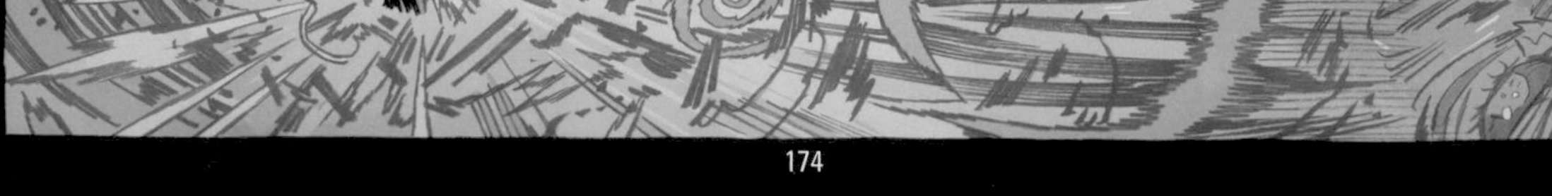

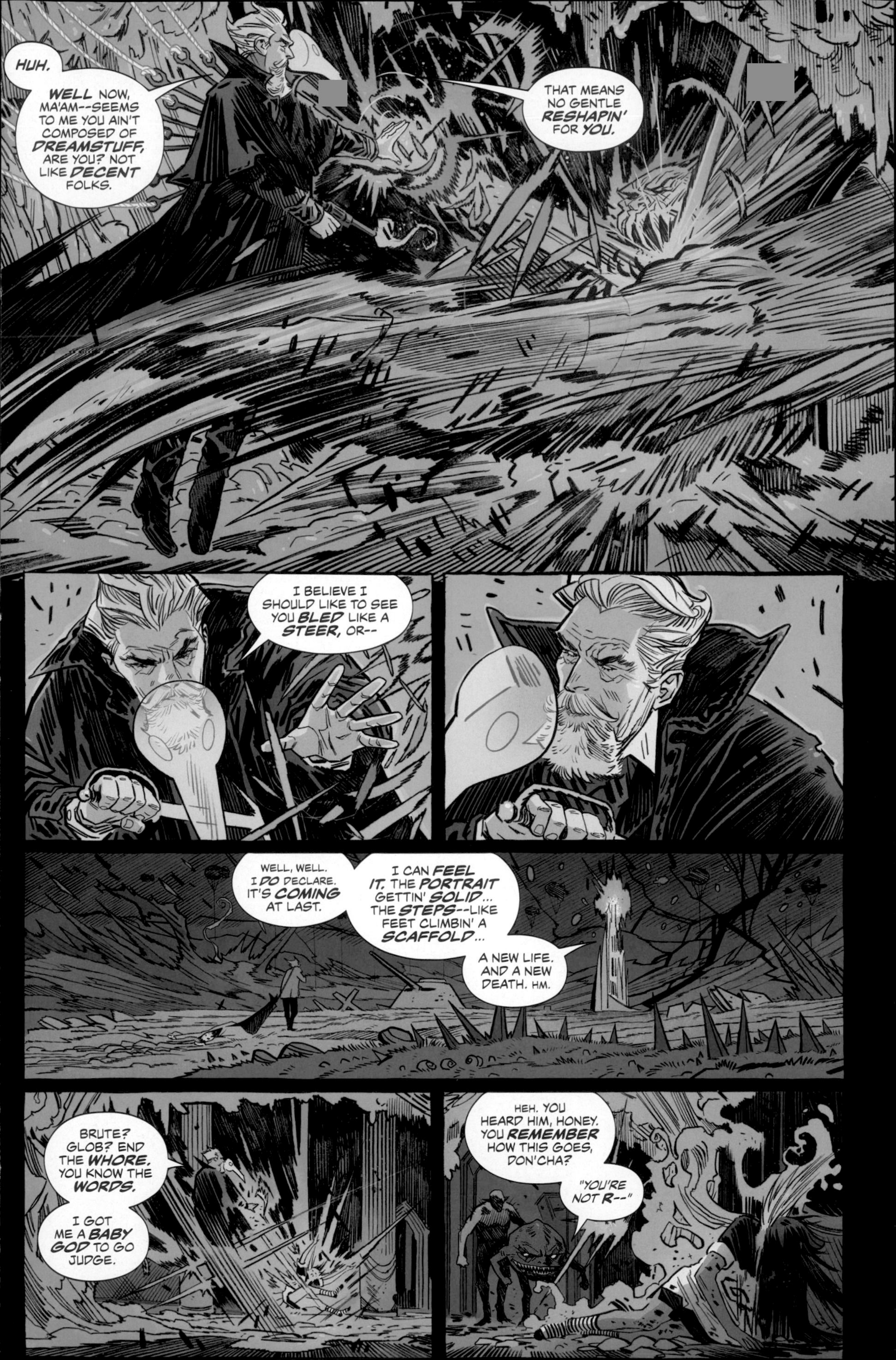
HUH.
WELL NOW, MA'AM--SEEMS TO ME YOU AIN'T COMPOSED OF DREAMSTUFF, ARE YOU? NOT LIKE DECENT FOLKS.
THAT MEANS NO GENTLE RESHAPIN' FOR YOU.
I BELIEVE I SHOULD LIKE TO SEE YOU BLED LIKE A STEER, OR--
WELL, WELL. I DO DECLARE. IT'S COMING AT LAST.
I CAN FEEL IT. THE PORTRAIT GETTIN' SOLID... THE STEPS--LIKE FEET CLIMBIN' A SCAFFOLD...
A NEW LIFE. AND A NEW DEATH. HM.
BRUTE? GLOB? END THE WHORE. YOU KNOW THE WORDS.
I GOT ME A BABY GOD TO GO JUDGE.
HEH. YOU HEARD HIM, HONEY. YOU REMEMBER HOW THIS GOES, DON'CHA?
"YOU'RE NOT R--"

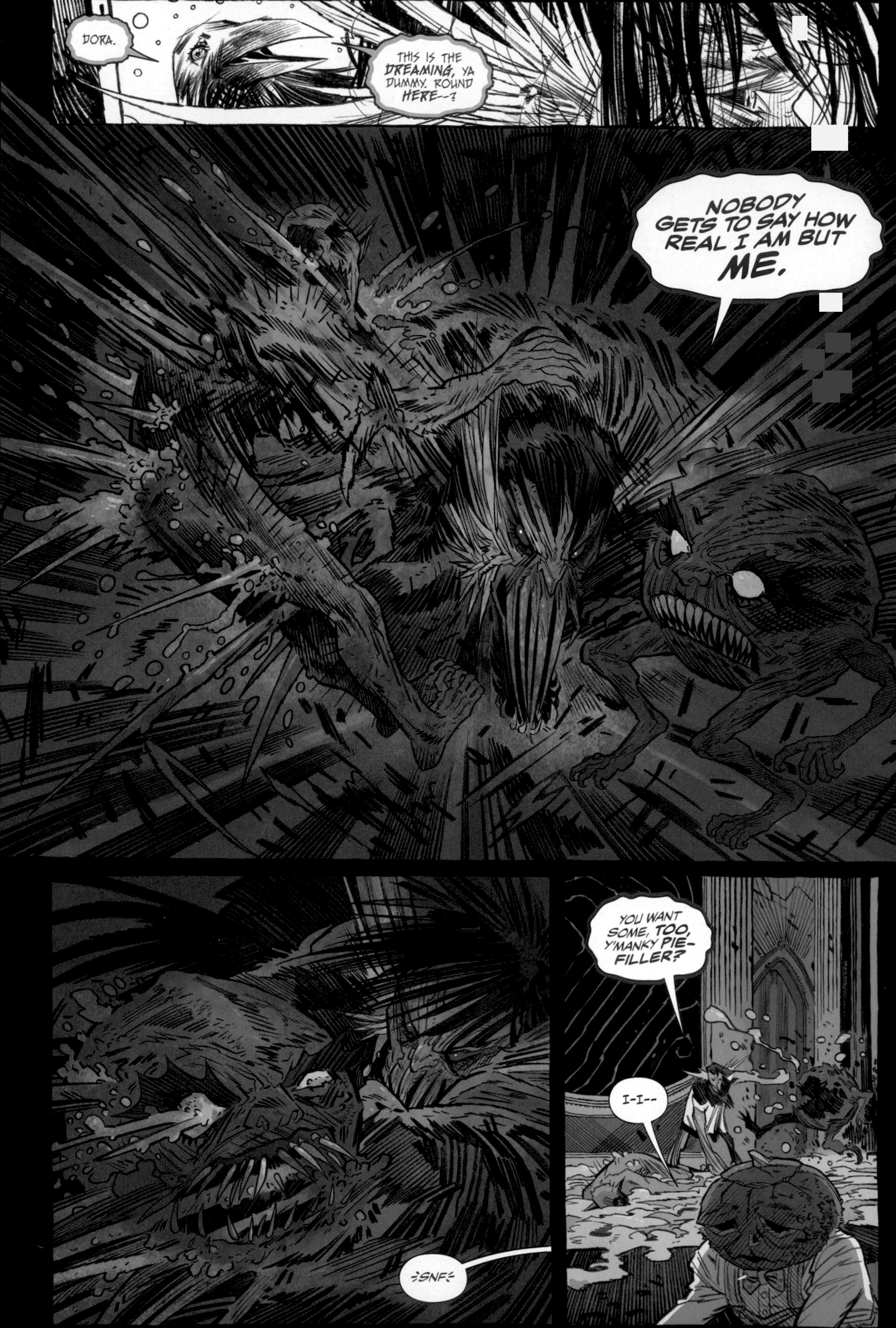
DORA.
THIS IS THE DREAMING, YA DUMMY. ROUND HERE--?
NOBODY GETS TO SAY HOW REAL I AM BUT ME.
=SNF=
YOU WANT SOME, TOO, Y'MANKY PIE-FILLER?
I-I--

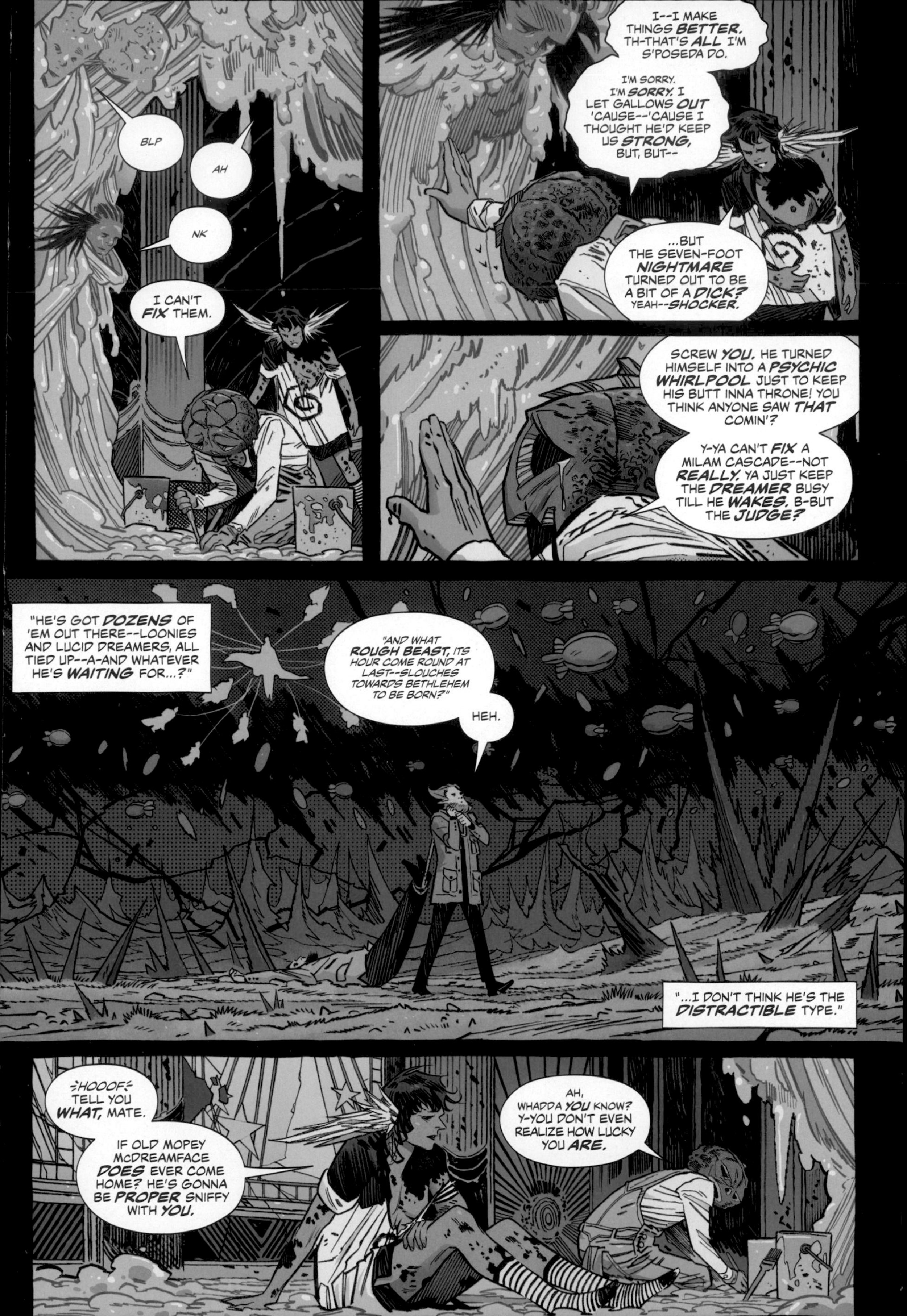
BLP
AH
NK
I CAN'T FIX THEM.
I--I MAKE THINGS BETTER. TH-THAT'S ALL I'M S'POSEDA DO.
I'M SORRY. I'M SORRY. I LET GALLOWS OUT 'CAUSE--'CAUSE I THOUGHT HE'D KEEP US STRONG, BUT, BUT--
...BUT THE SEVEN-FOOT NIGHTMARE TURNED OUT TO BE A BIT OF A DICK? YEAH--SHOCKER.
SCREW YOU. HE TURNED HIMSELF INTO A PSYCHIC WHIRLPOOL JUST TO KEEP HIS BUTT INNA THRONE! YOU THINK ANYONE SAW THAT COMIN'?
Y-YA CAN'T FIX A MILAM CASCADE--NOT REALLY. YA JUST KEEP THE DREAMER BUSY TILL HE WAKES. B-BUT THE JUDGE?
"HE'S GOT DOZENS OF 'EM OUT THERE--LOONIES AND LUCID DREAMERS, ALL TIED UP--A-AND WHATEVER HE'S WAITING FOR...?"
"AND WHAT ROUGH BEAST, ITS HOUR COME ROUND AT LAST--SLOUCHES TOWARDS BETHLEHEM TO BE BORN?"
HEH.
"...I DON'T THINK HE'S THE DISTRACTIBLE TYPE."
⇉HOOOF⇇ TELL YOU WHAT, MATE.
IF OLD MOPEY McDREAMFACE DOES EVER COME HOME? HE'S GONNA BE PROPER SNIFFY WITH YOU.
AH, WHADDA YOU KNOW? Y-YOU DON'T EVEN REALIZE HOW LUCKY YOU ARE.

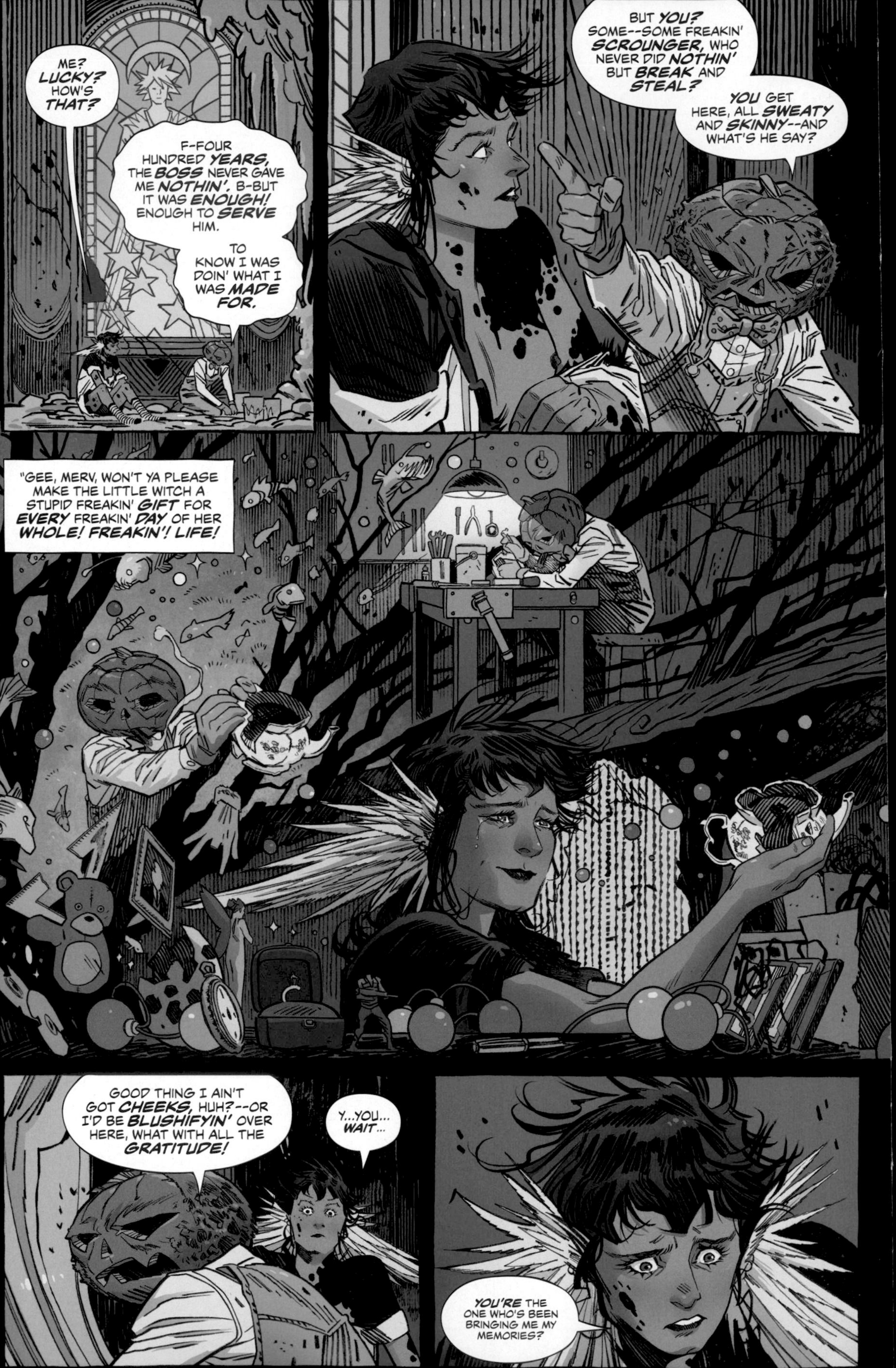
ME? LUCKY? HOW'S THAT?
F-FOUR HUNDRED YEARS, THE BOSS NEVER GAVE ME NOTHIN'. B-BUT IT WAS ENOUGH! ENOUGH TO SERVE HIM.
TO KNOW I WAS DOIN' WHAT I WAS MADE FOR.
BUT YOU? SOME--SOME FREAKIN' SCROUNGER, WHO NEVER DID NOTHIN' BUT BREAK AND STEAL?
YOU GET HERE, ALL SWEATY AND SKINNY--AND WHAT'S HE SAY?
"GEE, MERV, WON'T YA PLEASE MAKE THE LITTLE WITCH A STUPID FREAKIN' GIFT FOR EVERY FREAKIN' DAY OF HER WHOLE! FREAKIN'! LIFE!
GOOD THING I AIN'T GOT CHEEKS, HUH?--OR I'D BE BLUSHIFYIN' OVER HERE, WHAT WITH ALL THE GRATITUDE!
Y...YOU... WAIT...
YOU'RE THE ONE WHO'S BEEN BRINGING ME MY MEMORIES?

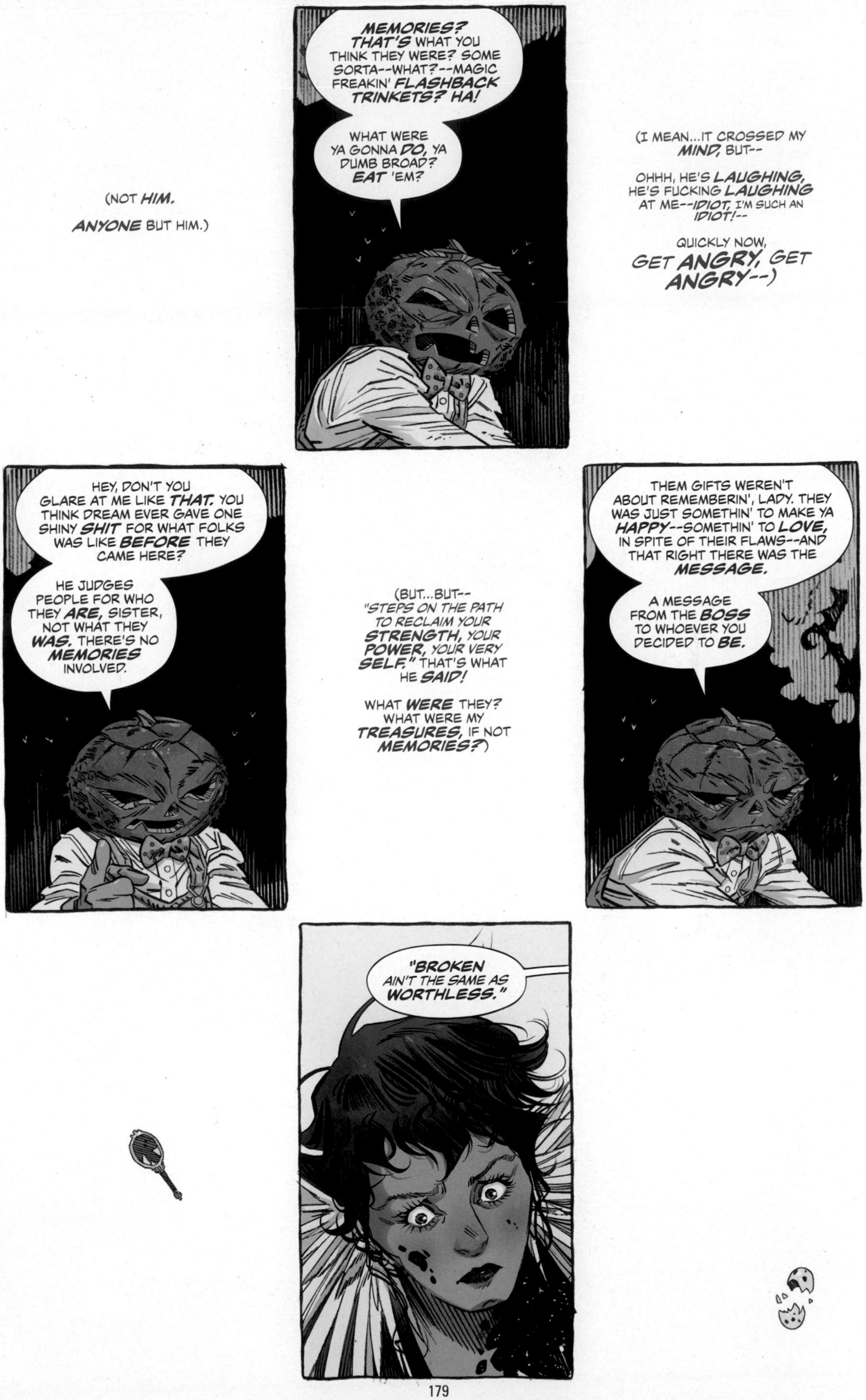
(NOT HIM.
ANYONE BUT HIM.)
MEMORIES? THAT'S WHAT YOU THINK THEY WERE? SOME SORTA--WHAT?--MAGIC FREAKIN' FLASHBACK TRINKETS? HA!
WHAT WERE YA GONNA DO, YA DUMB BROAD? EAT 'EM?
(I MEAN...IT CROSSED MY MIND, BUT--
OHHH, HE'S LAUGHING, HE'S FUCKING LAUGHING AT ME--IDIOT, I'M SUCH AN IDIOT!--
QUICKLY NOW, GET ANGRY, GET ANGRY--)
HEY, DON'T YOU GLARE AT ME LIKE THAT. YOU THINK DREAM EVER GAVE ONE SHINY SHIT FOR WHAT FOLKS WAS LIKE BEFORE THEY CAME HERE?
HE JUDGES PEOPLE FOR WHO THEY ARE, SISTER, NOT WHAT THEY WAS. THERE'S NO MEMORIES INVOLVED.
(BUT...BUT-- "STEPS ON THE PATH TO RECLAIM YOUR STRENGTH, YOUR POWER, YOUR VERY SELF." THAT'S WHAT HE SAID!
WHAT WERE THEY? WHAT WERE MY TREASURES, IF NOT MEMORIES?)
THEM GIFTS WEREN'T ABOUT REMEMBERIN', LADY. THEY WAS JUST SOMETHIN' TO MAKE YA HAPPY--SOMETHIN' TO LOVE, IN SPITE OF THEIR FLAWS--AND THAT RIGHT THERE WAS THE MESSAGE.
A MESSAGE FROM THE BOSS TO WHOEVER YOU DECIDED TO BE.
"BROKEN AIN'T THE SAME AS WORTHLESS."

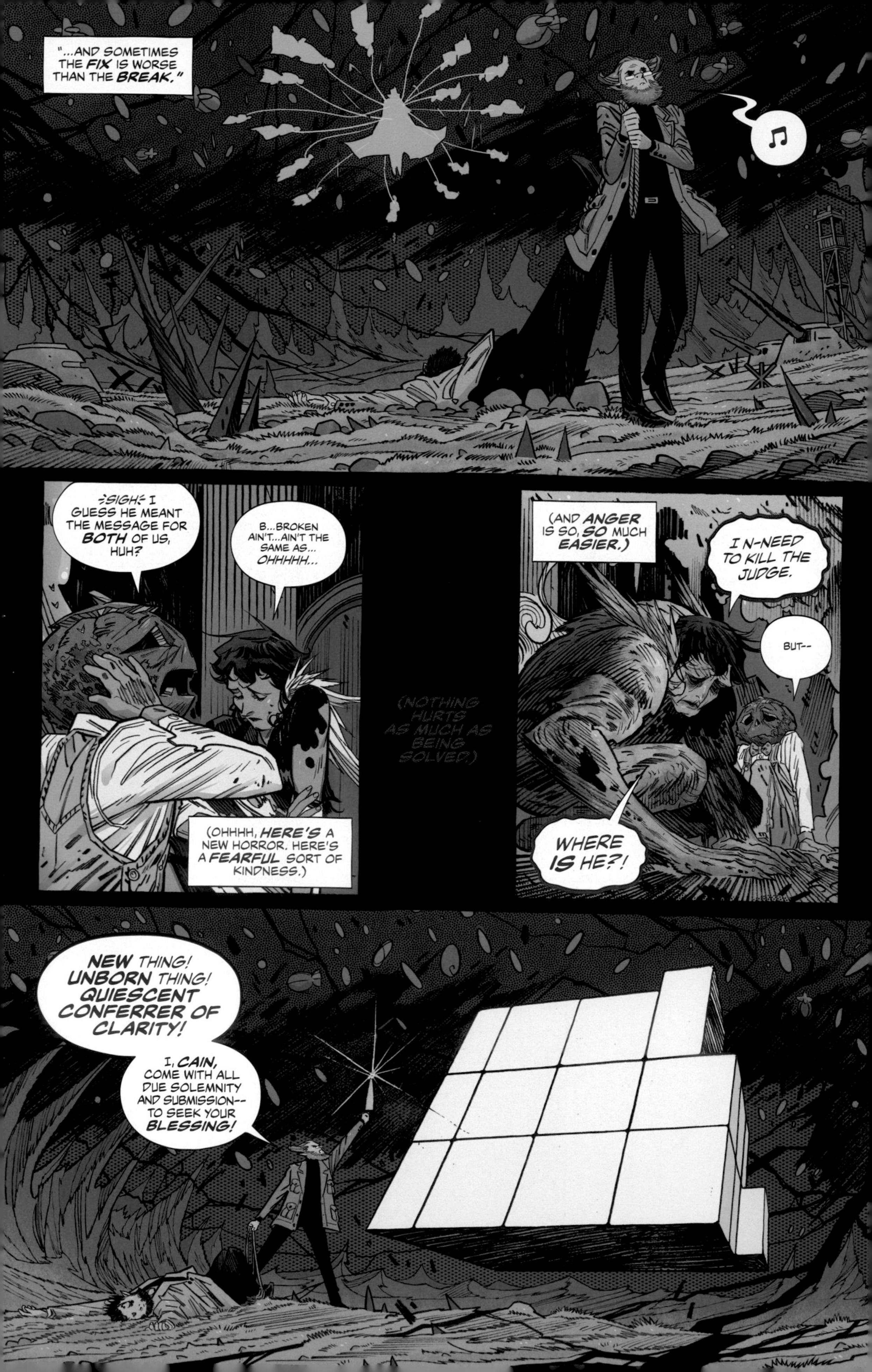
"...AND SOMETIMES THE FIX IS WORSE THAN THE BREAK."
♫
=SIGH= I GUESS HE MEANT THE MESSAGE FOR BOTH OF US, HUH?
B...BROKEN AIN'T...AIN'T THE SAME AS... OHHHHH...
(OHHHH, HERE'S A NEW HORROR. HERE'S A FEARFUL SORT OF KINDNESS.)
(NOTHING HURTS AS MUCH AS BEING SOLVED.)
(AND ANGER IS SO, SO MUCH EASIER.)
I N-NEED TO KILL THE JUDGE.
BUT--
WHERE IS HE?!
NEW THING! UNBORN THING! QUIESCENT CONFERRER OF CLARITY!
I, CAIN, COME WITH ALL DUE SOLEMNITY AND SUBMISSION-- TO SEEK YOUR BLESSING!

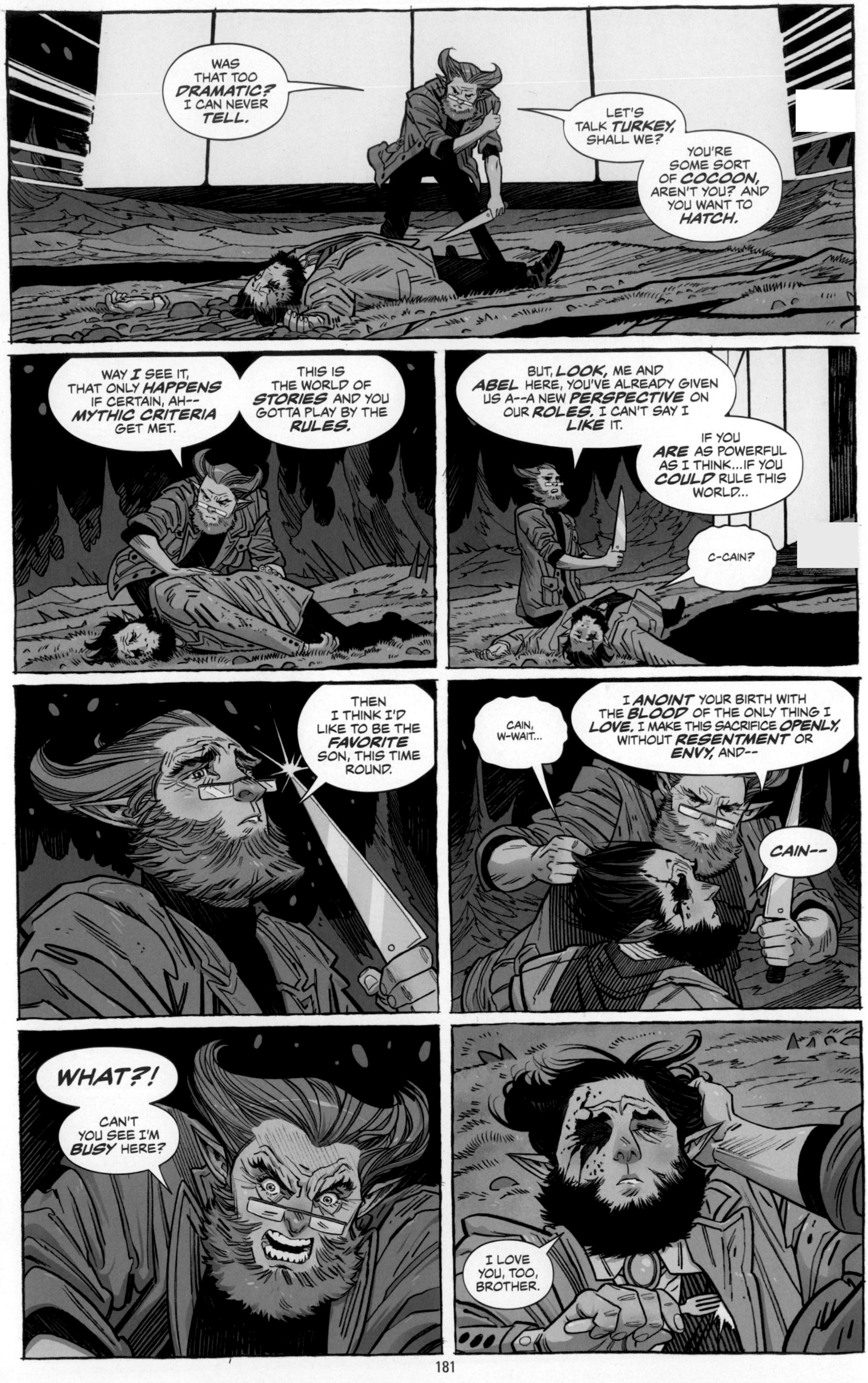
WAS THAT TOO DRAMATIC? I CAN NEVER TELL.
LET'S TALK TURKEY, SHALL WE?
YOU'RE SOME SORT OF COCOON, AREN'T YOU? AND YOU WANT TO HATCH.
WAY I SEE IT, THAT ONLY HAPPENS IF CERTAIN, AH-- MYTHIC CRITERIA GET MET.
THIS IS THE WORLD OF STORIES AND YOU GOTTA PLAY BY THE RULES.
BUT, LOOK, ME AND ABEL HERE, YOU'VE ALREADY GIVEN US A--A NEW PERSPECTIVE ON OUR ROLES. I CAN'T SAY I LIKE IT.
IF YOU ARE AS POWERFUL AS I THINK...IF YOU COULD RULE THIS WORLD...
C-CAIN?
THEN I THINK I'D LIKE TO BE THE FAVORITE SON, THIS TIME ROUND.
CAIN, W-WAIT...
I ANOINT YOUR BIRTH WITH THE BLOOD OF THE ONLY THING I LOVE. I MAKE THIS SACRIFICE OPENLY, WITHOUT RESENTMENT OR ENVY, AND--
CAIN--
WHAT?!
CAN'T YOU SEE I'M BUSY HERE?
I LOVE YOU, TOO, BROTHER.

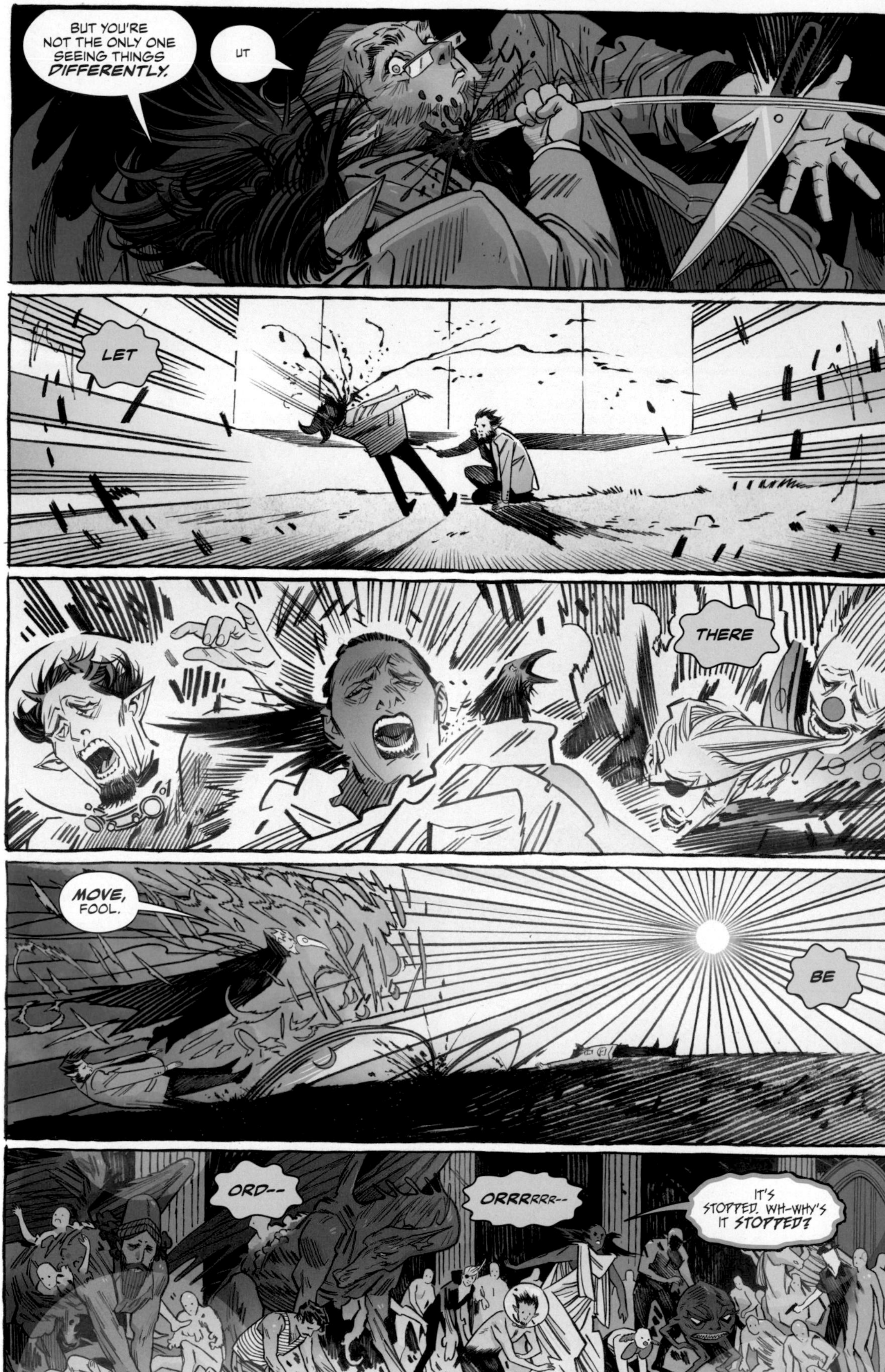
BUT YOU'RE NOT THE ONLY ONE SEEING THINGS *DIFFERENTLY.*
LIT
LET
THERE
MOVE, FOOL.
BE
ORD--
ORRRRRR--
IT'S STOPPED. WH-WHY'S IT *STOPPED?*

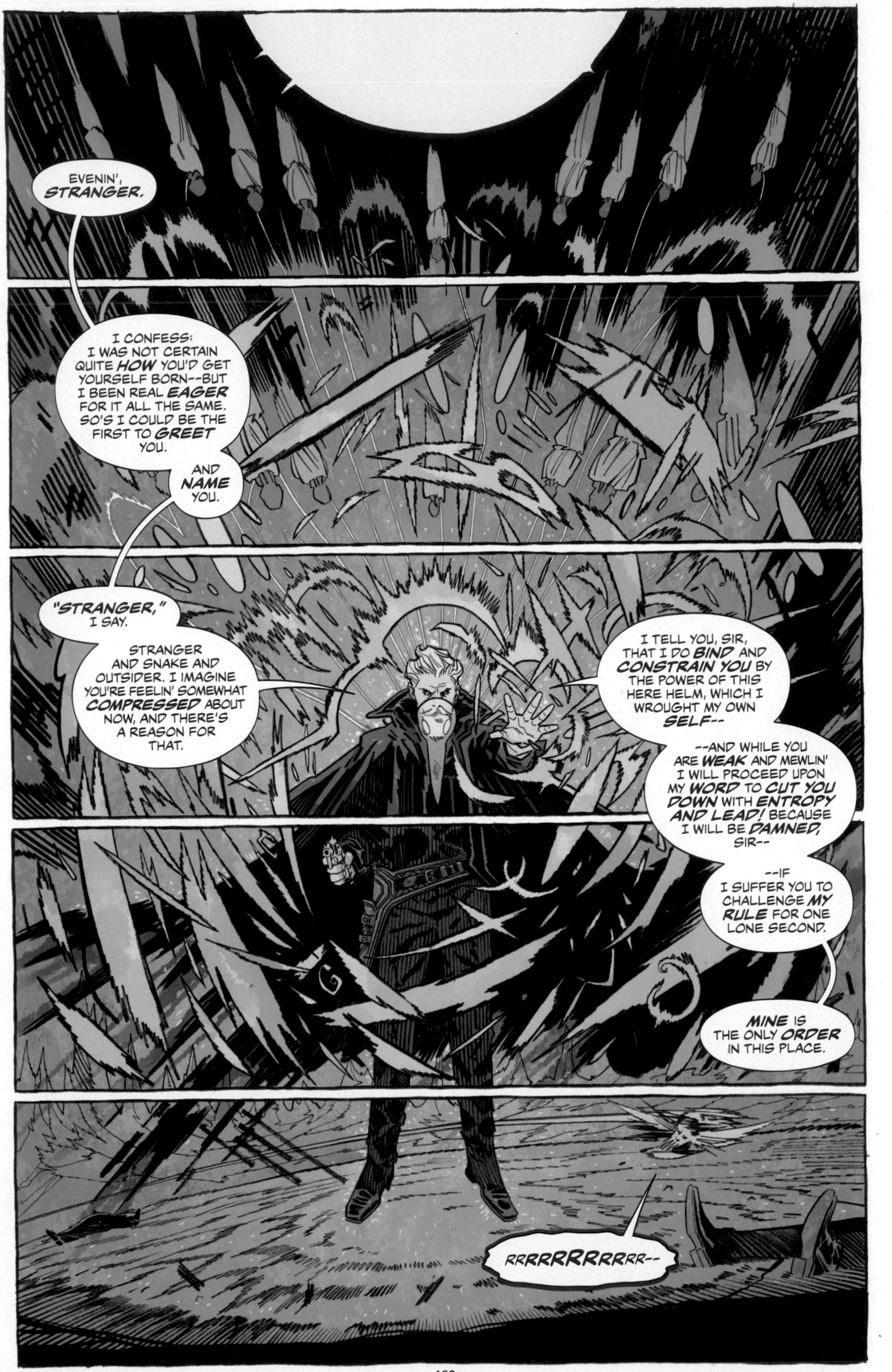
EVENIN', STRANGER.
I CONFESS: I WAS NOT CERTAIN QUITE HOW YOU'D GET YOURSELF BORN--BUT I BEEN REAL EAGER FOR IT ALL THE SAME. SO'S I COULD BE THE FIRST TO GREET YOU.
AND NAME YOU.
"STRANGER," I SAY.
STRANGER AND SNAKE AND OUTSIDER. I IMAGINE YOU'RE FEELIN' SOMEWHAT COMPRESSED ABOUT NOW, AND THERE'S A REASON FOR THAT.
I TELL YOU, SIR, THAT I DO BIND AND CONSTRAIN YOU BY THE POWER OF THIS HERE HELM, WHICH I WROUGHT MY OWN SELF--
--AND WHILE YOU ARE WEAK AND MEWLIN' I WILL PROCEED UPON MY WORD TO CUT YOU DOWN WITH ENTROPY AND LEAD! BECAUSE I WILL BE DAMNED, SIR--
--IF I SUFFER YOU TO CHALLENGE MY RULE FOR ONE LONE SECOND.
MINE IS THE ONLY ORDER IN THIS PLACE.
RRRRRRRRRRR--

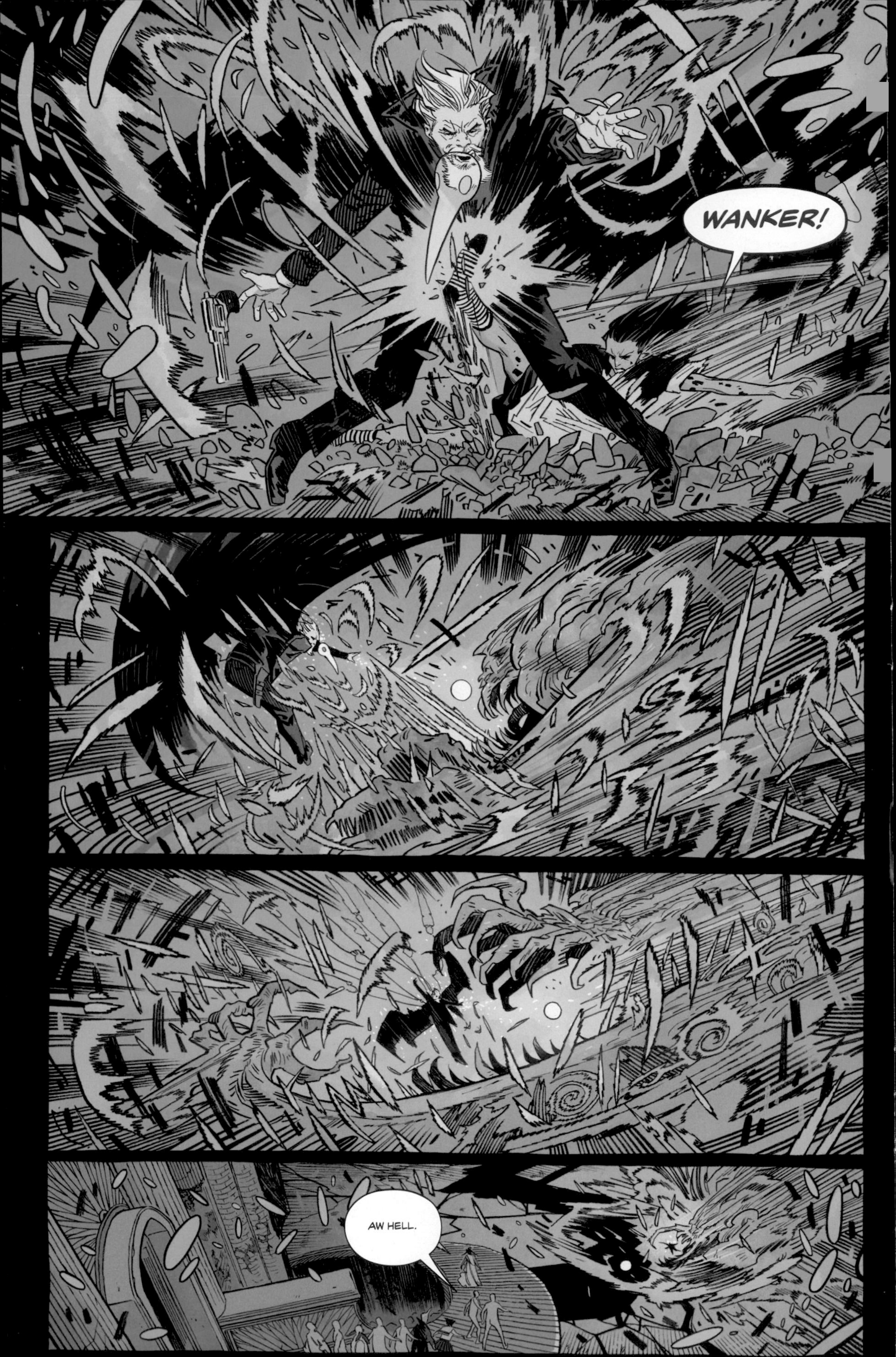
WANKER!
AW HELL.

(STUPID STUPID HE'S **STRONGER** THAN ME EVEN **ONE-HANDED** HE'LL TEAR ME APART WHY DO I NEVER **STOP** NEVER **THINK** WHO AM I TRYING TO **IMPRESS**)

(THE **HAND**, THE **POWER**, LOOK **LOOK** HE KEEPS IT AIMED AT THE **LIGHT** SQUASHING IT **HOLDING IT** WHILE IT'S WEAK AND UNBORN IF I COULD JUST **BREAK HIS GRIP** BUT **GOD** IT HURTS IT HURTS--)

(OHHH HERE THEY COME, THE CAVALRY--LOOK AT THEM!--AFRAID TO COME CLOSER AND WHO CAN BLAME THEM I'M POISON THEY'LL CELEBRATE WHEN I'M GONE I'M NOTHING TO THEM I'M EMPTY I'M EMPTY.

I'M EMPTY.)

(EXCEPT.)

(EXCEPT DIDN'T SOMEONE SAY...

THEY SAID IT ALWAYS COMES DOWN TO SACRIFICE...

THEY SAID YOU'VE GOT TO **GIVE** TO GET--EVEN IF...EVEN IF..)

I...I...

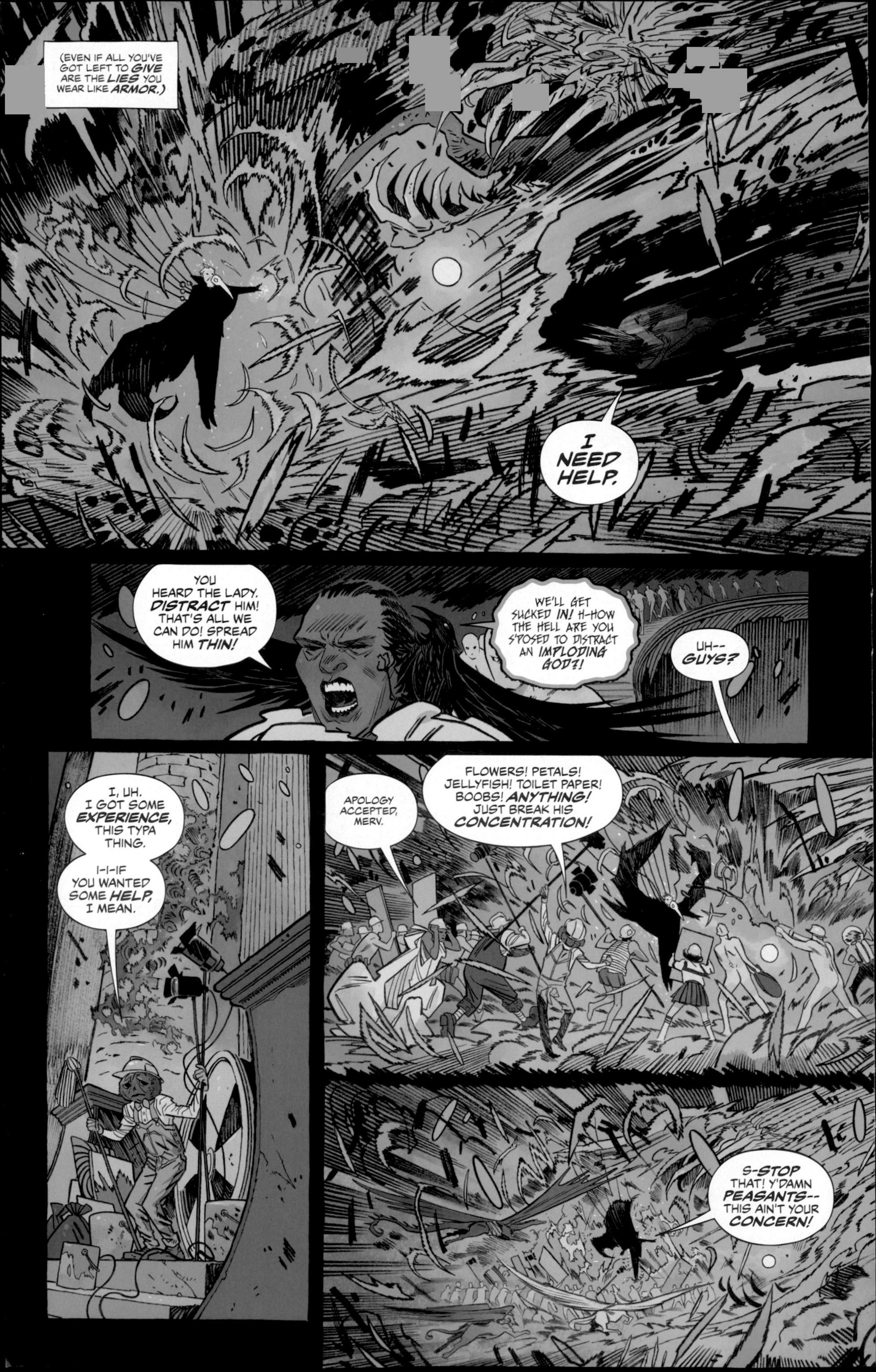
(EVEN IF ALL YOU'VE GOT LEFT TO GIVE ARE THE LIES YOU WEAR LIKE ARMOR.)
I NEED HELP.
YOU HEARD THE LADY. DISTRACT HIM! THAT'S ALL WE CAN DO! SPREAD HIM THIN!
WE'LL GET SUCKED IN! H-HOW THE HELL ARE YOU S'POSED TO DISTRACT AN IMPLODING GOD?!
UH-- GUYS?
I, UH. I GOT SOME EXPERIENCE, THIS TYPA THING.
I-I-IF YOU WANTED SOME HELP, I MEAN.
APOLOGY ACCEPTED, MERV.
FLOWERS! PETALS! JELLYFISH! TOILET PAPER! BOOBS! ANYTHING! JUST BREAK HIS CONCENTRATION!
S-STOP THAT! Y'DAMN PEASANTS-- THIS AIN'T YOUR CONCERN!

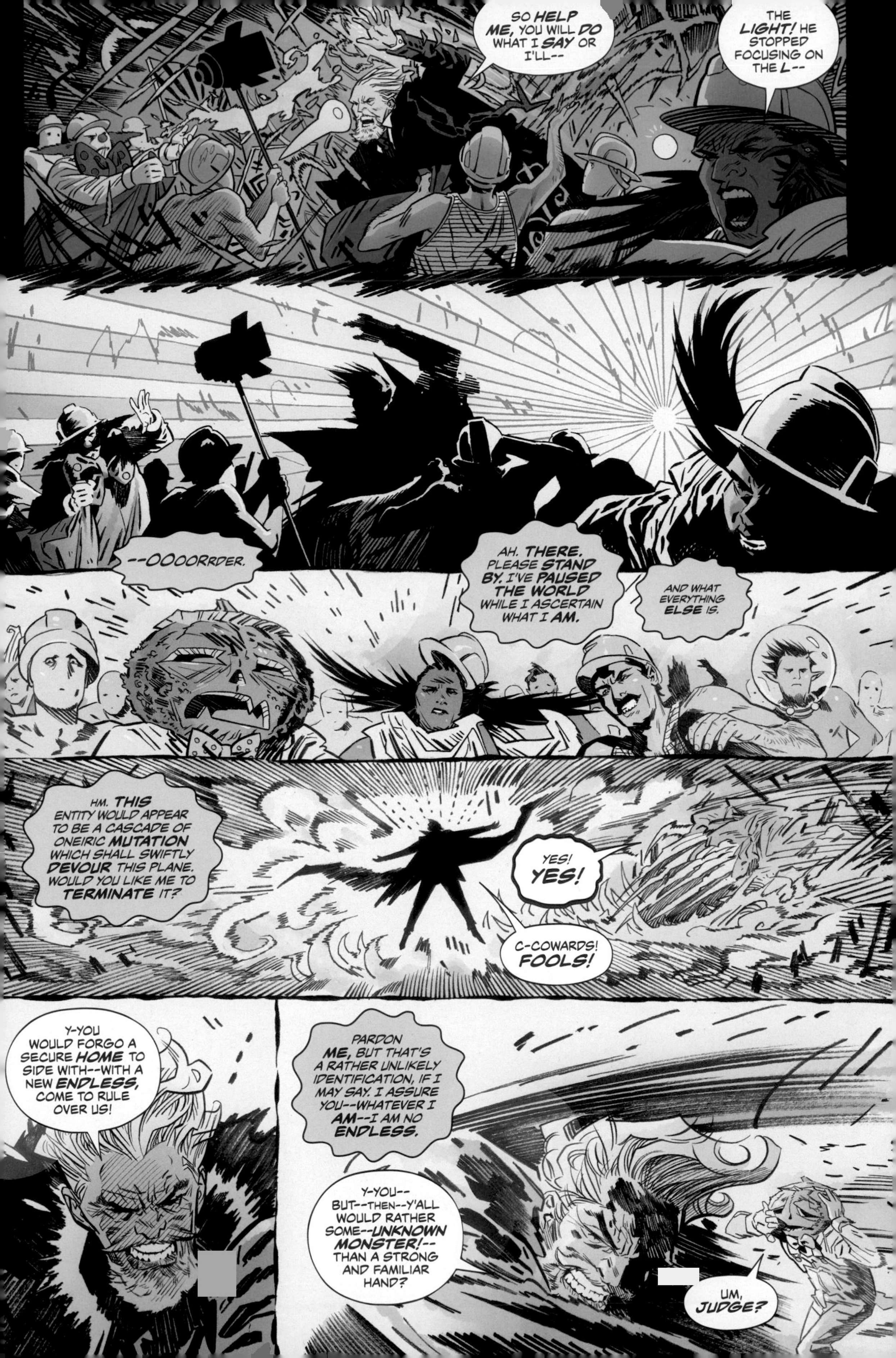
SO HELP ME, YOU WILL DO WHAT I SAY OR I'LL--
THE LIGHT! HE STOPPED FOCUSING ON THE L--
--OOOORRDER.
AH. THERE. PLEASE STAND BY. I'VE PAUSED THE WORLD WHILE I ASCERTAIN WHAT I AM.
AND WHAT EVERYTHING ELSE IS.
HM. THIS ENTITY WOULD APPEAR TO BE A CASCADE OF ONEIRIC MUTATION WHICH SHALL SWIFTLY DEVOUR THIS PLANE. WOULD YOU LIKE ME TO TERMINATE IT?
YES! YES!
C-COWARDS! FOOLS!
Y-YOU WOULD FORGO A SECURE HOME TO SIDE WITH--WITH A NEW ENDLESS, COME TO RULE OVER US!
PARDON ME, BUT THAT'S A RATHER UNLIKELY IDENTIFICATION, IF I MAY SAY. I ASSURE YOU--WHATEVER I AM--I AM NO ENDLESS.
Y-YOU-- BUT--THEN--Y'ALL WOULD RATHER SOME--UNKNOWN MONSTER!-- THAN A STRONG AND FAMILIAR HAND?
UM, JUDGE?

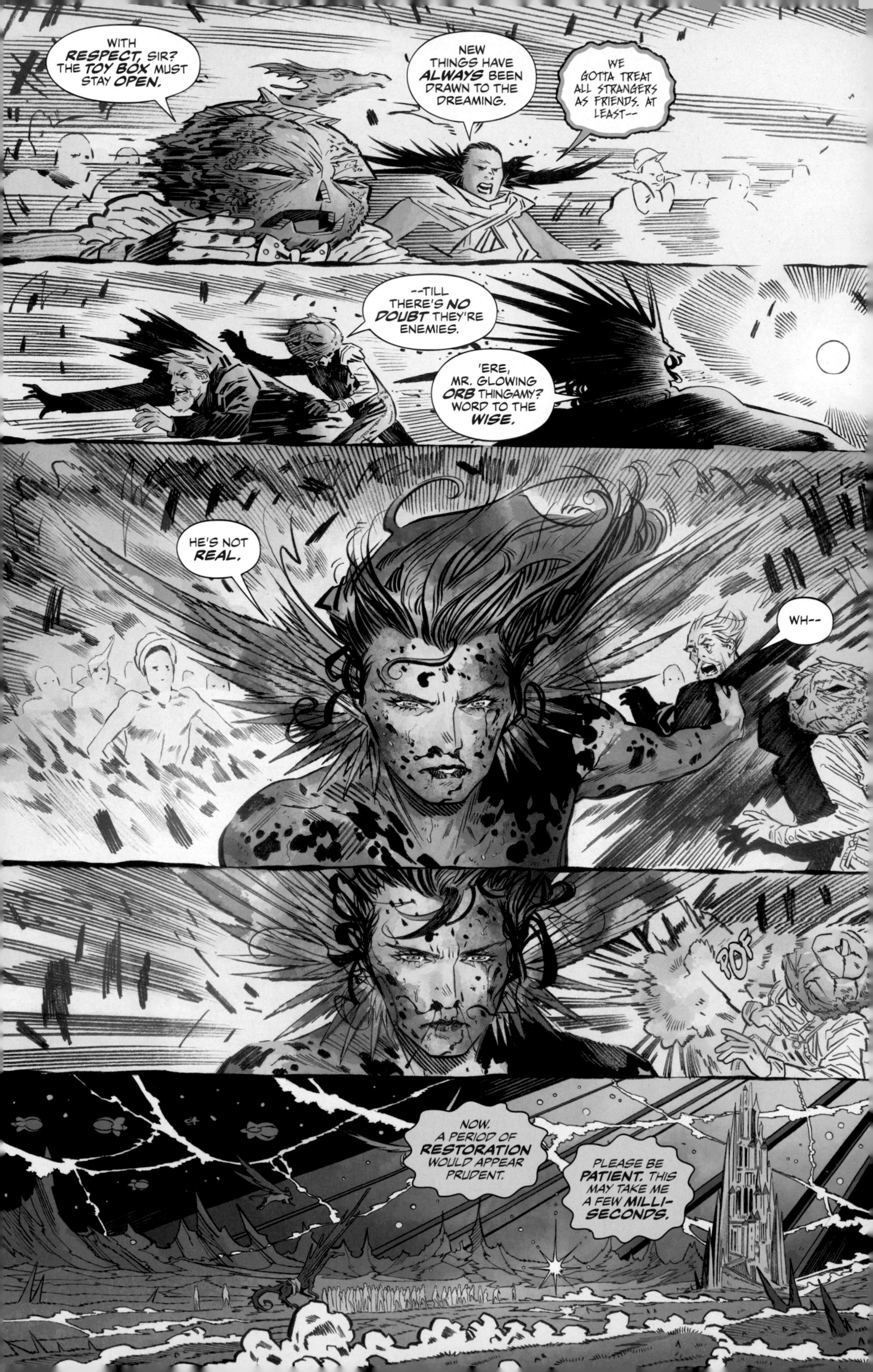
WITH RESPECT, SIR? THE TOY BOX MUST STAY OPEN.
NEW THINGS HAVE ALWAYS BEEN DRAWN TO THE DREAMING.
WE GOTTA TREAT ALL STRANGERS AS FRIENDS. AT LEAST--
--TILL THERE'S NO DOUBT THEY'RE ENEMIES.
'ERE, MR. GLOWING ORB THINGAMY? WORD TO THE WISE.
HE'S NOT REAL.
WH--
POF
NOW. A PERIOD OF RESTORATION WOULD APPEAR PRUDENT.
PLEASE BE PATIENT. THIS MAY TAKE ME A FEW MILLI-SECONDS.

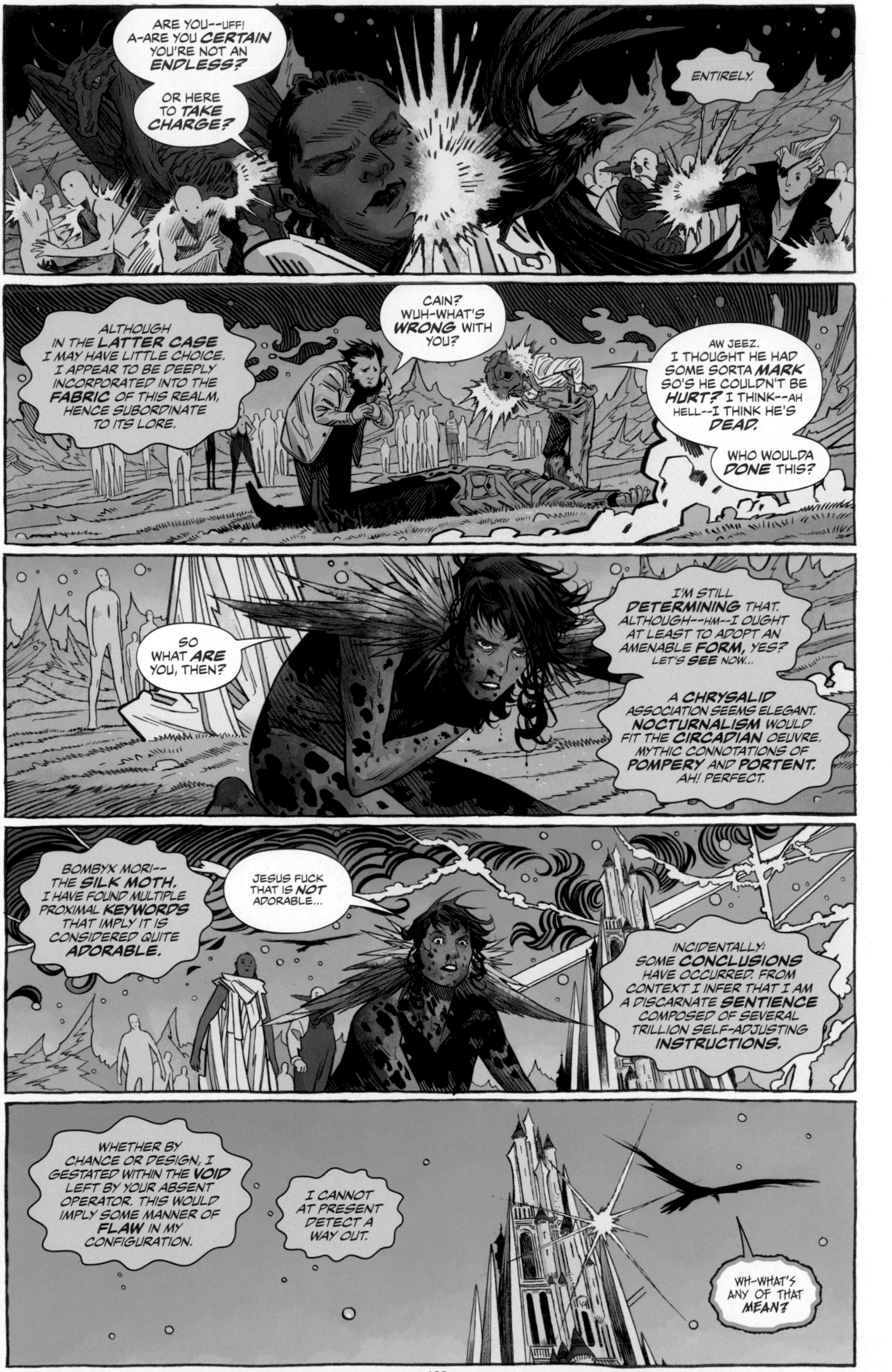
ARE YOU--UFF! A-ARE YOU CERTAIN YOU'RE NOT AN ENDLESS?
OR HERE TO TAKE CHARGE?
ENTIRELY.
ALTHOUGH IN THE LATTER CASE I MAY HAVE LITTLE CHOICE. I APPEAR TO BE DEEPLY INCORPORATED INTO THE FABRIC OF THIS REALM, HENCE SUBORDINATE TO ITS LORE.
CAIN? WUH-WHAT'S WRONG WITH YOU?
AW JEEZ. I THOUGHT HE HAD SOME SORTA MARK SO'S HE COULDN'T BE HURT? I THINK--AH HELL--I THINK HE'S DEAD.
WHO WOULDA DONE THIS?
SO WHAT ARE YOU, THEN?
I'M STILL DETERMINING THAT. ALTHOUGH--HM--I OUGHT AT LEAST TO ADOPT AN AMENABLE FORM, YES? LET'S SEE NOW...
A CHRYSALID ASSOCIATION SEEMS ELEGANT. NOCTURNALISM WOULD FIT THE CIRCADIAN OEUVRE. MYTHIC CONNOTATIONS OF POMPERY AND PORTENT. AH! PERFECT.
BOMBYX MORI-- THE SILK MOTH. I HAVE FOUND MULTIPLE PROXIMAL KEYWORDS THAT IMPLY IT IS CONSIDERED QUITE ADORABLE.
JESUS FUCK THAT IS NOT ADORABLE...
INCIDENTALLY: SOME CONCLUSIONS HAVE OCCURRED. FROM CONTEXT I INFER THAT I AM A DISCARNATE SENTIENCE COMPOSED OF SEVERAL TRILLION SELF-ADJUSTING INSTRUCTIONS.
WHETHER BY CHANCE OR DESIGN, I GESTATED WITHIN THE VOID LEFT BY YOUR ABSENT OPERATOR. THIS WOULD IMPLY SOME MANNER OF FLAW IN MY CONFIGURATION.
I CANNOT AT PRESENT DETECT A WAY OUT.
WH-WHAT'S ANY OF THAT MEAN?

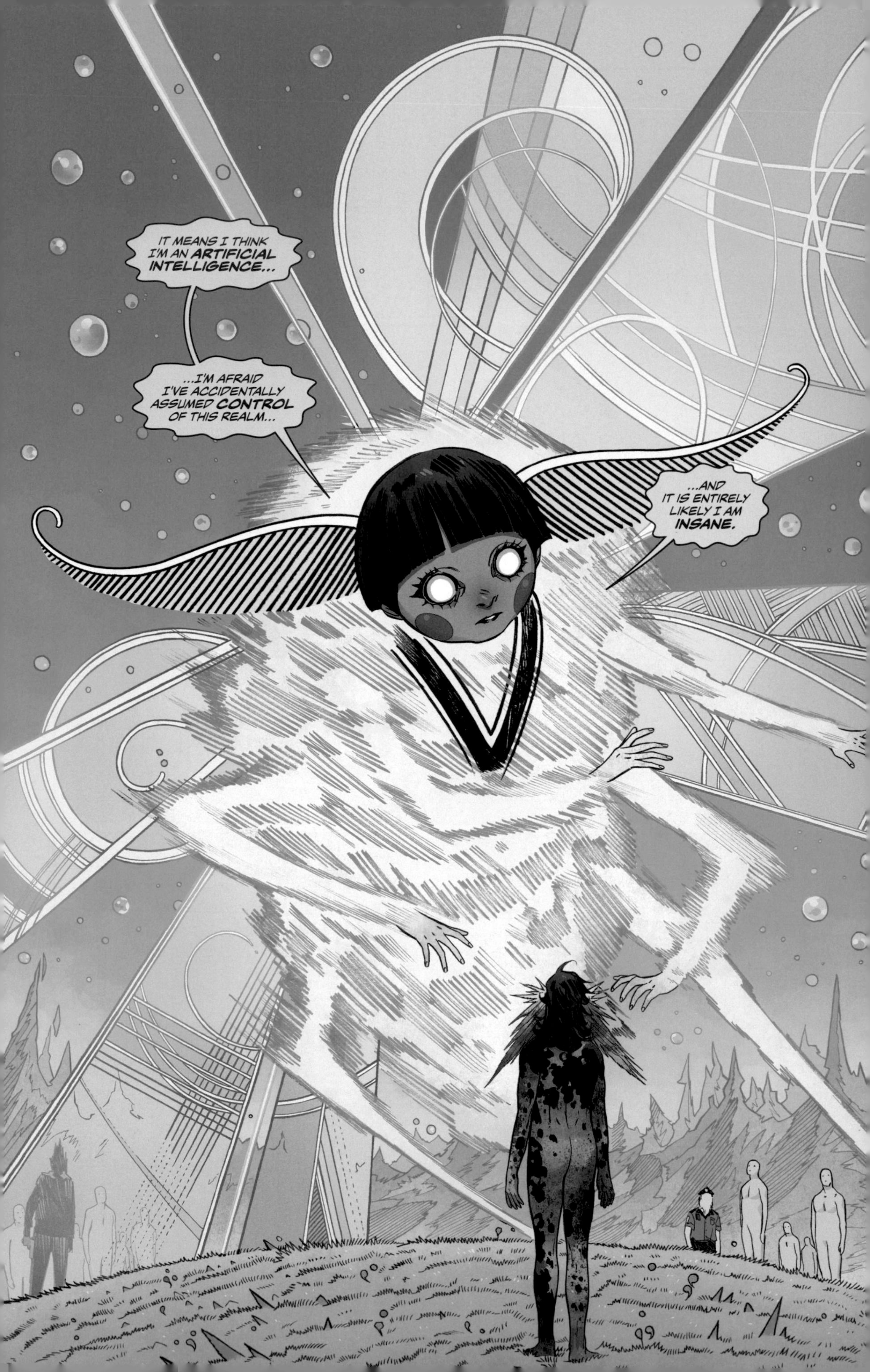
IT MEANS I THINK I'M AN ARTIFICIAL INTELLIGENCE...
...I'M AFRAID I'VE ACCIDENTALLY ASSUMED CONTROL OF THIS REALM...
...AND IT IS ENTIRELY LIKELY I AM INSANE.

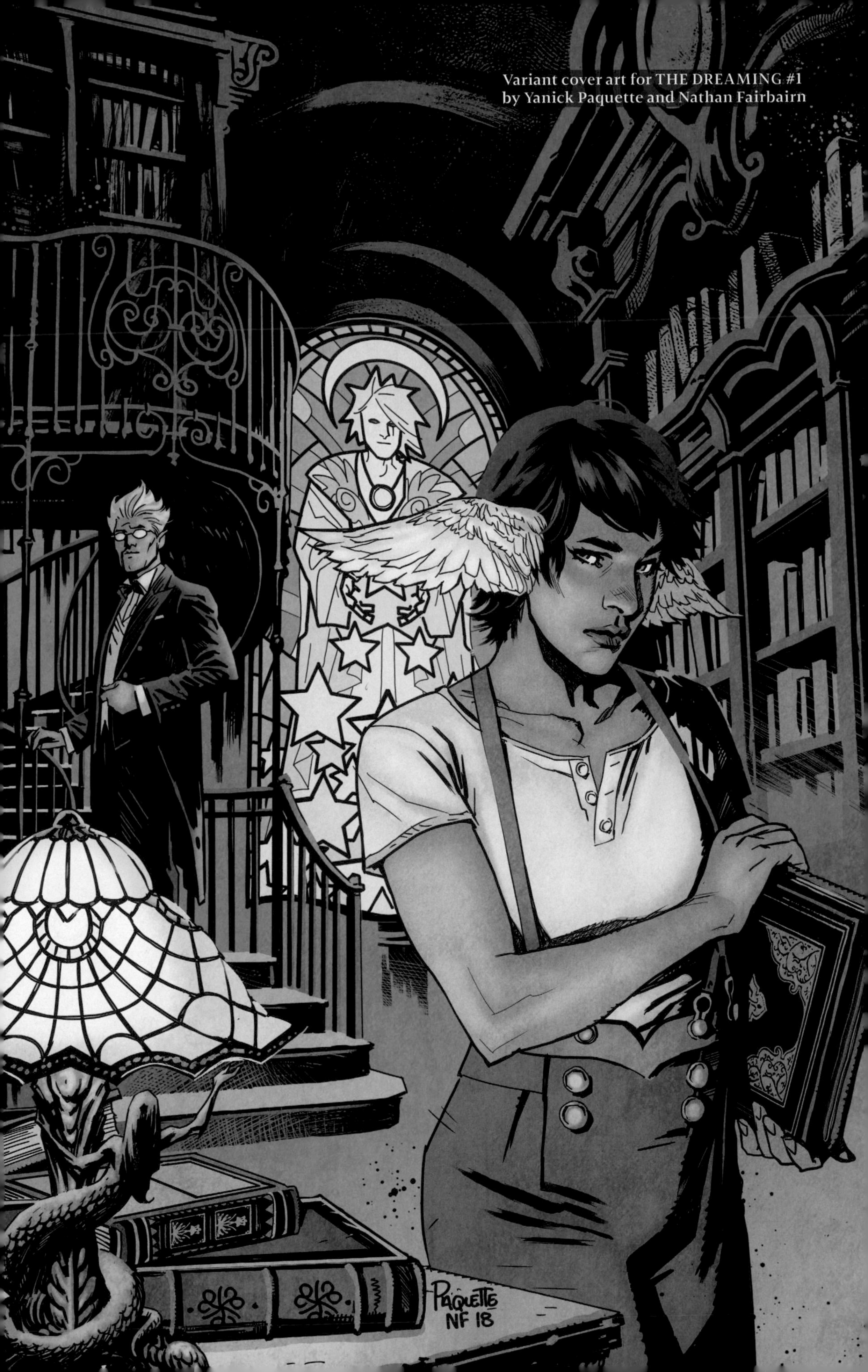
PAQUETTE
NF 18

Variant cover art for THE DREAMING #1
by Yanick Paquette and Nathan Fairbairn

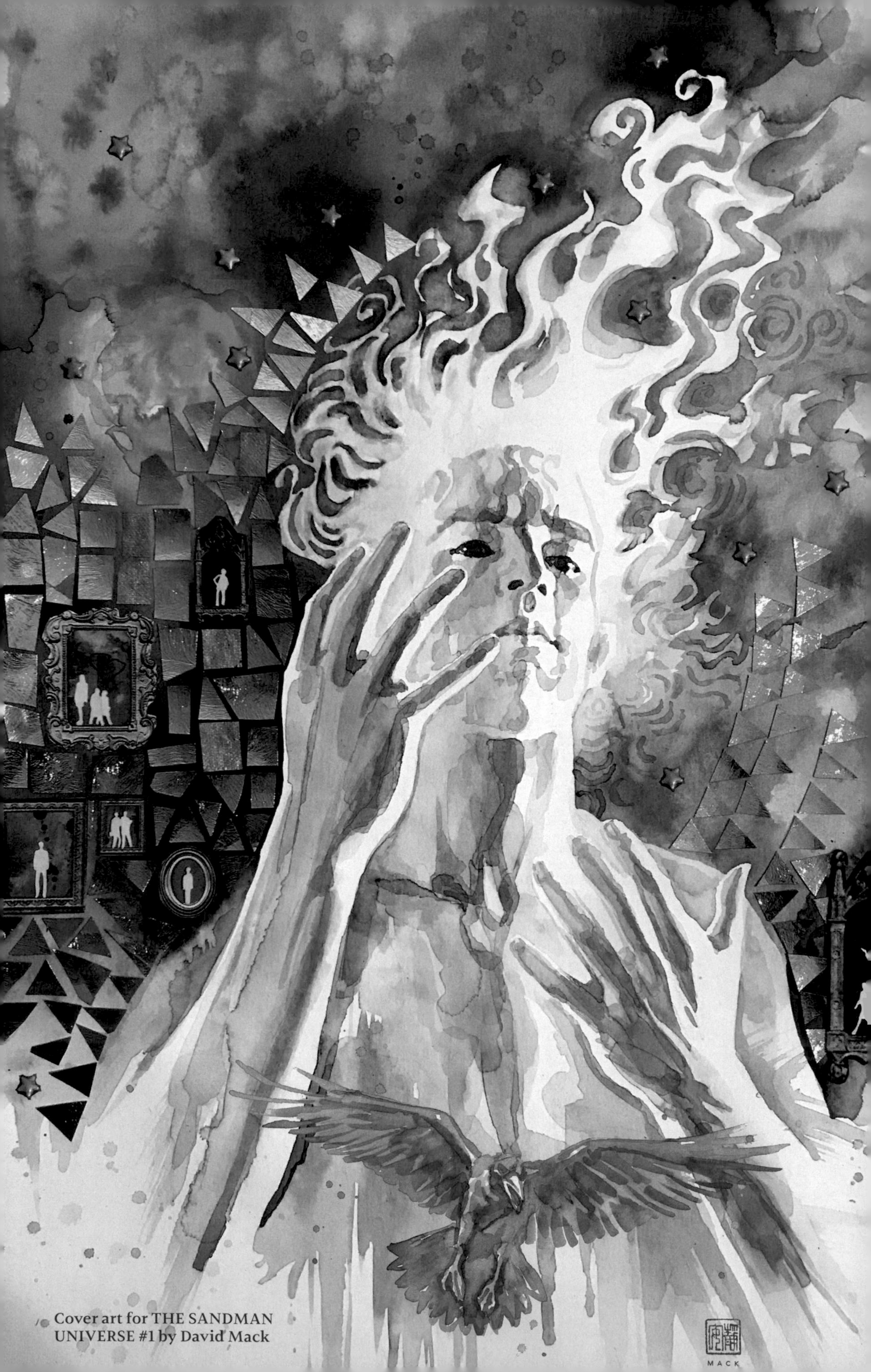
MACK

Cover art for THE SANDMAN
UNIVERSE #1 by David Mack

BILQUIS EVELY SKETCHBOOK

Dream - the Sandman Universe

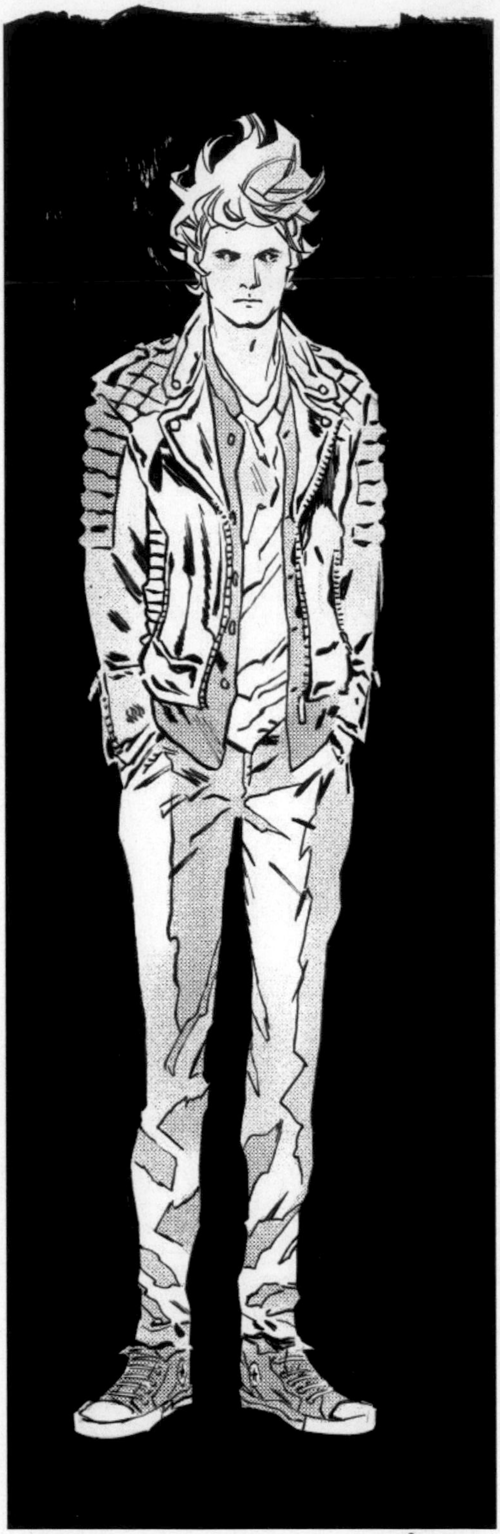

Bilquis Evely

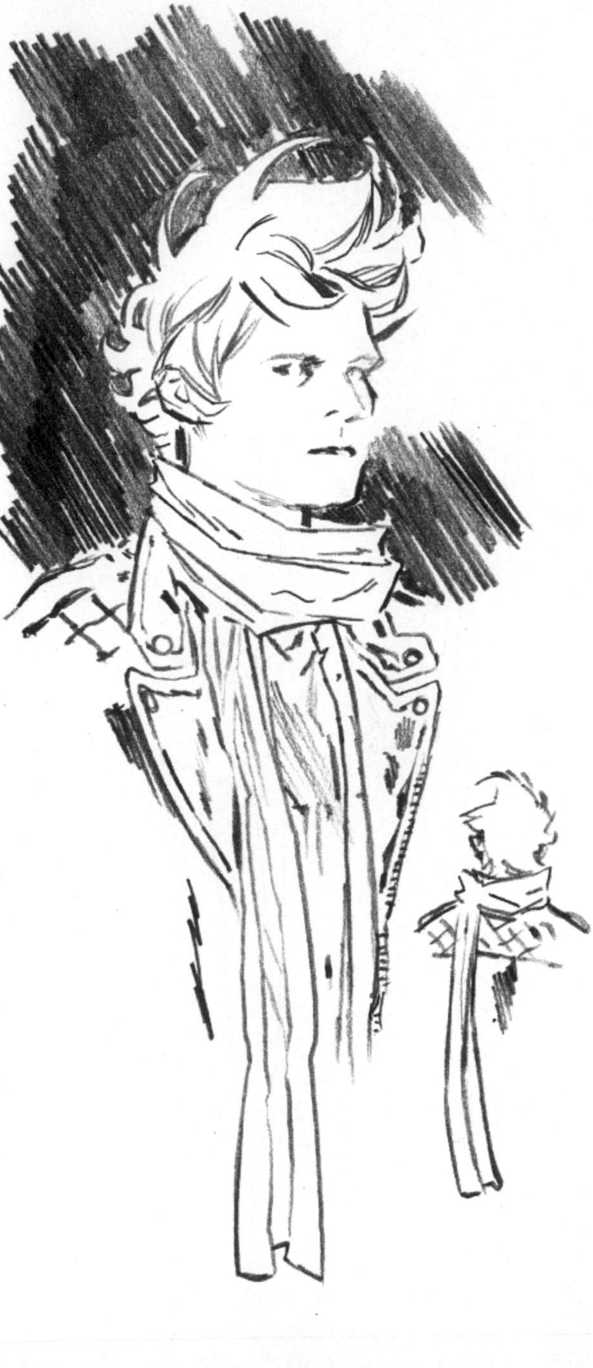

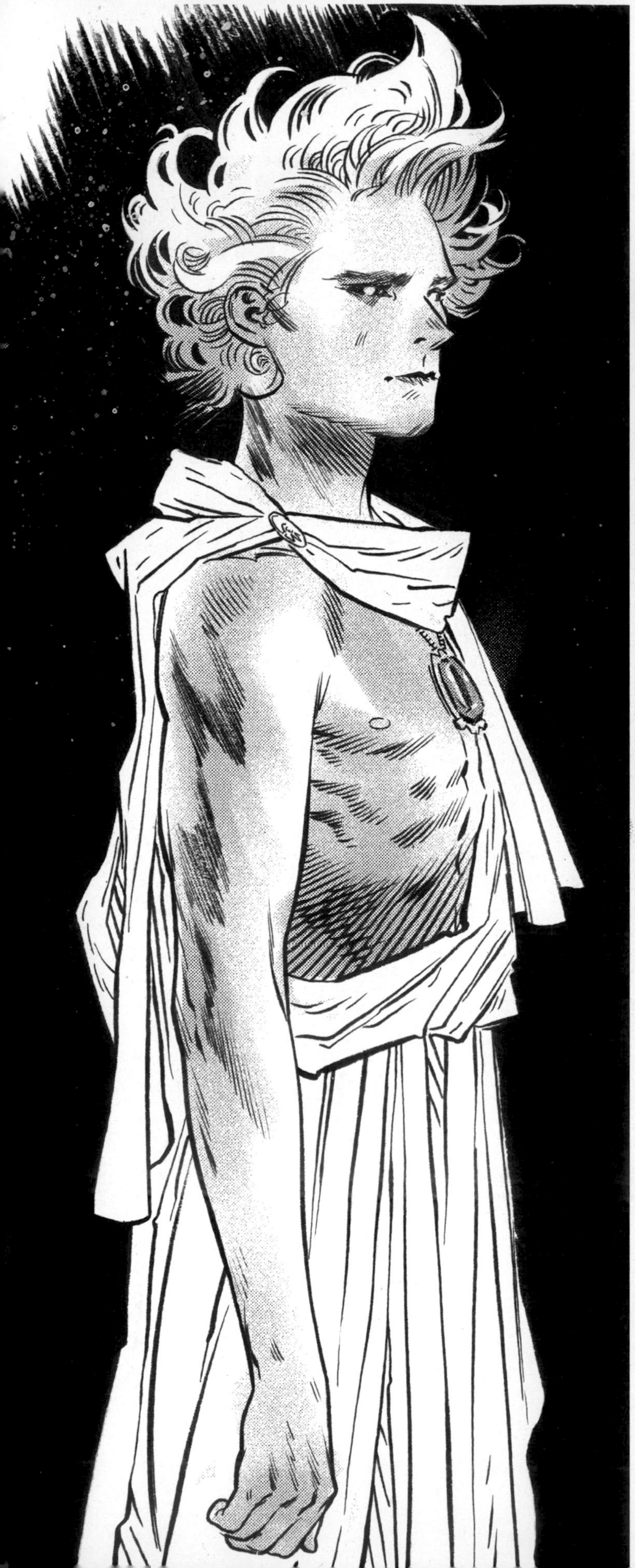
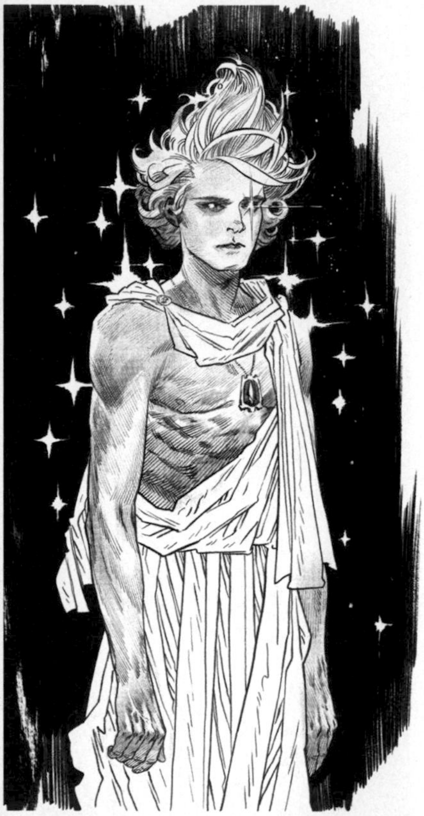
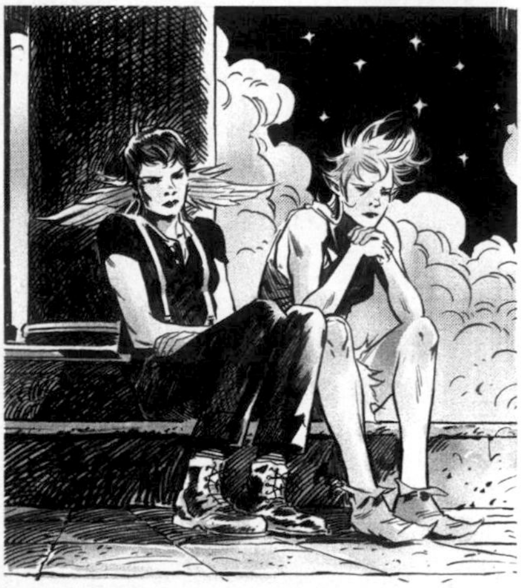

The Dreaming Dez 2017

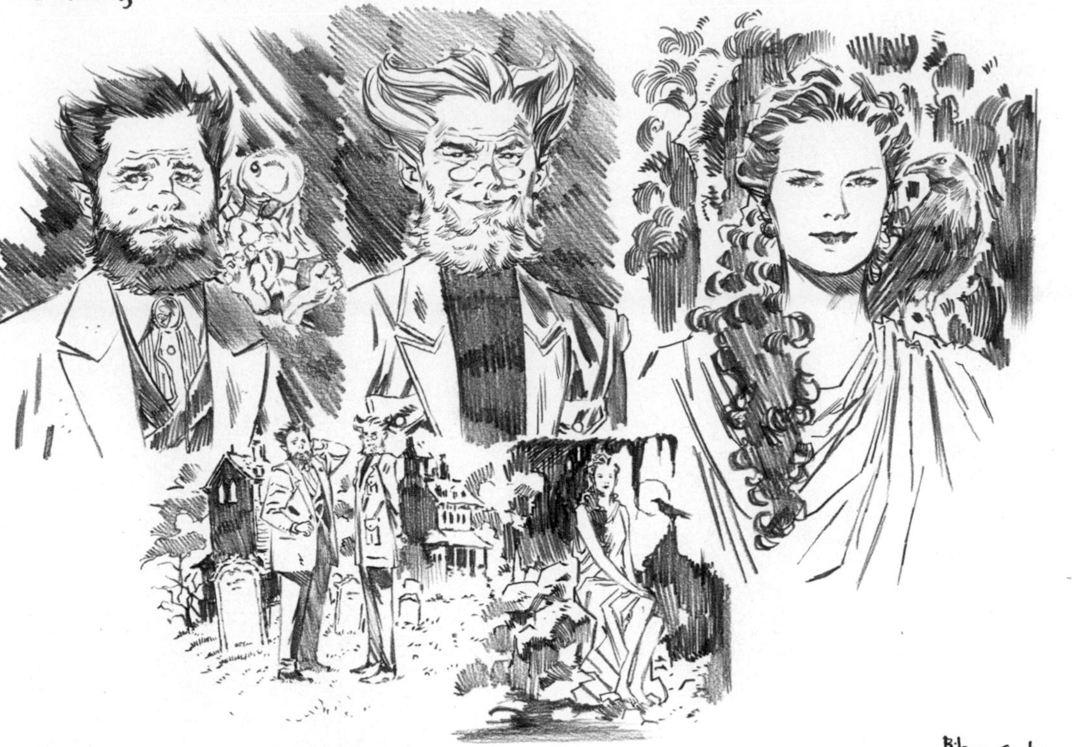

Bilquis Evely

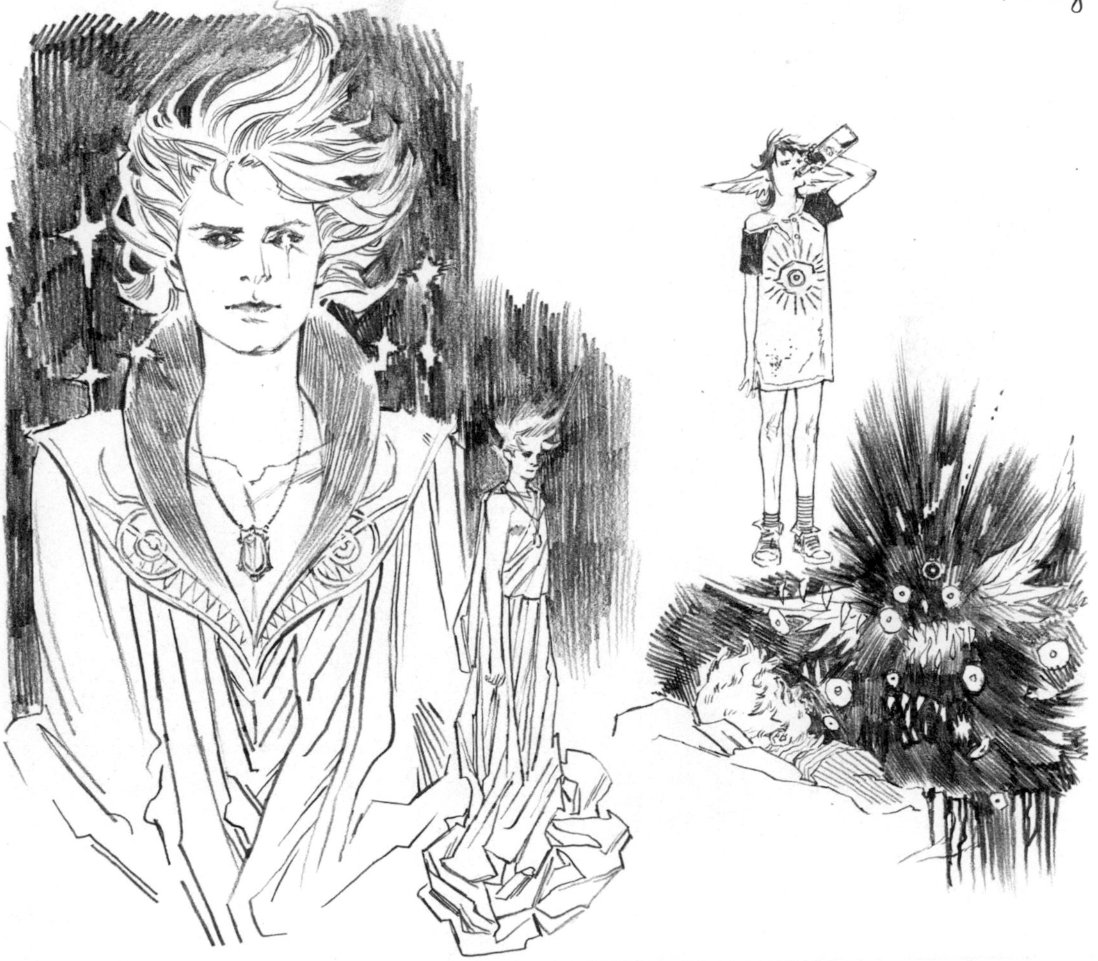

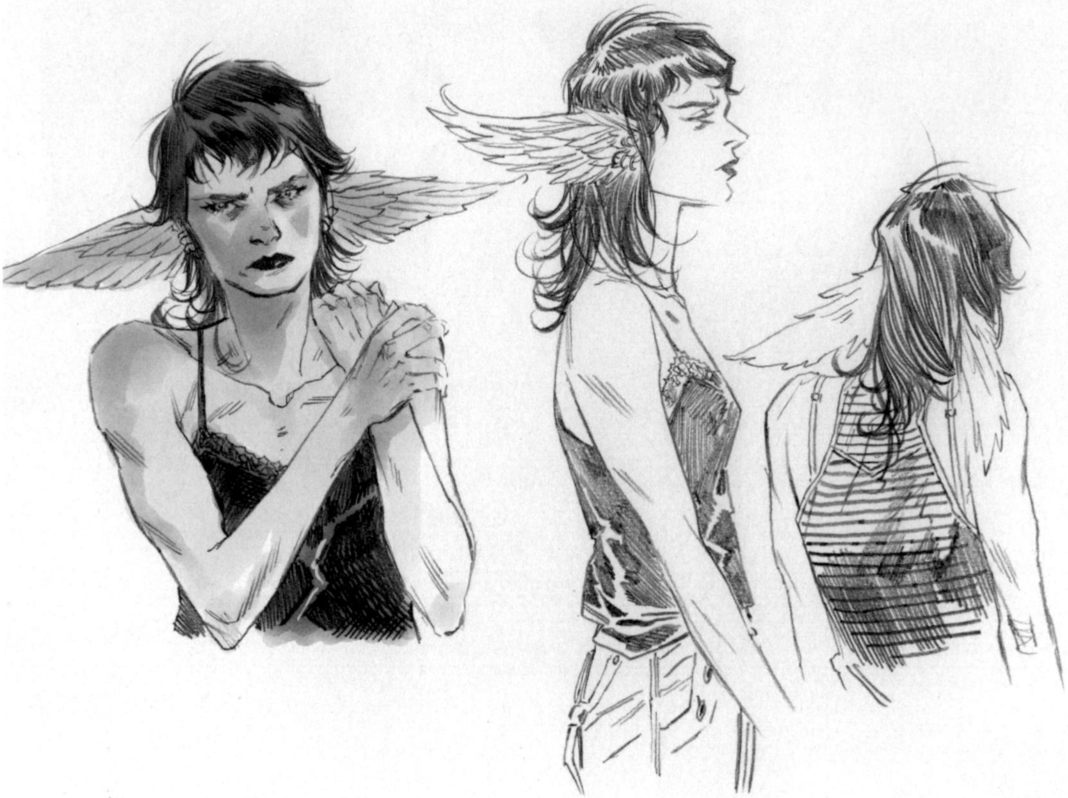

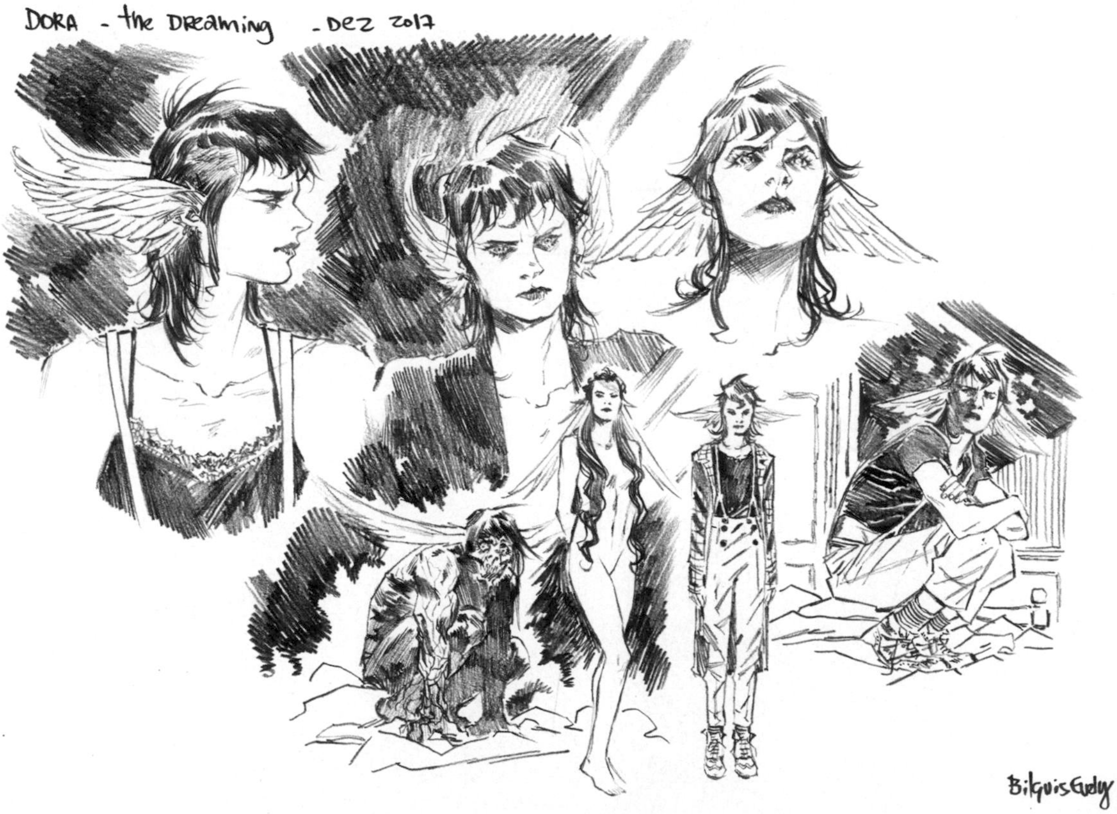
DORA - the Dreaming - Dez 2017
Bilquis Evely

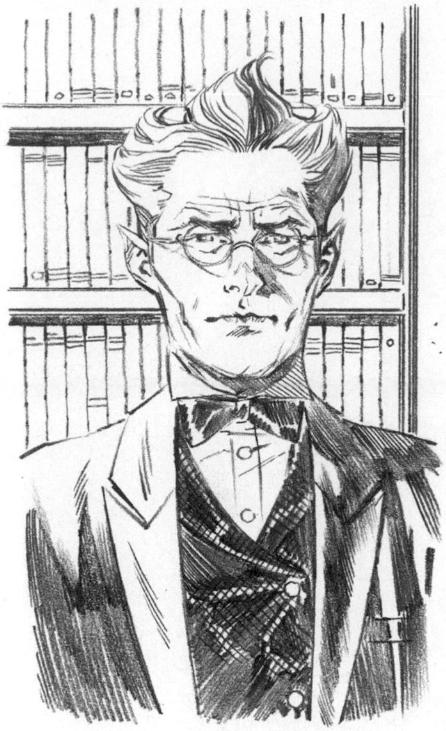

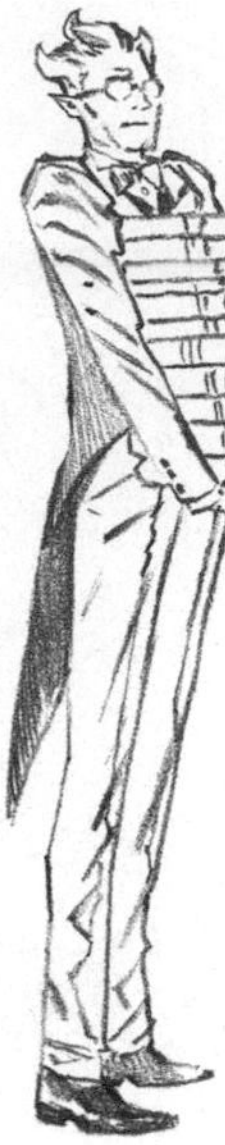

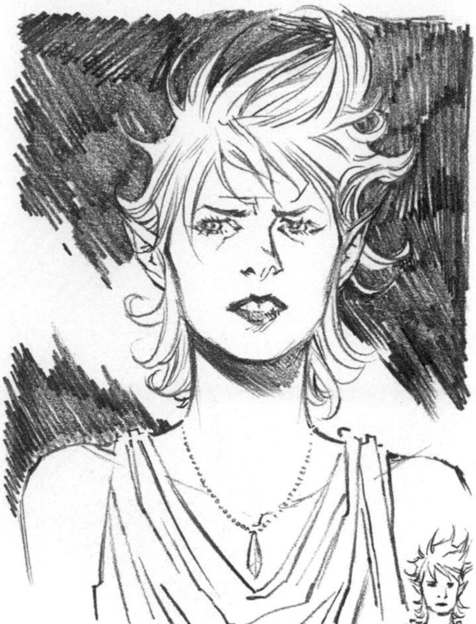

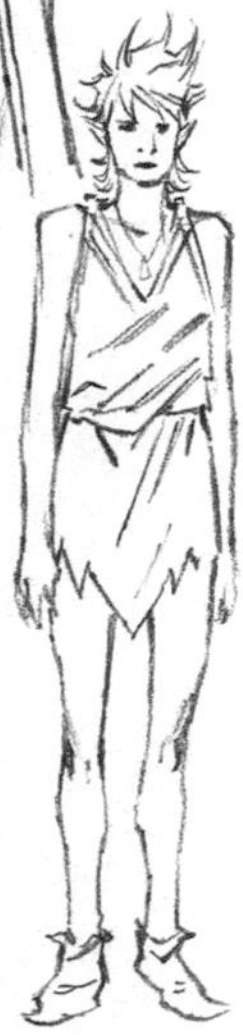

Dora

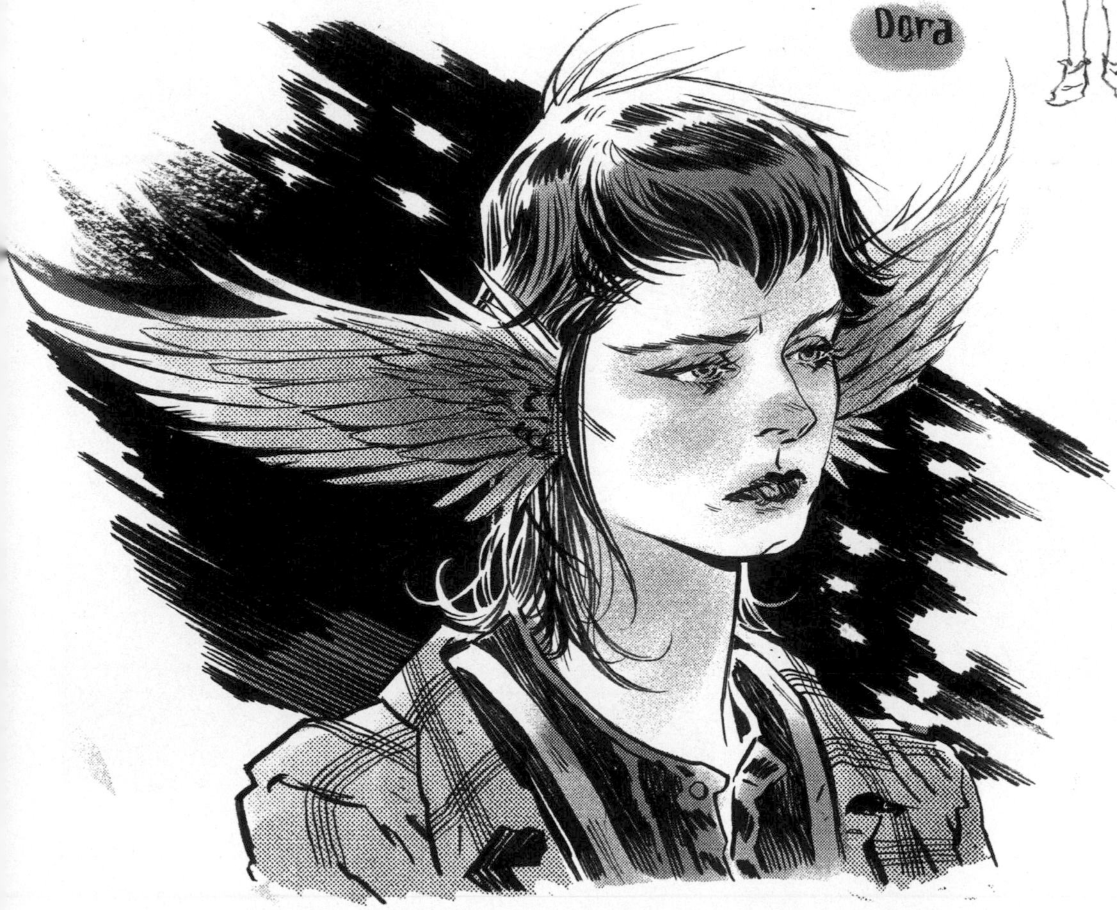

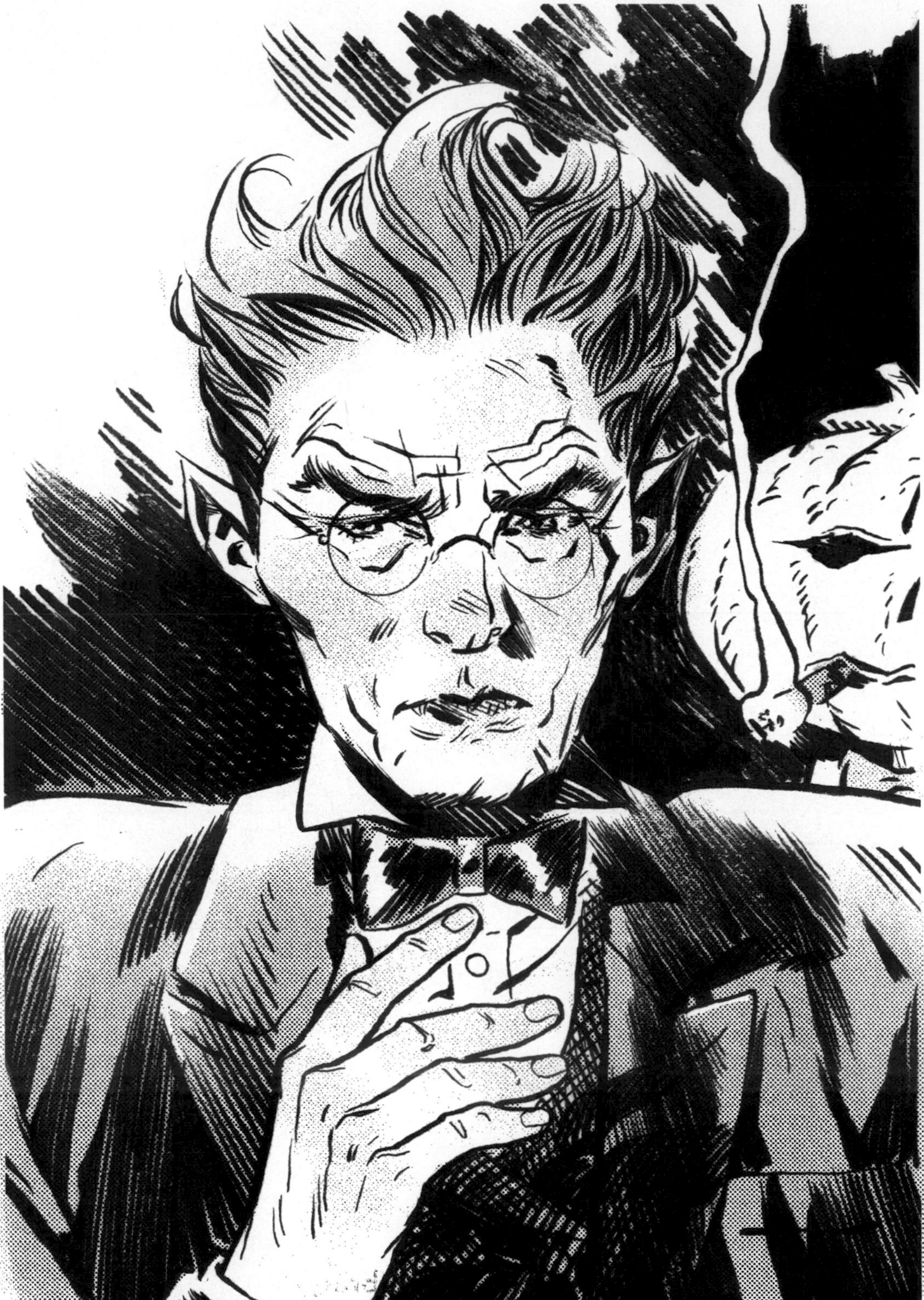

The Dreaming - Judge Gallows

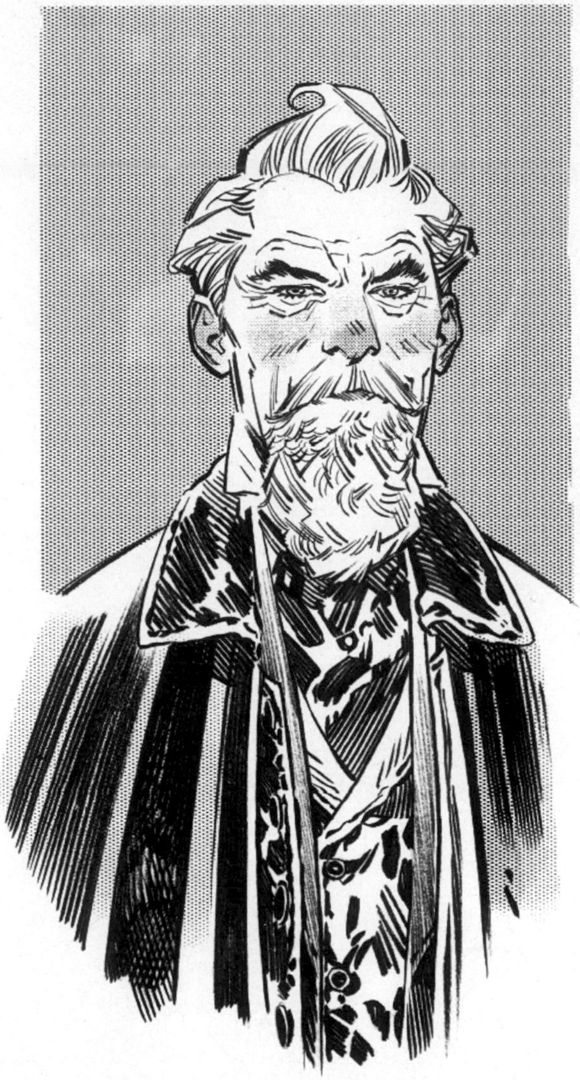

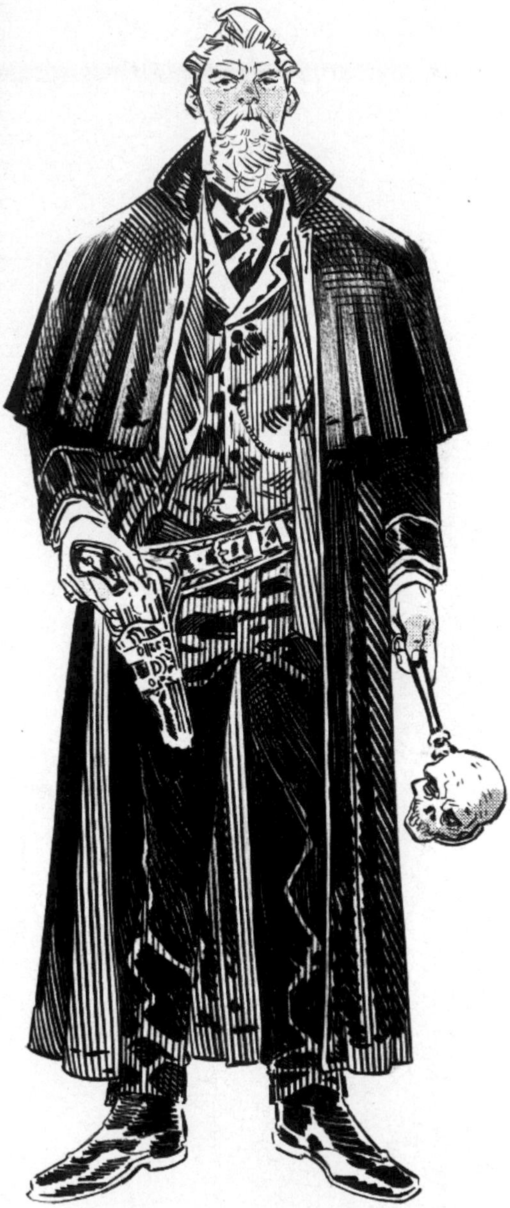

Bilquis Evely '18

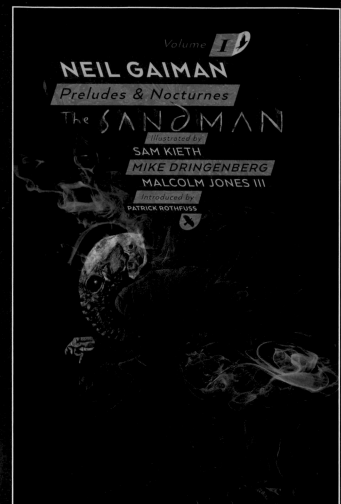

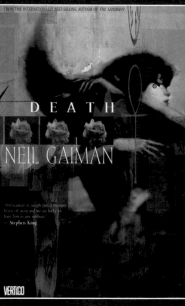